PEOPLE AND LAND IN AFRICA
SOUTH OF THE SAHARA

Readings in Social Geography

EDITED BY
R. MANSELL PROTHERO

NEW YORK
OXFORD UNIVERSITY PRESS
LONDON   1972   TORONTO

Second printing, 1974

Copyright © 1972 by Oxford University Press, Inc.
Library of Congress Catalogue Card Number: 72-82995
Printed in the United States of America

PREFACE

There are sound reasons, both academic and practical, for presenting this collection of geographical essays on population and land in Africa south of the Sahara. Since the end of World War II, the continent of Africa has become of considerable public concern and of great academic interest in the United States and other developed countries. With a lead from institutions such as Northwestern University, African Studies Programs have been developed in more than thirty-five American universities. Geography is part of a large number of these programs, and the geography of Africa is taught in many other universities and colleges where specific programs do not exist. In Britain the majority of university departments of geography offer courses on Africa, and it figures increasingly in the programs of institutions of higher education. Comparable developments have taken place in France, Germany, and other European countries. In Africa itself there have been major advances in the teaching of the geography of the continent during the last twenty years.

This academic interest has been stimulated by the active research work of geographers in Africa, particularly during the last two decades. Those from Britain have been associated with university and research institutions established for the most part in the late 1940s. With some notable exceptions, American geographers have come late to the African field, supported in their work by various national bodies and private foundations. Their contributions are already large in volume and of great academic significance (e.g. de Blij, 1964; Hance, 1964, 1967; Kimble, 1960; references are to the bibliography of this collection, beginning on p. 335).

The readings in this volume are concerned with various aspects of human geography; that is, the complex relationships between people and land, expressed particularly in agricultural practices and in agricultural systems, in land use, and in crop selection. These relationships are of crucial importance in Africa south of the Sahara, where most of the people depend directly upon the land for their livelihood.

There are a great many papers relevant to this theme from which to choose, which has made selection difficult. The final choice was inevitably personal, and anyone closely acquainted with the study of African population-land relationships would undoubtedly select and arrange differently. Selection has been governed particularly by the wish to make more widely available significant contributions to the study, but it has been limited by several factors. Each of the papers presented here was published originally in English. Many important contributions to the study of African population-land relationships have been made by authors writing in French, Flemish, German, Spanish, and Portuguese, but problems and costs of translation have made the inclusion of such work impossible. It should be noted, too, that though the study of African population-land relationships is multidisciplinary, involving agriculturalists, social anthropologists, economists, political scientists, and others, this collection includes for the most part the work of geographers, with the addition of a major essay by an agriculturalist.

This is no merely disparate collection, however. Many thematically relevant works would otherwise be left scattered among a variety of journals. Some of these journals are available only in large libraries and even their collections are often unable to fulfill the demands of ever-increasing numbers of university and college students.

Thanks are due to institutions, editors, and authors for permission to reproduce published papers. The figures and tables have been reproduced, but unfortunately it was impractical to include the original photographs. Details of the origin of each paper appear in the text.

THE ARRANGEMENT OF PAPERS

The papers in this volume are arranged in six groups. The first group concerns the physical environment as a determinant of population-land relationships and shows the potential that the environment offers for adjustment and adaptation as well as for exploitation. The papers in the second group illustrate successful adjustments in population-land relationships to unusual and particularly difficult environmental conditions, to increasing population, and to economic change resulting from the introduction or expansion of export crops. In contrast to these successes, there follow examples of maladjustment and its consequences. Rather more emphasis has been placed on successful adjustments since they point out the possibilities for future satisfactory development.

The colonial era in Africa was one of profound importance for population-land relationships. Direct influence occurred in areas alienated from African to European use exclusively, and although this situation no longer exists in Kenya, it continues in parts of southern Africa, with great political, social, and economic implications. The fourth group of papers deals with European influences. Africans have now settled on most of the land once allocated to Europeans, and directed readjustment is taking place in these areas as well as in areas where the design of resettlement is to promote productive land use or to open up previously unused land. Group five deals with these developments. The last group illustrates measurement and prediction in population-land relationships.

There is a logic in the grouping of the papers, but there are no definitive breaks between groups. For instance, a continuum, not a dichotomy, exists between adjusted and maladjusted population-land relationships; examples given are of relationships which are neither wholly satisfactory nor wholly unsatisfactory. No paper is exclusive to the group in which it appears, and a high degree of cross-relevance is evident throughout.

CONTENTS

PEOPLE AND LAND IN AFRICA
SOUTH OF THE SAHARA

RELATIONSHIPS BETWEEN PEOPLE AND LAND

The theme of this collection of papers is distinctively geographical. Relationships between people and land involve the physical and human branches of geography and provide a focus for consideration of the whole environment. The interplay between human and physical elements is complex and multidirectional and in no way does it express a crude pattern of environmental determinism (Brookfield, 1952). Thus in different locations, the relationships between man and land may be satisfactory or otherwise—depending on a variety of physical, social, economic and political factors.

Most of the people in Africa south of the Sahara are directly dependent on the land, although a purely subsistence economy is practiced only by groups in remote parts of the continent (Biebuyck, 1963; Dalton, 1964; Lehrer, 1964; McMaster, 1962a; Richards, 1958). Yet recent economic developments have affected people far beyond the confines of their villages, even of their countries, drawing them into networks of trade at local, regional, national, and international levels (Hance, 1964, 1968; Hance et al., 1961; Herskovits and Harwitz, 1964; Hodder and Harris, 1967; Green and Fair, 1962). This participation in the exchange economy has had considerable influence on population-land relationships (Bohannan and Dalton, 1962; Hodder, 1968). Increases in agricultural production and the introduction of new crops have had inevitable effects upon land and labor (Murdock, 1960), and frequently participation in the exchange economy at one level has stimulated involvement at another. For example, increased concentration on export crops may necessitate the import of food staples to supplement decreased local production (Morgan, 1956; White, 1956). Wider participation in the network of economic relationships in one area may affect circumstances in other areas, through the diffusion of ideas, techniques, implements and crops.

Whether expansion in economic involvement, which has been linked directly with European influence since about 1900, would have come about without colonial rule is a debatable point, but it is a fact that where Europeans settled permanently, gaining control of large areas of land, population-land relationships were considerably affected (Gann and Duignan, 1962).

One result of European contact has been the growth of the indigenous population. Medical services, though embryonic and thinly spread, have profoundly affected public health. The practice of preventive medicine in particular (Colbourne, 1963) has lowered death rates, yet birth rates have remained high. It is now forecast that Africa will have the highest rate of population growth in the world by the end of the century (U.N., 1966; Caldwell and Okonjo, 1968; Brass *et al.*, 1968). Even without complicating factors, such growth will make it difficult even to maintain present standards of living, sorely inadequate, for the most part, as they are.

That large numbers of people are a major factor in population-land relationships may be illustrated by the inability of traditional agricultural systems to cope with the rapid population growth of the last few decades (Steel, 1965, 1970). These systems were not always adequate in the past; shortages and famines were frequent in times of environmental stress or of political disruption (Brooke, 1967). Today, pressure from increasing population is coupled with wider economic involvement, and in some instances with land alienation. Population and land may never be in equilibrium for more than brief moments in time, because of the many highly dynamic factors involved. Change in one factor may trigger a complex chain reaction: even when it is possible to maintain a particular group of relationships over a period of time, it is likely that mobility—spatial mobility in particular—will be involved. For example, with ample land at their disposal, small groups of people may practice subsistence agriculture by shifting cultivation—which frequently involves shifting settlements as well (Watters, 1961). Yet circumstances favorable to shifting cultivation exist in few parts of Africa today (Allan, 1965). Increased demands on the land have led inevitably to increased fixation in land use and in the location of settlement (Grove, 1951b; Morgan, 1965).

Neither land nor people always adjust satisfactorily to change. Failures to adjust result in deterioration of the physical environment —soil erosion, which is usually insidious, may be spectacular, as in some parts of Eastern Nigeria (Floyd, 1965; Grove, 1951, 1956), and loss of fertility, indicated by falling crop yields, may occur. In areas of poor rainfall human activity may result in the growth of desert conditions. Maladjustments, too, are manifest among people who are either landless or short of land. The plight of these people has been a major factor in the development of migrant labor and the rapid growth of towns during the present century (Prothero, 1964; Steel, 1961).

By contrast, when adjustments are successful it becomes possible to support more people and to cultivate export crops. Progressively greater intensification in land use has eliminated wasteful periods of non-production as a means of restoring soil fertility, and in some areas of successful adjustment, the traditional dichotomy between herdsman and cultivator has been replaced by either a mutually advantageous symbiotic relationship (Mortimore, 1967) or the basic elements of a system of mixed farming (Pelissier, 1953). Apart from the social problems, the limiting factor in such developments is climatic: rainfall must be sufficient for cultivation; at the same time conditions must not favor the tsetse fly and animal trypanosomiasis, which inhibit or prevent the keeping of cattle (Davies, 1966; Deshler, 1963; Veyret, 1952).

Many successful adjustments have been made almost entirely without changes in technology: traditional crops and implements are still used, land for cultivation is still cleared by axe and fire. In areas of mixed farming, manure is used for fertilizer, but the cattle that provide it still may not be used for drawing plows (Coppock, 1966). Yields have improved through more intensive land use, not through the use of better varieties of crops. The staple foods cultivated may still be traditional ones (Johnston, 1958). Cash crops may be new, however, such as cocoa in West Africa (Dickson, 1968) or improved varieties, such as cotton in Northern Nigeria and in East Africa. Strains of rust-resistant maize and other improved varieties of staple crops are in use, but the real problem, as with many other potential agricultural improvements, is engineering diffusion and widespread adoption of new practices.

Because agricultural traditions are difficult to break down or even to modify, changes in population-land relationships are often spontaneous rather than the result of organized promotion. In areas where root crops are food staples, there has been spontaneous crop substitution, particularly of the higher-yielding and less-demanding cassava for yams (Johnston, 1958; Jones, 1959; Mabogunje and Gleave, 1964). All too frequently in recent decades organized attempts to promote change have met with limited success. Particularly unsuccessful were schemes involving large-scale production, in which inadequate appreciation of existing conditions contributed heavily to failure (Wood, 1950, Chambers, 1970): while the technical aspect of development was adequate, understanding of the human element was sadly lacking (Baldwin, 1957). Attempts to impose new developments rather than to integrate them with existing practices have been strongly resisted. Thus, in spite of revolutionary change—the development of irrigation in the Gezira region of the Sudan (Barbour, 1959; Hance, 1967) or the resettlement of the Kikuyu people in Kenya in the 1950's (McGlashan, 1958, 1960)—experience overall suggests that evolutionary progress is likely to be more acceptable and in the long run more successful.

The great problem is time: is there enough to permit gradual progress, given the present rates of population growth? Even before the growth rates started to rise, production barely kept pace with demand, and undernutrition and malnutrition were common. Living standards have risen and are manifest in improved nutrition and increased power to purchase consumer goods. Political stability has increased, permitting a better distribution of resources so that large-scale famines are now unlikely, yet the rise in living standards has affected few Africans—and in many areas malnutrition and even undernutrition are the norm.

Major breakthroughs are required to solve—even to alleviate—existing and potential problems of population-land relationships in Africa. Essential to consider are population control and disease control, changes in crops, the adoption of new production techniques on a large scale, improvements in transportation and storage methods, and means of livelihood other than agriculture (Jones, 1965; Brokensha, 1965; Hance, 1968). Without change in these areas, the prospects for the future are not particularly encouraging. All are a part of the relationships between people and land explored in the papers in this collection.

I. POPULATION-LAND RELATIONSHIPS: THE PHYSICAL ENVIRONMENT

In a flight from the worst of environmental determinism popular in the earlier part of the century, scholars have tended to give scant consideration to the influence of the physical environment. This trend may be noted in the work of social anthropologists and other researchers in Africa after World War II, who often studied people as if they existed in an environmental vacuum. Nowadays more balanced views are generally achieved, but economists still do not recognize that the physical environment matters—a disturbing attitude for those who have such a large say in plans for African development. In fact, the failure of some development schemes during the past two decades may be partially attributed to a prevalence of this attitude, and the experience has been costly. (Baldwin, 1958; Wood, 1950). Geographers have not helped to adjust this unbalanced view. In works encompassing the whole or large parts of the continent, environmental details have been presented indiscriminately and have been unsatisfactorily linked to the total geographic situation. The papers in this group give full recognition to the physical environment; at the same time they present a balanced perspective of its function. Mythical generalizations about the physical sameness of vast areas of the continent have been discarded by all but the ignorant: conditions in fact often change rapidly over short distances. It can be amply demonstrated that appreciation of these changes—which are sometimes quite subtle—and adaptation to them are essential to establishing satisfactory population-land relationships. Among African farmers this appreciation is intuitive.

Although its influence is pervasive, the physical environment in Africa is not totally controlling nor is it totally permissive in terms of human response. In many parts it is harsh—if not completely intractable—and severely limits development. But limitations may also exist because of restricted technology and lack of organization, and numerous examples, although small in scale, point the way by which these limitations may be overcome. This group of papers shows how people have adapted to different physical surroundings. Some of these adaptations have been naturally dictated by physical conditions, but more often they have depended on the availability of human resources and the nature of human needs.

The ability of people to adapt to and utilize the physical environment varies in space and time. In African studies, historical depth and perspective have been generally lacking—despite the long time span involved—and major advances in the study of African environments and human responses to them have taken place only recently. The most significant feature of this work is its interdisciplinary character; archaeologists, historians, anthropologists, and geographers are joining with linguists, botanists, serologists, and others in most unlikely combinations to reconstruct past physical and human circumstances. Light is being cast upon such things as former vegetation cover, agricultural origins, and the introduction of various crops, past movements of population, and patterns of settlement (Gray et al., 1962).

It has been possible to show for the Buboka District in Tanzania how various population groups have evaluated their distinct regional environments, shifting and changing points of emphasis over the centuries. Reflected in these shifts and changes are the levels, techniques and modes of life of the people. At present, problems stemming from population growth and from a cash economy based on coffee are plaguing the areas deemed most favorable for occupation. These problems could be alleviated, but at the expense of resettling population in areas requiring major environmental modifications to make them habitable.

The Buboka study and other research with similar historical perspective (e.g., Mabogunje and Gleave, 1964; Kay, 1964; Dickson, 1969) are important not only because they illuminate the past, but also because they point to possible future development.

1. Change of Regional Balance in the Bukoba District of Tanganyika

D. N. MC MASTER

In the life, development, and history of simple societies ecological factors are of central importance. Man, however, is an active agent in deciding and altering the ecological equations of which he is a part. These two facts soon become apparent to the geographer who works in tropical Africa, and the present study demonstrates their influence within a regional framework.

The general setting of Bukoba District is shown in Figure 1. The district lies in the extreme northwestern part of Tanganyika, bordered on the east by Lake Victoria and on the west by the Kagera River, which separates it from Ruanda-Urundi. On the northwestern border the Kagera turns abruptly eastward, and the artificial boundary that separates Tanganyika from Uganda crosses a belt of relatively low country north of the river. The southern boundary is purely an administrative one. The district thus defined has a land area of about 5900 square miles, with an African population in 1957 of 376,962.[1]

[1] Since this paper was written, Bukoba District has been divided for administrative purposes into two. Karagwe, formerly the westernmost chiefdom, has been given the status of a separate district. This division took effect on January 1, 1958.

From *The Geographical Review*, Vol. 50, 1960, pp. 73–88.

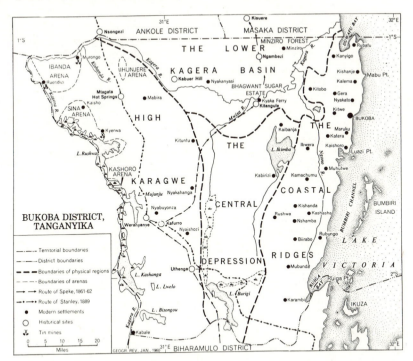

Figure 1.—Location map of Bukoba District, showing generalized physical regions. Topographic information based on maps supplied by the Department of Lands and Surveys, Dar es Salaam, Tanganyika.

Within this area are distinctive contrasts in landscape, deriving essentially from geological differences and accentuated by contrasts in rainfall. This indeed is country in which changes in geology are immediately and strikingly manifest in the scenery. The major contrast is that between the linear ridges of Bukoba sandstone overlooking Lake Victoria and the fluted downlands of the west, developed on Karage-Ankolean metamorphosed sedimentary rocks and standing high above lake level. In the north the lower Kagera Valley floored partly with later sediments and alluvium, forms a third unit; and the two highland areas are separated by a belt of lower country 15 to 30 miles in width. Thus the district can be subdivided physiographically into four units: (1) the coastal ridges, (2) high Karagwe, (3) the lower Kagera basin, and (4) the central depression.

It is the purpose of this paper to discuss the changing evaluations that man has put on these regions at various stages in his own development. The area is well suited to such a study; for by any standard the record of man's occupation is unusually long, and by tropical African standards it is unusually detailed. There is clear evidence that within the setting of these four regions man has been active from the very earliest times; and that at different epochs the balance of advantage for human occupation has shifted from one region to another, reflecting the levels, techniques, and modes of life of the occupants.

THE PHYSICAL SETTING

Figure 2 shows the geology, structure, and relief. The rocks of the coastal ridges are dominantly fine and well-jointed quartzitic

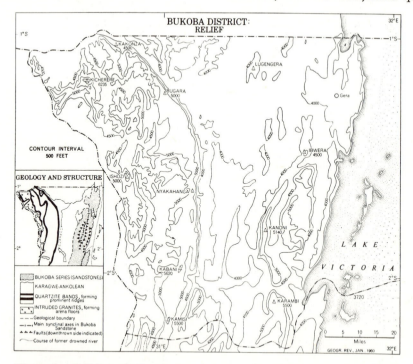

Figure 2.—Relief map of Bukoba District, with inset showing generalized geology and structure (after A. D. Combe). Topographic information based on maps supplied by the Department of Lands and Surveys.

sandstones, with some shaly bands. They are probably wholly pre-Cambrian [2] and were later intruded by numerous thick dolerite sills. Long ages ago they were gently folded, and later they were cut in places into long, narrow blocks by strike faults. The highland block between Kamachumu and Biirabo is a horst, and straight sections of the coast line probably reflect faulting. The present ridges, aligned south-southwest to north-northeast, are chiefly synclinal, and the intervening broad vales are excavated in the anticlines.[3] Three main ridge lines can be traced: that of Bumbiri and nearby islands, that of the coast ridge (in many places rising 400 feet above lake level in bold cliffs), and, west of the Ngono vale, that which can be traced through the summits of Karambi, Kanoni, and Ibwera. The ridgetops are planate and appear to display two erosion levels. The lower, at about 4100 to 4300 feet, dominates the sky line of the coast ridge; a higher and earlier surface is suggested on parts of the third ridge. The ridges carry bold scarps, in many places buttressed by jointed sandstone outcrops. Below these craggy buttresses the valley flanks are littered with detached blocks.

The central depression is an erosional corridor of relatively subdued relief. Its discontinuous hills are aligned north–south. The two major independent lakes of Bukoba District, Lake Ikimba and Lake Burigi, occupy basins between these hills.

The rugged scenery of high Karagwe results chiefly from the differential erosion of pre-Cambrian Karagwe-Ankolean rocks of varying resistance and the superposition of a south–north drainage system on an ancient, strongly folded structure. The bold ridges are developed on hard bands of quartzite. Like the ridges of the coastal region, these ridges are synclinal and display two summit surfaces, though at higher altitudes. The impressive scrap, 1000 feet or more in height, that defines the eastern edge of this highland reflects one such band. Its trend can be traced through the peaks of Kabani, Nyakahanga, Bugara, and Kakonza. The more sinuous crest lines to the west, culminating in Ishozi and Kicherere (6235 feet), are also developed on these quartzites. In the extreme northwest the denudation of the anticlines has exposed granite intrusions, which now form enclosed basins, termed "arenas," rimmed by quartzite ridges. Five such arenas occur wholly or partly in Karagwe (Fig. 1). Their margins are mineralized, bearing veins and stringers of tin.[4] On the flanks of the ridges phyllites are exposed and have been eroded into deep-cleft combes, or "kloofs," running down the hill slopes. They are a characteristic feature of Karagwe-Ankolean scenery.

The Kagera is a composite river. Its course and valley reflect a long and complex history of tilting, river capture, and fluctuating lake levels. Though these events had their beginnings long geological ages ago, early man seems to have witnessed some of the later, and by no means least important, episodes.[5] Tilting explains the drowned nature of much of the upper river, where the course is northerly. The permanent and copious flow of the lower river largely results from the capture of these headwaters. The lower Kagera is indeed among the west-coast feeders of Lake Vic-

[2] A. M. Quennell: The Bukoban System of East Africa, *Internatl. Geol. Congr., 20th Sess., Mexico, 1956*, "El sistema Cámbrico, su paleogeografía y el problema de su base," Vol. 1, Part 1, Mexico, 1956, pp. 281–307.

[3] A. D. Combe: The Geology of South-West Ankole and Adjacent Territories with Special Reference to the Tin Deposits, *Geol. Survey of Uganda Memoir No. 2*, Entebbe, 1932. Combe suggests that the Bumbiri Channel represents a drowned river valley (p. 92).

[4] G. M. Stockley and G. J. Williams: Explanation of the Geology, Degree Sheet No. 1 (Karagwe Tinfields), *Tanganyika Geol. Survey Bull. No. 10*, Dar es Salaam, 1938.

[5] Combe, *op. cit.* [see footnote 3 above], pp. 101–104; E. J. Wayland: Rifts, Rivers, Rains and Early Man in Uganda, *Journ. Royal Anthropol. Inst.*, Vol. 64, 1934, pp. 333–352.

toria in being a rapid, free-flowing river. This explains why early European travelers noted with some surprise the vigor of its current.[6]

The present Kagera, breaking free of the quartzite above Nsongezi, flows in an incised bed, above which rises a flight of alluvial and rock-cut terraces, flanked in their turn by the rubble-littered Pliocene pediments of dissected hills. Toward the mouth of the river the terraces broaden, the valley opens out, and marshy alluvial flats merge into the open waters of Lake Victoria.

Most of the coastal region receives abundant rainfall, well distributed throughout the year, and Bukoba records the exceptionally high mean of 80.46 inches

---

[6] J. A. Grant: A Walk across Africa (Edinburgh and London, 1964), p. 194; H. M. Stanley: Through the Dark Continent (2 vols., London, 1878), Vol. 1, p. 450.

(Fig. 3).[7] Annual variability is relatively low.[8] Two rainfall peaks reflect the influence of the trade winds, flowing into the intertropical convergence zone. The April peak is the more marked. Owing partly to the longer fetch of the northeast trades across Lake Victoria's broad waters, the isohyets show a decrease in annual totals south-southwest from Bukoba. July is everywhere the driest month, but no month here is really dry.

The remainder of Bukoba District suffers

---

[7] I am much indebted to the Tanganyika Department of Agriculture for making available to me rainfall statistics gathered over a period of years, and to Mr. A. C. McCallum, Agricultural Officer, West Lake Division, for his help.

[8] Compare Bukoba, 1920–1949: extreme maximum 105.38 inches, 1947; extreme minimum 61.16 inches, 1922 ("Collected Climatological Statistics for East African Stations," East African Meteorological Department, Nairobi, 1953).

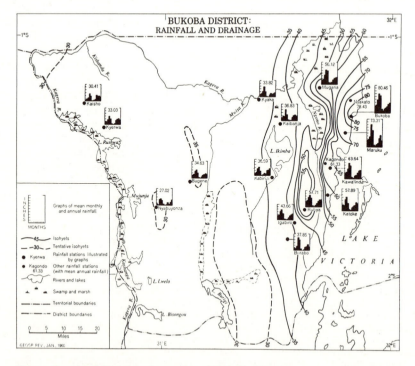

Figure 3.—Rainfall and hydrography of Bukoba District.

from the rain-shadow effect of the coastal ridges. Even the bold Karagwe scarps can wring little further moisture from the prevailing winds.[9] The mean annual rainfall is almost everywhere less than 35 inches, and probably less than 30 inches in the more southern parts of the central depression. Moreover, the seasonal regime is accentuated. The midyear dry season is more pronounced, and in the west a second minimum, in January and February, is becoming apparent.

On this basis of relief and rainfall the probable climax vegetation in early times can be suggested.[10] On the coastal ridges the favorable rainfall, allied to equable temperatures, was conducive to the growth of a rich climax forest, the affinities of which are generally regarded as montane rather than truly equatorial. Little such forest exists today, but small and scattered fragments remain. Today, on more open country, groves of the *musizi* tree (*Maesopsis eminii*) and the vigorous growth of acanthus shrubs corroborate the testimony to the climatic suitability of the area for forest growth.[11] High Karagwe probably carried a mixed savanna vegetation, characterized by *Acaccia stenocarpa, Combretum fischeri,* and, in the more open stretches, *Protea*

abyssinica and *Markhamia platycalyx*.[12] The combes supported dense thickets, in which *Albizzia* and *Erythrina* were frequent trees. The valley floors, seasonally inundated, still display in many stretches grassy or sedge-covered country, dotted with tangled thickets on innumerable termite mounds, with closer woodland strips along the more marked watercourses. Much of the central depression retains a similar aspect.

Gallery forest probably lined the Kagera River, with drier acacia bush on the terraces and hill flanks. In the lower valley patches of more extensive forest still remain (for example, the Minziro forest of the Uganda border). Papyrus swamp fringed the lakes and open water.

This is the domain into which man entered. These are the regions that have been successively the focus of his activities. We may take our cross sections in time at the three best-recorded epochs: the prehistoric period, the time of the coming of the early European travelers, and the present day.

The Kagera Valley is one of the greatest hearths of African prehistory.[13] Following the pioneer discoveries of Wayland at Nsongezi, excavations on one of the river terraces revealed a sequence of human occupation stretching back into the dimmest human past. The density of artifacts is incredible—a potential of 500 million artifacts has been calculated for the 100-foot terrace within a mile of Nsongezi![14] Spurr has recently added to this remarkable record as a result of work done between Kabuer

[9] High Karagwe is also partly shielded from Atlantic influence by higher ridges to the west, in Ruanda, where a foehn effect has been observed. See H. Scaëtta: Le climat écologique de la dorsale Congo-Nil, *Mémoires Inst. Royal Colonial Belge, Sect. des Sci. Nat. et Médicales,* Vol. 3, Brussels, 1934, pp. 198–200.

[10] A complication is introduced by the possibility of appreciable climatic changes since Pleistocene time. However, reference to Scaëtta (*op. cit.,* p. 328) and Wayland (*op. cit.* [see footnote 5 above], pp. 348 and 351) suggests that such changes have not been of an order to invalidate the general description given here.

[11] Both plants are active colonizers of forest margins. Furthermore, the musizi, being a short-lived tree, cannot be a remnant from the past. Cf. W. J. Eggeling: The Indigenous Trees of the Uganda Protectorate (revised and enlarged by I. R. Dale; Entebbe, 1952), especially p. 325.

[12] H. M. Lloyd: The Occurrence of *Glossina morsitans* in Tanganyika Territory in Vegetational Types Other Than *Isoberlinia-Brachystegia* Communities, *Bull. of Entomol. Research,* Vol. 29, 1938, pp. 77–98.

[13] C. van Riet Lowe: The Pleistocene Geology and Prehistory of Uganda, Part II: Prehistory, *Geol. Survey of Uganda Memoir No. 6,* 1952, p. 13. See also S. Cole: The Prehistory of East Africa (London, 1954), p. 125.

[14] Lowe, *op. cit.* [see footnote 13 above], pp. 44–45.

Hill and Nyakanyasi.[15] Today most of the lower Kagera basin is virtually uninhabited (Fig. 4).

The earliest European travelers in high Karagwe—Speke, Grant, and Stanley—found it the site of a strong pastoral kingdom. Since then the rich herds have dwindled and the population has decreased. Modern times have witnessed a further shift of focus to the coastal ridges, which today support 70 per cent of the total African population of Bukoba District.

We must now put forward explanations for such marked fluctuations in the importance of these regions.

THE PREHISTORIC PERIOD

The astonishing record of Nsongezi points to a factory site and also to the persistent attraction of the lower Kagera basin for prehistoric peoples through countless generations. It is easy to picture its advantages. The copious river attracted game animals to its banks, as it does today. The swift current bore down quartzite fragments from the hillside rubble, rolling them into pebbles, which man took from the river terraces to fashion his primitive tools. This supply must go far to explain the site of the Nsongezi "factory." Pleistocene climates fluctuated: in drier times the attraction of the river for game and for hunters and fishermen must have been reinforced. Men held to the river valley that provided water, sustenance, settlement sites on the terraces, and an avenue of intercourse.

We may surmise that before the days of agriculture the importance of the rest of Bukoba District was slight and its development rudimentary. Hunters and gatherers doubtless ranged the land, but life focused on the lower Kagera.

This pre-eminence cannot long have survived the development of agricultural tech-niques. A low rainfall, coupled with the incision of the river bed, severely curtailed the availability of water for crops. The terraces were of limited extent, and the rubble of the pediments was unpromising for cultivation. The depredations of game on planted plots would doubtless have been severe. The inhabitants had to look farther for their fields, and thus probably began the appreciable and increasing modification of the climax vegetation of high Karagwe.[16]

This has been such an important process, here as in other parts of tropical Africa, as to call for some elaboration. Doubt has sometimes been cast on the degree of human responsibility involved. Michelmore in particular has advanced strong arguments for a belief that many of the high-level grasslands of Africa may be largely natural, rather than man-made.[17] Certainly the tree-lessness of much of Karagwe in the nineteenth century was so striking as to induce comment from all the early European observers, including Emin Pasha and Stuhlmann.[18] However, it seems probable that, whatever the cogency of Michelmore's arguments regarding other localities, the grassland of high Karagwe was largely man-made. Scaëtta, concerned with similar ecological problems in neighboring Ruanda, presents a convincing case for believing that human activities have there been the main cause of forest recession and grassland formation, and that fire has been the princi-

[16] It may have begun even before agriculture became firmly established; for the use of fire in game drives is a long-established hunting technique (cf. Maximilien Sorre: Les fondements de la géographie humaine, Vol. 2, Part 2 [Paris, 1950], p. 616). Such practices persist in East Africa today.

[17] A. P. G. Michelmore: Observations on Tropical African Grasslands, *Journ. of Ecol.*, Vol. 27, 1939, pp. 282–312.

[18] I am indebted on this point to an unpublished report on "The Development of the Ankole Tsetse Belts" by J. Ford, of the East Africa Tsetse and Trypanosomiasis Research and Reclamation Organization.

[15] A. M. M. Spurr: Archaeology—The Kagera River Valley, *Records Geol. Survey of Tanganyika*, Vol. 4, 1954, p. 42.

pal agent.[19] Furthermore, the last 60 years have witnessed a vigorous growth of bush and savanna trees in Karagwe as the interference by man has been reduced.

Many generations of agriculturists must have ranged over high Karagwe, seeking empirically the better soils, moving on as their primitive techniques lowered soil fertility, clearing zones around their settlements and fields as a protection against wild animals. Thus the climax vegetation was ravaged, and the grasslands and open stretches multiplied. The soils of high Karagwe are varied, but except on the quartzites and the granites they are almost everywhere of fair quality. The problem is water supply. Centuries ago the Bantu cultivators must have appreciated these problems of the environment and settled themselves about the flanks of the ridges and arenas and near the mouths of the combes. Under such conditions settlement cannot have been close, but the vegetation was degraded over much wider areas.

Similar processes can be envisaged as operating over a broad band of savanna west and northwest of Lake Victoria. A grassland avenue was opened up through which waves of cattle-owning peoples migrated southward, conquering the agriculturists and setting up pastoral kingdoms. Among later waves were the Hamitic people variously called the Bahima, Bahuma, or Batussi. Certain authors trace their affinities to the Galla of southern Ethiopia. Vastly superior to the indigenous Bantu, the Banyambo, in political organization, military prowess, and mobility, the Bahima were able to establish themselves over a sedentary peasantry whose scattered agricultural settlement militated against effective organization and resistance. In opening the grasslands and reducing the bush, with its dan-

gers to cattle from game and insect pests, the agriculturists had fashioned a rod for their own backs.

The relationship in Karagwe between the ruling Bahima and the Banyambo peasantry was not uneasy. Both groups had well-ordered places in a symbiotic relationship.[20] Numerically the Bahima were only a fraction of the total population. The reports of early observers, whose contacts were largely with this ruling group, may give an exaggerated idea of their number. The thoughts and affairs of the Bahima centered on their long-horned cattle, on whose products they largely subsisted, but their economy was supported on the broad base of the agricultural production and the services of the Banyambo. Heavy grazing, burning, and agricultural activities kept the grasslands open and healthy.

THE NINETEENTH CENTURY AND THE PRESENT DAY

Such was the aspect of high Karagwe when Speke, Grant, and Stanley first viewed it.[21] Some four hundred thousand cattle grazed the broad upland pastures; groves of bananas and patches of millet grew on the valley slopes and in the better-watered spots. From the capital at Weranyanye, the Kingdom of Karagwe dominated the surrounding lands. The Kagera Valley formed a march zone, separating Karagwe from neighboring pastoral kingdoms and, in its lower stretches, from the power of Buganda.

[19] H. Scaëtta: Les famines périodiques dans le Ruanda: Contribution à l'étude des aspects biologiques du phénomène, *Mémoires Inst. Royal Colonial Belge, Sect. des Sci. Nat. et Médicales*, Vol. 1, Part 4, 1932. See especially Plates 6–15.

[20] There is much useful comparative information in K. Oberg: The Kingdom of Ankole in Uganda, *in* African Political Systems (edited by M. Fortes and E. E. Evans-Pritchard; London, 1940), pp. 121–162. Oberg estimates the Bahima in Ankole as "only one-tenth" of the total population (p. 126).

[21] J. H. Speke: Journal of the Discovery of the Nile (Edinburgh and London, 1863), pp. 195–272; Grant, *op. cit.* [see footnote 6 above], pp. 137–187; Stanley, *op. cit.* [see footnote 6 above], Vol. 1, pp. 450–482. Speke's route is shown on Figure 1. In 1876 Stanley took a closely similar route in the reverse direction.

Kitangule alone seems to have been of some significance. Then, as now, it was the site of an important ferry, and large royal herds were grazed and watered nearby.[22] The coastal ridges were largely tributary to Karagwe, though tenuously held. They were far from ideal for cattle and were separated from high Karagwe by the poor country of the central depression. Considerable agricultural settlement existed, but it was still mainly of a subsistence character.

The collapse of the power of Karagwe was sudden and devastating. Several factors contributed to it, some of them political. Rumanika, the strong ruler, died, and the cement of the state crumbled.[23] But worse was to follow from natural causes—in the weakened country. The cattle "monoculture" of the Bahima suffered the classic misfortune of a new disease. In 1890 or 1891 the sweeping scourge of rinderpest, a cattle disease new to Africa, hit Karagwe. It has been estimated that nine-tenths of the cattle died.[24] To the pastoral Bahima this was utter disaster. They were thrown on the Banyambo for their very survival, but this group also suffered badly in the disintegration of a well-ordered society. Into this devastation entered two further biological plagues: jiggers (*Tunga penetrans*) and a smallpox epidemic. These, besides their directly fatal effects, further depleted through debilitation the manpower available for cultivation.[25] The power and population of Karagwe were broken. No longer could

a depleted population, with few cattle, maintain the open grasslands. The bush grew away from them and created a habitat favorable to invasion by the tsetse fly (especially *Glossina morsitans*), which, advancing by way of the central depression and the Kagera Valley, was not slow to enter the domain. Such is the delicacy of ecological balances that the consequent condition of high Karagwe was in some ways worse than its original state before the entry of man. Early man had had the advantage of virgin soils, and it is reasonable to assume that the Bahima entered into tsetse-free pastures. Today the reclamation of high Karagwe faces greater difficulties; the problems posed by the tsetse fly and soil depletion are accentuated in the presence of a disintegrated human society.

Figure 4, which shows the present distribution of the African population in Bukoba District, confirms the pre-eminence of the coastal ridges in contemporary affairs. Thanks to the native-grown coffee crop, the economic leadership of those areas is also unchallenged. The lakeside location early brought the coastal ridges under German control, and today it facilitates transportation and communication. Thus position has favored the development of coffee production, which was, however, broadly based on the past agricultural development of the region.

From early times the forested coastal ridges must have been subjected to the probings and experiments of agriculturists. High forest, apparently indicative of high fertility, is still frequently sought by the African cultivator. But the forest concealed the fact that the soils of the coastal ridges are variable, as Milne showed 20 years ago.[26] For the most part the sandstones, poor in bases, yield a difficult soil. When the climax forest has been destroyed, this soil breaks down under the heavy rainfall.

[22] Speke, *op. cit.*, p. 262.

[23] It is of interest in this respect to compare Stanley's first account of Karagwe, in 1876, with his second, written 13 years later (see H. M. Stanley: In Darkest Africa [2 vols., London, 1890], Vol. 2, pp. 373–379). Stanley's route of 1889 is shown on Figure 1.

[24] R. W. M. Mettam: A Short History of Rinderpest, With Special Reference to Africa, *Uganda Journ.*, Vol. 5, 1937–38, pp. 22–26.

[25] There is a good assessment of these influences in J. Ford and R. de Z. Hall: The History of Karagwe (Bukoba District), *Tanganyika Notes and Records*, No. 24, 1947, pp. 3–27.

[26] G. Milne: Essays in Applied Pedology, III: Bukoba—High and Low Fertility on a Laterised Soil, *East African Agric. Journ.*, Vol. 4, 1938, pp. 13–24.

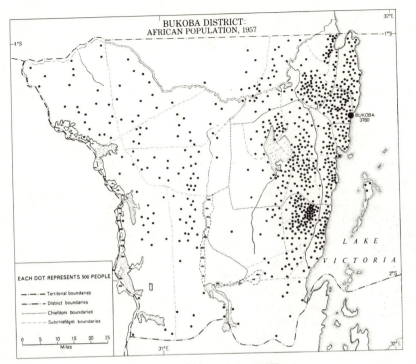

Figure 4.—African population of Bukoba District, 1957.

The resultant impoverishment has been so severe in many parts that the land will support only coarse grasses of low nutritive value, and a natural return to the former forest growth is virtually inhibited. Thus man has created the poor grasslands, or "rweya," which clothe large expanses of the coastal ridges today. They furnish a further graphic example of the delicacy of ecological balances.

Better soils were to be found in perhaps one-fifth of the region. These were developed on the shale bands and dolerites or in places where, through denudation, weathered products from these rocks were mixed with soils from the poor sandstones. The productive soils thus occurred apparently haphazardly on the planate ridgetops, on valley flanks, and along the discontinuous coastal fringe. The natives learned this lesson empirically through centuries of de-

forestation, of trial and error. The rweya are in part the result; but there was also a credit side to man's endeavors. On the better soils he established an agricultural system that not only maintained, but to some degree even enhanced, the fertility of the land. The banana was a staple crop—a perennial plant able to prevent excessive leaching, providing an umbrella from the rain and a mulch from its dead leaves. Cattle, a traditional token of wealth, were carefully tended, and their manure was used to enrich the cultivated land. This care of the land was encouraged by a tradition of permanent heritable tenure of the banana gardens.[27] In these ways indigenous man had established, before the coming of the European, an advantageous balance with

[27] H. Cory and M. N. Hartnoll: Customary Law of the Haya Tribe (International African Institute, London, 1945).

the environment. This is now threatened by the rapid growth of population, commercial coffee production, and the development of a cash economy.

Coffee has grown in Bukoba District from time immemorial. The local variety, *bukobensis*, may even be indigenous, though this view has been questioned.[28] The dried beans were an article of local commerce before European time; commercial development, however, has been the direct result of European stimulus. Under the German administration certain coffee trials and experiments were carried out and limited alienations of land on the coastal ridges were made for estates. Beyond the coastal ridges German control made much less impact. A stronger development of native production set in under the British mandate, and today the great bulk of the coffee crop is grown by Africans, the seven remaining estates making only a small contribution.

Coffee has brought prosperity to Bukoba. It has also created problems. In effect, a new crop, not ideally suitable like the banana, jostles for increasing space on the limited fertile land. With commercial coffee production has come an increasing conversion to a cash economy. Once the people looked on their cattle as the measure of their wealth. Poor though the beasts were, subsisting chiefly on the grasses of the rweya, they nevertheless represented a vital contribution to balanced agriculture. Today there is no doubt that cattle keeping is declining: the African thinks more of his cash from coffee. His response to a natural desire for self-betterment and to fluctuations in market price is to plant more coffee. The rweya still contribute little. It is easy to criticize African agriculturists regarding the rweya, but a number of years of scientific agricultural research has not yet solved all the problems of their utilization.

The African population of Bukoba District is still increasing: at the 1948 census

[28] T. S. Jervis: A History of *Robusta* Coffee in Bukoba, *Tanganyika Notes and Records*, No. 8, 1939, pp. 47–58.

it was about 300,000; at the 1957 census it was almost 368,000, an increase of 23 per cent. Pressure is of course most acute on the coastal ridges, where, with the exception of fishing on the coast, there are few immediately promising alternatives to agriculture. Thus the pressure on the land now poses a formidable problem.

It is such considerations that are prompting yet another reappraisal of the relative resources of the regions of Bukoba District. High Karagwe now carries 15 per cent of the African population of the district. Since 1924 small-scale tin mining along the granite margins has given some new stimulus to development and communications, but progress depends on the current carefully integrated agricultural resettlement schemes. The future of these deeply concerns administrator and cultivator alike: they hold the key to the redevelopment of high Karagwe.

The lower Kagera basin now carries 7 per cent of the African population. It is difficult to see great prospects here. Over much of the region the bush is thick and tsetse-infested. The river, however, is still an asset. It is navigable for barges as far as Nyakanyasi, but traffic is light. The Bhagwant Sugar Estate, north of Kyaka Ferry, is a recent Indian venture, which will have to rely for success on water from the river for irrigation. Some settlement is seeking favored spots on the flanks of the lower valley, but it is of modest proportions.

Somewhat surprisingly, the central depression now exceeds the lower Kagera basin in population, supporting 8 per cent of the total. This is largely due to new agricultural settlement, especially around Lake Ikimba and centered on Kabirizi. More of the overspill from the coastal ridges is likely to swell the population, and, as high Karagwe also develops, the importance of the central depression as a link region is likely at last to be increased.

A new regional balance is in the making. Sauer has pertinently directed attention to the relationship between man's cultural attainments and his changing appraisals of natural resources.[29] The regions of Bukoba District have been successively re-evaluated in such a way. Modern developments and

[29] C. O. Sauer: Agricultural Origins and Dispersals, *Amer. Geogr. Soc. Bowman Memorial Lectures Ser. Two,* New York, 1952, pp. 2–3.

European technical innovations are increasing the power of man to alter the ecological equations here in his own favor. Nonetheless, these equations remain an underlying reality, and an understanding of them provides a valuable background to the problems of development and resettlement.

The regions of differing environment discussed in the Bukoba study are minor compared with the vast area of savanna and forest that extend latitudinally throughout West Africa. The latter have offered a great variety of challenges and opportunities to their inhabitants and display marked contrasts in agricultural systems, crops, population distribution, and settlement patterns (Forde, 1953). The interchange of products between the forest and the savanna, extending far back in time, has had important social and political consequences (Hodder, 1965, 1969; Tricart, 1956). The people who live in these two major regions—the savanna and the forest—are by no means mutually exclusive. Some groups have moved southward from the savanna adapting their economy and culture to the forest environment; former inhabitants of the savanna, such as the Yoruba in Southwest Nigeria and Dahomey, are now distributed in both regions (Ojo, 1967).

Controversies continue over differences in vegetation between forest and savanna in West Africa (Hopkins, 1965). Some arguments attribute the development of the savanna to the degradation of forest by biotic factors. Research in Western Nigeria is attempting through air-photo-interpretation and fieldwork to study the geographic differences between the two zones, to measure accurately variations in the boundary between them, and to determine and evaluate the complex factors responsible for differences. The results to date are only tentative, but suggest that forest degradation has not been responsible for extension of the savanna, and that overall the evidence of physical controls is stronger than might have been expected (see also Moss and Morgan, 1970; Moss, 1968).

Research of this nature offers a good opportunity for inter-disciplinary work. The practical implications for economic development are great, in regions supporting some of the highest densities of population in West Africa (Church, 1969; Morgan and Pugh, 1969).

2. Savanna and Forest in Western Nigeria

W. B. MORGAN AND R. P. MOSS

The savanna-forest boundary in West Africa is one of its most remarkable geographical features. The clarity with which the boundary is defined, whether seen from the air or from ground level, is, throughout most of its length, most striking. Moreover, the most casual observer will discover that many other features, particularly of settlement and of agriculture, reach the limit of their distributions at about the same location. Not the least significant feature, in sharp contrast with many other zones of vegetation change, is that the boundary is not an *ecotone*, or zone of gradual change in floristic composition and community structure in response to equally gradual changes in habitat character, but "a mosaic of communities representative of each region." [1] The zone of change consists of islands, salients, and enclaves of forest and savanna, sharply separated from one another. Only one community, the "transition woodland," [2] may in any sense be considered an ecotone. Even this, in some instances at least, may be a more or less transient sub-seral community, in view of the fact that forest trees within it are generally young, whereas the savanna trees are old.

The savanna-forest boundary thus appears very clearly, especially on vertical air photographs, and may in consequence be accurately mapped and studied in relation to other features in a number of locations. Such study has the full support of the Special Commission on the Humid Tropics of the International Geographical Union, which is especially concerned with understanding, defining, delimiting, and subdividing the humid tropical environment, and which regards the savanna-forest boundary

as one of its most interesting and significant problems. A symposium on the ecology of the boundary was held under its auspices in Venezuela in May 1964, and a major symposium to discuss the geography of the humid tropics is planned for 1968.

Nowhere is the boundary more clearly defined than in Western Nigeria, where the authors already have considerable field experience and where the new infra-red vertical air photographs, taken by Canadian Aero Services during the 1961–2 and 1962–3 dry seasons, provide prints of superb quality especially suitable for the study of vegetation communities in considerable detail. [3] The origin of the boundary here, as elsewhere, is a matter of considerable ecological debate. Some authorities stress the importance of burning and cultivation as dominating biotic influences. [4] Others assign more importance to climatic controls, such as rainfall, dry season length, and relative humidity, often with an emphasis on the importance of climatic change. Edaphic factors, related to soils, water table levels, and drainage, are also emphasized by some authors. [5] More recent work has related major features of the floristic composition to climate, while considering physiognomy, accompanied by some floristic change, as the product of cultivation and burning. [6] The relative importance of these factors in Nigeria has yet to be determined, but it may

[1] Keay, 1951, p. 64.
[2] Ibid., p. 63.

[3] Canadian Aero Services, Ottawa; photography on a scale of 1:40,000 taken under the Canadian Government Technical Aid Program.
[4] Aubréville, 1949; Macgregor, 1937; see also the important paper on the Central African savannas, Vesey-Fitzgerald, 1963.
[5] Clayton, 1958; Chevalier, 1909; Moreau, 1933 and 1938; Cole, 1963. Many other references might be cited to illustrate the points made under notes 4 and 5.
[6] Taylor, *et al.*, 1962, ch. iii, pp. 6–11.

From *Africa*, 35, 1965, pp. 286–293. Reprinted by permission of the International African Institute, London.

be noted at this stage that the generalized boundary approximately follows the orientation of the isohyets, and that dry-season relative humidity increases sharply on the forest side.

The savanna and forest environments provide different fallows for the agriculturalist, sometimes serve locally as indicators of major soil differences, and provide different conditions for settlement siting in relation to such considerations as defense and local land use. Many of the larger Yoruba towns are grouped in a crescent-shaped zone some 20 miles in width which follows the boundary quite closely. These towns contain markets traditionally concerned with the interchange of savanna and forest produce amongst other forms of exchange. Such interchange has long been one of the major elements of Yoruba commerce, and modern developments, particularly the expansion of cocoa planting, have served only to emphasize rather than to reduce the commercial contrasts between the two environments. Traditionally therefore Yorubaland has a dual character which provides such contrasts as that between the religious capital of Ife in the forest and the former political capital of Old Oyo in the savanna. Thus Fage could write: "Ife, which may possibly have come into existence about A.D. 1000, lies in the northern fringes of the forest, remote from trade and other contacts with the great states of the Sudan. These were doubtless more in evidence in Oyo, one of the most northerly Yoruba kingdoms, which in fact became famed for the power of its cavalry." [7] Speculation on Yoruba history has frequently suggested an important role for vegetation in influencing population movement. Despite Yoruba traditions of origins at Ife in the forest, such speculation has connected the foundation of the Yoruba kingdoms with the migration of peoples across the savannas, entering the forest only at a late period of their history. For example, Lloyd has claimed: "The early an-

cestors of the people we now call the Yoruba migrated in one or more waves southwards from the savanna belt into their present abode, bringing with them the arts of pottery, iron smelting, yam cultivation and perhaps the institution of kingship. Slowly they penetrated the forest, already probably inhabited by people whose economy was based on hunting and gathering. By continual cultivation the limits of dense forest were pushed southwards." [8] Similarly Forde wrote of the penetration of the forest belt from the savannas and suggested ". . . the tendency of linguistic frontiers to correspond with the savanna-forest margin suggests an early and important cultural differentiation between these two zones. In the savanna, where until recently the human movement over considerable distances was so much easier than in the forest, we find that a series of distinct subgroups have expanded over compact areas." [9] Unfortunately, we do not know with certainty that the movement of peoples some centuries or even millenia ago was in fact easier in the savanna than in the forest, nor do we know with certainty that savanna environments were preferred to forest environments by earlier agriculturalists.

It is important to point out also that, although botanists have generally tended to stress the importance of both fire and cultivation in producing the present savanna plant communities, the actual effectiveness of grass burning and of different forms and intensities of cultivation in destroying or modifying forest communities are alike unknown. A recent paper [10] has drawn attention to this fact and points out that less than a dozen ecological experiments involving the study of the effects of different types of burning or of fire protection have been conducted in the whole of West Africa, and some of these cannot be considered absolutely reliable because of deficiencies in experimental or statistical techniques. As

[7] Fage, 1962, p. 89.

[8] Lloyd, 1962, p. 51.
[9] Forde, 1953.
[10] Ramsay and Innes, 1963.

a consequence of this, speculations so far made on the early history of West Africa in relation to the character of the vegetation rest upon highly generalized and equally speculative ecological evidence and conclusions.

For example, the linguistic frontiers have been described as tending to correspond with the savanna-forest margin, but in Western Nigeria the frontiers between the Yoruba, Bariba, and Nupe languages lie some 40 to 70 miles to the north and west of the present margin. They more nearly correspond with the probable limits of "climax forest" as indicated by forest outliers in the "derived savanna," but if we are to suppose a relationship between language and vegetation, must we claim that ecological conditions further to the north and west were unsuited to Yoruba farmers, or that it was Yoruba settlement in the "climax forest" which resulted in the reduction of a portion of it to "derived savanna"? If such claims are to be made further evidence must be sought to substantiate them, rather than leave the present generalizations with all their implications to go unchallenged. Or can one see historic difficulties in supposing that migrants across the savannas penetrating the formerly more extensive forests only with great difficulty could find no cultivators from amongst their number able or willing to plant crops in the savannas from which they came? One might on the other hand suppose the borderland between Yoruba, Bariba, and Nupe to represent at least in part a balance of power between rival communities, but what relationship can this have to "derived savanna" and "Guinea savanna"?

The savanna-forest boundary is clearly a feature of great interest to students in many disciplines and the attempt to solve the several problems raised will ultimately need the co-operation of research workers in all those disciplines. Such co-operation, however, does not need to be simultaneous. The first task is clear definition of the feature in its varying character and distribution, replacing

the present generalized view and making possible an accurate picture of its true character. This task alone may provide answers to some of the questions already raised, while at the same time posing new problems. It is this primary task of definition and delimitation which the authors have set themselves, with reference, in the first place, to the region between the Dahomey border and Ibadan. Two separate sets of vertical air photographs are available for the area, giving complete stereoscopic coverage for two dates approximately eight years apart. The older set, at a scale of 1:25,000, are panchromatic prints made from photography flown in 1953 and 1954 by the Federal Survey Department, and the newer set, taken under the Canadian Technical Air Program, dates from 1962 and 1963. The latter set was taken using infra-red film, with an A.V. 2·2 filter, and, though the haze-penetration properties of the film were the primary reason for its use, the so-called "chlorophyll effect" produced by its sensitivity to green tones makes it especially suitable for use in vegetation and land use studies. For the present study, the fact that the habit of the plants composing the vegetation markedly affects the film response made it relatively easy to differentiate grass fallow from the early herb stage of the woody fallow succession, the grass areas appearing much darker owing to the more upright habit of the dominant plants. Furthermore the physiognomy of the vegetation may also be readily seen on the photographs, and a number of distinct vegetation-land-use communities may be distinguished directly from the prints without actual field-work. At a later stage field-work will be necessary in order to check the photo interpretation, and also to facilitate closer definition of the distinct units distinguished from the prints, but, in the zone embracing the forest-savanna boundary, the actual dividing line can be mapped in all its detail and complexity for 1962 and 1963 directly from the photographs.

Similar maps can be made from the earlier

photographs, though not so readily, since the prints are of much more variable quality, largely as a result of the poorer haze-penetration of the panchromatic film. It is relevant to point out the peculiar difficulties of aerial photography in this part of the tropics. During the wet season, and even at the beginning and end of the rains it is almost always too cloudy to make extensive photography from an aircraft a practical possibility, and for much of the dry season, even when the harmattan is not strong, the ground haze is sufficiently thick seriously to impair the quality of the photographs. For consistently good prints, therefore, film with good haze penetration is essential.

By plotting from both sets of photographs on the same scale, using simple photogrammetric equipment, it will be possible for the first time to make a direct comparison of the actual position and character of the savanna-forest boundary for two fixed dates. Actual movements and changes which have taken place in the intervening period will thus be quite clear. An additional advantage of the air photographs as a source of information is that it provides a ready means of relating the features in which one is primarily interested to others which may be important; frequently also the juxtaposition in the photograph of two features which had not previously been thought to be connected suggests important relationships.

It may be objected that 8 to 10 years is too short a period to show any significant changes. Considered in terms of general, gradual, ecological development this may be true, though even with reference to this problem it is not unlikely that suggestive evidence may emerge. In relation to the immediate effects of cultivation, burning, and population pressure, however, important trends should be readily apparent, since the most marked increase in Nigeria's population, according to census evidence, occurred in the 1950's. This increase is quite evident in the area of study, and is clearly shown on the photographs by the expansion and proliferation of towns, villages, and minor settlements between the dates of the photography. It may also be pointed out that burning experiments usually yield significant results after only 10 to 11 years,[11] though a longer period of fire protection is obviously desirable for really conclusive results.

If therefore there is any close relationship between density of population, intensity of cultivation, burning, and the character or position of the forest-savanna boundary, it is reasonable to expect that some evidence of it will be seen even within the 10-year period. Absence of such evidence would strongly indicate that no close connexion in fact exists.

Work on the photographs is in progress, but some preliminary observations and tentative conclusions may be offered on the basis of the investigations so far made, principally of the infra-red prints.

BURNING

Burned patches are clearly defined on the infra-red photographs. Owing to the fact that the prints cover a period of some two to three months in each of two dry seasons, no accurate measurement of the total area burned in any one season can be obtained from the prints, but nowhere is there evidence of the wholesale destruction of large areas of vegetation in any one season. Burning always occurs in scattered small patches, very occasionally rectilinear, possibly as a result of pulling the grasses before burning in order to destroy their roots, but more often amorphous, suggesting that the fire is not controlled, and has spread, and stopped, of its own accord. There is no evidence at all to suggest that fires once started spread either rapidly or far. Furthermore, the most extensive burned patches occur principally on shallow, rubbly soils, associated with hard laterite pavements, on which a quite distinct grass vegetation is characteristic (with *Ctenium newtonii*).[12] On these the

---

[11] Ramsay and Innes, op. cit.
[12] Taylor, *et al.*, op. cit., ch. viii.

burned area stops abruptly at the "break-away" at the edge of the pavement, where the deeper, heavier soils are associated with a woodland, or sometimes a forest community,[13] and this abrupt cessation of burning is found invariably where the fire has come up against a salient or outlier of forest.

The evidence suggests that some notions of the extent and destructiveness of savanna fires are rather exaggerated. In particular the idea of an annual burn which affects a large proportion of the area in each year would seem to be quite false. It is more likely that some patches, peculiarly susceptible to fire, as a result of edaphic or biotic influences upon the character of the community itself, are repeatedly burned, whereas others are hardly, if ever, affected. It is perhaps unfortunate in this connexion that fire-protection experiments have almost always been conducted on the most degraded communities to be found in the Guinea savanna.[14] It is also important to note that there is no evidence anywhere along the forest fringe, whether of the main forest zone or of outliers and salients, to suggest that fires sweep into the forest, effecting notable destruction of forest trees. Such comparisons as have been made so far indicate that there has been little retreat of the forest fringe, even around the forest outliers well away from the main belt of forest. Indeed, in some areas, especially on the northern fringe of the Ijaiye and the Osho Forest Reserves, to the north of Olokemeji, the forest seems to be extending into the savanna and also to be increasing in vigour.

FOREST "OUTLIERS"

Large forest "outliers" are numerous throughout the extensive area of "derived savanna" shown on the air photographs.

They are much larger and more common than had been realized from ground-level observation. They consist not only of streamside forest of the "gallery" type and of patches of forest on steep slopes perhaps unsuitable for cultivation, but of extensive islands of forest on comparatively level land, within which there is no apparent physical advantage other than perhaps that of deeper or heavier soil. Moreover, such islands of forest contain larger continuous areas of apparently more intensive cultivation than the adjacent savannas. Such cultivation produces fallows of woody plants as cultivation within the forest areas proper does. These forest islands are not just rings of forest allowed to remain or deliberately encouraged around savanna towns or villages. Several of them each contain a number of villages within or just fringing their perimeters. The forest islands are therefore not as easily explained as some authorities would insist. Schnell, for example, follows Aubréville in describing a savanna with clumps of high dense forest some hundreds of metres in width on the edge of the equatorial forest domain, but claims that normally the centre of each is occupied by a village: "Couramment, le centre de ces bosquets est occupé par un village, comme si les habitants avaient cherché (pour des raisons traditionelles ou pratiques) à maintenir autour de leurs agglomérations leur milieu forestier primitif."[15] Perhaps the islands are remnants of forest surrounding central settlements which have since disappeared? Perhaps—but no supporting evidence has appeared yet for those examples seen. Rather do these great patches of forest and woody fallow appear capable of resisting very intense levels of cultivation without being reduced to savanna. As such they do not appear to be the product of settlement. The reverse appears to be the case—that settlement has moved into or near the forest islands because of the agricultural advantages of the associated soils and perhaps also for the timber and fruit available. This

[13] For a description of the soils of this particular area and a discussion of breakaway features at the edge of hard laterite sheets, see Moss, 1965.

[14] Ramsay and Innes, op. cit.

[15] Schnell, 1957, p. 90.

phenomenon has been noted elsewhere by Jones, even much further north, within the Guinea savanna.[16] His observations were limited by problems of movement, distance, and terrain. Now it becomes possible to gauge the extent of the phenomenon. It would appear perhaps that within the southern savannas (southern Guinea and "derived") islands of the forest type of environment may be more attractive to settlement than the savannas themselves. One wonders whether this is recent or long established. Some of the islands have been examined in detail on both earlier and later photography and show over the past 10 years very little, or in most cases, no alterations in their boundaries, despite the obvious increases in the sizes of their associated villages.

The evidence suggests that biotic factors, in the form of cultivation and burning, are not at the present time capable of effecting any rapid degradation of forest or of areas subjected to woody fallows, despite an increase in population, even in the case of forest outliers a considerable distance from the main forest-savanna boundary. This in turn suggests two intriguing alternatives. On the one hand it may be that edaphic controls are critical, or on the other it may be that there is a delicate balance between population and the plant community, with a "threshold," or critical level, at which population density, with associated pressure on the biological resources, becomes sufficient to produce rapid degradation from forest and woody fallow to savanna and grass fallow. Until this level is reached increased pressure merely produces a reduction in tree growth, but does not encourage invasion by savanna grasses and shrubs. This may itself imply some edaphic control of the forest outliers which remain.

AGRICULTURAL PATTERNS

There are some notable differences between field sizes, and even, in certain instances, shapes between savanna and forest. Fields

are generally larger, in several cases much larger, in the savanna. The arrangement of fields in ring patterns [17] is so far only apparent in the savannas. Corridors seem more characteristic of the forest, but this observation is extremely tentative and much more study must be done. Certainly rings of a type already described chiefly in the Sudan and northern Guinea savannas are also quite common in the "derived savanna" of Western Nigeria. Usually there is a ring of woodland or of forest around settlements, even around isolated compounds. There are problems in comparing agricultural patterns between forest and savanna, particularly in the forest areas where part of the ground is hidden by the trees themselves. Nevertheless wherever woodland or forest has reestablished itself after cultivation that fact is often readily apparent in the markedly rectilinear patterns of the vegetation.

THE SAVANNA-FOREST BOUNDARY

The existence of such a complicated mosaic of plant communities makes the location of the "boundary" difficult to define. In practice it is not impossible, for on the photographs it is usually fairly easy to draw a line which represents the points at which savanna with forest ouliers becomes forest with savanna inliers, and changes in the location of this line must be as important to define as the complexity of the community pattern in the border zone. Demonstration of stability or movement must await more detailed measurement and analysis of the border pattern, but random sample studies indicate that it has shown little general movement in the past ten years.

Furthermore, the actual pattern of distribution of forest with woody fallow and savanna with grassy fallow along this generalized boundary line is not homogeneous. For example, in the area between Meko and Aiyetoro, in the western part of the area being investigated, the pattern is strikingly

---

[16] Jones, 1963.

[17] For a major study with a useful bibliography, see Sautter, 1962.

related to the soils, for the grass and savanna communities found on the flat tops of the hills are associated with the outcrops of hard laterite pavements, while forest communities and woody fallows are associated with the deeper more clayey colluvial soils immediately below the "breakaway," even on the less steep slopes, which are in some cases heavily cultivated. Elsewhere, such edaphic control is not immediately apparent.

In conclusion it may be said that these preliminary investigations suggest that the forest-savanna boundary in this area seems to be relatively stable, both in general and in detail, despite the increase in population which has taken place in the last ten years. There is rather more evidence of minor forest advances, particularly in the vicinity of forest reserves, than of forest retreat, and the importance of edaphic factors as critical controls is strongly indicated. Nevertheless the complexity of the pattern, both in its morphology and in its dynamics, cannot be overemphasized, and generalizations concerning the whole boundary are dangerous and must wait the results of more detailed examination. The complexity of the factors involved is considerable, and they operate with a different balance at different times and in different places. The sum total of the effect determines the location of the boundary at any one time. The changes taking place at present, and those which have taken place in the past, must not be conceived as the progressive complication of an initial homogeneous vegetation pattern by the influence of man, both directly and indirectly. Rather they must be visualized as the evolution of a complexity of a different kind from an initial situation which may well have been no less complex. Diversity is not the product of human intervention; it is an inherent property of the pattern. Isolation of the important factors and study of their influence with reference to particular times and particular locations is indispensable to any understanding of the general principles governing balance and stability or movement. It is hoped that the continuation of the study here reviewed will serve to elucidate some of them.

REFERENCES

Aubréville, A. 1949. *Climats, forêts, et désertification de l'Afrique tropicale.* Paris.

Chevalier, A. 1909. "L'extension et la regression de la forêt vierge de l'Afrique tropicale," *Comptes rendus, Acad. Sci. Paris,* cxlix. 458–61.

Clayton, W. D. 1958. "Secondary Vegetation and the Transition to Savanna near Ibadan," *Journ. Ecol.* xlvi. 217–38.

Cole, M. M. 1963. "Vegetation and Geomorphology in Northern Rhodesia: An Aspect of the Distribution of the Savanna of Central Africa," *Geog. Journ.* cxxix. 467–96.

Fage, J. D. 1962. *An Introduction to the History of West Africa.* Cambridge. 3rd edition.

Forde, Daryll. 1953. "The Cultural Map of West Africa: Successive Adaptations to Tropical Forests and Grasslands," *Trans. N.Y. Acad. Sci.,* series 3, xv. 206–19.

Jones, E. W. 1963. "The Forest Outliers in the Guinea Zone of Northern Nigeria," *Journ. Ecol.* li. 415–34.

Keay, R. W. J. 1951. "Some Notes on the Ecological Status of Savanna Vegetation in Nigeria," *Commonwealth Bureau of Pastures and Field Crops Bull.* xli. 57–68.

Lloyd, P. C. 1962. *Yoruba Land Law.* London.

Macgregor, W. D. 1937. "Forest Type and Succession in Nigeria," *Empire Forestry Journal,* xv. 234–42.

Moreau, R. E. 1933. "Pleistocene Climatic Changes and the Distribution of Life in East Africa," *Journ. Ecol.* xxi. 415–35.

—— 1938. "Climatic Classification from the Standpoint of East African Biology," *Journ. Ecol.* xxvi. 467–96.

Moss, R. P. 1965. "Slope Development and Subsoil Morphology in a Part of South-western Nigeria," *Journ. Soil Sci.* 1965, no. 1.

Ramsay, J. M., and Innes, R. Rose. 1963. "Some Quantitative Observations on the Effects of Fire on the Guinea Savanna Vegetation of Northern Ghana over a Period of Eleven Years," *African Soils,* viii. 41–85.

Sautter, G. 1962. "A propos de quelques terroirs d'Afrique occidentale, essai comparatif," *Études rurales,* vi. 24–86.

Schnell, R. 1957. *Plantes alimentaires et vie agricole de l'Afrique noire.* Paris.

Taylor, B. W., Baker, R. M., Leefers, C. L., and de Rosayro, R. A. 1962. *Report on the Land Use Survey of the Oyo-Shaki Area, W. Nigeria.* (Mimeographed, Min. of Agriculture and Natural Resources, Ibadan.)

Vesey-Fitzgerald, D. F. 1963. "Central African Grasslands," *Journ. Ecol.* li. 243–74.

The recognition of the importance of the physical environment in recent years is amply demonstrated in the following paper, a geographer's contribution to an interdisciplinary research project in the social sciences. *The Culture and Ecology in East Africa Project,* carried out early in the 1960's, also involved social anthropology, economics, and psychology in a controlled comparative study in which the geographical base was treated as an independent variable (Goldschmidt *et al.,* 1965). Porter discusses the environment in terms of opportunities offered for exploitation, but states that it must also be considered "at a further remove, a potential for shaping culture," thus indicating acceptance of its considerable and wide-ranging influence.

Temporal variations are significant in respect of rainfall probability and variability, both major environmental parameters to which detailed attention has been given in East Africa (Kenworthy, 1964). Porter also discusses spatial variations. One of the situations described illustrates significant environmental variation over short distances resulting from changes in altitude and relief. The changes are considerable enough to cause discontinuity, rather than a continuum, in the opportunities they offer, permitting multiple-environment use and reciprocal economies that spread the risks resulting from environmental variability. Among the different environments identified, intensity of land use is very low in the one offering the least opportunities. Because agriculture provides inadequate subsistence, gathering and hunting assume greater importance in the economy. A minimum of human interference and modification of the environment give correspondingly greater rewards from collection and from the chase.

Porter views man as an active causative factor in change. His example of one cultural group utilizing several contrasting environments involves a time element; as the need of the group changed, different zones were successively exploited. This historical perspective may be compared with that given by McMaster for Bukoba where, through time, differing cultural groups have exploited different environments depending on their needs and capabilities.

3. Environmental Potentials and Economic Opportunities—A Background for Cultural Adaptation

PHILIP W. PORTER

My task in this cooperative research has been to examine environment and to express the varieties of environment as potentials for different subsistence uses. The environment is thus seen as a potential for exploitation by man, and at a further remove, a potential for the shaping of culture. In order to relate environment and subsistence forms to one another in a meaningful way we use the concept of subsistence risk. In outline, first we discuss environmental parameters in East Africa and explain subsistence risk; second, we examine two environmental gradients, a steep one in Pokot, and a gentle one in Kamba country; and third, we conclude with some suggestions as to what these environmental types and gradients mean for economic exploitation and cultural adaptation.

The environmental setting with which we are concerned is equatorial highland and lowland. The Pokot of west-central Kenya and the Wakamba also of Kenya in the area east of Nairobi lie within a degree of the equator, the Pokot to the north, the Wakamba to the south. The elevations of settlements range from 10,000 to 3,000 ft. in Pokotland; from 7,000 to 2,500 in Ukambani. There is a clear relationship between rainfall and elevation in East Africa (see Fig. 1). It increases with altitude with such regularity that a simple regression equation allows fairly precise calculation of rainfall from elevation. An important feature of the rainfall is its distribution through the year, which is most closely tied to the equinoctial overhead passage of the sun, and precipitation resulting from local convectional storms in the train of this overhead passage (see Fig. 2). Where rainfall is ample these peaks may not be important, but as rainfall amounts decline, the concentration of precipitation in the bimodal peak periods, and the spacing of the maxima with respect to one another, do become important. Still another variable is the reliability of rainfall, which generally can be said to decrease as the amount of rainfall decreases.

Granting that technology can extend the range of a subsistence activity, we can see (Fig. 1) that there is a zone in which the growing of bananas would be possible (the requirements are over 44 inches of rainfall per annum, evenly distributed); next comes a zone in which the growing of grains, finger millet and maize, is favored. These are water demanding crops if they are to do well. Moving on to drier areas it becomes necessary to rely more heavily on quick-maturing water-conservative plants such as bulrush millet, sorghum, castor, pigeon peas, and cowpeas, as well as tuberous famine crops like sweet potatoes and cassava. At some point even these drought resistant plants cannot be relied upon, and subsistence becomes based on the grasses and browse plants which can sustain livestock in very dry environments.

Now to add another variable to this altitudinal profile: we must remember that temperature as well as rainfall has been changing with altitude, at about 3.5° f. per thousand feet. The interrelations of heat and moisture provide zones in which the vectors of two important livestock diseases can flourish. Roughly, one can say that well-watered areas between 4,000 and 7,000 ft. are both warm and moist enough to support tick populations, the vector of East Coast Fever. There is a tendency for livestock diseases to be associated with particular kinds of vegetation. In the case of East

From the *American Anthropologist*, Vol. 67, April 1965, pp. 409–420.
Reprinted by permission of the American Anthropological Association.

Generalized Altitudinal Profile

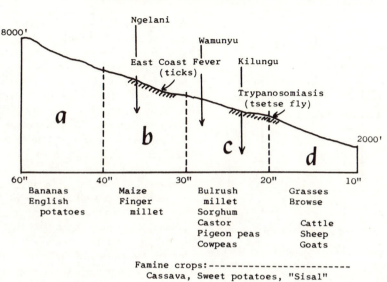

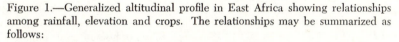

Figure 1.—Generalized altitudinal profile in East Africa showing relationships among rainfall, elevation and crops. The relationships may be summarized as follows:

1. The higher, the wetter. 2. The lower, the hotter. 3. The less the mean annual rainfall, the greater the variability. 4. The importance of the bimodal rainfall regime increases with decreases in altitude. 5. The bimodal regime merges into a single maximum with increases in latitude.

Coast Fever in Kenya it is with combretaceous woodland and forest. The other great livestock menace, trypanosomiasis, is found in areas suited to the tsetse fly. The necessary habitat involves heat, moisture, and shade, all in close proximity, and accordingly moist lowlands and drier plains areas of thicket and dense *Acacia* thorn scrub near perennial streams are commonly tsetse infested. Since livestock disease is associated with vegetation types, the boundaries between infested and free areas are often sharp. The Pokot and Wakamba know which areas are infested and the times of year it is unsafe to run livestock there. The environmental limits for crops, however, are seldom so clearly stated in nature, a point to which we will presently return.

We can, I hope, see that this over-all gradient in rainfall, heat, and the presence or absence of livestock diseases represents a continuum or profile of environmental types wherein differing subsistence activities are possible depending on the technology and will of the people. But these types merge, one into the other, and we are hard pressed to know where to draw boundaries between types. By tampering with the slope of the altitudinal profile, I now introduce another variable, one that is peculiarily spatial (Fig. 3). It is a distance factor, related to the range of movement of people under normal primitive circumstances. An abrupt change in elevation, on the order of two to three thousand feet in a few miles, can effectively collapse or eliminate certain environments

Water Balance Diagram

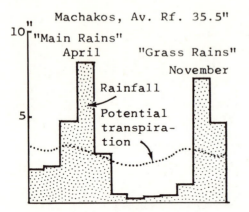

Figure 2.—Water balance diagram for Macha-kos, Ukambani. The rainfall has a bimodal regime which is characteristic of areas close to the equator. The year is thus divided into four alternating periods of rainfall surplus and defi-cit. The moisture deficit is partly met by mois-ture stored in the soil.

and place very different environmental types so close to one another as to be within walk-ing distance. It is reasonable to expect that the subsistence economy in an area of en-vironmental diversity would differ from that in a zone of environmental uniformity.

Steep Altitudinal Profile

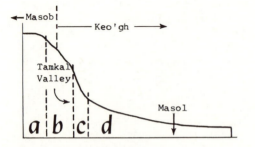

Figure 3.—A steep altitudinal profile in West Pokot District places different environmental zones close to one another.

SUBSISTENCE RISK

All human activities involve risk. Men have devised individual and institutional strate-gies to cope with these dangers. The un-certainties connected with farming and herding in East Africa are proverbial. The Masai lost 400,000 head of cattle from drought during 1961, when our field season was just starting. In large measure, subsis-tence uncertainty can be traced to vagaries of climate. Tick populations, pests such as army worms, stalk borers and dioch-bird swarms are related to climatic conditions. Agricultural (as well as pastoral) risks are not everywhere the same. It is, I feel, in a geography of subsistence risks that a mean-ingful link can be forged between subsis-tence economies and environmental poten-tials. Subsistence risk is not given in nature, it is a settlement negotiated between an environment and a technology. Just how much risk an individual or a community can tolerate, how often a failure of crops or decimation of herds can be borne, is a prob-lem that each culture must solve. A com-munity has institutional and technical means of coping with risk. It can tighten its belt, develop surpluses, or raid neighboring terri-tory. Danger to the individual can be de-creased by sharing out risks, through dis-persal of fields, timing of harvests, cattle deals, and the like. We may assume that in the degree to which the situation is tenuous, adjustment to risk is the essential element in the articulation of subsistence with environ-ment.

The way in which I thought the geog-raphy of subsistence risk could be subjected to rigorous analysis was to map rainfall probabilities. We can describe this as a method for determining water need/water supply relationships for various agricultural seasons. Water need, the term which mea-sures the transpiration requirement of in-coming radiant energy, has been based on the work of Penman (1948, 1963) and Thornthwaite (Thornthwaite 1948; Thorn-thwaite and Mather 1957, 1962). The calculation of rainfall probabilities is patterned after studies by Manning (1956), Glover, Robinson and McCulloch (Glover and McCulloch 1958; Glover, Robinson and Henderson 1954; Kenworthy and Glover 1958; Robinson and Glover 1954) except that they generally deal in rainfall *per se*, rather than its relationship to plant transpiration requirements.

Against the water need was compared the water supply (rainfall) over a number of years. The number of years in which a season showed a positive water balance, divided by the total number of years, gives the probability of transpiration demands being met. Where the water balance is a negative value, that is, need exceeds supply, it is argued that plants wilt and die, and crops consequently fail or the harvest is severely reduced.

By studying the temporal as well as spatial variability of environment we at last touch the reality of what is going on between people and environments. We see a way of grasping and using process, of taking into account secular change. We find, in short, a way of coping with that flux which people term "ecology."

The Pokot. Pokotland shows an extremely steep environmental gradient. Basically there is *keo'gh* the hot country, and *masob*, the cold country; but within these climates are several explicitly named and managed zones: valley bottoms, steep lower hill slopes, and land higher up on a bench at about 7,000 ft. (Figs. 3 and 4). There are specific crops, irrigation, and other agricultural techniques for each zone. People are organized within the *korok*, which geopolitically is a space laid out to include these several zones. People commonly have farms in all zones. The timing of planting, weeding, irrigating and harvesting is carefully worked out so that there is a constant movement between zones and no intolerable peak load of work in any month. In the Pokot view, life in Tamkal could hardly be

contemplated except as one based on the use of several zones.

Much of the work is communally shared. Large fields (called *parahgomucho*) involving even 30 people are cut from bush, burned, fenced, irrigated and protected from birds and animals on a communal basis. Year by year there is a constant recurrence of opening new farms and letting used fields revert to bush. This creates a kaleidoscopic involvement of kin and neighbors, for the personnel of one *parahgomucho* is different from the next. Since the head of a household will have 4 to 6 fields in crop and 20 others in fallow, this means that his fortunes and risks are inextricably enmeshed with those of the community at large.

The use of multiple environments does not stop at having farms at different elevations. Abutting on the escarpment walls are wide plains covered with poor thorn *Acacia*. Although tsetse infested along the perennial rivers, the Masol plains elsewhere are marginally suitable for livestock. There can be no question of agriculture here. These dry plains are less than a day's walk from farming communities in the adjacent hills. A long established trade in milk, livestock, and grain flourishes between the two sectors. A mutually beneficial specialization of economic activity exists along this steep environmental gradient. Because of the abruptness of the environmental change, the Pokot have not been in a position to argue with nature; subsistence adaptations here are explicit and successful. The probability of agricultural success or failure changes so precipitously that it is a discontinuity, not really a gradient.

Ukambani. We turn now to the Wakamba. Here our interest centers on the gradual transition in rainfall probabilities from the high potential areas in the west, which change imperceptibly with loss of altitude to the southeast (Figs. 1, 5 and 6). We will examine three points along this gradient, the two extremes being the communities in which Dr. Oliver worked. In the

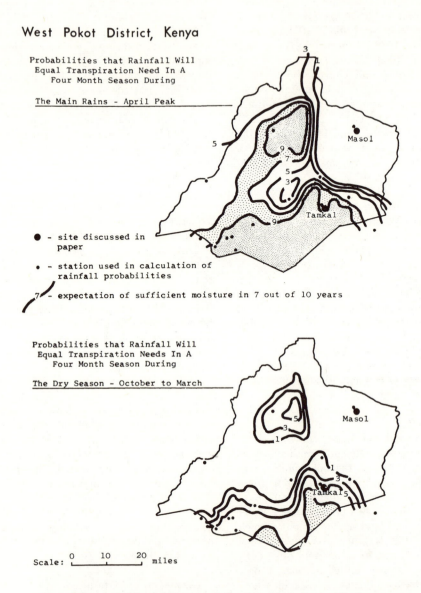

Figure 4.—Maps showing the probability of transpiration needs being met in four-month crop seasons during the main rains and during the dry season in West Pokot District. The isolines describe the certainty a farmer has of obtaining sufficient moisture for crops for particular seasons and places. Note the steep gradient between Tamkal and the plains to the northeast.

time available, I have no choice but to adopt a telegraphic even stream-of-consciousness delivery by which to create an image of the subsistence and its technology.

Ngelani. The farming community is in the western hills at elevations of 5,500 to 6,500 ft. Rainfall exceeds 35 inches and is bimodal, being concentrated into the November-December grass rains, and the March-May main rains (Fig. 2). The probability of obtaining adequate moisture to satisfy transpiration needs is 0.8 in four months in the grass rains (Fig. 5), and over 0.9 in four months in the main rains (Fig. 6).

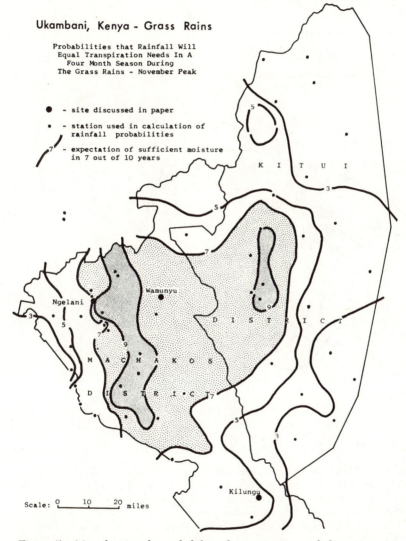

Figure 5.—Map showing the probability of transpiration needs being met during the grass rains (November peak) in Ukambani, Kenya. The isolines describe the certainty a farmer has of obtaining sufficient moisture for crops. Note the gentleness of the probability gradient between Ngelani and Kilungu.

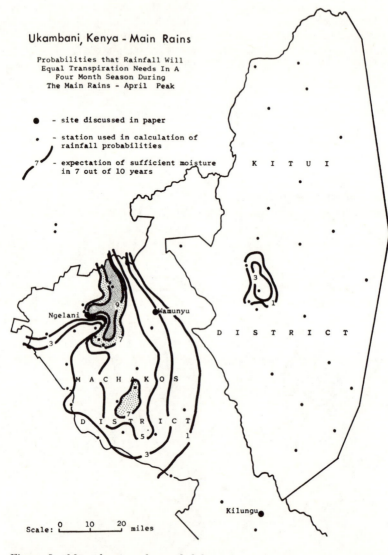

Figure 6.—Map showing the probability of transpiration needs being met during the main rains (April peak) in Ukambani, Kenya. The isolines describe the certainty a farmer has of obtaining sufficient moisture for crops. Note that although the gradients have steepened over those shown for the grass rains (Fig. 5), the gradient is still more gentle than in the area cited in West Pokot District (Fig. 4).

Population density is high, some sub-locations achieving values of 1,600 people per square mile. Land is individually owned, sold and inherited. Land values in this area are about 2,000 shillings per acre; this compares with the average annual income in the district for a man—about 1,600 shillings. Land transactions are the subject of much litigation and secrecy.

The typical farmer has from 4 to 7 acres in crop. The crops are few, but water demanding: maize, beans, peas, and Irish (English) potatoes. Yields are high. Technology involves ox-drawn steel plows, cultivators, terraced land, use of manure and insecticides. Seed selection, planting, and weeding are done with reasonable care, but without specific concern for drought and moisture conservation. Livestock are owned, but generally kept elsewhere, on lower adjacent plains.

Wamunyu. Wamunyu represents a zone of medium potential along the gradient. Elevations are here all within a few hundred feet of 4,000 ft. The rainfall is nearly 30 inches and shows the same marked concentration into two seasons. The probability of water supply equalling water need for four months in the grass rain is about 0.85; in the main rains, only 0.3 (Figs. 5 and 6). The density of population is between 150 and 300 persons per square mile. The crops here are more numerous and increasingly of a sort that do well in drought: maize and beans, of course, but also sweet potatoes, pigeon peas, cowpeas, bulrush millet, and cassava. Livestock are much more heavily depended on. Commonly one brother in a family will assume responsibility for the cattle of everyone, for the livestock must be driven great distances for graze.

The farmer who uses bench terraces and manure, who plants early and weeds early (to reduce transpiration and conserve soil moisture) obtains good and nearly certain yields. Most farmers, however, do poorly. They plant maize because it is easier than the traditional bulrush millet and is not susceptible to bird damage, like millet and

sorghum. Their yields are poor; the second season maize usually fails altogether. This part of the district has some of the worse mangalata, or devastated land, in Africa— the result of overgrazing and planting row crops (maize) on easily gullied slopes. Grazing beyond the carrying capacity of the land denudes it of vegetation, prevents the annual grass firing to keep back the bush, and this allows rain to etch out gullies, which in turn lowers the water table and makes the re-establishment of a grass cover difficult. This is an area of chronic crop failure and famine. From 1943 to 1961 the district had to import maize in 15 out of 19 years, and in 7 of these years there was severe famine.

In describing the environmental parameters earlier, we left out what is perhaps the most important one—man. Machakos District, the western and populous portion of Ukambani, in the past 44 years increased its population fourfold, from 120,000 to 570,000, an annual increase of 3 percent. As a consequence, an agriculture that worked well in the moist hills in the west has been successively pushed out into areas where the chances of failure are greatly increased, with devastating effects on the environment, as we have seen. There is great fluidity and uncertainty in the Wakamba use of environment in this area. The environmental gradient is gentle; the agricultural limits are not clear; and despite various tactics to spread risk and create a viable subsistence, the people have not yet found a workable solution.

Kilungu. The third, and most pastoral, site lies at an elevation of about 2,500 ft. The rainfall averages just under 25 inches and is very unreliable. The rainfall profile is again bimodal, but the November-December grass rains are definitely better. The likelihood of having enough rainfall to meet transpiration needs in four months in the grass rains is a little better than even, about 0.65 (Fig. 5); but for the main rains, less than 0.1 (Fig. 6). Population density is between 50 and 150 around Kilungu; but by and large the *Acacia-Commiphora* and

Acacia tortilis areas of Ukambani support densities under 25 people per square mile.

The Mkamba here uses huge quantities of land on a shifting cultivation basis. Land is owned, but not sold or inherited. "Who would want his father's land? It is all used up and worthless." New bush is there for the taking. Fields are deployed great distances from one another, over 10 miles sometimes. A multitude of crops, many of them quick-maturing, hardy and drought-resistant, is sown in what appears to have been a fit of temporary insanity. Seeds are all thrown together and worked into large dryland clearings that are virtually unmappable. Here is a list of crops from one field: maize, beans, cowpeas, groundnuts, red millet, sorghum, castor, bulrush millet, cassava pumpkins, calabashes, and pigeon peas. Six kinds of millet are grown here. The great number of crops, mixed sowing, placement of fields far apart—all are attempts to reduce the risk the individual takes. Care is taken to plant before or with the rains; indeed the second planting is done amongst standing unharvested crops from the grass rains. This second crop is usually a forlorn hope. Early weeding is done; timing is most important. The tools are simple, there being no plow, no use of draft animals, almost no manuring or terracing. The basic implements are: hoe, panga, ax, and over large parts of Kitui District, the digging stick. Agriculture is insufficient of itself as a subsistence base. The people are heavily involved with livestock; indeed, they think of themselves as herders. In the community studied, the average family holding in stock was 20 cattle, 9 sheep, and 28 goats. The drier the realm, the greater becomes the dependence on livestock. There is greater emphasis also on gathering and hunting, as evidenced by the importance of honey, gum arabic and poaching in the local economy.

In this paper we have examined some East African environments in three ways: 1) according to the variety in types of environment, 2) according to their spatial arrangement, that is, the steepness of gradient be-

tween types, and 3) according to their inherent secular variability. By way of conclusion we make six assertions:

1) It is evident that there are not two types of environment in East Africa—one for farmers and one for herders—but many, each having its own peculiar set of subsistence possibilities and problems. A complex pattern in which agricultural and pastoral activities are either symbiotic, competitive, excluded, or integrated is therefore to be expected.

2) A steep environmental gradient provides positive advantages by allowing people to use multiple environments and even to form specialized reciprocal economies as a means of combating the uncertainties of nature.

3) In semi-arid uniform environments a greater premium is placed on mobility. This favors pastoralism as a subsistence mode, but even agriculture may reflect it by a greater dispersion of fields. People will attempt to be more internally self-sufficient; their subsistence mode may be unstable because the environmental limits are not clear.

4) An effective adjustment of agricultural subsistence to the environmental demands of semi-arid areas can be achieved only by the most meticulous management of the available resources. The constraints of a rigorous agricultural timetable tend to restrict movement and other activities. This may be competitive with pastoral pursuits.

5) Where environmental potentials are high and subsistence risks are minimal or absent, the population increases, densities become high, settlements are permanent, and internal disputes over land become likely.

6) A model which seeks to describe culture as adaptive, through subsistence, to environmental potential cannot ignore man himself as a causative agent of environmental change. The circuitry of the model should allow for reciprocal energy flows, for feedback. In saying this we confirm rather than deny the value of the truly ecologic

approach, and highlight the need to proceed historically in any study of a specific culture.

We would claim that the study of environmental potential is enhanced by an appreciation of the spatial arrangement and temporal variability of environmental types. We therefore suggest that the use of rainfall probability gradients and the involvement of subsistence risks offer a promising way to relate environment realistically to actual subsistence technologies, and thereby to the kinds of life that people fashion for themselves.

REFERENCES

Glover, J. and J. S. G. McCulloch. 1958. The empirical relation between solar radiation and hours of sunshine. Quarterly Journal of the Royal Meteorological Society 84:172–175.

Glover, J., P. Robinson, and J. P. Henderson. 1954. Provisional maps of the reliability of annual rainfall in East Africa. Quarterly Journal of the Royal Meteorological Society 80:602–609.

Kenworthy, Joan M. and J. Glover. 1958. The reliability of the main rains in Kenya. East African Agricultural Journal 23:267–271.

Manning, H. L. 1956. The statistical assessment of rainfall probability and its application in Uganda agriculture. Research Memoirs, No. 23, pp. 460–480. London, Empire Cotton Growing Corporation.

Penman, H. L. 1948. Natural evaporation from open water, bare soil and grass. Proceedings of the Royal Society of London (A), Vol. 193, pp. 120–145.

——— 1963. Vegetation and hydrology. Technical Communication No. 53, Commonwealth Bureau of Soils, Harpenden, vide pp. 40–43.

Robinson, P. and J. Glover. 1954. The reliability of the rainfall within the growing season. East African Agricultural Journal 19: 137–139.

Thornthwaite, C. W. 1948. An approach toward a rational classification of climate. Geographical Review 38:55–94.

Thornthwaite, C. W. and J. R. Mather. 1957. Instructions and tables for computing potential evapotranspiration and the water balance, C. W. Thornthwaite Associates, Laboratory of Climatology, Publications in Climatology, Vol. X, No. 3, pp. 181–311.

Thornthwaite, C. W. and J. R. Mather (eds.). 1962. Average climatic water balance data of the continents, Part I. Africa, C. W. Thornthwaite Associates, Laboratory of Climatology, Publications in Climatology, Vol. XV, No. 2, 287 pp.

Geological, paleobotanical, geomorphological, and archaeological evidence is available concerning major climatic fluctuations in the distant past, but minor fluctuations in recent times are difficult to identify and evaluate, since climatological data are limited and at best are available for the present century only. During the 1930's strong views were expressed on the widespread encroachment of desert in West Africa, which to some signalled climatic retrogression (Stamp, 1940). Other research suggests that apparent desiccation in areas such as Northwestern Nigeria must be related to seasonal fluctuations in climate, with important changes in the appearance of the landscape where there are short wet seasons and long dry seasons.

If the quality of an environment diminishes, human activity rather than climatic change is likely to be the cause. Deterioration may result from factors such as maladjustment in population-land relationships brought about by increased numbers of people, or from unsatisfactory repercussions caused by economic development in another area. In the valleys of the Rima basin of northwestern Nigeria increased runoff and flooding indicate that changes in the river regimes may well have been influenced by the expansion of cropland in the upper reaches and watersheds of the basin (Ledger, 1961).

Human malpractice may permanently impair the quality of the environment (e.g., by removal of the soil through gully and sheet erosion), but more frequently man's damage is only temporary. In northwestern Nigeria in the mid-1950's there was some evidence that deterioration had been slowed down, if not arrested.

4. Some Observations on Desiccation in North-Western Nigeria

R. MANSELL PROTHERO

Only in comparatively recent times has man come to modify the environment of West Africa significantly, and there is little evidence of human modifications of the environment to consider before the present century. Although the last sixty years are but a fraction of the ages through which the West African environment has passed the changes and modifications that have taken place in recent times are of the greatest importance. They have created many problems for which solutions are urgently required. Amongst these problems are those which result from increases in the numbers of people who, in turn, exert increasing pressure on resources to provide for their needs. In West Africa where the internal and external economies still depend very largely on farming it is obvious that increasing human needs will exercise very important modifying influences both directly

and indirectly on the environment. More land is required for cultivation and for grazing and the demand for timber for fuel and other purposes increases. Depending on the man/land relationships in different areas changes may become necessary in agricultural practices. These are only the more important of the influences at work.

These influences are particularly significant, and the changes that result from them often all too apparent, in the northern parts of West Africa, on the northern fringes of the Sudan Zone and throughout the Sahel Zone (Aubreville 1937, Dundas 1938). (Figure 1). These areas are characterized by low totals of annual rainfall (under 750 mms., c. 30 inches) which is uncertain and variable in amount and incidence. The fall is concentrated into periods of from two to five months with almost complete dryness for the rest of the year. For several months

From *Erkunde, 16*, 1962, pp. 112–119. Reprinted by permission.

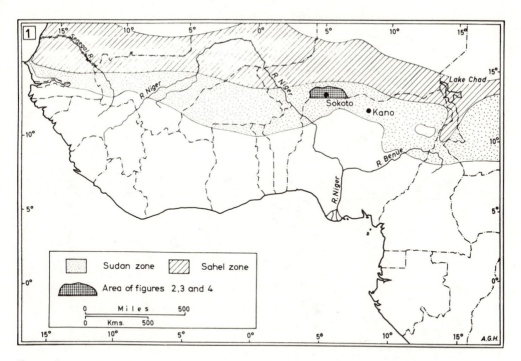

Figure 1.

desiccating winds blow down from the Sahara. The contrasts between wet and dry seasons in these areas are remarkable and it is possible to obtain an erroneous impression of conditions if the changes in the appearance of the landscape from one part of the year to another have not been observed. The rainfall of these areas presents problems to both cultivators and pastoralists, restricting the activities of the former to a limited period of the year and requiring the latter to move seasonally with their flocks and herds in search of pasture and water. Under normal conditions successful cultivation is possible during the few months of the rains without supplementary irrigation. But it is virtually impossible to designate what are normal conditions. Average rainfall is of no significance where totals may vary by up to 50 per cent from the average from one year to another. Incidence is of far greater importance than amount. At Sokoto in north-western Nigeria

(Figure 2) with an average rainfall of about 675 mms. (c. 27 inches) good harvests have been recorded with a well distributed annual total of only 400 mms. (c. 16 inches); while near-famine conditions have resulted from a poor harvest with an annual total of 1,000 mms. (c. 40 inches) which has been badly distributed. The problems of these areas are not confined to variable and uncertain rainfall, during the dry season there is also the problem of water supplies for human and animal populations and to allow a comparatively small, but nevertheless important, amount of dry season cultivation by irrigation.

From the average density of population (under 8 per square km., c. 20 per square mile) these areas would appear to be only sparsely populated. Average figures, however, have very little meaning and in some parts there are relatively dense concentrations of people in spite of the difficult physical conditions. To some extent these

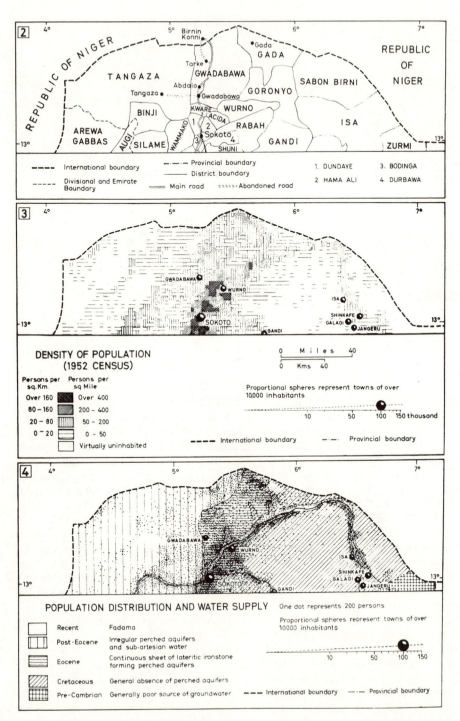

Figures 2, 3, 4.

concentrations occur in areas which are relatively better endowed from the point of view of the physical environment, but political, historical, social and economic factors have also influenced their development. In the northern parts of Sokoto Province, particularly in the vicinity of Sokoto town and northwards from there to the frontier with the Republic of Niger, population densities average over 80 per square km. (c. 200 per square mile) and rise in limited areas to over 160 per square km. (c. 400 per square mile). (Figure 3). There is a marked tendency for the population to concentrate near to water in the valleys of the Sokoto River and its tributaries. At the same time the whole of this area is underlain by sedimentary formations which yield water in varying amounts from perched aquifers near the surface and from the permanent water table which generally lies at depths of less than 30 metres (c. 100 feet). (Figure 4). Although the physical environment is relatively favourable it has by no means been exclusively responsible for attracting the large numbers of people. Sokoto town was founded as the capital of the powerful Fulani Empire which flourished during the nineteenth century and in this role must have exerted a great focal influence. Since the establishment of European administration in the area at the beginning of the present century and the demarcation of a Franco-British frontier which had no physical or ethnic significance, there has been very considerable immigration from what is now the Republic of Niger into Nigeria. This immigration is a continuing process and between 1944 and 1954 accounted for part of the increases in the populations of Gwadabawa, Gada and Sabon Birni Districts which were between 25 and 35 per cent. The changes and modifications brought about by increases in population over the last sixty years have been considerable and have brought in their train a wide range of problems.

Before the establishment of settled conditions under European administration the greater part of the districts mentioned above and nearly the whole of Tangaza District, which remains sparsely populated to the present day because of poor water supply, were covered with woodland. Gwadabawa town was founded only in 1875 and in 1905 it was reported that settlement in the district was for the most part restricted to near the road which runs northwards from the town to Birnin Konni. People concentrated for protection in or very near to large towns. The areas which could be farmed with safety were restricted and comparatively intensive farming methods must have been employed in order to produce the food required by the population from limited areas of land, even if allowance is made for the fact that then the numbers of people were less than at the present day. The advent of peaceful conditions coupled with increases in the population have led to a dispersal of settlement over a much wider area. This dispersal has been accompanied by a widespread clearance of land for farming so that today the areas of woodland remaining are very small. Farming methods appear to have changed with this dispersal, becoming more extensive on the greater amounts of land available. They have been responsible for much indiscriminate and unnecessary clearing. In the early stages of the dispersion of population there was sufficient land available to accommodate extensive cultivation, but with a steady increase in the numbers of people population pressure and land hunger have become apparent.

The people have responded in several ways to these changed circumstances. There has been some permanent emigration to sparsely populated districts in the south of Sokoto Province though this has been more than balanced by further immigration from the north. More significant is the large scale seasonal migration of labour from these areas prompted, in part at least, by the need to conserve food supplies and to supplement incomes (Prothero 1957 and 1959). Particularly disastrous in the districts have been the attempts to meet the needs of the increasing population by keeping the land under cultivation for longer periods and reducing the length of recuperative fallow without providing any alternative means of maintaining fertility. In the districts adjacent to Sokoto town which carry an even denser population (over 160 per square km., c. 400 per square mile) and have done so for a much longer time, though there are problems of population pressure much of the farmland is cultivated each year with provision being made for maintaining fertility by various forms of manuring.

Evidence of the evils which may occur during these stages of transition is not hard to find in northern Sokoto. For example, around Gwadabawa town the top soil, having become unstable through complete clearing, has been eroded away leaving the less fertile sub-soil. In other areas even the subsoil has been eroded down to the underlying indurated ironstone which is useless for agriculture. A short distance to the west of Gada town an area of between one and two square miles of good farmland is being eaten away by a system of erosion gullies developed on a slope no steeper than 2° to 3°. The main gullies are up to 3 metres (c. 10 feet) deep and up to 9 to 12 metres (c. 30 to 40 feet) wide. Far from anything being done to prevent extension of this erosion all the land right up to the edges of the gullies is cultivated and where the gully walls have slumped they have been planted also. Such examples of active gully erosion are fortunately not very common but in many areas paths and tracks, particularly those used by cattle, develop as minor eroded areas.

The coarse sandy soils which are found over the greater part of these districts are inherently of low fertility. The amounts of potash and phosphorous in them are on the whole good, probably because there is insufficient rain to leach them out, and it is due to these that growth is possible. Crop yields are low and fall off very rapidly if inadequate provision is made to maintain

what little fertility the soils possess. An insidious practice is the burning of animal manure and crop refuse for fuel, due either to the shortage of wood or, as is sometimes the case, to laziness on the part of the people. Small areas of woodland which remain have been reserved by the Forestry Department as Communal Forest Areas to be cut on a rotational system for fuel supplies, but in these it is a common practice for the people to cut indiscriminantly outside the parts which have been demarcated for cutting.

The combined effects of these malpractices are to reduce the carrying capacity of the land to a very low level or to render it incapable of production or even to make the restoration of fertility virtually impossible.[1] In areas where cultivation has been abandoned the extent of deterioration is evident from the very sparse and poor fallow cover that is established. Such land may have the appearance of semi-desert in the dry season and may seem to indicate that natural processes of desiccation are at work if the history of land use and agricultural practices in the area are not known. Indeed to an observer who has not seen the cultivated land during the rains much of it may seem to be in the same category at the height of the dry season. The soil is completely dried out and bare and soil particles drift on the surface if there is a strong wind blowing.

On several occasions in the last half century various evidence of desiccation in northern Sokoto has been presented and consideration given to the factors, producing it.[2] Bovill (1921), discussing "the encroach-

[1] Experiments by the Department of Agriculture from 1940 to 1950 to restore the fertility of a farm established on degraded and eroded soils at Tarke in Gwadabawa District proved abortive and were abandoned. Annual manuring was found to be neither practical nor economical: in 1945 1.6 hectare (c. 4 acres), manured in the previous season with 2 tons of animal manure per acre, produced a total of only 250 kilos (c. 500 lbs.) of millet.

[2] Renner (1926) and Stamp (1940) present critical summaries of various published papers.

ment of the Sahara on the Sudan," offered particular evidence of this fact from Sokoto Province. He referred to a regular decline in rainfall since records were begun in 1903 and the reduction of water in lakes and wells. His inferences cannot be substantiated from the available rainfall records which are few and fragmentary. With regard to water supplies from wells he was writing at a time when they were undoubtedly at their poorest, not because of deficiencies in the rainfall and inadequate replenishing of the aquifers but because of changes in social conditions. Prior to the establishment of British rule the digging and maintaining of wells was carried out by slave labour because of the risks involved. With the abolition of slavery this labour was no longer available and there seems to have been a consequent decline in the yield of water from wells due to lack of attention (Jones 1938). In the latter years of the 1920's the construction of permanent concrete-lined wells was commenced by the Geological Survey in Sokoto Province and these activities were extended subsequently throughout Northern Nigeria. Surveys prior to construction suggested, and from the construction of wells it was proved, that ample supplies of groundwater existed in northern Sokoto, both in perched aquifers (many of the native wells tapped these only and were liable to be exhausted during the dry season) and from the permanent water table (Raeburn 1928, Jones 1938). Well construction has continued on an increasing scale.[3] Since 1945/46 it has been controlled by the Rural Water Supplies section of the Public Works Department and was financed very considerably by money from the Colonial Development and Welfare Fund. Now water supplies from wells are without any doubt, incomparably better

than at any time in the past not only in Sokoto Province but throughout Northern Nigeria. The majority of the wells are sunk to the permanent water table and yield water throughout the year. It is a fact, however, that even when provided with a deep well people may prefer to obtain their water from stagnant pools or from shallow wells which are very liable to pollution in order to avoid the effort of hauling up water fifty feet or more.

Bovill (1921) maintained that a general southward drift of people was taking place as a result of increasing aridity. Certainly Sokoto Province and particularly the northern districts have gained very considerably in population as a result of immigration from further north but these migrants have been attracted by the economic possibilities and amenities (particularly the provision of permanent wells in the last thirty years) available here, rather than being driven by any intensification in aridity. A bad season with a poor harvest may cause a temporary acceleration in the numbers of migrants but often people who move in response to such conditions will return to their villages when conditions are better (Grove 1957). There is certainly no large scale movement from the overcrowded northern districts of Sokoto Province to the comparatively empty areas in the south (Prothero 1957 and 1959). The Adarawa people are found on either side of the northern frontier between Sokoto Province and the Republic of Niger and they move freely backwards and forwards across it; but there is no evidence that they are moving progressively further south and being replaced by Buzai and Tuareg people as Bovill (1921) said was happening.

In the 1930's the causes and problems of desiccation received the greatest attention; Stebbing (1935, 1937a, 1937b, 1938a, 1938b) wrote at considerable length, if not always with the greatest accuracy (and his observations were made in the dry season only), of the threat to the West African colonies of a southward moving Sahara desert resulting from a natural deterioration

[3] 447 wells were constructed in Sokoto Province between 1929 and 1946; 1437 were constructed in the decade 1947–56. For the whole of Northern Nigeria the figures are 1992 and 7520 respectively.

in the environment.[4] "The people are living on the edge, not of a volcano, but of a desert whose power is incalculable and whose silent and almost invisible approach must be difficult to estimate."

On Stebbing's estimate (1935) the most northerly parts of Northern Nigeria should have been overwhelmed by Saharan sand by the present day. This has not happened. He noted (1937a) in these areas ". . . real evidence of the desert—sand invasion with the typical goriba or dom palm (*Hyphaene thebaica*) . . ." There are areas in the northern districts of Sokoto Province, for example a few miles to the north of Gwadabawa town in the vicinity of the villages of Gwombilla and Melle, which exhibit these features at the present day. There is goriba scrub and little other vegetation during the dry season and the landscape has a desertic appearance. But this is no invasion of the desert for only a little distance to the north the goriba scrub disappears and the desertic scene changes.[5] Rather this is an over-farmed area of degraded soils which are blown about in the dry season because of the absence of vegetative cover. In the wet season they still yield crops and they receive small amounts of manure. This particular area has a population density of over 100 per square km. (c. 250 per square mile).

An Anglo-French Forestry Commission (1937) which investigated the evidence for desiccation in the most northerly area of

Northern Nigeria and in the adjacent lands of the Republic of Niger, strongly refuted any ideas of climatic retrogression and placed responsibility for any deterioration of the environment on human activities. They found no evidence of any large scale movement of sand or of any lowering of the permanent water table. Sand dunes occur in Sokoto Province in a zone some ten to fifteen miles wide south of the international frontier but they originated in conditions of much greater aridity in the Quaternary era (Grove 1958). They are firmly anchored and frequently provide the sites for villages as the lower-lying land around may be flooded periodically during the wet season.

Reference has already been made to the superficial displacement of the sandy soils. The drifting sand collects particularly on roads. The old motor road between Gwadabawa and Tangaza (Figure 1), along which the writer trekked in 1955 had been abandoned three years previously when a new road was built and in the meantime had become impracticable for all motor traffic due to the large amounts of sand which had accumulated on it from the surrounding land. For the same reason sections of the road from Birnin Konni to Dogon Doutchi were difficult to negotiate by car in 1955. Here the practice of clearing the land of vegetation for some distance back from the road plays an important part in allowance a freer movement of wind-borne material. These are examples only of the inconvenience that may be caused by sand drift, its effects are much more serious when it occurs on farmland. The Anglo-French Forestry Commission (1937) reported that this was occurring around Birnin Konni and around Tahoua further north. At this time also farmers in the northern districts of Sokoto Province were complaining that they were having to sow seed up to six times owing to the smothering of young sprouting corn by wind-blown sand. This menace can be counteracted by the planting of shelter-belts and the maintenance of trees on the

---

[4] In a more recent work, following a visit to the Sudan in 1947 but concerned in general terms also with the zone between 13° and 15° N. latitude, Stebbing (1953) reaffirms his belief in desert encroachment but at the same time emphasizes more the influence of human activities in the processes of desiccation.

[5] Collier and Dundas (1937) state, with reference to *Hyphaene thebaica, Ziziphus, Balanites aegyptiaca* and *Commiphora africana*, "The species named are typical of their localities and show that one is approaching the desert and not that the desert is encroaching." and Keay (1954) "*Hyphaene thebaica* is a very conspicuous feature of the Sudan zone and sometimes forms pure stands, particularly where the soil is somewhat saline."

farm-land to break the force of the wind. The planting of the boundaries of farm plots with gamba grass (*Andropogon Gayanus*), a feature of the farmlands in the intensively cultivated zone around Kano, is particularly effective. The cultivation treatment given to these light sandy soils is also important. Before the first rains of the wet season the land is too hard to be prepared for planting but after the first substantial fall of rain the ground is broken for each seed with a long-handled hoe, the seed is placed in the hole and covered over. If any extensive hoeing is carried out once the seed has sprouted, but before it has become a sturdy plant, there is the danger, if there is a period with no further rain, that the surface layers of the soil will dry out and in a friable condition will be liable to movement by the wind and may smother the plant. Late hoeing, when the plants have grown beyond the stage when they can be affected in this way, is an obvious solution which has been recommended and accepted by the people. In another respect, however, late hoeing is unsatisfactory. During the long dry season the surface soil dries out into a hard crust which the early rains in April and May are not able to penetrate easily unless it is broken up. With late hoeing, therefore, there is the danger that the moisture supply to the soil will be impaired at a time when this can be ill-afforded.

In the 1930's at the same time as evidence was being produced to illustrate the processes of desiccation at work, there were reports from the northern districts of Sokoto of excessive flooding in the valleys of the River Rima and its tributaries the Bunsuru and Gagere which necessitated the abandoning of farmland and the re-siting of settlements. The majority view at the time was that human changes and modifications of the environment were responsible for producing the features of desiccation and it is probable that this flooding was, paradoxically, a part of the same process. The streams of the Rima system have their head-waters in Katsina and Kano Provinces and flow through relatively narrow valleys cut in the crystalline rocks in the eastern districts of Sokoto Province. In the 1930's these areas were developing the cultivation of cotton and groundnuts for cash crops. These developments were attracting population and it seems likely that altogether there was considerable clearance of land taking place here at this time. This would result in increased run-off into the streams in their upper courses and so to flooding further downstream where the valleys, cut in softer sedimentary rocks, are wide with extensive flood plains.

In addition to seasonal fluctuations in the permanent water table, overall rises have been recorded in parts of Northern Nigeria over the last three decades.[6] In the northern districts of Sokoto Province there is ample evidence of the appearance of increased amounts of surface water.[7] This was noted in 1940 and was stated to have been occurring over the previous ten years though, at the same time, it was incorrectly stated that these were manifestations of a climatic change (Bond 1940). Increased amounts of water in fadama (the flood plains of rivers and low-lying areas which become waterlogged or flooded during the rains) were making rice cultivation difficult. Low-lying areas with heavier soils which generally collected sufficient moisture to allow the cultivation of guinea corn (in an area where soil and moisture conditions are generally favourable for the cultivation of millet only) were being flooded and cultivation made impossible. At the same time the increased amounts of surface water meant the retention of soil moisture in the fadama for a longer time into the dry season and therefore increased the possibilities for the cultivation of sugar cane, sweet potatoes, cassava, onions and wheat, crops which depend on this soil moisture supplemented by irrigation.

[6] Personal communication from the Director, Geological Survey of Nigeria.
[7] This feature has also been noted in western Bornu (Grove 1961).

A particular instance of the increase in surface water has been observed over the years at Tarke, a village in Gwadabawa District. The Provincial Agricultural Officer noted at the end of December 1939 that "Water is still lying in the fadama . . ." and the following year that "Water stood in the fadama all through the dry season for the first time seven years ago and this year it has risen higher than last year."

It is not known whether there has been a steady increase in the amount of water remaining throughout the dry season but in June 1955, after more than eight months without rain there was over an acre of open water in this fadama.

Increases in the amount of surface water remaining throughout the dry season have interfered with communications in northern Sokoto. The motor road from Sokoto town northwards to Birnin Konni had to be re-aligned in 1940/41 because the increase in the depth of water in a fadama immediately to the north of Gwadabawa town made the passage of vehicles impossible. (Figure 2). In February 1955, along the line formerly taken by the road there was over six feet of water and the fadama could only be crossed by canoe. Further north along the old road the ford through the fadama at Abdalo was negotiable on horseback but would certainly have been impracticable for most motor traffic—in the middle of the dry season!

One obvious explanation for these increased amounts of water is that they are due to climatic change but the rainfall records for this area suggest that this explanation is unsatisfactory. Alternative explanations have been advanced. An Administrative Officer at Tarke in 1949 reported (Muffett 1949) ". . . the fadama has now been in existence for more than twenty years and apparently owes its origin to the sinking of a native well which either struck a spring or a sub-artesian rise." This explanation is unsatisfactory for Tarke and certainly could not be applied to the other examples of increased surface water of

which only a few are referred to here. There is very little sub-artesian water in Sokoto Province, the depths at which it occurs are unlikely to have been reached by a native well and if it were a subartesian rise the water not have reached the surface. These increases in surface water are not associated with climatic change but are indirectly related to human activity.[8] Like the flooding in the river valleys they are the result of increased run off due to widespread clearing of the land.

Although flooding in the wide river valleys may have serious effects on farm land and settlement advantage may be taken of the increased amounts of water in small fadama to increase the amount of land that can be cultivated during the dry season. There are many such areas in the northern district of Sokoto which are either unused or which could be further developed for this purpose. Such development might require the construction of small scale earthworks, both drainage and irrigation channels, but the people should be able to construct them if given some direction in what was needed. There is, however, a human element in this development also to be considered. In one village where there was fadama that might be developed, when asked why this was not undertaken to reduce, at least to some extent, the need for a considerable proportion of the male population to migrate during the dry season in search of work, the reply was that aikin fadama (dry season cultivation) was arduous and demanding work and that they preferred to go away. The motives for seeking work in other parts of Nigeria are in fact much more complex than this (Prothero 1957 and 1959).

Overall, in spite of continued population increases, environmental conditions in the northern districts of Sokoto Province do not appear to have progressively deteriorated during the last decade or so. An Adminis-

[8] Jones (1938) noted increases in surface water in other parts of Nigeria, suggesting that they were associated with a cycle of wet years though not with any climatic change.

trative Officer, competent to assess the situation, reported (Johnston 1952) "Knowing Gwadabawa before the war and hearing that since then its population had increased by a third . . . I was apprehensive. On the whole I have been pleasantly surprised by what I have seen." At the same time it is not suggested that conditions have much improved but they seem to have reached their lowest level during the 1930's. There is room for much improvement in standards of living which are low and which are only maintained at their present level by the absence of between 30 and 40 per cent of the male population during the dry season. In years in which the harvest is poor near-famine conditions may still result, though with the facilities that now exist for buying in food from other areas the possibility of a devastating famine is very remote. The pressure of population on the land is so great that no land can be given over to the cultivation of cash crops and so there is no prospect of increasing income from them.

There is above all else the need for an increase in the amount of land which is cultivated each year and where fertility is maintained by manuring. At the present time most of the animal manure which gets on to cultivable land comes only from indiscriminate grazing over the stubble during the dry season. In the conditions of great heat and low humidity the manure is soon desiccated and its value greatly reduced. On the other hand in the wet season a large proportion of the cattle are taken northwards into the Republic of Niger where the population densities are lower and there is more land for grazing. Between the cultivators and the herdsmen who remain in the northern districts of Sokoto during the wet season there are frequent troubles due to cattle damaging crops. The much needed symbiosis between pastoralist and cultivator is lacking here as it is in so many other parts of tropical Africa.

The evidence indicates that farmers in Northern Nigeria and elsewhere in tropical Africa will intensify their methods of cultivation and adopt measures of conservation only when they are forced to by extreme population pressure on the land. These improved methods are in use on the intensively farmed lands in Kano Province where there are population densities which range from 200 to 400 per square km. (c. 500 to 1,000 per square mile). The real dangers of land deterioriation seem to be greatest where the population densities are between 80 to 100 per square km. (c. 200 and 250 per square mile), as in the areas which have been discussed.[9] These figures indicate a critical transition stage between lower densities which allow cultivation under a system of land rotation and higher densities which demand the permanent cultivation of a large proportion of the cultivable land. In this transition stage, in lands where the rainfall is low and uncertain, processes of desiccation, which are essentially induced by human activities, will develop (Wayland 1940). If this development is allowed to proceed then the fertility and productivity of the land may be permanently impaired. In these circumstances there is much to be said for attempting to accelerate this stage in order to conserve land which is capable of supporting greater numbers of people under a more efficient system of cultivation.

NOTE

Field work on which this paper is based was undertaken while the author was a research fellow of the West African Institute of Social Economic Research.

REFERENCES

Aubreville, M. 1937. The Niger Colony forestry expedition September-December 1935. Translated, Forestry Department, Ibadan, Nigeria.

Bond, W. E. T. 1940. A climatic change—its

[9] Cf. Farmer (1957) with reference to chena cultivation in Ceylon. "To judge by the Kala Wewa area the critical density is about 200–250 per square mile; but further field research is needed."

effect on agriculture in northern Sokoto. Unpublished ms.

Bovill, E. W. 1921. The encroachment of the Sahara on the Sudan. J. Afr. S. 20, 174–185 and 259–269.

Dundas, J. 1938. Vegetation types of the Colonie du Niger, Institute Paper No. 15, Imperial Forestry Institute, University of Oxford.

Farmer, B. H. 1957. Pioneer peasant colonization in Ceylon. Royal Institute of International Affairs, London.

Collier, F. S., and Dundas, J. 1937. The arid regions of Northern Nigeria and French Niger colony. Emp. For. J. 16, 184–194.

Grove, A. T. 1957. Land and Population in Katsina Province. Government Printer, Kaduna, Northern Nigeria.

———— 1958. The ancient erg of Hausaland and similar formations on the southern side of the Sahara. Geog. J. 124, 528–533.

———— 1961. Population densities and agriculture in Northern Nigeria. In K. M. Barbour and R. M. Prothero (eds.), Essays on African population.

Johnston, H. A. S. 1952. Notes on the economy of Gwadabawa district. Unpublished ms.

Jones, B. 1938. Desiccation and the West African colonies. Geog. J. 91, 301–423.

Keay, R. W. J. 1954. An outline of Nigerian vegetation. Lagos.

Muffett, D. J. 1949. Intensive census of Tarke hamlet. Unpublished ms.

Nigeria. 1937. Report of the Anglo-French forestry commission, 1936/1937. Sessional Paper No. 37, Lagos.

Prothero, R. M. 1957. Migratory labour from northwestern Nigeria, Africa, 27, 251–261 and (1959) Migrant labour from Sokoto Prov-

ince, Northern Nigeria. Kaduna.

Raeburn, C. 1928. The Nigerian Sudan: some notes on water supply and other cognate subjects. Geological Survey of Nigeria, Pamphlet No. 1.

Renner, G. T. 1926. A famine zone in Africa: the Sudan. Geog. Rev. 16, 583–596.

Stamp, L. D. 1940. The southern margin of the Sahara: comments on some recent studies on the question of desiccation in West Africa. Geog. Rev. 30, 297–300.

Stebbing, E. P. 1935. The encroaching Sahara: the threat to the West African colonies. Geog. J. 85, 506–524.

———— 1937a. The forests of West Africa and the Sahara. London.

———— 1937b. The threat of the Sahara. J. R. Afr. S. Supplement (May).

———— 1938a. The man-made desert in Africa. J. R. Afr. S. Supplement (January).

———— 1938b. Africa and its intermittent rainfall: the role of the savannah forest. J. R. Afr. S. Supplement (August).

———— 1953. The creeping desert in the Sudan and elsewhere in Africa, 15° to 13° latitude. Khartoum.

Wayland, E. J. 1940. Desert versus forest in eastern Africa. Geog. J. 96, 329–341.

Note: There is an extensive literature in French on the problem of "désséchement," the following papers contain bibliographical references.

Pelissier, P.: Sur la déssertification des territoires septrionaux de l'A.O.F. Cahiers d'Outre-Mêr, Jan/Mars, 1951, 80–85.

Monod, Th. Autour du problème du désséchement africain. Bulletin I.F.A.N. XII, 2, 1950, 517–523.

Disease is a part of the environment, functioning both as a dependent and as an independent variable. It is thus a factor in population-land relationships, both influencing and being influenced by them. Geography has contributed to the epidemiological study of disease in Africa in respect of river blindness (Hunter, 1966a), sleeping sickness (trypanosomiasis) (Langlands, 1966), and malaria (Prothero, 1965). Further studies of the interactions between disease and population-land relationships could result in considerable practical gain.

Human and animal trypanosomiasis inhibit economic development over large areas of tropical Africa, either independently or in combination with one another. Sleeping sickness (human trypanosomiasis) limits areas of human settlement (Gillman, 1936; Hilton, 1959); animal trypanosomiasis limits the keeping of cattle, which results in a lack of animal protein and reduced possibilities for mixed farming (Deshler, 1962; Turner and Baker, 1968).

In many areas the balance of environmental conditions favorable to tsetse flies—the vectors of trypanosomiasis—is delicate. Problems are complicated by considerable seasonal variation in climate, an important factor in the movements of stock in both East Africa and West Africa (Stenning, 1969). In the past, depopulation resulted in increased growth of vegetation and new infestations of tsetse flies. While these disease carriers may multiply with depopulation, an increase in population and a lowered incidence of trypanosomiasis may bring about concentrations of humans and/or animals with consequent pressure upon resources. A conflict of interest may develop between those concerned with eradicating disease and those bent on developing the most efficient and economic system of land use. Predictably, the former will want to reduce vegetation cover, the latter (e.g., forestry interests) to preserve and increase it. Satisfactory accommodation can be achieved, provided liaison between the two interests is close.

In Karamoja in Northeast Uganda, the harsh environment is marginal for human occupation. Population-land reltionships are precariously maintained, and the incidence of trypanosomiasis is high. Interactions between vector, pathogen, livestock, and herders are complex and present problems in development for which there are no easy solutions.

5. *Livestock Trypanosomiasis and Human Settlement in Northeastern Uganda*

WALTER DESHLER

In large parts of Africa south of the Sahara the spread and density of population are restricted by trypanosomiasis. Both human beings and their domestic livestock can be afflicted by this disease, and in both cases human settlement is affected. In East Africa livestock trypanosomiasis infests much of the potential grazing country—more than half of the total area of Tanganyika, a third of Uganda, and a quarter of Kenya. This paper treats the impact of the disease on one cattle-keeping tribe and that tribe's adjustment to the problem during three decades.

TRANSMISSION AND CONTROL

Trypanosomes are single-celled organisms of the phylum Protozoa. They are flagellates, moving by means of the vibratory motion of permanent filaments along their bodies, and they are parasites, adapted to life in the blood stream of a vertebrate host. In Africa they are largely parasites of game animals, which have generally become immune.[1] However, from their game hosts they may be transmitted to domestic animals and to man. These new hosts have not yet developed resistance, and to them certain of the trypanosome species are pathogenic. Several forms of the disease infect livestock. In the acute form there is high temperature, which is quickly followed by anemia, progressive weakness, and death.[2] In the form most common to cattle there is varying temperature, a dry coat, gradual wasting of the animal, extreme weakness,

and death usually after about three months. The mechanism within the host animal is not well understood, but there is the possibility that in some forms of the disease the trypanosomes increase rapidly in number, in the absence of an antibody, until the animal dies.[3]

Five or six principal species of trypanosome cause the wasting disease in domestic animals, among them *Trypanosoma vivax*, *T. congolense*, and *T. brucei*. Humped East African zebu cattle have little or no resistance to trypanosomiasis and cannot be kept in infested areas without a prophylactic treatment that is not generally available to herders. Goats, sheep, and some species of West African cattle are partly resistant to one or more of the trypanosome species, and on exposure most of a herd may escape without developing acute symptoms.[4]

The trypanosomes are carried and transmitted by biting flies. The commonest carrier is the tsetse fly, but other biting flies such as the camel fly and the horsefly may also be carriers. The fly obtains the trypanosome from infected animals. Among the common game hosts are the buffalo, the wart hog, the giraffe, and the elephant, and some of the antelope. The trypanosomes pathogenic to cattle can be carried by more than one species of fly.

There are some twenty species in the tsetse-fly genus, *Glossina*, each with its affinity to particular terrain, vegetation associations, or plant species. The trypanosomes that infest man are carried by flies

---

[1] T. W. M. Cameron: Parasites and Parasitism (London and Toronto, 1956), pp. 23–35.

[2] P. Z. Mackenzie and R. M. Simpson: The African Veterinary Handbook (London, Toronto, Nairobi, etc., 1953), pp. 60–64.

[3] Cameron, *op. cit.*, p. 28.

[4] "The Improvements of Cattle in British Colonial Territories in East Africa," *Colonial Advisory Council of Agric., Animal Health and Forestry Publ. No. 3*, 1953, p. 16.

From *The Geographical Review*, Vol. 50, 1960, pp. 541–554. Copyright © 1960 by the American Geographical Society of New York. Reprinted by permission.

that inhabit riverine and lacustrine environments, and human trypanosomiasis is largely limited to areas that have permanent water. The numerous carriers of livestock trypanosomiasis are less restricted and range into semiarid country, though not into deserts.

Topography is a further limitation to the area occupied by the livestock disease. In northern Uganda at least, the fly avoids the uplands and is found in the usually dry river valleys. In some cases this is explained by the association of vegetation and topography; for example, *Acacia hebecladoides*, which harbors tsetse, is found in the valleys and not generally in the hills. In tropical highland country the fly may be found at considerable elevations, often 4000 to 5500 feet, but also in the valleys.

Control of a disease with such a train of transmission is not possible within the framework of an indigenous African cattle-keeping culture, but it has been undertaken within the last several decades by the European administrations of the territories afflicted. Control measures have been directed toward breaking the train of transmission by eliminating the host, the carrier, or both from the infested area.

Among the measures taken to control the host have been construction of electric and other fences to restrict the movement of game, firing of guns to frighten game from the area, and shooting of game populations in an infested area. The first two methods have often been ineffective, and the third, though undoubtedly effective, has brought opposition from persons concerned with game conservation.

Measures taken to control the fly carrier comprise direct use of insecticide sprays, removal of the host, or removal of the fly habitat.[5] Clearance of selected species of

vegetation or of all the herbaceous vegetation in belts ranging in width from a few hundred yards to several miles has proved effective as a barrier to the fly carriers. Among the vegetation that is cut and burned along drainage lines are thickets and large shade trees, including *Ficus* and *Kigelia* species. In the broad valleys stands of *Acacia hebecladoides* are removed. But this control measure also has its debit side; removal of the vegetative cover on extensive parts of a watershed results in accelerated erosion. Any tsetse clearance measure alters the existing ecological balance.

TRYPANOSOMIASIS IN NORTHEASTERN UGANDA

An example of the results of tsetse infestation can be found in Dodos [6] County of Karamoja District in Uganda. Dodos is the northeasternmost administrative unit in Uganda. It extends from the Nyangeya Mountains on the west to the Kenya boundary on the east (Fig. 1), and from the Sudan boundary on the north to Jie County of Karamoja District on the south. It is a semiarid highland of some three thousand square miles occupied by seasonally nomadic, cattle-keeping, Nilo-Hamitic tribes.

The settled area is 4000 to 6000 feet in elevation. Residual mountain masses rise to 7000 feet or more; some reach 8000 feet, and one, Morongole, is more than 9000 feet

---

[5] For general background on the problems of tsetse control and on control methods evolved, see the Annual Reports, 1950 through 1958, of the Uganda Protectorate Tsetse Control Department and of the East African Tsetse and Trypanosomiasis Research and Reclamation Organization (East Africa High Commission), and E. A.

Lewis: Land Use and Tsetse Control, *East African Agric. Journ.*, Vol. 18, 1953, pp. 160–168.

[6] Although governmental sources use the spelling Dodoth, it is not local usage. During my residence of more than a year in the area, I observed that *s* and *th* as enunciated by tribal members are difficult to distinguish, but I heard the tribal name almost always as Dodo*s*. Doris Clark, a missionary with 25 years of residence in Karamoja and a fluent speaker of the language, asserted that Dodos is correct. See also Pamela and P. H. Gulliver: The Central Nilo-Hamites (Ethnographic Survey of Africa: East Central Africa, Part 7; International African Institute, London, 1953), p. 9.

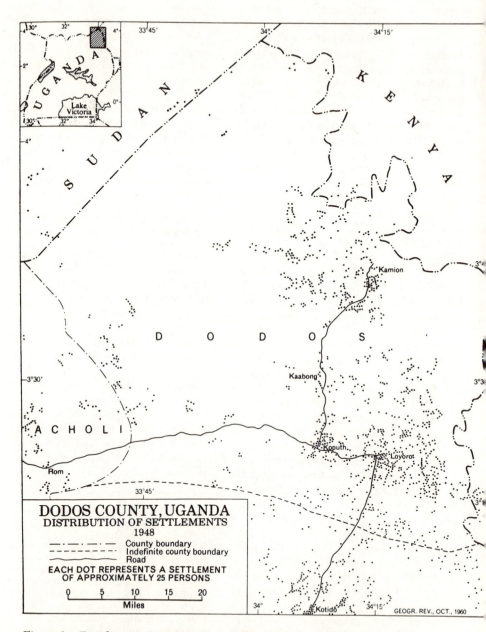

Figure 1.—Distribution of settlements in Dodos County, 1948, showing the pattern of settlement during the wet season, when the herds are in the home area. All streams shown are intermittent. Source: appropriate sheets of the 1:50,000 map series published by the Directorate of Colonial Surveys, Uganda, and based on aerial photographs taken in 1947–1948.

high. Broad, pedimented valleys lie between the Nyangeya Mountains and the mountain masses of the north and east. The river valleys of the west carry a fire-altered vegetation consisting of scattered broad-leaved trees and grasses that grow to five or six feet. This area is favorable for grazing. The eastern valleys carry some relict patches of a drier phase of scattered tree-grassland, useful for light grazing, and more extensive areas of man-induced scrub thicket, which, however, contains large patches bare of vegetation for much of the year. Rainfall ranges from about 40 inches annually in the west and in the highlands of the north to 15 to 20 inches in the southeast.

The county is occupied by about twenty thousand Dodos people in the eastern half, and by about three thousand Napore and Nyangeya people along the Nyangeya Mountains of the west. The distribution of the population, however, is not what one would expect from the environmental setting (Fig. 1). Two-thirds of the people are clustered in the southeastern quarter of the county, the poorest lands; 90 per cent are in the eastern third. This anomalous distribution is for the social scientist one of the more interesting and provocative aspects of Dodos settlement.

The Dodos live in homesteads that shelter all the members of an extended family. A common arrangement consists of a father with his wives and unmarried children plus his married sons with their wives and children. The homestead has a corral for the family herd and a series of fenced yards, one for each wife and her sleeping house and granaries. The whole is surrounded by a thorn fence.

In order to subsist, the Dodos combine gathering and shifting cultivation with cattle keeping. From a European point of view the country presents an unproductive base for any of these activities. Rainfall is erratic, crop and animal yields are low and variable, food shortage is common late in the dry season. During much of the six-month

annual drought vast areas are waterless. Late in the dry season, only a few water holes remain, deep within the sandy beds of the larger rivers. The grass cover in the east, long overgrazed, is thin, and here the seasonal migration of herds is essential to their survival.

The Napore and Nyangeya live in somewhat smaller homesteads, which contain nuclear families (parents and children) and a few older widowed dependents. The homesteads consist of houses and granaries within a thorn fence, the family herds are corralled separately, usually high in the mountains. Napore-Nyangeya country has a heavier and more reliable rainfall than that in the east, and the people are able to depend more on cultivation than the Dodos. However, gathering and livestock keeping are practiced.

THE TSETSE INFESTATION IN DODOS

The tsetse fly first appeared in Dodos early in the 1920's. Before that, in 1916, it had been reported to the north, in the Kidepo Valley of southern Sudan.

In the early 1900's the Napore-Nyangeya people formed an effective barrier to tsetse penetration from Sudan south into Dodos. They were settled in the highlands near the border, and they hunted in the valleys; their relatively small cattle herds were usually kept in the hills. Since the tsetse fly feeds on game animals, the presence of human population, especially hunters, by making an area unattractive to game tends to limit tsetse penetration. In any case, the area was settled, and tsetse was not a problem. Throughout the first decade of the century there was frequent raiding of cattle between the Didinga tribe of Sudan and the Dodos. Moreover, a migration of the Napore and Nyangeya southward into Dodos resulted in conflict between them and the Dodos.

In order to eliminate the raiding across the Sudan border, the King's African Rifles, the military arm of the Uganda Protectorate, carried out a series of police actions against the Napore and Nyangeya and the Didinga between 1909 and 1913.[7] The disturbances continued, however, and the administration's next step was to move small groups of Napore and Nyangeya to the south whenever they became especially troublesome. During 1924–1925 some 1500 people were moved out of northwestern Dodos County to the south, in what amounted to an effective evacuation of the area (Fig. 2).[8]

As people left, game and tsetse fly moved in. Buffalo were reported on the increase in western Dodos and northern Jie in 1924, and the natives requested permission to exterminate them, giving as a reason that the buffalo was a carrier of tsetse.[9] As early as 1922 there had been indications of tsetse in west-central Dodos, and by mid-1924 it had progressed as far as 80 miles south of the Sudan border into Jie County. During the next three years the fly appeared in numbers throughout the valleys of western Dodos. By this time the infested area amounted to about 1500 square miles, half the area of the county (Fig. 3).

For more than thirty years this fly infestation has been a dominant factor in Dodos settlement, because of its impact both within the fly belt and over large areas still fly-free.

IMMEDIATE AND LONG-TERM EFFECTS

At the onset of the infestation cattle keepers within the tsetse belt were confronted with deaths in their herds, which constituted a threat to subsistence. They solved the problem in diverse ways.

In the far west the tsetse belt ended at the front of the Nyangeya Mountains. The people who were settled along the mountain front had to make only a slight adaptation to tsetse. They moved their herds

back into the mountains, which were fly-free, and kept them there the year round. They maintained unchanged their settlements and cultivation patches along the mountain front.

The central part of the tsetse belt, largely the north-south river valleys of western Dodos, was deserted by man and livestock after the infestation. This area of calcareous soils had been among the best dry-season grazing grounds in the county, but since it lacks dry-season water, it had never contained permanent settlers.

The eastern part of the tsetse belt, extending well into central Dodos, was also emptied of cattle and nearly deserted by man after the infestation. This area has year-round water and had supported permanent settlement. It was from this area that repeated reports of cattle deaths came. Most of the inhabitants moved with their herds eastward out of the fly belt; a very few gave up cattle keeping and remained behind, living in the hills adjacent to the best cultivable land. They were able to keep flocks of goats within the fly zone.

Within a short time the fly belt, about half of Dodos, was nearly deserted by man. Except in the mountain areas of the far west, no cattle grazed within the 1500 square miles of the high-rainfall country of western Dodos County. Cultivation was limited to the high pediments of the western margin and a few scattered patches elsewhere.

Not only was the more fertile part of Dodos County nearly emptied of settlement, but the influence of the fly reached out well beyond the infested area into eastern Dodos, which received many refugees. Local population increases resulted in crowding in the southeast, and to a smaller extent in the northeast, because the refugees did not settle evenly over the county but moved to areas where they had relatives or close friends and to the few areas of reliable year-round water supplies. In this fashion the drier parts of Dodos came to carry most of the population (Fig. 1). Densities in the

---

[7] Hubert Moyse-Bartlett: The King's African Rifles (Aldershot, 1956), pp. 233–256.

[8] Karamoja District Officer, Annual Report to the Provincial Commissioner, 1924.

[9] *Ibid.*

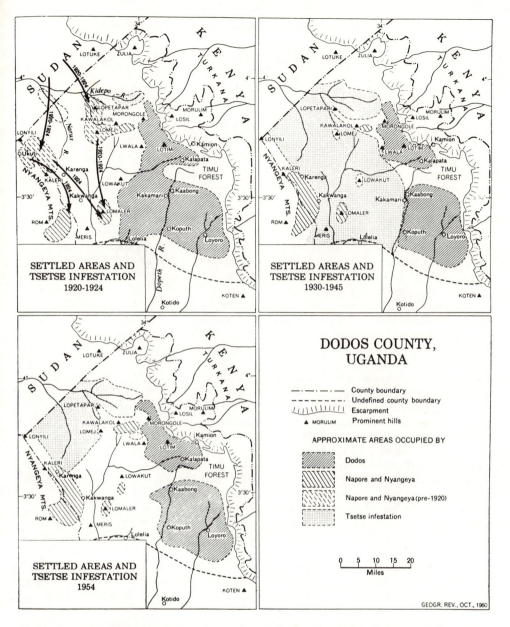

Figure 2. (upper left). Distribution of people and tsetse immediately before the tsetse infestation. Arrows indicate population movements. (Source of all three maps, government files, Moroto.)

Figure 3. (upper right). Distribution of people and tsetse during the period of maximum infestation.

Figure 4. (lower left). Distribution of people and tsetse at the time the tsetse clearance consolidation line was established. The tsetse position in late 1957 was about the same.

crowded areas became extremely high for this semiarid country.

The change in grazing pattern was equally catastrophic. Before the infestation cattle had grazed throughout Dodos, and the well-grassed lands of the west had been heavily used in season. After the infestation the entire cattle population was compressed into the grazing lands of drier eastern Dodos, and pressures here increased well beyond the carrying capacity of the land. There were no practical possibilities for further movement of people or livestock. The eastern margin of the fly belt became the western boundary of the Dodos tribe, and expansion in all other directions was inhibited by the presence of hostile tribes with land problems of their own. Warfare, a common solution before the British imposed peace, was no longer possible on an extended scale.

From the mid-twenties on, the tsetse problem received increasing attention from the Karamoja administration.[10] In 1935 tsetse clearance was studied by the Uganda Director of Veterinary Services, and a plan was devised, but the program was delayed by World War II. Clearance began in 1946, and in 1953 and 1954, when the writer was in the field in Dodos, fly clearance by the Uganda Tsetse Control Department was well under way. By early 1954 the southern two-thirds of the fly belt had been largely cleared (Fig. 4).

The principal method used in clearance was the removal of herbaceous vegetation by cutting and burning. Buffalo, one of the main hosts of trypanosomes in that area, were exterminated within the tsetse belt. The tsetse-control people worked to estab-

[10] Karamoja District, about 10,000 square miles of semidesert, was administered before World War II by one or two European district officers with their small African and Asian staffs, and usually by one European police officer with a small number of native police. The Dodos tsetse area is located 130 miles or so northward along a dry-weather track from Moroto, the district headquarters.

lish a buffer zone patrolled by hunters to prevent re-entry of game and of tsetse from the areas to the north that were still infested. By 1956 the southern part of the fly belt was sufficiently cleared to permit grazing of cattle.

At the time of observation the land within the belt was in good condition. Former erosion gullies had been arrested and were covered with vegetation. The stands of grass were thick during the wet season. The vegetation, burned by annual grass fires, was fire-conditioned and consisted of fire-resistant trees such as *Combretum* and *Terminalia,* with an understory of grasses with seeds that resist fire by burying themselves within the earth. The grazing supported herds of game, among them large groups of hartebeest, smaller herds of eland, some waterbuck, several groups of giraffe, zebras, gazelles, bush pigs, rhinoceros, elephants (on migration), and lions on the plains and leopards in the hills. There were also lesser buck and hyenas.

Signs of man's occupance before the infestation were largely effaced, though abandoned grindstones were to be found throughout the formerly settled areas, and from air photographs regular lines of trees that probably outlined former corrals could be read.

The first cultivators to return to the southern part of the former fly belt obtained crop yields of about five bushels per acre in place of the one or so that their relatives thirty miles to the east in the drier part of Dodos obtained in the same year. Clearly, the most important long-term effect of tsetse within the area of infestation was to make possible adequate fallow for the restoration of the tillage and grazing land, by forcing out man and his domestic livestock.

In contrast with the restored tsetse belt, southeastern Dodos, which had supported heavy densities of people and livestock since the late 1920's, was a wasteland in 1954. Population densities in the main settlement cluster were as high as 60 to 80 persons per square mile, on land that had received less than 13 inches of rainfall in 1953. Crop failure was widespread, and local grain supplies lasted for only about four months after the harvest. Cattle died of starvation.

The general picture was desolate. Vast areas were bare of vegetation and supported only ephemeral grasses for a few weeks during the rains. Much of the remainder of the southeast was covered with deciduous thicket in regions which had become so unproductive that they had been abandoned. Around the crowded areas near the sources of year-round water, soils that were not bare were covered with a thicket of thorny succulents—aloes, sansevieria, euphorbia, and the like.[11] This pattern of vegetation was almost certainly induced by cultivation and grazing. The most badly deteriorated areas were near permanent water, where the grazing pressure was highest. Old men among the Dodos asserted repeatedly that in the past the crowded area of the southeast had been superior grazing country, and similar assertions have been made to other observers. The European cattle buyer who had visited Dodos for nearly a week every month for twelve years stated that the deterioration had been progressive within his experience. C. A. Turpin, writing in 1916 from the northern garrison at Morungole (Morongole), remarked: "There is no comparison between the excellent grazing grounds of Loyoro and the jungle district of Morungole."[12] The condition during the mid-1950's was the reverse of that described by Turpin.

Cultivation also contributed to the deterioration. The Dodos practice a shifting

[11] See A. S. Thomas: The Vegetation of the Karamoja District, Uganda, *Journ. of Ecology*, Vol. 31, 1943, pp. 149–177.

[12] Manuscript report (p. 1 missing) from C. A. Turpin, Northern Garrison, Morungole, Feb. 29, 1916. (In Karamoja District files, Moroto.)

cultivation, and their procedures are extractive of nutrients in the soil. The cattle and small stock make no large return of manure to the soil. There are chance droppings as the animals feed in the field after the grain harvest, but these are slight. In the crowded areas fallow periods had been so shortened because of land shortage that fields appeared to be in cultivation every other year and in some places every year. Soil restoration under indigenous African practice comes largely from prolonged bush fallow, but in Dodos this was inadequate. The scars of accelerated erosion were commonplace throughout the cultivated areas.

Although the deterioration is largely man- and cattle-induced, it is not all attributable to the tsetse infestation Dodos is a land where settlement appears to have been precarious throughout the short period of record. The tsetse infestation was only one of numerous disasters. There have been famines caused by drought or by livestock disease; there have been wars and epidemic diseases of man. The present landscape bears the marks of all these, attenuated by the passage of time. The tsetse infestation, being the most recent, is the most readily noticed.

The evils of the tsetse infestation in Dodos have not ended; they will go on for decades. Land deterioration as severe as that in eastern Dodos is not quickly remedied. Even if the damaged land were to be completely abandoned to fallow, the newly cleared lands of the west are not adequate to support the total population without rapid deterioration or to support the present population over a long period.

The most marked effect of the tsetse infestation was found outside the fly belt, in the areas into which refugees fled. The disease restricted human settlement over areas much larger than that covered by the infestation.

II. POPULATION-LAND RELATIONSHIPS: ADJUSTMENT

Adjustment may be achieved when people are able to come to terms with, if not to solve fully, the problems confronting them in their attempt to make a reasonable livelihood from the land. Moderately successful adjustment and the achievement of balance in relationships between people and land may be observed in a variety of ways.

Few areas in Africa offer better opportunities for observing the growth and the concentration of population than Southern and Northern Nigeria. Both stand out markedly on maps of population distribution and of crude population density (Trewartha and Zelinsky, 1954). Average crude density in the most closely settled parts of Southeast Nigeria approaches 1,000 persons per square mile (Floyd, 1969; Udo, 1963). In the close-settled zones around Kano city in the North, the average is 500 persons per square mile, rising to a maximum of about 900. The latter area is a major producer of groundnuts for export (White, 1963). Adjustments in agricultural practices, settlement pattern, and land tenure have been made to accommodate the needs of increasing numbers of people and the demands of a cash crop economy. These changes were not made independently of one another; instead they were closely related.

The paper on cocoa in Ghana specifically illustrates adjustments to the cultivation of a non-indigenous cash crop introduced to the Gold Coast and other parts of West Africa late in the nineteenth century (Anyare, 1963; Dickson, 1969). Highly specific adjustments may also be required in certain well defined physical environments. Highland regions, for example, present problems related to altitude, relief, and associated physical factors. And in areas of intense aridity, where annual rainfall is insufficient to support permanent settlement and cultivation, the need for specific adjustment may be even more sharply defined.

The area surrounding Kano illustrates adjustment in population-land relationships in a savanna environment where population densities are high (Forde, 1953; Grove, 1961). Cereal crops are the characteristic food staples, and the low incidence of animal trypanosomiasis during the dry season permits the grazing of cattle. Most of the cultivable land is intensively used, with fallowing either reduced or totally eliminated. Soil fertility is restored and maintained by the use of organic manures and, increasingly, artificial fertilizers. Cattle dung is available, but quantities are limited because cooperation between cultivators and livestock raisers is limited—and mixed farmers represent only a small proportion of the total farming population (Coppock, 1966).

The settlement pattern contributes further to the intensity of land use in the Kano close-settled zone: dispersed hamlets and individual compounds, together with large villages and towns functioning as market and service centers. The rural areas benefit from the central location of Kano city, the focus of a complex network of rural-urban linkages (McDonnell, 1964; Mortimore and Wilson, 1965).

Intensification has necessitated changes in land holding and land tenure. With permanent cultivation, plots have assumed a more regular, rectilinear shape and their boundaries are usually demarcated. Individual titles have replaced traditional communal holdings, permitting the pledging and leasing of land and outright sales and transfer. To accommodate such changes, Muslim land law (which recognizes sale and private ownership) has been substituted for customary land law, which recognizes communal ownership with the right of the individual to acquire sufficient land to meet his needs.

The cultivation of groundnuts for export has developed notwithstanding the demand for food staples made by the dense population. Although commercial production of this crop may result in a food deficit, it provides cash for the purchase of staples from other areas.

Population-land relationships in the Kano region are reasonably well balanced, yet stress is evident. The claim that population pressure on resources is manifest in net out-migration and in large-scale seasonal migration (McDonnell, 1964), has been challenged (Mortimore and Wilson, 1965), though movements for comparable reasons have been identified in other parts of Northern Nigeria (Grove, 1957; Prothero, 1957c; 1959).

6. Land and Population Pressure in the Kano Close-Settled Zone, Northern Nigeria

M. J. MORTIMORE

The population of tropical Africa is at present just over 200 million and, with a prospective rate of increase of 2.4 per cent per annum, is expected to reach 295 million by 1980. According to the FAO Africa Survey of 1962, "unless action is taken to accelerate economic progress, this increase will mean added unemployment and underemployment and consequent malnutrition, misery and social unrest." [1] The average density of population in tropical Africa is about 25 persons per square mile, or 9 per square kilometre, not a high figure by world standards. But increasing population threatens in many areas to upset the balance of population and resources, which often depends upon maintaining soil fertility by systems of land rotation, such as shifting cultivation and bush fallowing. These require that a large proportion of available agricultural land shall always be in fallow. In certain parts of tropical Africa, however, much higher densities of population have been achieved using traditional techniques of peasant agriculture: such as the Lake Victoria basin, the highlands of Ruanda and Burundi, and the Kano close-settled zone in Northern Nigeria. In such areas, land rotation has been largely replaced by permanent or annual cultivation based upon intensive techniques such as the use of animal manure, double cropping, or the rotation and interplanting of crops. It has been suggested that farmers only intensify their methods of cultivation when forced to do so by land shortage.[2] In the Kano close-settled zone the density of rural population rises to over 600 per square mile in the centre and to over 900 in places. This paper attempts to explore some of the ways in which the agricultural economy has responded to, and been modified by, an exceptionally high density of population.

THE KANO CLOSE-SETTLED ZONE

The Kano close-settled zone is an outstanding feature in the distribution of population in Northern Nigeria.[3] Within Kano Province, the dominance of the close-settled zone is equally marked (Fig. 1). It contains about 2.4 million inhabitants out of a provincial total of 4.3 million, at an average density of about 500 persons per square mile, excluding Kano itself. The close-settled zone is provisionally defined here as having a population density of 350 or more per square mile.

The evolution of the close-settled zone is customarily attributed to a combination of favourable historical and natural (mainly pedological) conditions. Kano has been one of the chief centres of power in Hausaland for a thousand years, and the most important economic centre for at least a century. A large sedentary population grew in the shadow of a stable and highly organized Emirate which was firmly based upon the organized production of widely traded craft goods, and Kano's nodality with respect to continental trade routes.[4] Those areas with a density of population in excess of 350 per square mile lie within the limits of distribution of soils which are classified as brown or reddish-brown soils of arid or semi-arid regions (Fig. 1).[5] Situated on a gently undulating plain at about 1500 feet above sea level, and drained by seasonal rivers, these soils have developed on windblown sands derived from acid crystalline rocks of the Basement Complex. They are light, freely draining sandy loams, which have proved highly amendable to intensive cultivation. In depressions and alongside the larger rivers, alluvial and colluvial soils with a larger clay/silt fraction and inferior drainage form a small but important group.

From *The Advancement of Science*, 23:118, April 1967, pp. 677–686. Reprinted by permission.

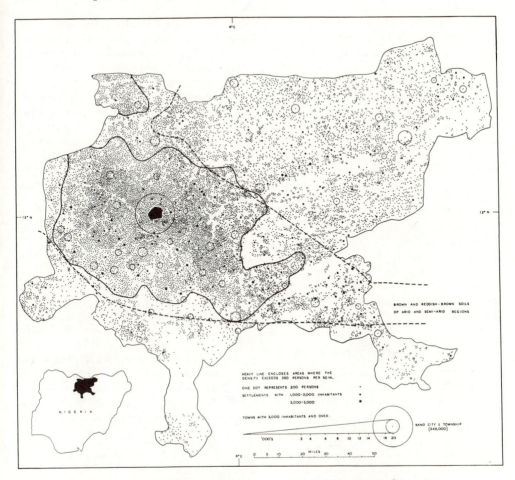

Figure 1.—The distribution of population in Kano Province, Northern Nigeria in 1962.

The agricultural growing season is confined to the rainy months, beginning in May and extending until September. The total annual rainfall averages 33 inches, with July and August the wettest months, but variability of both the annual and monthly distribution is a serious hazard to agriculture. For example, between 1945 and 1949 annual rainfall varied between 20 and 38 inches, and the monthly total for August between 8 and 19 inches. After the end of the rains the humid south-westerly airstream is replaced by north-east winds which bring the Harmattan, an extremely dry, dust-laden wind associated with low night-time temperatures. Except where irrigation is practised, agriculture is at a standstill from the end of the harvest in December until the planting rains arrive in the following May.

The material used here is drawn from a survey of three villages in the District of Ungogo and situated between 1 and 6 miles north of the urban area of Kano, which in 1962 had a population of 249,281.[6] They had a population in 1964 of 5103 at a

density of 915 per square mile. The first
of the villages includes the District Headquarters, a nucleated settlement of 1365
inhabitants (Fig. 2). In addition to the
District Administration, it has a market and
most of the public services provided for the
District, such as the dispensary and school.
Its focus is the District Head's house and
office, and outside the ruined wall a small
suburb is growing up. It is surrounded by
cultivated fields with dispersed family compounds such as those in the second village
(Fig. 3). In many other parts of Hausaland, the dispersal of settlement followed
the arrival of peaceful conditions with the
British administration in the early years of
this century, but in Kano it took place
much earlier. The third village was chosen
for study because it includes same valuable
dry season irrigated gardens along the banks
of a perennial stream.

POPULATION GROWTH AND MIGRATION

Family compounds contain either a close
family (a man, his wives and children) or
an extended family. In the latter event, it
is customary to divide the compound into
sections, separated with grass matting, in
each of which lives a married son or other
relative with his immediate dependants.
According to Muslim customs a man may
have up to four wives provided that he has
the means to support them. The "average"
number of wives per married man is, however, only 1.5, and the "average" size of
close families, defined as the inhabitants of
a compound section, is 4.5. Compounds
occasionally have six or more such sections
and a population of over 50, but the average
is two sections and a population of eight.

Between 1931 and 1964 the population
of the three villages doubled, and the rate
of growth accelerated from approximately
1.5 per cent per annum in the first two
decades to 3.1 per cent in the third. This
is somewhat higher than the probable rate
of natural increase, which is 2.5 per cent,
and seems to suggest net immigration. On
the other hand, the population of Ungogo
District as a whole is growing by only
1.3 per cent per annum, which is below the
probable rate of natural increase, and it
has been claimed that this and other central
districts of the close-settled zone are ex-
periencing net emigration.[7]

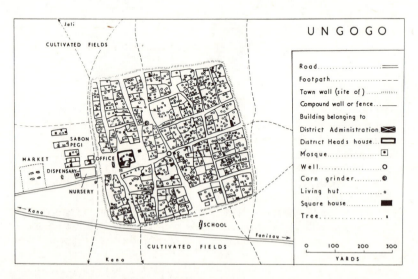

Figure 2.—Ungogo: nucleated settlement.

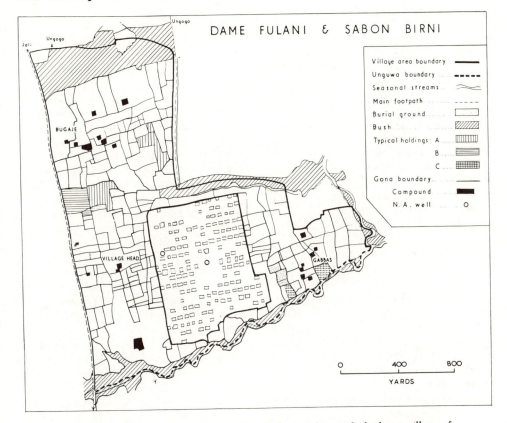

Figure 3.—Dame Fulani: dispersed settlement. The newly laid out village of
Sabon Birni occupies land in the centre of Dame Fulani purchased in 1943 to
resettle those affected by airport construction. Dame Fulani is an *unguwa*
(administrative subdivision) of Rafin Mallam village area. A *gona* consists of
one or more adjacent plots held by a single farmer. N.A.: Native Authority.

In these three villages, the most important type of migration is that of wives.
Each man seeks his wife on the basis of his
personal contacts in other areas. Altogether
408 immigrants wives of all ages were
counted, of whom the majority came from
other villages in the neighbourhood but a
few from distances of more than 100 miles.
Against these, 265 women were traced who
had left the villages as wives. Other migrants were few in number: 27 male immigrants and 23 temporary visitors against 23
male emigrants, both temporary and permanent (the survey was conducted during

the dry season when seasonal emigrants
were away). Migration is thus of small
importance in the total demographic situation, except for a small net gain of wives
from outside the villages.

THE DIVISION OF LAND

The impact of an acute shortage of agricultural land is shown both in the pattern
of land use and in the organization of land
holdings. In less densely populated parts of
Northern Nigeria, the zone of permanently
cultivated fields and short grass fallows

around the village is in turn surrounded by secondary woodland or scrub vegetation extending as far as the village boundary, in which farmers are allocated land by the Village Head. In the environs of Kano these reserves of "bush" are almost exhausted, being limited to rocky outcrops, or narrow strips of scrub or grassland along the village boundaries (Fig. 4). The latter frequently coincide with stream courses or topographical depressions where seasonal water-logging renders agriculture unprofitable. Such residual land occupies only 7.5 per cent of the total area, no less than 83.8 per cent being land under cultivation. This figure rises to about 85 per cent if garden land is included, which lies within the bounds of settlements and compounds.

The cultivated area is divisible into two main categories: upland, which comprises 79.6 per cent of the total area, and fadama land, which comprises 4.2 per cent. Cultivated upland is distributed on the broad, flat or gently sloping interfluves. It is the basis of the agricultural economy, on which the staple crops, guinea corn, millet, groundnuts and cowpeas are grown. Fadama land is important because although often only a few feet lower than upland, it enjoys a high water table or a perennial stream and often has alluvial soils replenished by frequent flooding. While arable upland dries hard and dusty during the dry season, year-round growing of crops is possible in the fadama.

Land tenure has a double ancestry, in traditional Africa concepts of communal ownership and in Islamic land law, which recognizes individual tenure. Islamic law has been superimposed upon earlier traditions and has encouraged the evolution of an orderly, closely defined and carefully regulated pattern of landholding. Allocations of land are made by the Village Head, as the representative of the community, but since very little unused land still exists, his chief importance is as a registrar of inheritances and transfers. In theory all land belongs to the Emir of Kano. Land left unoccupied reverts to the Village Head for re-allocation. The impossibility of rotating land in agriculture has encouraged the trend towards individualization of land tenure, and this is expressed in a considerable degree of permanency in the pattern of landholdings. Plots are rectangular in shape, with boundaries orientated north-south and east-west, and planted with thatching grass, henna bushes or other economic plants. The boundaries of landholdings in Dame Fulani are shown on Fig. 3.

A second important result of land shortage is the increasing frequency of alienation by sale. Pledging and loaning of land have long been recognized, but exchange by sale, a concept inconsistent with African traditions of communal ownership, has become generally accepted only during the last thirty years Land values have increased from little more than £1 an acre, twenty years ago, to £10–20 an acre, giving many family holdings a value of £100–200.

The formalization of landholdings and the growth of commercial transactions in land have brought land tenure closer than is usual in Africa to the English concept of freehold. Landholdings were the basis of taxation in the central districts of Kano Emirate until very recently. In 1932 a survey of all farm boundaries, and a record of all landholders, was made which permits some instructive comparison with the survey of present-day farm boundaries shown in Fig. 3.[8] The changes which have taken place illustrate the operation of a cycle of fragmentation and consolidation which is adjusted to the normal growth and subdivision of families (Fig. 5). As a farmer increases his wealth he attempts to increase the size of his holding by purchasing adjoining plots, or, if these are not available, distant ones, if necessary outside the village boundary. His sons on marriage, or shortly before, are given outlying parts of the father's holding, numbered 2–5 on Fig. 5. On these they grow cash crops independently, while continuing to work under the father's direction on the main farm and

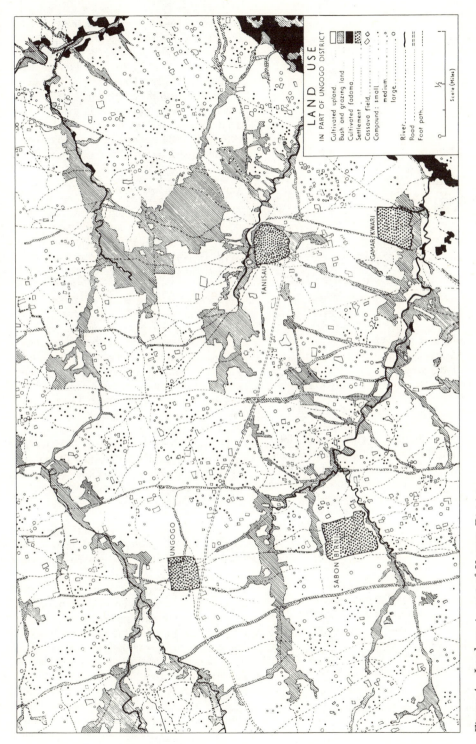

Figure 4.—Land use in part of Ungogo District.

HOLDINGS IN
JANGARU

Footpath		----
Compound		▦
Uncultivated		▨
Tree		⋮
① JANGARU I:	Main holding	
② ,,	Son 1	
③ ,,	Son 2	
④ ,,	Son 3	
⑤ ,,	Son 4	
⑥ JANGARU 2		

YARDS 0   100   200   100

Figure 5.—Some farm holdings in Jangaru. Jangaru 1 (29 acres) is farmed full-time by an extended family; Jangaru 2 (2½ acres) is farmed part-time by a weaver and his close family.

thereby contributing to the family food supply. On the death of the father, Islamic law provides for the subdivision of the holding between the heirs, or its sale intact and the subdivision of the proceeds. This fragmentation is followed by further consolidation or enlargement as the sons in turn attempt to increase the size of their holdings.

Between 1932 and 1964, the number of separately occupied plots in the 448 acres which were surveyed increased by 42 per cent to 185. The number of landholders also increased from 95 to about 115.* During the same period the cultivated area was increased by the clearance of 26 acres of bush, mostly marginal land situated in

* Unfortunately the number is not known precisely because of the frequent duplication of proper names.

depressions and low in productivity. Of all the plots registered in 1932, 41 per cent had been subdivided by 1964, while only 16 per cent had been consolidated with adjacent holdings. Thus subdivision gained at the expense of consolidation. Fragmentation is also increasing. The average plot decreased in size by 22 per cent between 1932 and 1964, whereas the average holding decreased by less than 11 per cent.[9]

AGRICULTURAL INTENSIFICATION

The intensification of agriculture has been a further response to land shortage. Estimates of the average size of landholding in Northern Nigeria suggest about 4 acres per adult male or about 8 acres per family.[10] In these villages in Ungogo District only 2.6 acres of cultivated land are available for each adult male and the average size of holding in the area surveyed is between 3.3 and 3.7 acres. However, the common practice of holding land outside the village boundary, and of outsiders holding land within it, suggests that family holdings are somewhat larger than this. The area of cultivated land per head of the population is only 0.6 of an acre.

The most important form of agricultural intensification is the substitution of manure for fallowing as the principal means of maintaining soil fertility. The manure is produced by goats, sheep, donkeys, and other domestic animals and combined with household refuse. Arrangements are made between farmers and passing Fulani herdsmen for the kraaling of cattle on the fields at night, but this is an unimportant source in quantitative terms. The average application of manure is in the neighbourhood of one and a half tons per acre per annum, either heaped around the feet of the growing plants, or spread before sowing. The production of manure in the villages is insufficient for requirements and considerable quantities are purchased from Kano City, whose animal population is enormous. One group of farmers spent an average sum of 13s. 4d. per acre on buying manure each year. Yields vary sharply according to the amount applied, which is partly determined by the farmer's cash resources at the end of the dry season.

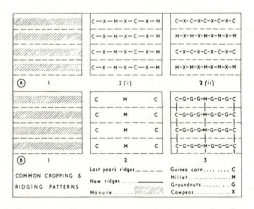

COMMON CROPPING &
RIDGING PATTERNS

Last years ridges _ _ _ _   Guinea corn C
New ridges _____   Millet.................M
Manure ....▨▨▨   Groundnuts .... G
                              Cowpeas X

Figure 6.—Some common cropping and ridging patterns. In the upper row, 2(i) and 2(ii) are alternatives.

Whereas little evidence of the regular rotation of crops was obtained, intercropping is a general practice. Sometimes groundnuts, the cash crop, are planted in patches alone, but the two grain staples, guinea corn and millet, are always intercropped with each other or with cowpeas or groundnuts. Some common cropping patterns are shown in Fig. 6. Guinea corn and millet are the first to be planted; groundnuts are planted a few days later and can be put in between the growing plants. Cowpeas are planted in July. The beneficial effect of the legumes upon plant growth, and of the nitrogen-fixing cowpeas, is thus recognized in general practice.

Farm work is done entirely by hand using the hoe, of which there are two types adapted for weeding and for ridgemaking. In the Kano area, the sandy nature of the soils makes ridging before planting unnecessary, except for groundnuts planted alone. Since the soil is too hard for working until after heavy rain has fallen, this facilitates quick sowing of the grain crops, which is essential in an area of low rainfall. Bullock ploughing, which is gaining acceptance in some parts of Northern Nigeria, has not been successfully introduced because the shortage of land makes viable holdings difficult to achieve, and there is insufficient pasture for the animals.

In most parts of Northern Nigeria the size of farm holdings is largely a function of the size of the labour force available at peak periods. Despite the small average size of holdings in Ungogo, the regular labour force of adult males is often insufficient. On one example (shown in Fig. 5), a large holding having a resident labour force of seven adult males, the women and children, despite Muslim custom, were recruited to help with the sowing, and hired labourers provided about 680 man-hours in excess of the family labour capacity, chiefly during the first two hoeing periods.* Such labourers are usually farmers whose holdings are too small to keep them fully occupied, or who need cash urgently. Harvesting, which was spread out from August until December, presented no labour problems.

The need for cash has forced a limited abandonment of the subsistence economy. Almost every farmer grows groundnuts for sale, and the production of grain for home consumption frequently falls short of actual requirements and the deficit has to be purchased. This seems to be more profitable than attempting to grow more food crops, and in any case it is essential to have cash to pay taxation; providing this is the most important function of the groundnut harvest. Kano Province grows half of Nigeria's groundnuts; thus shortage of land has not discouraged widespread response to commercial incentives.

The greatest intensification and commercialization of agriculture is apparent in

* In Katsina Province, where conditions are comparable in several respects, hired labour was found not to be an economic alternative to family labour.[11]

the fadama, where irrigation from perennial streams, using the shaduf, enables market gardening to continue throughout the dry season. Land values are three or four times as high as those of upland, and the holdings are commonly a fraction of an acre in size. Labour inputs are at a maximum since in addition to normal agricultural operations many hours must be spent in lifting and controlling water. Almost the whole output is sent to the markets in Kano, or exported, and consists chiefly of vegetables; but at a greater distance from the urban area, lower valued crops which are less dependent upon market accessibility, such as sugar cane, rice and wheat, are of greater importance. Despite this heavy emphasis upon commercial production, every fadama farmer also has an upland farm on which he grows subsistence crops during the wet season, when the fadama, which is frequently flooded, is relatively neglected. This defines the impact of commercial agriculture in what, for Northern Nigeria, are optimum conditions.

SECONDARY OCCUPATIONS

The exploitation of secondary sources of income is encouraged by a widespread, though small, deficit in the production of food crops, the existence of a large urban market near by, and a relatively idle period of four or five months during the dry season. Weaving is the most important, and brings in about £ 30 a year to those families seriously committed to it. The cloth, woven on a narrow loom, is principally for the Kano market. There is some association between weaving and smallholdings, and many of the weavers have sufficiently small agricultural responsibilities to enable them to continue weaving throughout the year. However, the peak period of the industry is during the dry season. Despite competition from manufactured cotton, weaving is an important economic outlet because it requires smaller capital resources than the purchase of additional land for farming.

Other important secondary sources of income are wage labour, which has been mentioned already, services such as butchering and laundering, crafts such as leather- and woodworking, and various forms of trading. All secondary occupations except for farm labour, are most active during the dry season, and it can be seen that irrigated agriculture in the fadama fits into the same pattern. Almost every family derives some income from secondary sources, although the amount involved varies from £ 25–30 per annum to £ 1–2 for some of the humbler types of trading. Differences in opportunities and in individual aptitudes have much to do with the variable importance of the non-agricultural sector of the rural economy.

RURAL-URBAN RELATIONS

An essential part of the growth and functioning of the Kano close-settled zone is the symbiotic relationship which Kano enjoys with its rural environs. The importance of urban markets for the sale of the products of rural industry, and of fadama agriculture, has been mentioned. It seems likely that in former times the rural areas supplied surplus grain to the urban population, but there is no longer a surplus and Kano's food supplies come from farther afield, with the exception of those produced by City-dwelling farmers. The largest element in present-day relations between Kano and its immediate environs is the exchange of two commodities in large demand in town and country respectively, namely firewood and manure.

The consumption of firewood in the City alone, which contains two-thirds of Kano's inhabitants, has been estimated to be of the order of 15,000 donkey loads per week.[12] Quantities are brought from a distance by lorry, but every week during the dry season approximately 13,000 donkeys converge upon Kano from all directions, carrying firewood obtained by felling some of the many farm trees which give its rural

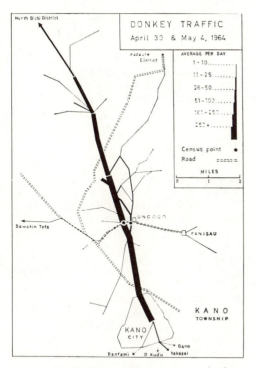

DONKEY TRAFFIC
April 30 & May 4, 1964

| AVERAGE PER DAY |
| 1 - 10 |
| 11 - 25 |
| 26 - 50 |
| 51 - 100 |
| 101 - 250 |
| 250 + |

Census point •
Road ======

MILES
0   1   2

North Bichi District

Kazaure District

Dawakin Tofa

UNGOGO

FANISAU

KANO
TOWNSHIP

KANO
CITY

Gano

Danfami   D Kudu   Yakasai

Figure 7.—Donkey traffic on one of about eighteen routes radiating from Kano, on April 30th and May 4th 1964.

environs their characteristic parkland aspect. Wood may thus be viewed economically as a cash source of some importance.

The greater part of this traffic comes from distances of less than 10 miles from Kano, and on their return trip in the afternoon many of the donkeys carry loads of manure from the City which is distributed over the farms within the same area. Figure 7 shows the daily donkey traffic on one of about eighteen routes at the end of the dry season. Between January and April, when the demand for manure is greatest, the traffic leaving Kano in all directions amounts to at least 9000 donkey loads per week, representing approximately 1000 tons of manure. On the assumption that the average application of manure is the same as in the villages studied, i.e. 1.5 tons per acre per annum, or slightly lower, it

may be said that Kano supplies during the course of the year 10–15 per cent of the manure utilized within a radius of 10 miles.

This traffic, like all other non-agricultural activities, is busiest during the dry season; the need for manure ends with the beginning of the growing season and farmers are too busy to fell trees. Donkey traffic concerned with other commodities, and a large volume of pedestrian traffic, add to the intimacy of contact between town and country. But it is noticeable that commuting from rural or peri-urban residences to urban employment is almost absent.

The high population densities in the heart of the Kano close-settled zone appear to be maintained by natural increase and to be neither alleviated nor exacerbated to a significant extent by migration. The pattern of land use reflects the pressure of population in the virtual disappearance of fallow and the devotion of 85 per cent of the surface area to permanent or annual cultivation. Land tenure is becoming more individualized, and the rising value of land, together with the influence of a commercial economy, has forced the acceptance of increasingly frequent alienation by sale. The subdivision and fragmentation of landholdings is proceeding at a greater rate than consolidation and enlargement.

The intensification of agriculture has replaced fallowing by heavy manuring, and regular intercropping with high labour inputs (especially in the fadama) is practised. Technological advance, in the form of bullock ploughing, appears not to be viable at present. There is a small but significant deficit in food crop production, mainly as the result of the cultivation of cash crops. Secondary occupations, especially weaving, based principally upon the urban market, provide sufficient income to make up for any deficiencies in agricultural production. The exchange of manure and firewood on a large scale has increased the interdependence of urban and rural communities. The continental space relations of precolonial Kano have suffered drastic change during the last sixty years, but the close web of economic ties between town and country survives intact. It has played an essential part in the growth of the Kano close-settled zone and in the process of urbanization.

REFERENCES

[1] United Nations, Food and Agriculture Organisation. 1962. *FAO Africa Survey,* 16, Rome.

[2] Prothero, R. M. 1962. "Some observations on desiccation in north-western Nigeria," *Erdkunde, 16,* 111–19.

[3] Prothero, R. M. *Northern Region, Nigeria,* 1:1,000,000 *Population Distribution,* and *Northern Region, Nigeria,* 1:1,000,000 *Population Density* (maps compiled from 1952 Census of Northern Nigeria), Directorate of Overseas Surveys, Tolworth, Surrey.

[4] Barth, H. 1858. *Travels and Discoveries in North and Central Africa, 2,* 97–147.

[5] Information supplied by G. M. Higgins and K. Klinkenberg, Soil Survey Section, Institute for Agricultural Research, Ahmadu Bello University, Zaria.

[6] Mortimore, M. J. and Wilson, J. 1956. *Land and People in the Kano Close-settled Zone; a Report to the Greater Kano Planning Authority.* Department of Geography, Ahmadu Bello University, Zaria, Occasional Paper No. 1. This study followed the approach of Grove, A. T. (1952): *Land and People in Katsina Province,* Government Printer, Kaduna.

[7] McDonnell, G. 1964. "The dynamics of geographic change: the case of Kano," *Annals of the Association of American Geographers, 54,* 355–71.

[8] MacBride, D. F. H. 1938. "Land survey in the Kano Emirate, Northern Provinces, Nigeria," *Journal of the Royal African Society,* 37, 75–91.

[9] Rowling, C. W. 1952. *Report on Land Tenure, Kano Province,* Government Printer, Kaduna, also reported subdivision.

[10] Baldwin, K. D. S. 1963. "Land tenure problems in relation to agricultural development in the Northern Region of Nigeria," in Biebuyck, D. (ed.) *African Agrarian Systems,* 65–82, Oxford. Federal Department of Statistics (1961), *Agricultural Sample Survey, Bulletin* 3, agrees with this if the term "farmer" is taken to be equivalent to an adult male.

[11] Luning, H. A. 1961. *An Agro-economic Survey in Katsina Province,* Government Printer, Kaduna.

[12] Based upon information in Wilson, J. 1964. *Social Studies with special reference to Housing,* Greater Kano Planning Authority, Kano.

The forest environment of southeastern Nigeria contrasts in many respects with the savanna lands around Kano, yet there are notable similarities in the ways the agricultural systems of the two areas have met the demands of large numbers of people. Intensive use of the cultivable land, dispersed rural settlement (Udo, 1965a), land holdings, and patterns of land tenure are all comparable. Complications posed by laws of inheritance, as well as by increased demands for land and by the intensity of its use, have contributed to the fragmentation and areal reduction of holdings.

The oil palm is the main cash crop in the southeast. It rarely occupies land exclusively, and annual crops may be grown between the trees. Nonetheless, some areas have food deficits, and must import staples. There has also been a reduction in food crops that make the heaviest demands on soil fertility; the cultivation of cassava has increased and fewer yams are grown. Further indications of population pressure are the local migrations of farmers in search of land (Udo, 1964) and the widespread dispersal of the Ibo people over the whole of Nigeria. The latter situation has, of course, been considerably modified by the political upheavals and civil war in recent years.

7. *Farming Practice, Settlement Pattern and Population Density in South-Eastern Nigeria*

W. B. MORGAN

In 1951 A. T. Grove read a paper before the Society on the badly eroded country of Iboland in the Eastern Region of Nigeria.[1] In conclusion he pointed to the need for further research amongst the Ibo, particularly in the contrasting environments of the lowlands. The following paper represents an attempt to develop such research and is based on field work from the centres of Port Harcourt and Aba in 1954. The major part of the work is concerned with conditions in Aba Division, especially in that part of it termed Aba Ngwa County, whilst the study made in the area north of Part Harcourt, that is in Diobu District, is used to provide a comparison.

The farmer of south-eastern Nigeria is essentially a hoe cultivator; his work has the character of gardening rather than farming, since it is small scale and permits individual attention to the plants grown. Since holdings are small a large number of people per unit area is possible upon farmed land with resulting high rural densities. However, the chief problem of the south-east is that in many parts the population densities are very much higher than the present system of land holding would appear to allow. Grove has already shown

the problem in the Awka-Orlu uplands and the Udi Plateau. South of these the lower and more level regions, stretching down to the deltas of the Niger and Cross rivers and to the lagoons and bars of the firmer ground between, appear to be divided into two density zones characterized by Aba Division with 347 to the square mile and Ahoada, which includes Diobu District, with 143 (Fig. 1). It was felt therefore that an investigation of the conditions around Aba and in the area adjacent to Port Harcourt might shed some light on density problems and in particular on the carrying capacities of the lands concerned.

The normal practice amongst the Ngwa and Ikwerri divisions of the Ibo-speaking peoples in Aba Division and Diobu District respectively is to plant their crops in two types of land—farm land, which is the major food producer, and compound land, which serves the purpose of a kitchen garden. Farmland is divided into holdings consisting of "farms" which may be further divided into plots. Generally, holdings average less than 3 acres per family plus another ½ acre of compound land.[2] The cultivating unit is the family grouped into settlements whose pattern reflects the nature

From *The Geographical Journal, 121*, 1955, pp. 320–333.
Reprinted by permission of The Royal Geographical Society.

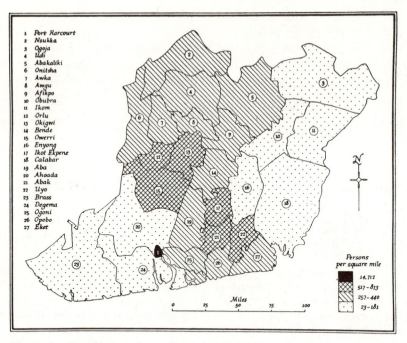

1　Port Harcourt
2　Nsukka
3　Ogoja
4　Udi
5　Abakaliki
6　Onitsha
7　Awka
8　Awgu
9　Afikpo
10　Obubra
11　Ikom
12　Orlu
13　Okigwi
14　Bende
15　Owerri
16　Enyong
17　Ikot Ekpene
18　Calabar
19　Aba
20　Ahoada
21　Abak
22　Uyo
23　Brass
24　Degema
25　Ogoni
26　Opobo
27　Eket

Persons
per square mile

14,712
517 - 813
257 - 440
23 - 181

Miles
0   25   50   75   100

Figure 1.—Distribution of population by Divisions in the Eastern Region of
Nigeria.

of the cultivation, since agriculture is the basis of existence. Here a contrast is immediately apparent amongst the Ngwa and Ikwerri. In Figure 2 it may be seen that the settlement pattern near Aba consists of scattered compounds entirely devoid of nucleation. The Ngwa in fact have no villages in the accepted sense. In Diobu, however, whilst compounds rather than individual huts are still characteristic, they are normally grouped together in well-defined villages of which that of Atako (Fig. 3) is an excellent example. The contrast in pattern apears to be related to a contrast in the form of local authority. Amongst the Ngwa, compounds are larger than those of the Ikwerri and house what may be described as an extended family or *onumara* —that is, not only a man and his wife or wives and children as represented by the *ezi* or smallest unit; but his sons, their wives and their children and often brothers and cousins. Even within this unit of closely related families, each family undertakes its own farm work and, whilst some assistance may be given by one to another, the labour is in no sense communally performed.[3] Groups of compounds inhabited by kinsfolk together form a larger unit called a "village" or *mba* in which unrelated family groups may be permitted to settle if land is available. "Village" affairs are discussed at a common meeting place. The connecting paths or *ama* are thus of vital importance in such administrative system as exists, and furthermore link the compounds for trade purposes. Their importance is stressed by the common occurrence of the word *ama* in Ibo settlement names[4] and, as will be shown, they have left an imprint on the agricultural pattern. The paths are vital also for water supply, since convenience with regard to agricultural land and not the location of water is the most

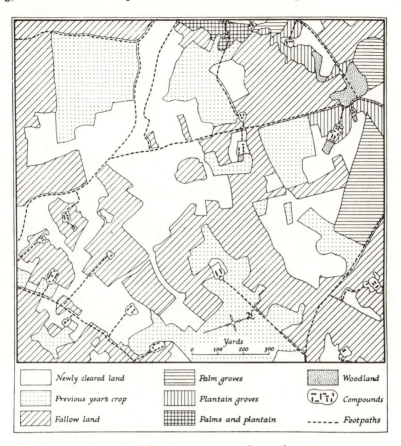

Figure 2.—Settlement and land use in Umu Ocham, Aba.

important factor in determining the settlement site: this is so despite the scattered distribution of water, due to the porous nature of the sub-soil with its low dry season water-table, and despite the difficult descents to streams. Distances of 8 miles to water are not unknown. Each household provides itself with a clay-lined catch pit which, however, is usually too foul for drinking purposes. With the exception of location near local springs arising from the few laterite outcrops, Ngwa settlement tends to be away from streams with their steep valley slopes, steep high banks in the dry season and lack of flood-plain. This seems to be a common Nigerian phenomenon, for

the chief concentrations of population are all on watersheds. Well-digging amongst the Ngwa was rare until the introduction of European techniques, owing to the liability of collapse of excavations and the great depths needed. In Diobu, by contrast, whilst the village also tends to be a kinship group, it is in effect comparable to a gathering together of the scattered *onumara* of its Ngwa counterpart. Local authority is vested in a chief who appears to have a greater control over village and compound affairs, and many agricultural activities are performed on a communal rather than an individual basis. Here the paths no longer have as their main function the linking of

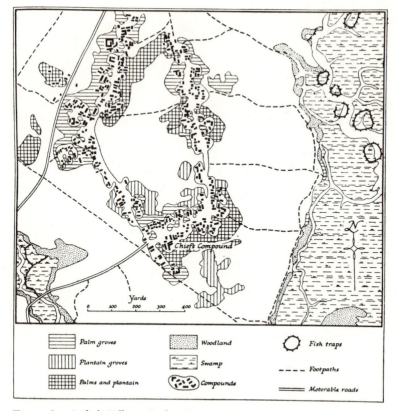

Figure 3.—Atako's Village, Diobu District

compounds, but radiate out from the village to the "farms." In the Port Harcourt area the comparatively level surface of the older alluvia is much lower and the dry season level of the water-table is nearer the surface. The descent to streams is less than at Aba and waterside locations are common both for fishing and for trading purposes. Thus one has the surprising contrast of evenly dispersed settlements in a region of restricted water supply and highly localized, nucleated settlement in a region offering easier conditions.

The effect of village organization and settlement pattern on agricultural practice is immediately apparent from a comparison of the cultivated area depicted in Figure 2 with that depicted in Figure 4. The scat-

tering of settlement in the Umu Ocham area of Aba Division is paralleled by that of the small blocks of cultivated land, whilst the nucleated settlement type of the Diobu area is accompanied by large cohesive blocks. Land utilization amongst both groups of Ibo is based broadly on six types of land:

1. The village or compound area with its accompanying kitchen garden land.

2. Farmland under cultivation and various stages of fallow, bearing oil palms in addition to annual crops.

3. Oil palm groves, usually close to the village or compound, and occasionally cropped.

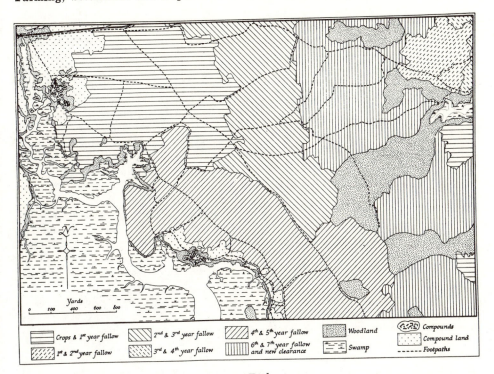

Crops & 1st year fallow   2nd & 3rd year fallow   4th & 5th year fallow   Woodland   Compounds

1st & 2nd year fallow   3rd & 4th year fallow   6th & 7th year fallow and new clearance   Swamp   Compound land   Footpaths

Figure 4.—Settlement and land use in eastern Diobu

4. Woodland, divided into (a) timber and firewood reserves including a windbreak round the settlement; (b) sacrosanct land, i.e., cemetery or religious shrines; (c) boundary demarcation lots, of which there is a good example in the northern-eastern quarter of Figure 4.

5. Plantations, generally of oil palms, a recent innovation due to European influence.

6. Wasteland, including swamp, steep slopes and areas of infertile soils.

Of this classification farm land clearly occupies the greater part of both areas depicted, with most of it in fallow. The fallow period in Umu Ocham generally lasts three years, and in eastern Diobu six to seven years. Only a small proportion of the farmed land is therefore productive in any one year. The confusion of fallow and farmed land in Umu Ocham illustrates the effect of farming from a variety of centres and this confusion is made worse by the development of land ownership and fragmentation due to inheritance.

The greater part of the area shown in Figure 4, illustrating conditions in February 1951, is farmed from the village in the north-western corner whose limits are marked by the woodland belt stretching with small breaks eastwards in a broad curve from Amadi. In Amadi village farming is restricted to the narrow riverain stretch of compound land since its people are Okrika whose main occupation is fishing. The outstanding feature of the farm-land is the division into large blocks each representing two years of cultivation. The normal practice is to clear scattered patches in fallow of the sixth and seventh years. Figure 5 shows the haphazard arrangement over an eighteen-day period in February

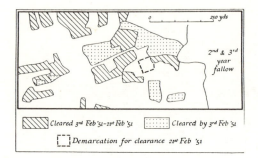

Figure 5.—Sample 18-day clearance pattern in eastern Diobu.

1951. Community needs take up approximately half the area available. Since, however, there is insufficient land to continue the process of scattered clearance indefinitely, the remainder of the block must be cleared the following year and the chief and elders must advise on the equitable division of the land. Thus the pattern of cultivation pursued is one combining random clearance with the thoroughness needed by a people who must cultivate all the land locally available. The remaining blocks, therefore, consist of various two-year stages of fallow, plus a block having the previous years' planting of cassava and the first year of fallow weeds and bushes. But in Umu Ocham (Figure 2, depicting March conditions) only small patches of community land exist, the greater part being privately held by each compound. Private or *okpulo* land as opposed to community or *egbelu* land has always been regarded as that to which an individual or family has a possessory title comparable to that of an absolute freeholder except that it cannot be permanently alienated.[5] Land may be pledged indefinitely for a loan, but it can always be redeemed without compensation for any improvements affected. With increasing shortage of land there has been a tendency for individuals to acquire private holdings in order to ensure a sufficient share of the area available. Custom has tended to weaken so that pledging is often virtually a sale. In

addition a system of renting has developed. Community land is still divided by the decision of the elders, but scattered clearance is impossible since the blocks available are so small. Moreover, fragmentation due to division amongst heirs is reducing the size of holdings and of individual blocks still further. Although the figures are not available to provide a detailed comparison there is every indication that population density is higher in Umu Ocham than in Diobu and is partly responsible for the contrast in agricultural patterns.

Figures for population density, areas of holdings and periods of fallow are difficult to obtain and of doubtful value. Nevertheless the subject is important enough to warrant the study of such material in order to obtain at least an indication of the nature of the situation. Figure 6 shows the distribution of population by Local Council areas in Aba Ngwa County. There are two main regions of high density; (i) the north with 931 to the square mile in Mbutu, and 685 in Ntigha and Ovukwu; (ii) Aba district with 1180 in Aba na Ohazu, 793 in Uratta and 701 in Amavor. The extremely high densities to the north-west and south of Aba are partly due to urban growth under European influence and the development locally of "market gardening." Generally the two main population regions are favourable to Ibo farmers since they are abundantly provided with the light, sandy brown earths which are preferred for farmland and for the growth of oil palms. Towards the south with lower altitude and slightly heavier rain these earths tend to become more acid. Moreover, the surface of the country becomes more highly accidented (Fig. 7). It is the steep slopes of the valley of the Aba river which are primarily responsible for the comparatively low density of Ahiaba na Abayi. Occasionally very sandy and useless patches of soil occur bearing only spear grass as in Amaise and Ngwaobi. However, a large part of the explanation of the various densities of population may be found in the historical

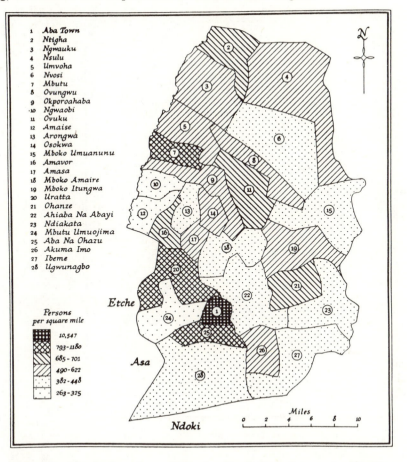

Figure 6.—Distribution of population by Local Council areas in Aba Nwa County.

evidence. According to reports compiled by District Officers,[6] the Ngwa entered the region from the north-west making their founder settlement in Ngwauku and driving back the former Ibeme and mixed Ibo and Ibeme inhabitants. Other invasions of the north followed, and as these first settlements developed and more land was sought, numerous "colonial" villages, each taking the name of the parent settlement, were founded to the south and east. The Mboko district in the east was never overrun by the Ngwa, which may explain the lower density figures recorded by the three

Mboko Local Council areas. The population density of the southern area and of the Etche, Asa and Ndoki groups was reduced by slave raiding for the merchants of Bonny and Opobo. British rule has not only brought slavery to an end, but has tended to prevent further Ngwa migration, resulting today in numerous land disputes particularly on the eastern border of the Ngwa against the Ibibio. The practice of renting land has also developed, particularly on the western fringes of Mbutu Umuojima and in the lightly peopled portions of Etche, Asa and Ndoki districts where there is still land

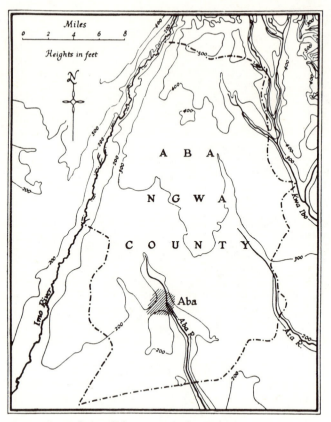

Figure 7.—Relief and drainage of Aba District.

to spare. Hence the modern phenomenon of bicycle cultivators daily proceeding to their rented holdings from the crowded lands around Aba. Cultivators in the area west of Aba have holdings averaging less than 3 acres per family. In Nvosi (density 436) the average appears to be nearer 4 acres, whilst in Ndoki (density 148) holdings of 10 acres or more are common. Fallow periods are as low as three years in Umu Ocham, a time considered locally to be insufficient for satisfactory soil recuperation. The most common fallow period amongst the Ngwa, however, is five years and this is typical in Nvosi, Amaise, Mboko Itungwa and Ahiaba na Abayi. In Ndoki and the Ogwe district of Asa (density 306) seven-year fallows are usual, whilst in

Etche (density 187) fallow periods are often of nine to fifteen years.

All the districts of Aba Ngwa County and even parts of Asa Local Council area are crowded and the central and northern portions with their short fallows and temporary migration may be described as overcrowded. An approximate calculation shows that 3 acres per family of seven with a three-year fallow means that 12 acres are needed for the family's continued support giving a density on farmed land alone of 373. Many people depend on outside resources and here one should note the movement of Ibo in search of work throughout Nigeria, many of whom remit money home. Comment by Ngwa agriculturalists suggested that five years' fallow is the satisfactory minimum and the four districts already known to have this have densities of 436, 263, 490 and 382 respectively. Amaise with 263 has exceptional soil conditions so that is not typical of the region. The remainder suggest a critical density figure at approximately 382 to 490. It is interesting to compare this figure with Grove's suggestion of 300 to 400. Of the twenty-seven Local Council areas comprising Aba Ngwa County only three have lower densities than 382 and two of these have been shown to have exceptional adverse physical conditions. If Aba Ngwa County is a fair example of the land immediately south of the Awka-Orlu highlands then there is no room here for immigration from the badly eroded parts of the latter.

One result of crowding is the development of rectilinear plot patterns, although even in areas with plentiful land there is occasionally a rectilinear tendency due to attempts to economize in the work of clearing fallow. Figure 8 shows examples from both Umu Ocham and eastern Diobu. The narrow plot frontages combined with great

length indicate the importance of access to paths. Paths are often arranged in rectangular patterns at even distances apart, thus enabling easy measurement of newly cleared land by mere pacing of plot frontages for the purpose of division. One area was found to be cut by parallel paths a little over 200 yards apart. Each plot was thus 100 yards long and had approximately 9 yards of frontage giving an area of approximately one-fifth of an acre. Even on community land the scattered patches to be expected from the fragmentation of private holdings is prevalent. The distances apart of both community and private farms may be as much as 5 miles: a problem of dispersal offering serious difficulty to the introduction of European concepts of farming. The size of the plots into which the farms are divided varies. Calculation from aerial photographs and pacing in the field shows that of 75 plots in Umu Ocham the largest was 0.44 acres and the smallest was 0.07 with a mean of 0.25. In eastern Diobu, of thirty-eight plots the largest was 1.35 acres and the smallest

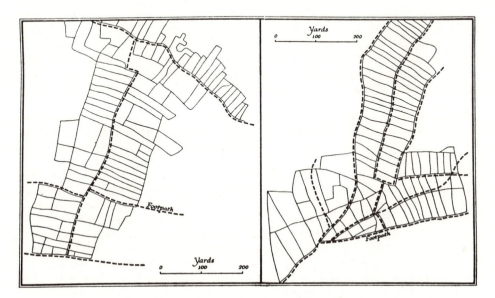

Figure 8.—Plot patterns in (left) eastern Diobu and (right) Umu Ocham.

0.12 with a mean of 0.35. The district with the larger plots also has longer fallow periods and a lower population density.[7] With increase in the area of private land a degree of permanence in plot shape is beginning to emerge, for many of the plots near Aba have presumably reached the minimum useful size. This permanence is reflected in the common occurrence of fencing on both farm and compound land in order to protect the crops from the depredations of goats, sheep, cattle, pigs and fowls.

Crowding has brought with it the problems attached to fixing a system originally dependent on regular movement. Villages and compounds now occupy almost permanent sites. Cultivation similarly is restricted to rotation over a fixed area instead of a widespread "shifting" throughout the bush. This tendency to permanence has been encouraged by the development of a modern administrative system combined with fixed trading centres and routes. In the south of Aba Division, for example, artificial village councils or groups had to be formed in order to obtain "a workable administrative system," [8] thus introducing a new rigidity to the old social order. Fixed paths and compound spaces have resulted in gullying. Hut foundations are often exposed and village churches and compounds undermined. Reduction in fallow period must lead eventually to lower returns per acre and possibly accelerated soil erosion. Fixed compounds must also mean fixed disposal of human excrement with a consequent danger to health. Present practice is to make cesspits on compound land which is also heaped with household refuse often making cultivation on such land possible without a fallow period. Manuring in this way is developed to the extent of heaping refuse around the trees, particularly palms and fruit trees, thus providing compound land with the richest "black" soil. In the past, plots near living quarters have become overgrown and the occupiers have been forced to move.[9]

Changing circumstances may demand changes in agricultural technique, but all suggestions for improvement must face the fact that Ibo farming practice is careful and based on long experience and that the environmental conditions offer limitations unknown to Europeans. Generally amongst the Ngwa and Ikwerri the men plant and tend those crops and trees needing most attention, leaving the remaining food production to the women. Thus men's crops include yams, pineapples, oil and raffia palms, coconut palms, plantains and bananas, and oranges, African pear, kola, oil bean and "vegetable leaf" trees. Women's crops are cassava, maize, cocoyams, beans, groundnuts, pumpkins, calabash, melons, okra, chillies and peppers. After careful storage seed yams are planted in April before the "former" rains, in holes dug with a special hoe, and the earth is heaped up to form mounds usually over 1 foot high and 2 feet in diameter—the spacing between plants varying from 2 feet 6 inches to 5 feet. It has been claimed that contour ridges are superior to mounds and that the latter encourage soil erosion. However, yams need aeration, a good depth of soil and adequate drainage. Ridges would require more work to produce the same conditions and, moreover, where the quantity of the top soil available is limited, could not be made to provide the same depth of tilled earth around the plant. Cassava in interplanted in July and August before the "latter" rains and when yams have already developed a good growth. Such interplanting, which includes maize and vegetables, usually in part only of the plots, ensures not only a protective cover for the soil, but an extended period of harvest from the same piece of land. It also confers some of the benefits of crop rotation and, by including plants of variable needs, guarantees that at least one crop will succeed in the varying weather conditions. Compound land is the chief vegetable producer and is often planted to cocoyams which will produce some crop even if the rainfall is extremely low. Yams and cassava are the bases of the diet whilst other crops are either flavouring elements or provide some variety. Soils are carefully selected for planting and both the Ngwa and Ikwerri have their own classification.

The distinction of soil types and the recognition of the value of manuring are both evidence of careful farming. The few animals kept are allowed to graze on the fallow. Of these only goats and sheep appear to thrive. Cattle are of the dwarf trypanosomiasis-resistant variety, poor in both meat and milk yields. Grass fallows might provide increased and better quality fodder, but would entail considerable work in the suppression of encroaching shrubs and would not give the great volume of vegetable matter considered essential by the Ibo for burning before resuming cultivation. Burning supplies nutrition to the soil in the form of ash and reduces the number of insect pests. Small plots make possible individual attention to plants thus maintaining within the limits of the technique a high production per acre. Suggestions for farming on a larger scale must face the possibility of reduced production per acre in an overcrowded land. Fewer plot boundaries and the introduction of ploughlands would threaten the soil with rapid erosion from heavy showers. At Aba on 10 July 1950, 2.3 inches were recorded and on September 10, 2.8 inches. The following year 2.4 inches fell on May 5, 3.2 inches on September 2 and 3.0 inches on October 10. Occasionally rainfall totals differ considerably from normal. Whereas in 1933, 106.2 inches were recorded, in 1950 there were only 60.5 inches. Concentration of the total likewise varies. The 1950 total fell in ninety-eight rainy days, i.e. days with more than 0.01 inches, whilst in 1947 94.0 inches fell in eighty-five rainy days.[10] The reavy rains of 1955 resulted in the presence of unusually large numbers of insect pests at the time of planting, whilst the delayed rains of 1945 set back the maize crop and reduced the size of the yams. Two years later hot weather combined with heavier rainfall gave good returns of cassava and cocoyams, but maize again declined and so did vegetables. The 1952 fall, the heaviest for five years, gave good yams and early maize, but fostered rust amongst many late crops.

Despite the restrictions imposed by physical conditions and despite a conservative outlook, Ibo farmers are gradually changing their methods in response, firstly to changing social and economic circumstances, and secondly to the influence of Government Departments, particularly the Department of Agriculture. The expansion of trade has offered improved markets for palm products, the export of which from Aba Division has increased with fluctuations to a 1952 total of 39,427 tons of oil and 21,523 tons of kernels. The oil palm is the most valuable asset of the Ibo farmer since it is not only a source of cash, but provides food (in the form of fats which would otherwise be lacking with a shortage of animals), building materials and, together with the raffia palm, the staple alcoholic drink of "palm wine." Before the present large scale development of the palm oil trade, planted palms or palms on compound land were privately owned. Since the introduction of direct taxation in 1928, however, all palms must be open to fruit cutting by the whole community, generally for a period of three months in the year, in order to give everyone a means of paying tax, and thus inhibiting the establishment of palm plantations.

Cassava, and to a limited extent yams, copra, fruit and wild rubber have also become sources of cash. Cultivation of cassava has been encouraged by rising food prices with the increase in the proportion of non-agricultural population. Yams have become a rich man's food, but with the greater labour involved in their cultivation it is generally reckoned that more money may be obtained from the growth of the cheaper cassava sold in Aba Township or sent in the form of flour or *gari* to Port Harcourt and

Calabar Province. The trade formerly depended chiefly on the markets of Enugu and Onitsha and was stimulated during the war by a "plant more cassava" campaign. Since the war, however, these markets have found cheaper sources of supply. The export of food from the Aba Division is balanced by the import of yams, cocoyams, fruit, fish and meat from surrounding districts. The *gari* trade has resulted in the expansion of cassava growing at the expense of yams. Other factors have also contributed to an apparent decline in yam cultivation. Firstly, whilst women are keen traders and spend a proportion of their time away from the farms, men also are taking an increasing interest in trade and in transportation by bicycle competing with motor lorry traffic. In addition many men seek employment as labourers or clerks whilst others have probably had their attention drawn from farming by military service. There has been therefore a decreasing interest in farming amongst men, which has led to a decline in the production of the chief men's crop—yams. Both men and women are on the whole devoting less time to farming and therefore tending to concentrate more on cassava since it is the easiest crop to plant and tend. Moreover, cassava has become a cheap, easily transported food of increasing popularity amongst the major part of the employed population, has the advantage of harvest in May and June when no other fresh food is available, and is generally more productive on land with short fallows.

With regard to the cheapening of goods and the improvement of market facilities by trade the introduction of tarred road surfaces and the opening of the railway from Port Harcourt to Enugu in 1916 have had obvious effects. However, the old river routes of the Imo and Aba still compete via Opobo for palm oil traffic and are the chief means of conveying building sand and gravel. The improved facilities for export have also brought imported goods particularly cloth, metal ware, stockfish, kerosene,

salt and soap. The old weaving and metal industries and the salt trade have declined. The increasing dependence on overseas markets has also made the Ibo farmers subject to world price fluctuations and wartime shortages.

Attempts directly to modify agricultural and related social conditions came firstly with the suppression of slave raiding, which dated from the establishment of the first consular post at Obegu in Ngwa territory in 1895 and from the Aro Expedition of 1901–2. This was followed by the acquisition of land by urban authorities, missionary societies and the Forestry Department. Although these acquisitions are small compared with the whole, nevertheless the local problems they have created have been sufficient for many Ngwa and Ikwerri farmers to place the blame for overcrowding on the authorities concerned. In Diobu compensation claims and litigation have persisted since 1913 when the chiefs sold a large part of their land to the Government for the development of Port Harcourt. Direct interest in the agriculture of Aba Division began with experiments to improve the oil palm by the establishment in 1927 of 27 acres of experimental palm plots. In 1928 Regulation 20 enforced grading and inspection by Government agents of palm oil and kernels. The Agricultural Department followed with the issue of palm seedlings to farmers and, despite the difficulties incurred by communal culting, the encouragement of palm plantations; this was combined with the introduction of hand-operated oil presses. Experiments have been made to improve kola nut production and the growing of fruit, particularly oranges, has been fostered. During the war rubber planting and tapping boomed and the Department extended its interest to food in addition to commercial crops. This interest developed into an attempt to modify the entire agricultural system. In 1945 and 1946 an economic survey by individual sample villages was undertaken whilst a policy of all-round improvement in agricultural technique was laid down in Sessional Paper No. 16 of 1946 and confirmed by the Agricultural Ordinance No. 37 of 1948. In 1946 lime was issued to farmers and the construction of palm-oil mills began at Owerrinta and Azumini. There was a fear locally that the building of mills meant that the Government was going to take over the palm trees. Further post-war schemes include trials of fallow plants, of Chinese yams and rice, experiments with lime and artificial fertilizers and the establishment of Demonstration Farm Centres, Nurseries and Experimental and Demonstration Plots. The well-digging programme which had been commenced before the war was intensified. Pioneer Oil Mills proposed to establish a network of mills throughout Aba Division each sited 8–10 miles from one another. This plan has been followed despite demonstration against mill construction and opposition to the Agricultural Bill. In 1951 five mills were in production and four more building, artificial fertilizer was distributed to farmers and approximately 10,000 palm seedlings and 951 fruit trees planted, the latter encouraged by the construction of a fruit juice factory at Umuahia. Furthermore, loans were given for the establishment of plantations of oil palms and rubber, and of poultry, sheep, and pig farms.

South-eastern Nigeria faces, in regions like Aba Ngwa County, a problem of overcrowding. On the southern fringes, in regions like Ahoada, there is still land available for migrant farmers, although even this is evidently being reduced. Moreover, any attempt at a general resettlement would involve social disruption since all available farm land in the latter appears to be occupied, although farmed on more extensive lines. Farmers like the Ngwa have reacted to their new conditions by migration, by the fixing of settlement and associated farmland, by the reduction of farm size and fallow period, by changes in cropping and land tenure and even by the introduction of rules governing harvesting.

The influence of world markets and the need felt to improve agricultural technique has prompted Governmental attempts to introduce further modifications, abandoning in effect the old policy of Indirect Rule. Whilst it is true that rapid changes are disrupting the old institutions and introducing new problems which Government authorities can do much to solve, it is also evident that too rapid a promotion of new policies can also produce chaos. Similarly whilst the criticism can be raised that many more improvements are needed—for example, the planting of grass in all compound spaces around buildings could do much to prevent gully erosion—it is again evident that there is a danger in undertaking new methods of not fully appreciating the milieu or the results. Every improvement in agricultural technique and every increase in capital expenditure will tend to fix cultivators more and more to certain holdings. Whilst it has been shown that the amount of movement required for farming is decreasing, it would be unwise to push the process too far by proposals involving increased expenditure on the land, until the questions raised by fixed agriculture in inter-tropical conditions have been answered.

ACKNOWLEDGMENTS

The author wishes to acknowledge the help received from District Officers, Officers of the Agricultural Department and the many Ibo cultivators interviewed in the areas concerned, and also the loan of aerial photographs by the Nigerian Survey Department.

NOTES

[1] Grove, A. T., "Soil erosion and population problems in south-east Nigeria," *Geogr. J. 117* (1951) 291–306.

[2] Estimates of sizes of holdings have been made from observations in the field and from surveys made in Aba Division by Assistants of the Agricultural Department. They are no more than approximations to the truth. The size of a "family" is generally reckoned to be seven

persons, *i.e.* a man, his two wives and four children.

[3] See Green, M. M., "Land tenure in an Ibo village" (1941), published for the London School of Economics and Political Science. Monographs on Social Anthropology No. 6, particularly p. 11.

[4] Note that *Ama uku* signifies a meeting place. Similarly the fact that most settlements are founded from a common centre is illustrated by the prefix *umu* or "children."

[5] See Elias, T. O., "Nigerian land law and custom" (London), 1951, p. 93.

[6] Allen, J. G. C., "Notes on the customs of the Ngwa Clan" (1934); "Supplementary reports on the Ngwa Clan."

Jackson, J., "Intelligence report on the Ngwa Clan, Aba Division."

Kelly, E. J. G., Supplementary memorandum to J. Jackson's report.

[7] The indication is similar to that provided by the author's experience in Nyasaland. (Morgan, W. B., "The Lower Shire Valley of Nyasaland:

a changing system of African agriculture," *Geogr. J. 119* (1953) 459–469), where it was found that increase in population density is followed firstly by a reduction in the length of fallow period and secondly by the reduction in the size of holdings by reduction in the area of each plot.

[8] Notes on the customs of the Ngwa Clan.

[9] On the movement of habitations in relation to oil palms and the formation of "black" soils, see also Waterston, J. M., "Observation on the influence of some ecological factors on the incidence of oil palm diseases in Nigeria," *Journal of the West Africa Institute for Oil Palm Research,* No. 1, September 1953, pp. 24–59.

[10] For a diagram of rainfall reliability at Aba and discussion of rainfall reliability in Nigeria see Pugh, J. C., "Rainfall reliability in Nigeria," Proceedings of the International Geographical Congress: Commission on Periglacial Morphology and Section on Climatology (1952), pp. 36–41.

The adaptation of population-land relationships to accommodate the cultivation of export crops is illustrated by an example from the forest environment. The Ghana study is concerned with the introduction and spread of cocoa, a non-indigenous perennial tree crop which occupies land to the exclusion of other crops after the early years of growth (Wills, 1962). Cocoa was first grown in Ghana in Akwapim and spread toward the West and the Northwest by a process of spontaneous diffusion activated by two groups of local entrepreneurs (Hill, 1963). The differing social organizations of the groups, which influenced their methods of acquiring and developing land for cultivation, are expressed in the landscape in a variety of ways. Recognition of these social structures is important to comparisons of the agricultural systems and land-use patterns, for differences emerge even though the physical environment can be held as a constant factor and the main objective of both groups—to expand cultivation of cocoa—has been the same.

The migration to develop new areas for cocoa continues, strengthened by a regression in areas of earlier exploitation. The cause of the latter is the "swollen shoot" disease, which has fundamentally disrupted cocoa cultivation in the Southeast of Ghana. As a result, there have been substantial changes in some aspects of population-land relationships (Boateng, 1966; Hunter, 1961).

8. Cocoa Migration and Patterns of Land Ownership in the Densu Valley near Suhum, Ghana

JOHN M. HUNTER

The town of Suhum, with a population of about 10,000 in 1960, lies some 39 miles, as the crow flies, north-north-west of Accra, in latitude 6°02′ north and longitude 0° 27′ west (Fig. 1). The area around the town is typical of much of the eastern forest of Ghana in its economic and social geography. The exact extent of the area of investigation was determined by the availability of Department of Agriculture farm-plans, some explanation of which is called for here. These plans are produced by the Survey Branch of the Cocoa Division in order to facilitate the payment of grants for cutting out diseased cocoa trees and replanting with new ones. In the Suhum area, where there was almost total devastation by disease, every farm has been surveyed and registered, and official farm-plans produced on the scales of 88 yards to the inch and 8 inches to the mile. A simplified representation of these plans is given in Figure 4.

The survey area contains 5605 separately registered farms covering an area of 16,297 acres (25.46 square miles). The first aim of the investigation was to determine the place of origin of each registered farm owner. Official registers were consulted by courtesy of the Department of Agriculture; and, in difficult cases, information sought from Liaison Officers of the Cocoa Division. Once each farmer's place of origin was known, land ownership was tabulated and mapped (Table I and Fig. 5) and a flow-diagram of the migration constructed (Fig. 6). In 1960, chiefs and elders in twenty-six villages and hamlets around Suhum (Fig. 3) were interviewed, through interpreters, on the details of their migration and settlement. The results of the field work and map analysis are presented below.

THE COCOA MIGRATION

Ghana is the world's largest producer and exporter of cocoa. Widespread commercial cultivation of the cocoa tree began in the late eighteen-nineties in the forests of the Densu basin where the first farmers were not indigenous Akim but immigrants. Those who established the industry belonged chiefly, but not entirely, to two groups: Adangbe-speaking Shai and Krobo, and

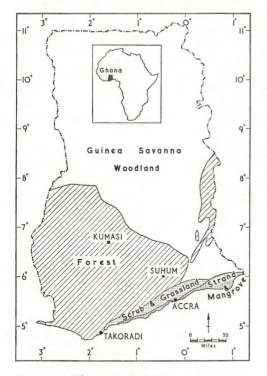

Figure 1.—The position of Suhum. Vegetation zones are based upon C. J. Taylor, *The vegetation zones of the Gold Coast* (Accra, 1952).

From *Transactions*, Institute of British Geographers, 33, 1963, pp. 61–87. Reprinted by permission.

Twi-speaking Akwapim. Both groups migrated westwards: the former from the Accra Plains and the latter from the Akwapim Ridge.

Prior to the cocoa migration, both groups were already looking westwards because of the need for more foodstuffs. The Krobo and Shai lived on the dry and infertile Accra Plains whose hard environment compelled them to turn to the more productive soils of the humid forest. According to M. J. Field, Krobo migrants began to establish subsistence food farms in the forest in the mid-nineteenth century.[1] The other major source-area, the Akwapim Ridge, although salubrious and defensible, was too narrow and steep-sided to provide enough farmland for its line of growing towns, hence an agricultural hinterland just beyond the west-facing flanks of the Ridge was developed.[2] But with the advent of cocoa, the modest demands for subsistence farmland in the west were suddenly swamped by demands for space for the new cash-crop, and thus the great migration began.

The outlines of this migration have been well described by Polly Hill[3] who has shown that several factors jointly contributed to the scale and speed of movement: (1) the Shai, Krobo and Akwapim already looked west to tributary food-producing regions; (2) these people had already gained a small amount of capital and commercial "know-how" through an early association with the trade in palm-oil between the forest and the coast; (3) the first cocoa trees were introduced by the Basel Mission on the Akwapim Ridge, hence the first seedlings were available there, and techniques of cultivation were first learnt there; (4) the Densu forests which the migrants entered, although belonging to the Akim, were virtually empty; (5) the Akim chiefs were willing and, in many instances, anxious, to sell off large tracts of stool land for ready cash, rather than attempt to cultivate cocoa themselves.

The basic method of migration can be likened to leap-frogging. A farmer purchased a piece of virgin forest, commonly within a day's walk of the starting-point

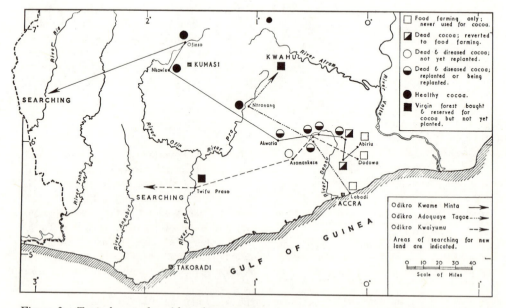

Figure 2.—Typical examples of leap-frog migration.

of the migration, cleared and cultivated it, and then re-invested any income accruing in the purchase of a second piece of land farther west. By this process of continuous re-investment, the farmer moved steadily westwards during the course of his lifetime, acquiring one new land after another.

The Suhum area was usually reached on the second "leap" from the starting-point, as the following summary of eighteen individual case-histories shows:

	1st	2nd	3rd	4th	7th	"leap"
Individual						
examples	2	9	3	3	1	

The migratory process continued beyond Suhum. The eighteen individuals referred to above (at first accompanying their fathers and then travelling alone) made an aggregate of 75 leaps to establish 75 new cocoa farms. One made 9 leaps, but 3 or 4 leaps were more common:

Total number of cocoa farms established	1	2	3	4	5	6	7	8	9
Examples (18 farmers)	0	2	6	5	2	1	0	1	1

Three typical examples of leap-frog migration are presented in Figure 2 which is examined more closely later. It will be observed that the farmers' never-ending search has now taken them as far west as the Ivory Coast frontier. Another point of interest, clearly evident in the map, is the progressively lengthening leap of the migrant. The first farm would lie within a day's walk of the starting-point; the second within easy reach of the first, and so on; but the advent of motor transport in the 1922s freed the farmer to range as widely as he wished.

In an illiterate society with few documentary records, it is not easy to ascertain precise dates, but, because of the value placed on oral tradition and memory, one can, without too much difficulty, fix certain events in relation to one another. This was a method employed with success in the 1962 Population Census of Ghana. For the present survey, a list of thirty-three events of known date was used, commencing with the invasion of Kumasi and capture of Prempeh (1896) to the granting of independence (1957). It is remarkable how vivid may be farmers' memories of certain events. One, for example, remembered buying a certain piece of land at the time of the Prince of Wale's visit (1925); another recalled moving at the beginning of the "Kaiser War" (1914); yet another purchased one of his farms at the time of the cocoa "hold-up" (1937–38).

Two events were of particular importance around Suhum: an influenza epidemic which took countless lives (1918) and the coming of the railway which reached Nsawam in 1910, Pakro in 1912, Mangoase near Suhum in 1913 and Koforidua in 1915. Thus, for example, a farmer may recollect that he migrated to the Suhum area after the railway reached Mangoase (1913) but before "the influenza" (1918). Further questioning might pin-point the date more accurately. A good example is the head farmer of Obuom, west of Suhum (Fig. 3), who recalled migrating during the "Kaiser War" two years before "the influenza" (that is, in 1916).

In many instances, settling on and cultivating the land did not immediately follow the act of purchase. The Kofi Gya land, east of Suhum, was bought in 1896 and settled in c. 1903–05; that of Niifio, north of Suhum, was bought in 1902 and settled in 1908; the corresponding dates for the Amanokrom land around Suhum are 1904 and c. 1908. With the sole exception of Kofi Gya, which seems to have been very early indeed, effective settlement of the Suhum area, from the evidence collected, falls into the decade 1907–17.

On arrival, each migrant built himself a house, and thus the pattern of "stranger villages" began to emerge (Fig. 3). Praprabida, one of the first, was established by Shai from Agomeda in 1907, Aponapon II by Dodowa Shai in 1911, Otwe Bediadua

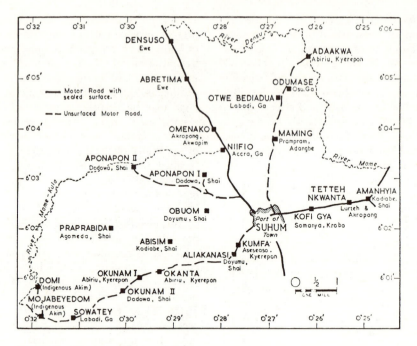

Figure 3.—Stranger villages of Suhum survey area.

by Ga from Labadi in 1912, Adaakwa by
Kyerepon from Abiriu also in 1912. Suhum, soon to become the leading settlement, was founded c. 1908 by Akwapim
from Amanokrom. Tradition has it that
when the first Amanokrom came, there was
only a solitary dilapidated hut belonging
to an Akim hunter. The founders of other
villages claim that they found no Akim
settlements at all, not even hunting lodges.
The migrants were true pioneers of the
virgin forest. The only indigenous Akim
villages in the survey area are Domi and
Mojabeyedom in the far west. Two Ewe
villages north of Suhum, Densuso and
Abretima, form a special case which will
be discussed later.

The boundaries of the registered farms
of the survey area are indicated in Figure
4; and a classification of land ownership
by place of origin is given in Table I and
Figure 5. The latter shows a fine degree
of intermingling of migrants from different
source regions. The closest mixing is immediately north of Suhum town where the
Amanokrom sold uncleared forest to later
migrants. Also apparent is the relatively
small amount of land owned by indigenous
Akim: west of Suhum only 225 acres or
1.4 per cent of the survey area, and east of
Suhum 3399 acres or 20.8 per cent of the
survey area. Migrant farmers thus own
77.8 per cent of the total area and indigenous Akim only 22.2 per cent. But
the latter figure, which relates to ownership
and not occupancy, conceals the important
fact that the Akim of the Apedwa Stool,
who own a large part of the survey area
north of Suhum, are, by and large, absentee
landowners. Their land is occupied and
farmed by immigrant Ewe labourers,
Densuso and Abretima being Ewe villages
(Fig. 3). Only the Akim of the Apapam
Stool, in the extreme west of the survey
area, personally occupy their land. Thus,
in terms of occupancy, migrants cultivate

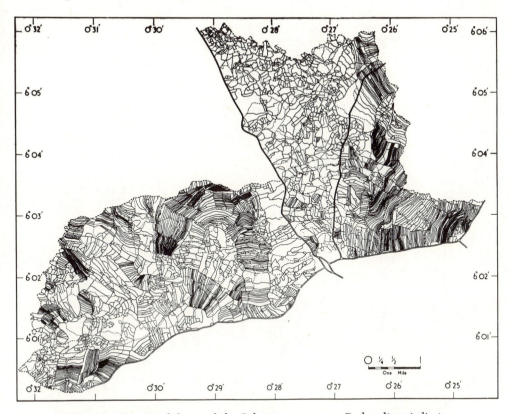

Figure 4.—Registered farms of the Suhum survey area. Broken lines indicate boundaries of 'blocks' within each of which all individual farms have been surveyed and registered. There are 179 blocks containing 5605 separately registered farms in a total area of 16,297 acres (25.46 square miles). For practical reasons connected with survey and registration, blocks were fixed before the survey of farm boundaries; hence, as the map clearly shows, block boundaries cut indiscriminately across farmland causing an artificial fragmentation of ownership. The total number of 5605 registered farms is certainly two to three times in excess of the actual number of farms. For this reason, analysis of farm data has been confined to acreages and ownership, not numbers of farms.

98.6 per cent of the land, and indigenous farmers 1.4 per cent.

The largest immigrant groups, with the proportion of land they own indicated in parentheses, are: matrilineal Akwapim (21.3 per cent), Shai (19.2 per cent), Kyerepon (14.2 per cent), other Guan mainly Larteh (7.8 per cent), Ga (7.1 per cent), and Krobo (4.3 per cent). (See Table I.)

A simple flow diagram of this movement is presented in Figure 6. Two principal source regions are shown: first, the Akwapim Ridge, a range of hills some 1500 feet above sea-level; and secondly, the Accra Plains stretching from the lower Densu to the Volta. From the ridge-top, the matrilineal Akwapim, Kyerepon and Larteh advanced to claim 42 per cent of the survey area, whilst from the coastal fishing villages

TABLE 1. PLACE OF ORIGIN OF REGISTERED FARM OWNERS OF SUHUM SURREY AREA[a]

Major language group[b]	Related groups of languages	Political divisions: traditional native states	Town or village of origin of farm owner[c]	Fig. 5 Code No.	Inheritance and succession	Number of registered farms in survey area		Acreage		Percentage of total acreage	
TWI		Akim Abuakwa	Apapam	11	Matrilineal	93		225.0		1.38	
			Apedwa	12	Matrilineal	853		3,251.3		19.95	
			Other[d]		Matrilineal	31	997	147.7	3,624.0	0.91	22.2
		Part of Akwapin[e]	Akropong	21	Matrilineal	504		1,890.1		11.60	
			Amanokrom	22	Matrilineal	208		986.2		6.05	
			Aburi	23	Matrilineal	169		516.9		3.17	
			Afwereasi	24	Matrilineal	5		13.9		0.09	
			Berekuso	25	Matrilineal	28	914	59.1	3,446.2	0.36	21.3
			Mamfe	26	Patrilineal[g]	19		42.7		0.26	
			Mampon	27	Patrilineal[g]	6		17.8		0.11	
			Obosomase	28	Patrilineal[g]	1		3.8		0.02	
			Tutu	29	Patrilineal[g]	36	62	96.4	160.7	0.59	1.0
		New Juaben	Jumapo	31	Matrilineal	1		3.9		0.02	
		Kwahu[h]	Mpraeso	32	Matrilineal	11		40.6		0.25	
		Fanti	Cape Coast	33	Matrilineal	3	15	4.0	48.5	0.03	0.3
GUAN	Kyerepon	Part of Akwapim	Awukugua	41	Patrilineal	278		625.7		3.84	
			Abonse	42	Patrilineal	12		12.4		0.08	
			Aseseaso	43	Patrilineal	180		314.7		1.93	
			Abiriu	44	Patrilineal	412		1,280.4		7.86	
			Apirede	45	Patrilineal	4		6.3		0.04	
			Adukrom	46	Patrilineal	50		67.9		0.42	
			Odawu	47	Patrilineal	14	950	8.3	2315.7	0.05	14.2
	Other Guan		Larteh[k]	51	Patrilineal	324		929.0		5.70	
			Boso	52	Patrilineal	74		299.5		1.84	
			Anum	53	Patrilineal	10		24.3		0.15	
			Krachi	54	Patrilineal	5	413	13.0	1,265.8	0.08	7.8
GA-ADANGBE	Ga	Ga	Accra	61	Patrilineal	90		529.4		3.25	
			Osu	62	Patrilineal	70		191.8		1.18	
			Labadi	63	Patrilineal	59		378.2		2.32	
			Teshie	64	Patrilineal	27	246	56.3	1,155.7	0.35	7.1
	Adangbe	Shai	Dodowa	71	Patrilineal	519		1,034.7		6.35	
			Agomeda	72	Patrilineal	115		280.4		1.72	
			Doyumu	73	Patrilineal	209		508.8		3.12	
			Kodiabe	74	Patrilineal	470		1,061.3		6.51	
			Ayikuma	75	Patrilineal	83	1396	241.6	3,126.8	1.48	19.2

Group	Town	Code	Inheritance	Farms	Acreage	%	Group farms	Group acreage	Group %
Krobo	Somanya	76	Patrilineal	390	675.5	4.14			
	Odumase	77	Patrilineal	9	25.6	0.16	399	701.1	4.3
Other Adangbe	Prampram	78	Patrilineal	44	90.3	0.55			
	Ningo	79	Patrilineal	57	79.0	0.48			
	Ada	710	Patrilineal	50	85.9	0.53			
	Osudoku	711	Patrilineal	32	46.0	0.28	183	301.2	1.8
EWE[l]		8	—	30	82.0	0.50			
NORTHERN[m]		9	—	18	45.3	0.28			
OTHER[n]		91	—	2	4.1	0.03			0.8
Indigenous (Akim Abuakwa)				977	3,624.0	22.2			
Immigrant				4,628	12,673.1	77.8			
Grand total				5,605	16,297.1	100.0			

a Farm registers of the Coca Division of the Department of Agriculture were examined, by kind permission of the Head of the Division, in order to determine each farmer's place of origin. Information was also obtained, where necessary, from Liaison Officers of the Cocoa Division who, between them, knew most of the farmers personally by reason of their official liaison duties. Once place of origin had been ascertained, individual farm acreages were grouped together to produce the above table, together with a map of ownership (Fig. 5) and a flow diagram of the migration (Fig. 6).

b The placing of farmers' home towns into classificatory groups presents certain difficulties. Three different criteria, each giving a different result, may be employed, namely: political organizations (that is, traditional native states), or ethnic groups, or language groups. In this table, language has been chosen (see Columns 1 and 2) with results which are sufficiently satisfactory for our purposes, although the towns of the Akwapim Ridge are very mixed (see Note (e) below).

c The positions of these towns and villages are indicated in Figure 6.

d Other Akim Abuakwa registered farms, with code numbers relating to Figure 5 in parentheses, are: Kibi (13) 18, Amangfrom (14) 8, Tetteh (15) 2, Dompin (16) 1, Akwatia (17) 1, Nkronso (18) 1, Total 31 farms.

e The traditional native state of Akwapim embraces Twi- and Guan-speaking towns, with both matrilineal and patrilineal forms of inheritance and succession. See 1. Wilks, The growth of the Akwapim State: a study in the control of evidence (in press), and D. Brokensha, "Notes on the history and ethnology of Akwapim," Appendix I (iv) in Polly Hill, The migrant cocoa farmer of southern Ghana (in the press).

f Reference to Figure 6 will indicate the southerly position Berekuso. The village lies on the borders of matrilineal Akwapim and patrilineal Ga territory. For reasons connected with intermarriage and trade, it is bilingual and seems to practise a mixed form of inheritance and succession, neither purely matrilineal nor purely patrilineal. Since it is of Akwamu origin, as stated by Wilks (Note e), one may suppose that an originally matrilineal system of inheritance has been progressively modified through contact with the Ga. However, preliminary investigations by Polly Hill do not reveal that this is obviously the case [op. cit., Appendix VII (iv)].

g According to Christaller, the four Twi-speaking towns of Mamfe, Mampon, Obosomase and Tutu spoke Guan before approx. 1750: see J. G. Christaller, A Dictionary of the Asante and Fante language (Basel, 1881). The Guan origin of these towns is also indicated by their patrilineal system of inheritance.

h Kwahu registered farms are: Mpraeso 10, Obo 1, Total 11 farms.

k The town of Larteh, which speaks a dialect of Guan, belongs to the Akwapim State (see Note e above).

l Ewe registered farms are: Adidome 5, Tefle 4, Kpandu 4, Abotia 2, Ahave 2, Agbeve 1, Agrave 1, Nkwanta 1, Tsibu 1, not ascertained 9, Total 30 farms.

m This section covers different language groups. Northerners' farms are: Zabrama 4, Moshie 7, Chamba 2, Wangara 3, Hausa 2, Total 18 farms.

n Other registered farm owners: Nigeria (Lagos) 1, British West Indies 1, Total 2 farms.

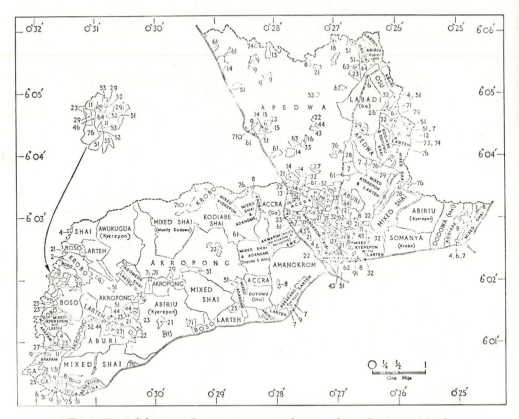

Figure 5.—Subdivision of survey area according to place of origin of land
owner. The code numbers on this map relate to the fifth column of Table I.
For example, all Kyerepon are 4, Awukugua being 41 and Adukrom 46. Similarly all Ga are 6, Accra being 61 and Labadi 63. A single digit represents a
mixed group. Thus 7 represents mixed Adangbe.

and homesteads of the dry plains, the Shai,
Krobo, Ga and Adangbe moved in to a
share of 32 per cent of the land.

Northerners (Zabrama, Moshie, Chamba,
Wangara and Hausa) and Ewe own less
than 1 per cent of the survey area. They
came as labourers and, by dint of hard
work and frugal living, managed to purchase small farms from insolvent migrants.

Ewe and northerners' farms are indicated in Figure 5 (code numbers 8 and 9
respectively). It seems significant that, in
the Apedwa area of Ewe tenancy, there
are no Ewe-owned farms, only northerners'

farms. Similarly, in the Apapam area, one
notices only northerners' farms. Ewe farms,
on the other hand, are not uncommon in
Akwapim and Adangbe areas. The explanation may lie in the reluctance of an
Akim landlord to mortgage or sell a farm
to one of his own Ewe *abusa* labourers,
preferring to raise money from "outsiders"
with whom he is not fettered by any previous contractual obligation.

Abusa tenancy is widespread throughout
Ghana. It is a form of tenancy in which a
share of the usufruct is paid as rent, the
word *abusa* indicating tripartite division.

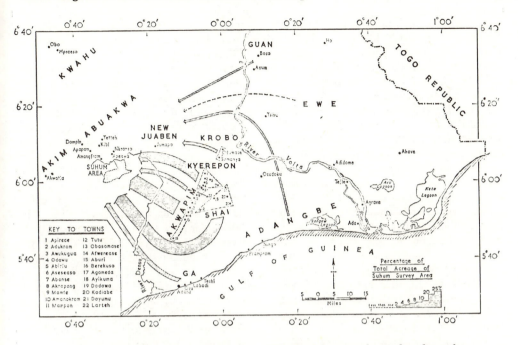

Figure 6.—Origin of migrant farmers. This flow-diagram shows the place of origin of migrant farmers in the survey area. The width of the arrows is in proportion to the amount of land owned in the survey area, as indicated in Table I. The main groups of migrants are Akwapim from the Akwapim Ridge, Shai and Krobo from the Accra Plains, Ga and Adangbe from the coast, and Guan from across the Volta. The Shai, Krobo, Ga and Adangbe all moved from a savanna environment into the forest (Fig. 1).

Thus an Akim landowner, lacking the manpower or the inclination to cultivate his land enters an *abusa* agreement with a labourer, usually a land-hungry migrant. There are many variations of *abusa,* and there are also other systems of employing farm labour, which need not be discussed here.[4]

Attacks on the cocoa by an unknown virus, causing a disease later to be known as "swollen shoot," began in the area in about 1937, were aggravated by capsid infestation and fungus, and ran unchecked throughout World War II. As a consequence, by the early nineteen-fifties, all the cocoa farms around Suhum were so seriously diseased that production became negligible. What had been, with Koforidua,

the leading production centre of the east was now moribund. The farmers' evidence, although probably exaggerated, is graphic: the Odikro (Chief) of Kofi Gya (Fig. 3) claimed that his harvest fell from 500 loads [5] to nil; the Mankrado (Deputy-Chief) of Otwe Bediadua said that his production fell from 200 loads to nil. All the farmers, large and small, told the same story.

The Ewe *abusa* tenants of Densuso and Abretima turned to food-farming as the cocoa died, still handing over two-thirds of the usufruct to the Akim landlords. The foodstuffs produced on the former cocoa farms include cassava, corn, plantain, cocoyam, ground-nuts, sugar cane, okro, garden eggs, tomatoes, peppers, beans, oranges, pawpaw, mangoes and coconuts. Palm wine and gin are also produced. These are fermented and distilled, respectively, from the sap of the oil palm which has, by natural regeneration, largely replaced cocoa trees in the most heavily devastated areas.

Throughout the survey area, food-farming has, for the time being, substantially replaced the cocoa industry. The transition was favoured by the rapid growth of the Accra market for foodstuffs and the increased use of road transport. Feeder roads built with voluntary local labour obviated much of the head-loading and made commercial production possible for many formerly isolated villages. The road to the west from Suhum reached Okanta in 1950 and Sowatey in 1954 (Fig. 3); Adaakwa, in the north-east, was reached in 1954, and Aponapon II, in the north-west, a year later. Amanhyia had been linked with Suhum in 1923; the road south-eastwards from Amanhyia to Mangoase was opened in 1937, and that north-eastwards to Koforidua in 1948. The main north–south road through Suhum was opened as early as 1915.

At present the cocoa industry of the survey area is at the beginning of an up-swing, gaining in strength year by year as more land is rehabilitated. Encouraged by Government grants, and also acting privately on their own initiative, farmers have begun to cut out the remaining diseased trees and to plant specially selected Amazonian seedlings. A second cycle of cocoa development has commenced on formerly derelict land. It is almost like a new industry. The extent of this rehabilitation is indicated in Figure 7. It will be seen that the greatest strides have been made west of Suhum, especially on Akropong and Shai land (compare Figs. 5 and 7). Good progress is also being made on Shai, Krobo and Kyerepon land due east of Suhum but, as yet, the general picture is one of widespread food-farming (Classes 3 and 4 in Fig. 7). Understandably, the diseased cocoa areas (Class 2) are of very limited extent today. An interesting feature of the map is the coincidence

of the major food-producing area with Ga ownership, the Ga being, by tradition, a diligent food-farmer.

We have seen that the average migrant came from the Akwapim Ridge, or the Accra Plains, reaching Suhum on his second leap, in the decade 1907–17; and that the migratory process of continuous reinvestment in new cocoa lands continues today. Specific examples of this are given in Figure 2. Odikro Kwaiyumu, a Shai from Dodowa, has three farms, excluding his home-town farm, and is now searching for a fourth near the Ankobra river. His Suhum farm is diseased but is being replanted; that at Asamankese has not yet been rehabilitated whilst the one at Twifu Praso in the west consists of uncleared forest. Odikro Kwame Minta, a Kyerepon of Abiriu (with his father in the early stages), made seven leaps to acquire seven new farms, and is now searching for land in the Bia basin near the Ivory Coast frontier. Two of his cocoa farms in the west are completely free of disease, three are diseased but are being rehabilitated, and the remaining two are now given over to food-farming, probably permanently.

Where a farmer owns more than one farm, it is obvious that he must become, in a limited sense at least, an absentee farmer. Often responsibility for various farms is delegated to sons, but in the case of derelict cocoa land, Ewe *abusa* food-farming tenants may be permitted, so as to leave the farmer and his family free to give their full attention to good cocoa land in the west. A case in point is Jonathan Donkor of Praprabida, a Shai from Agomeda. He has leased four of his dead cocoa farms to Ewe *abusa* tenants for food-farming. Donkor's two wives supervise the collection and sale of the usufruct from these widely scattered farms, all of which lie to the east of Suhum in the very oldest cocoa areas. Under the *abusa* system, supervision of tenants' activities is usually not very close.

Some landowners so completely neglect

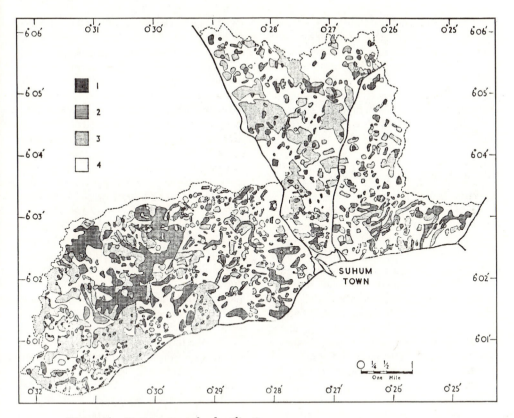

Figure 7.—Contemporary land utilization.
1. Healthy cocoa on rehabilitated farms; diseased trees have been cut away and new trees planted (1959).
2. Diseased cocoa; mostly small patches of dying trees. It will be observed that this category forms only a very small proportion of the survey area. Swollen-shoot virus, capsid lesions, and fungus are the prime causes of morbidity.
3. Food-farming on land with a few isolated and diseased cocoa trees remaining.
4. Intensive food-farming on land entirely denuded of cocoa trees. A comparison with Figure 5 will show the degree to which various groups of farmers practise food-farming, or have rehabilitated their land for cocoa.

their dead cocoa land that it stands as a temptation to others and is sometimes illegally encroached upon for food-farming. One such landowner declared to the writer that he was "about to take action," but one felt that a restitution of rights was not being sought with any great degree of urgency, because of the diffusion of interests which results from owning a large number of separate holdings, and because the land in question was not producing cocoa.

It is common for migrant farmers to hold a parcel of land for a lengthy period before cultivating it. Two of the farms in Figure 2, for example, remain unplanted although they were purchased many years ago. At the time of the survey (1960) three of the farmers interviewed stated that they were only just beginning to clear virgin forest, in the west, which they had bought in 1922, 1928 and 1935, respectively, that is, 38, 32 and 25 years previously. In some instances, land intended for cocoa has subsequently been reserved by the Forestry Commissioners.

PATTERNS OF LAND OWNERSHIP

Certain exceptions apart, the migrant farmers of the Densu basin can be classified into two groups, between which broad distinctions may be drawn. On the one hand there are the Twi-speaking Akwapim, with a matrilineal system of inheritance socially organized in what may be called the "extended family" and, on the other, the Adangbe-speaking Shai and Krobo, with a patrilineal system of inheritance, organized, for migratory purposes, into what is known as a "company." The basic differences between these two groups is apparent in the patterns of land ownership; family lands show a patchwork quilt or mosaic pattern whilst company lands are indicated by parallel strips (Fig. 4). These broad differences between matrilineal and patrilineal groups have been examined and reported upon by Polly Hill.[6]

If one bears in mind the distinction between strips and mosaics, and carefully examines the farm map (Fig. 4) in conjunction with the place of origin map (Fig. 5), one can attempt to reconstruct, albeit imperfectly, the blocks into which the pioneer farmers subdivided the forest. Such an attempt was made on a scale of eight inches to the mile; the results are presented in a somewhat simplified form in Figure 8. Because of considerable practical difficulties in confirming map and documentary evidence, Figure 8 is necessarily schematic: it involves guess-work on points of detail, but the general picture it presents cannot be far from the truth. There appear to have been several scores of blocks in the

12,673 acres (19.80 square miles) of forest occupied by the stranger-farmers. The exact number of blocks is not significant since the boundary of the survey area cuts through several of them, as, for example, along the road one and a half miles west of Suhum. The arrows on the map indicate the probable direction of clearing and cultivation and, in the case of company land, the direction of strips. The predominant movement is westward, but minor cross-currents, leading from the roads, can also be observed. The largest block on the map is about 400 acres; others are 200, 100 and 50 acres; there is no uniformity of size.

The Twi-speaking matrilineal Akwapim of Aburi, Amanokrom, Akropong and elsewhere (Table I and Fig. 6), have largely migrated by the "family system," that is, members of a family group travel, live and work together under the leadership of the head of the family. The high degree of social cohesion peculiar to the group stems directly from the indigenous concept of the extended family. In its purest form it is remarkably egalitarian. The head of the family (the chief) serves as a trustee of the family land, from which individual members of the family may take unsufruct according to their individual efforts, but over which no individual ownership can be exercised. The extended family gives food, shelter and farmland to any member of the family who may be in need of them, and thus, in a sense, it provides a form of insurance against personal misfortune.

Under traditional laws of inheritance in the extended family, a man's property, if he should own any, may pass to a younger brother and then, not to a son, but to the eldest sister's eldest son, that is, to a matrilineal nephew. Leadership of the family is passed down in the same way, and, with that leadership, trusteeship of the family land. A family land must be regarded as a whole. It will be subdivided into a number of usufructuary holdings each serving for the span of a cultivator's lifetime, but it is essentially single entity.

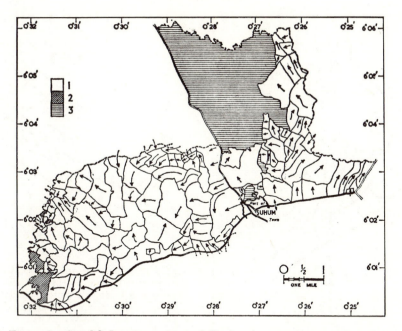

Figure 8.—Simplified reconstruction of blocks of virgin forest purchased by pioneer groups of cocoa farmers.

1. Land sold to, and occupied by, groups of migrant farmers. Arrows indicate probable direction of first clearing, and direction of strips on company land. Comparisons should be made with Figures 4 and 5 showing farm boundaries and ethnic origins, respectively. Block-size ranges up to a maximum of about 400 acres. Some blocks have been severed by the boundary of the survey area.
2. Land owned and farmed by indigenous Akim of the Apapam Stool.
3. Land owned by indigenous Akim of the Apedwa Stool but largely occupied and farmed by Ewe *abusa* labourers. Densuso and Abretima, indicated on Figure 3, are mainly Ewe villages.

A typical family land, Akotuakrom, south of Suhum, has been examined by the writer.[7]

In some instances, during the registration for the cutting-out and replanting campaign fairly large parcels of family land, embracing more than one usufructuary holding, have been recorded and mapped as a single farm, but fortunately, in most cases, separate usufructuary holdings have been mapped as separate farms. Official farm plans, therefore, give a useful guide to usufructuary subdivision in family lands.

On "pure" family land, holdings are characteristically small and irregular in shape, tending to be compact and concentric, and giving one the impression of a mosaic or patchwork quilt. In Figure 4 the contrast between linear and mosaic patterns is much in evidence. A small family land of 54 acres is shown in Figure 9. There are 32 holdings, the largest being 5.2 acres, the smallest 0.1, and the mean 1.7. The farmers are Akwapim from Akropong. A peripheral strip, cut to secure the western boundary of the family land in the early days, may be observed.

However, not all matrilineal family lands

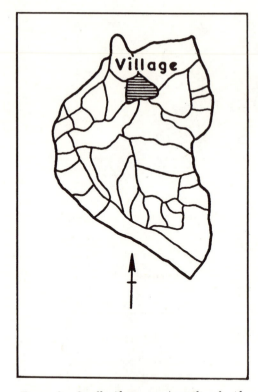

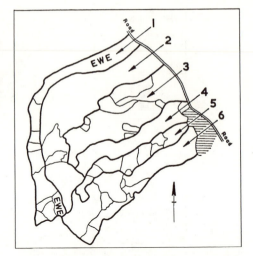

Figure 10.—Large Amanokrom (matrilineal Akwapim) family land. As in Figure 9, a peripheral strip securing the outer boundary can be
observed. Ownership of two parcels in this
outer strip has passed to Ewe farmers. The
general pattern of holdings is not completely
typical of family land in that broad, roughly
shaped strips (numbered 1 to 6) are discernible.
These divisions correspond to an initial subdivision between six brothers who founded the
land c. 1908. Farm boundaries in matrilineal
family land are characteristically irregular since
ownership of land is vested in the family as a
whole, not in individuals, and there is therefore
no need for a careful determination of internal
boundaries. Individual farmers enjoy usufructuary, not freehold, possession. The chief is
the trustee of the family land. The sizes of the
large strips in acres are: 1, 64.0; 2, 113.0; 3,
75.3; 4, 35.1; 5, 37.2; 6, 76.4. Altogether there
are 42 holdings in a total area of 401.0 acres.
The largest holding is 81.2 acres and the smallest 0.6. Approximate position: 6° 02′ 20″ north,
0° 27′ 30″ west. See Figure 4.

Figure 9.—Small Akropong (matrilineal Akwapim) family land. This small matrilineal
family land of 53.8 acres contains 32 holdings:
the largest is 5.2 acres, the smallest 0.1 and
the mean 1.7. There is a peripheral strip to
secure the western boundary, but otherwise a
normal patchwork quilt pattern prevails. Settlement is nucleated. Approximate position: 6°
02′ 50″ north, 0° 28′ 10″ west. See Figure 4.

show a simple mosaic pattern. In several
there are broad, roughly shaped strips
within each of which a mosaic has developed. A case in point is the Amanokrom
land near Suhum (Fig. 10). Here six strips
are divided into 42 holdings covering a
total area of 401 acres. Again, a boundary
strip is noticeable. This atypical combination of mosaics within strips results from
an initial division of the land between six
founder-brothers in c. 1908, a division
which obtains today, representing a modification of the family system.

Matrilineal peoples, then, do not always
adhere strictly to the family system. One
occasionally comes across large rectangular
blocks within normal family land. Around
Suhum at least, this seems to have been a
practice of the Akropong. Figure 11 shows
two 40-acre Akropong blocks which have
been carefully surveyed by chain and compass. One also finds, although compara-

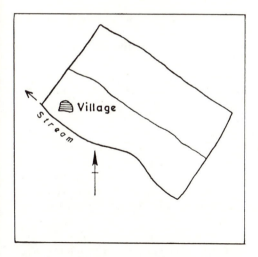

Figure 11.—Akropong (matrilineal Akwapim) blocks. These two rectangular blocks, which show evidence of having been surveyed by chain and compass, stand out prominently in an area of irregular matrilineal holdings. The upper block covers 39.4 acres and the lower, 42.0. Ownership of these blocks is vested in individuals, not in the extended family, thus indicating a departure from customary practice. Approximate position: 6° 01′ 40″ north, 0° 30′ 50″ west. See Figure 4.

tively rarely, matrilineal peoples making use of the company system. Figure 12 shows a small Amanokrom land of 68 acres containing the straight farm boundaries so characteristic of company land.[8]

Whereas, generally speaking, the matrilineal Akwapim migratory process functioned within the existing social framework of the extended family, the patrilineal Shai and Krobo created a special organization of their own for migration known as a "company."[9] A company is simply a band of farmers who, through their appointed leader, buy a tract of land from an Akim or any other chief. The land is then subdivided between company members according to the size of their individual contributions towards the total cost of the land. Once the subdivision is effected, each member enjoys complete freehold possession of his individual share of the land, and

the company, having served its purpose, is dissolved. As a corporate body, then, the company is purely transitory: it comes into being to arrange the purchase and subsequent division of land, and it is dissolved as soon as this end is achieved. It was, and remains today, the stranger-farmers collective bargaining device.

The system works somewhat as follows. A leader, perhaps accompanied by a few members of the company, travels west to meet an Akim chief with a piece of land for sale. The company leader inspects the land and makes a personal estimate of its worth, bearing in mind size, soil fertility and the proportion of swamp, rock outcrops and over-steep slopes. Bargaining takes place and a price is agreed upon. At this stage the area of the land is not known,

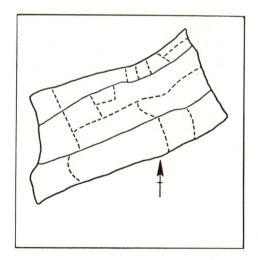

Figure 12.—Small Amanokrom (matrilineal Akwapim) company land. Matrilineal Akwapim occasionally reject the idea of communal ownership of family property in order to migrate by the company system, which confers individual freehold possession. In this example we see three strips (upper 11.8 acres, central 29.6, lower 26.5) covering a total area of 67.9 acres. Subsequent division, both longitudinal and transverse, has produced 17 holdings: the largest 13.6 acres, the smallest 0.7. Approximate position: 6° 02′ 40″ north, 0° 27′ 50″ west. See Figure 4.

only its boundaries. If the leader is wealthy he may purchase the land outright or, alternatively, secure it on a deposit collected from the company members. These company members do not figure in the purchase of the land. They are represented by the leader who deals personally with the vendor chief.

As the money is handed over, a bargain-sealing ceremony is performed. Normally the transfer of ownership is solemnized by the tearing of a leaf as the money changes hands. The chief and the company leader, seated hand under leg, each retain a half of the leaf. Sometimes a rope is cut instead. Sheep are slaughtered and a libation poured. Empty gin or rum bottles may be buried at the corners of the land. Customary ceremonies of this sort seal the transaction so effectively that written documents are considered unnecessary.[10]

When the land is bought, a straight line, known as a base-line, is cut through the property near the boundary and its length is measured. The unit of measurement is the "rope" which is discussed later. Once the length of the base-line is known, the share-out between the company members can proceed. Let us say, for example, that the agreed price, including incidentals such as libation, is £100 and that the base-line is 20 ropes in length. The price to the company therefore is £5 per rope. If the leader has bought the land himself he may keep 10 ropes for his own use and sell the remaining 10 ropes. If a deposit has been paid, then, when the price per rope is known, a distribution of land is arranged through mutual discussion and agreement. A very simple case would be 10 ropes for sale at £5 each. Farmer A says he would like to buy 5 ropes, Farmer B, 3 ropes and Farmer C, 3 ropes. Each has put down a deposit and has ready cash. One farmer may agree to take one less, or Farmers B and C may take 2½ ropes each. A number of alternatives are possible but, at any rate, demand is arranged to equate with supply. Occasionally, a farmer may withdraw his

deposit if he is not satisfied with the proposed share-out.

In a large company, the procedure is slightly different. The base-line is cut and measured. Let us say that there are 100 ropes at £2 10s. per rope. The leader and the "nucleus," that is the more active sponsors, may take 50 ropes and the remainder may be sold off to a large number of farmers in the home town most of whom would have given their prior approval to the venture but who need not necessarily have committed themselves financially. In a small company the idea of a nucleus does not apply.

Measurement under the company system is linear. There is no indigenous unit of area measurement. But it would be incorrect to deduce from this that no concept of area exists. The farmer is well aware that, provided the base-line is square to the major or minor axis of the land, and is accurately divided, a fair division of area will follow. Obviously the quantitative value of a rope will vary with the length of the land, but this lack of uniformity does not worry the farmer since he is only concerned with the division of one piece of land at a time. For him, an absolute scale of areal measurement is not necessary.

Rope length also varies from company to company. In fifteen cases, in the survey area, rope length varied as follows:

Company	Rope Length in Fathoms			
	24 fm.	22 fm.	12 fm.	Total
Shai	5	1	2	8
Krobo	–	–	1	1
Ga	–	1	2	3
Kyerepon	2	–	–	2
Mixed Larteh-Akropong	–	–	1	1
Total	7	2	6	15

A 24-fathom "rope" could be represented by a purchased nautical rope of that length, by a bush rope made of various creepers tied together, or simply by 24 men standing, arms outstretched, fingertip to fingertip.[11] The choice of rope length—either 24 fathoms or 12 fathoms—varied from company to company for no apparent reason. The two cases of 22 fathoms indicated above are unusual. Surviving company members could give no reason for the choice of rope length.

After the base-line has been subdivided, marker trees are planted to indicate the limits of each member's newly acquired property.[12] The work of clearing and cultivation can then commence. Normally the farmers advance side by side from the base-line clearing a fresh piece of forest each year. Ideally, the advance is co-ordinated, quite voluntarily, so as to ensure that no strip "swells" in width at the expense of a neighbour's strip. Once the original forest cover has been removed and marker trees

Kofi Gya and Annanhyia was sold by the chief of Apedwa (the Apedwahene). In the north-east of the survey area, the land around Adaakwa and Odumase was sold by the chief of Asafo (the Asafohene). Otwe Bediadua was a disputed area. Ga migrants first bought the land from the Asafohene and then were obliged to pay a further sum to the Apedwahene who claimed the land as his.

It is difficult to ascertain the selling price of the land per unit of area since no two ropes, even of equal length, would necessarily correspond to the same size of strip. Prices of £5 and £6 per short rope of 12 fathoms were recalled; and £5 and £10 per long rope of 24 fathoms.

As regards size of company membership and numbers of ropes purchased, there was no uniformity, as the following examples illustrate:

Place of origin of members	Numbers of members in each company	Total number of ropes purchased	Length of rope in fathoms
Doyumu, Shai	11	31	24
Labadi, Ga	5	6½	22
Dodowa, Shai	12	48	24
Dodowa, Shai	6	17½	24
Dodowa, Shai	40	34	24
Kodiabe, Shai	30	30	12

planted along the sides of the strips, the risk of encroachment diminishes.

The Akim, into whose territory the migrants had moved, were politically organized into the Native State of Akim Abuakwa with the Paramount Stool at Kibi (Fig. 6) and lesser stools elsewhere. In only two instances in the survey area, namely Aliakanasi and Suhum, did migrants deal directly with the Omanhene (Paramount Chief) of Akim Abuakwa at Kibi; in all other cases the migrants dealt with lesser chiefs. Land west of the main road in the area of Okanta, Okunam, Sowatey, Aponapon, Obuom and Abisim (Fig. 3) was sold by the chief of Apapam, whilst that east of the road in the area of Tetteh Nkwanta,

Informants' memories were clear in the case of small companies, where details of individual personalities and holdings were readily recalled; but information on large companies was hard to come by. Some companies, it was claimed, had "about 100" members, although no degree of accuracy was claimed for such guesses.

Most companies were remarkably homogeneous, membership being recruited from the same town or village. However, there were a number of mixed companies. These could be of the same tribe such as mixed Krobo (for example, Somanya and Odumase) or mixed Shai (for example, Dodowa and Kodiabe) or, more rarely, of different tribes such as Ga mixed with Akwapim. In the survey area, the following examples of the latter category, were found:

as fair a result as could be expected under forest conditions.

Osu	(Ga)	with Abiriu	(Kyerepon)
Accra	(Ga)	with Aburi	(matrilineal Akwapim)
Larteh	(Guan)	with Mamfe	(patrilineal Akwapim)
Larteh	(Guan)	with Akropong	(matrilineal Akwapim)

In the last two cases, physical proximity might account for the mixing since farmers migrating westwards from Larteh would pass between Akropong and Mamfe (Fig. 6).

A few specific examples of farm-patterns produced in the survey area by the company system may now be considered.

The further that the shape of a piece of land departs from a rectangle, the less equitable is the company system of subdivision by ropes. An example of this is given in Figure 13 which shows a Kodiabe (Shai) company land lying between two streams. The total area is 97 acres and the distance along the base-line is 9½ long ropes. A fair subdivision would be about 10 acres per rope, but obviously a farmer owning land on the western boundary, north of the stream confluence, is more fortunate than one owning land along the shorter, eastern boundary. Incidentally, one of the strips has been sold to an Ewe.

Another example of the greater or lesser inequalities which result from irregularities of shape, is provided in Figure 14. Here we see that a Somanya (Krobo) company has purchased land abutting against a stream. The total area is, again, 97 acres, and the length of the base-line 8 long ropes or 16 short ropes. A long rope would thus give a 12-acre strip and a short rope 6 acres. On the plan there are actually 17 strips, not counting transverse subdivisions. It will be noticed that the greater width of the land nearer the stream has enabled some of the farmers, especially those in the south, to widen their strips. Meander loops, swinging quite impartially from side to side, favour alternate groups of farmers. Actual differences arising, however, are comparatively small. The division of this company land by the rope system has given

In Figure 15, a company land curves around the head of a small valley, and in Figure 16, another company land lies, block-like, in a flat area alongside a road. Streams are preferred as boundaries, but,

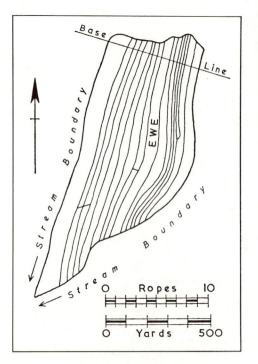

Figure 13.—Kobiade (patrilineal Shai) company land between streams. This company land of 96.8 acres is 9½ long ropes (i.e. 24-fathom ropes) along the base-line. It contains 15 strips subdivided into 19 holdings. There has been very little transverse subdivision, but longitudinal subdivision has reduced some strips to a mere 2½ acres. The largest holding covers 21.3 acres, and the smallest 1.0 acre. Tapering towards the stream confluence has given farmers at the western end of the base-line appreciably longer strips. Approximate position: 6° 00′ 30″ north, 0° 31′ 10″ west. See Figure 4.

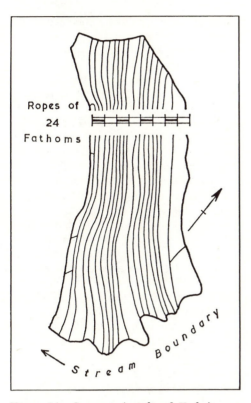

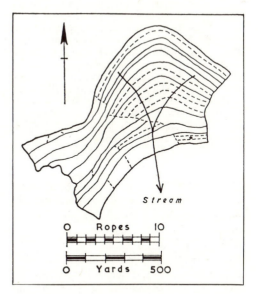

of the end strip (marked A in Fig. 16) which has poached some two to three acres from its neighbours.

Figure 16 also provided a good example of a typical company settlement, known in Adangbe as a *huza*.[13] Each farmer builds his house on his strip. At the beginning, a site near the base-line will be chosen, but, when all the land has been cleared, a more central position may be selected. Compounds are linked by footpaths in a typically linear settlement pattern which contrasts strongly with the nucleated, "family" villages of the Akwapim.

In the area we are examining, the company reaches its fullest development in Shai and Krobo society, but it was not their exclusive possession. Other patrilineal groups such as the Kyerepon and Larteh used the system (Fig. 17), as indeed

Figure 14.—Somanya (patrilineal Krobo) company land. This is an 8-rope company land of 96.9 acres abuttting against a stream boundary. There are 17 strips which, with transverse subdivision, given a total of 21 farms: the largest covering 9.6 acres, and the smallest 0.6. The value of a 24-fathom rope would be about 12 acres, and that of a 6-fathom rope, 6 acres, plus or minus the difference due to meander loops along the stream boundary. Approximate position: 6° 02' 10" north, 0° 31' 10" west. See Figure 4.

Figure 15.—Shai company land curving around head of small valley. Orientation along the contour lines ensures that farmers' strips are level and approximately equal in length. Subdivision of these strips is indicated by broken lines. Approximate position: 6° 02' 40" north, 0° 28' 30" west. See Figure 4.

where none exist, a road may be used, or, if necessary, a line of trees planted. The company land shown in Figure 16 is 23 ropes long and covers 194 acres, thus averaging 8.4 acres per rope. An idea of the degree of fairness of subdivision achieved under the rope system may be gained by comparing this average value of 8.4 acres with actual strips sizes which range from 7 to 10½ acres. Of interest is the swelling

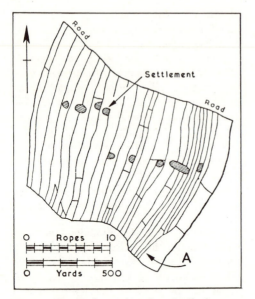

Figure 16.—Dodowa (patrilineal Shai) company land showing typical *huza* settlement pattern. This comparatively large company land of 23 long ropes covers 194 acres, giving an average of 8.4 acres per rope. Some of the strips have been subdivided transversely and others, noticeably in the east, longitudinally. Each farmer builds a house on his strip, hence a characteristically linear settlement pattern, known as a *huza*, develops. Linear settlements of patrilineal migrants contrast markedly with nucleated settlements of matrilineal migrants (compare nucleated settlement in Figure 9). Approximate position: 6° 02′ 45″ north, 0° 29′ 40″ west. See Figure 4.

did occasional groups of matrilineal farmers, as we have already seen. The company offered a farmer who wished to migrate two distinct advantages: first, the full weight of collective bargaining in the purchase of land without prejudice to individual freehold possession; and secondly, companionship in a strange forest through the growth of *huza* settlement. The method of areal subdivision by ropes along a base-line can be criticized, yet it was fair, in a rough and ready sense, and could hardly be bettered without the use of survey instruments, which would have been out of the

question under conditions obtaining in the forest fifty years ago.

Many of the pioneer company farmers who migrated into the survey area in 1907–17 have died, and, as is the custom in patrilineal societies, the land has passed to their sons. Some of these, in turn, have died and have been succeeded by their sons. Each death of a land-holder results in a division of the land between his sons. The strips are divided longitudinally and are thus becoming narrower and narrower. This is especially true of Shai and Krobo land in the survey area, as the evidence presented below will indicate, but less obviously the case in other patrilineal lands.

Land is not shared equally between sons but according to the number of wives. An actual example is presented in Figure 18. The farmer, a Shai from Dodowa living in Aponapon II, has three wives, A, B and C, and ten sons, four from one wife and three

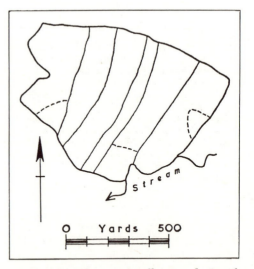

Figure 17.—Characteristically Broad Larteh strips. Larteh use the company system but do not measure their strips so carefully, or divide them so finely, as Shai and Krobo. In this example, there are only six strips in a total area of 108.5 acres: the largest covers 22.0 acres and the smallest 9.3. Approximate position: 6° 02′ 30″ north, 0° 31′ 00″ west. See Figure 4.

from each of the other two wives. He owns
a two-rope farm, 48 fathoms wide. When
he dies, the first-born son of each wife
will step up to the base-line which will
then be divided into three equal parts;
then each first-born son will divide his
part equally between himself and his full-
brothers. In this case, the sons of C will
receive less than those of A and B.

There is evidence of increasing subdivision of company land in the survey area
(Figs. 4, 13, 14, 15, and 16); and, with
the passing of each generation, the multiplication of strips increases. For example,
one Krobo farmer, a second generation
migrant, told the writer that his father
originally owned five short ropes. On his
father's death, the informant received one
rope. This informant in his prime, adding
to his family regularly. On his death, his
single short rope will be subdivided into
many parts, that is, if present intentions
are adhered to. Another informant, a
Kyerepon from Abiriu living in Okunam I,
where he owns a four-rope strip, will be
succeeded by no fewer than 23 sons (second example, below):

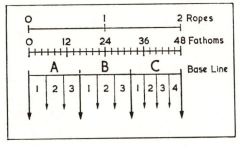

Figure 18.—An example of patrilineal subdivision.

some 1552 yards long and 4–14 yards
wide, is shown in Figure 19.

A further complication of farm ownership is the artificial fragmentation of holdings caused by the registration of farms
within survey blocks (see explanatory notes
relating to Fig. 4). It is true that ownership
is not necessarily affected but the fact that
a single farm may be split into two or
three parts, each separately demarcated
and registered, provides a ready-made
subdivision should one be contemplated

Farmer, still living	Land owned by Farmer		Farmer's Wives	Farmer's Sons	Intended division of land
	Short Ropes	Long Ropes			
Doyumu, Shai	—	5	4	10	Longitudinal
Abiriu, Kyerepon	—	4	6	23	Longitudinal and Transverse
Dodowa, Shai	—	1	1	5	Transverse
Doyuma, Shai	—	2	2	7	Longitudinal
Dodowa, Shai	—	2	3	10	Longitudinal
Kodiabe, Shai	—	5½	2	7	Longitudinal
Agomeda, Shai	2	—	2	10	Longitudinal
Labadi, Ga.	5	—	1	3	Longitudinal

Subdivision is, by tradition, longitudinal
but some strips have become so narrow
that recourse is had to transverse subdivision. A typically narrow strip farm,

(in connection with a mortgage for example).

With particular reference to Shai and
Krobo land, we may well ask: How long

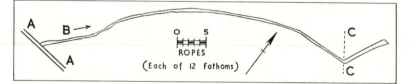

Figure 19.—A typically narrow strip farm. AA: Base-line along Suhum-Amanhyia road near Tetteh Nkwanta (see Figure 3). B: Direction of first cultivation of strip. CC: Reorientation and re-measurement of strip along supplementary base-line to accord with shape of company land. This strip belongs to a Dodowa (patrilineal Shai) farmer. It is 1552 yards long, 4–14 yards wide, and covers 3.4 acres. In terms of local measurement, it is half a short rope (or six fathoms) in width. Approximate position: 6° 02′ 45″ north, 0° 25′ 10″ west.

can such subdivision and multiplication of strips continue? It seems that a limit has already been reached in parts of the survey area. Some strips appear to be so small that one doubts if they are viable economic units. In the broader context of economic development in Ghana, capitalization of agriculture in order to raise productivity must be a major consideration, and thus the fragmentation of holdings presents a serious problem. Certainly from the point of view of cocoa-disease control as well as for agronomic reasons, the continued splintering of farms is undesirable.

FUSION OF ETHNIC GROUPS

The salient facts of the migration into the survey area have already been presented. It has been seen that there was an influx of Akwapim and Kyerepon from the Akwapim Ridge, of Shai and Krobo from the Accra Plains, of Ga and Adangbe from the coast, and of Ewe and Guan from across the Volta (Fig. 6).

Organized in companies of family groups, the migrants moved into a comparatively small area of 19.8 square miles (if one excludes the area of indigenous Akim holdings; Fig. 8). Subsequent division of their pioneer blocks has produced a bewildering pattern of small farms (Fig. 4) and a relatively fine intermingling of farmers of differ-ent origins (Table I, Fig. 5). A question naturally arising during the course of the survey, therefore, was: "To what extent has migration and mixing broken down ethnic barriers?"

Considering that the migration occurred fifty years ago, the farmer's ties with his place of origin, his home town, are remarkably strong. This is equally true of young farmers born in the survey area; so much so that, at first glance, the prospect that local loyalties will eventually displace loyalties to a distant traditional seat seems rather slight.

A major influence, which tends to perpetuate home-town loyalties at the expense of local assimilation, is the annual festival. Migrant Akwapim assemble in the ridge-top towns each September–October to celebrate *Odwira*. The chief of each town fixes the starting-date: Akropong is first, followed in turn by Aburi and the other towns. The corresponding Ga festival is *Homowo*, celebrated in August–September. Ningo and Prampram also celebrate *Homowo*. *Odwira* and *Homowo* are connected with the yam harvest and fishing seasons, respectively. The Yilo-Krobo of Somanya observe *Kotokro* in April, the Manya Krobo of Odumase *Nadu* and also *Maiyim*, the latter at the beginning of November, and the Shai *Ameyapam* or *Pamyam* in May.

These festivals include drumming, dancing, shooting of guns, pouring of libations, and remembrance of elders who have passed away. The home town is also visited for the performance of traditional wedding and funeral rites, and for the settling of family disputes.

One informant, a Ga of Sowatey, stated that he visited his home town, Labadi, about six times a year. Another Ga of Niifio visits Accra every fortnight because he is an elder of the Asere Division of the Ga State. A Shai informant of Abisim returns every four months to Kodiabe to see his mother. These few examples are quite typical of the general situation.

Education too, rather surprisingly, works as a separatist force, because many of the young children born in the survey area, especially the boys, are sent to their home towns to be educated. The custom which has developed is that children are sent first to the nearest 'primary school' in the survey area, and then away to a "middle school" in their home town. Thus a Sowatey farmer's children will be sent to a middle school in Labadi and a Niifio farmer's children will go to Accra. Our survey showed Aponapon children being educated in Dodowa, Abisim children in Kodiabe and Praprabida children in Agomeda. Indeed, one informant of Kumfa claimed that if he failed to send his son to the home-town school, in Aseseaso, the elders of that town would impose a £5 fine.

Custom, tradition and even education, have thus served to divert loyalties away from the local scene, and retard fusion of migrants. Language, too, reflects the deep emotional attachment of the migrant to his home town. The indigenous Akim and certain Akwapim speak Twi, the language of Akan, so that, in this group, no barrier exists (Table I). The Larteh, Boso, Anum and Kyerepon all speak dialectical variations of Guan, and, although there are difficulties, the obstacles in this group are not great. However, Twi and the various Guan dialects are not mutually intelligible.

The Adangbe language of the Shai and Krobo is related to the Ga language, but there are considerable differences. Ga-Adangbe, Twi and Guan form three distinct language groups. Similarly, the Ewe dialects, and the languages of the northern labourers, are quite separate elements. The linguistic scene, then, is heterogeneous to a degree.

Suhum town itself epitomizes the ethnic and linguistic heterogeneity which is a result of the cocoa migration. The chief of the town, the Odikro, is an Amanokrom (that is, a matrilineal Akwapim), his deputy-chief, the Mankrado, is an Aseseaso (that is, a Kyerepon), whilst below them are no fewer than *twenty-two* recognized tribal heads representing communities in the town from various parts of Ghana and West Africa including Dahomey, Togoland and Nigeria.

The cocoa migration brought together in a small area farmers of different origins, but, as we have seen, mere physical proximity does not automatically lead to a fusion of disparate elements. Small groups of settlers, scattered throughout the forest, still continue to look to the distant home town as the focal point of their social life. Only slowly are the forces of separatism—custom, tradition, education and language—beginning to weaken.

However, with the passing of time, and the rise of a second and third generation, a degree of fusion is taking place in innumerable small ways which have an increasingly important cumulative effect. Shai children, for example, may attend the same local primary school as Akwapim children. A Krobo farmer may regularly use a footpath crossing Kyerepon land. Ewe and Ga women jostle together in the same market. In the construction of feeder roads, communal labour is employed regardless of ethnic differences since all in the area will benefit equally.

Because of the services they provide, these feeder roads tend to bring changes in the settlement pattern. Farmers are tempted to desert their *huza* for a roadside location.

A new road acts as a magnet attracting farmers of different origins, thus many of the villages on the feeder roads of the survey area are quite mixed. Okanta is a good example. Primarily Kyerepon from Abiriu, it also contains Prampram, Anum, Somanya, Ewe and northerners, all living together under the leadership of an Abiriu.

Language is becoming less of an obstacle with the increasing use of English and Twi. English is the medium of instruction in middle schools and in the upper classes of primary schools. The growth of Twi is interesting since, in the survey area, those for whom Twi is a first language do not constitute a majority. The chief of Suhum, a Twi-speaking Akwapim himself, stated that Guan quickly learned to speak good Twi but that most of the Shai, Krobo, Ga, Ewe and northerners spoke only broken or "pidgin" Twi. Nevertheless this pidgin Twi is a *lingua franca* of the area.

Intermarriage is also helping to break down the barriers. As yet it is on a small scale, but examples are not difficult to find. The chief of Suhum, an Akwapim of Amanokrom, has a Kyerepon (Aseseaso) wife. The Mass Education Officer of the town, also an Akwapim or Amanokrom, has an Adangbe (Ada) wife. A Cocoa Liaison Officer, with whom the writer worked, an Akim of Apapam, has two wives: one is Kwahu and the other Akwapim from Akropong.

Suhum is thoroughly heterogeneous, but despite its large number of small, ethnically varied communities, some of which are physically separated into *zongos*, it is here, in the town, that one can observe the greatest degree of fusion. Trade and the functions of local and central government are largely responsible for this.

Suhum market is an important meeting place at which farmers from a wide area regularly congregate; the town's craftsmen (weavers, silversmith, lock-smiths, gunsmiths, gold-smiths, carpenters and mechanics) also provide services for the surrounding area, and, in so doing, assist in the growth of local identification. Its six middle schools attract villagers, as will the new technical college now under construction. Other regional foci are the health centre, soon to become a hospital, a rural training centre for women, and a social welfare community centre. Suhum is the headquarters of the South Akim Abuakwa Local Council, and of the Akim Abuakwa East Parliamentary Constituency. It also contains the Department of Agriculture mechanical workshops for the Eastern Region.

Through trade and the provision of services, as well as through the exercise of local and central government functions, Suhum town helps the migrant farmer to develop a feeling of local identification which is gradually challenging his other loyalties. Suhum is the focal point of the survey area, a place of social change, a melting-pot.

ACKNOWLEDGMENTS

The author wishes to place on record his deep appreciation of help received from officers of the Cocoa Division of the Ghana Department of Agriculture. He is also much indebted to chiefs and elders in the Suhum area for co-operating so willingly during the course of the survey. Lastly he is very grateful to Polly Hill for reading the typescript of this article and offering valuable criticism.

NOTES

[1] M. J. Field, The agricultural system of the Manya-Krobo of the Gold Coast," *Africa*, 14 (1943), 54–65.

[2] J. G. Christaller gives a list of Akwapim food-farming hamlets in the forest between the Ridge and the Densu; see his *A Dictionary of the Asante and Fante language* (Basel, 1881), Appendix.

[3] Polly Hill, "The history of the migration of Ghana cocoa farmers," *Transactions of the Historical Society of Ghana* 4 (1959), 14–28; and "The migration of southern Ghanaian cocoa farmers," *Bulletin of the Ghana Geographical Society*, 5 (1960), 9–19.

[4] For a discussion of abusa and other cocoa

labourers, see Polly Hill, *The Gold Coast cocoa farmer: a preliminary survey* (1956).

[5] The standard head-load is 60 lb.

[6] The writer has been privileged to read, comment upon and discuss, with particular reference to his own field work, the draft typescript of Miss Polly Hill's book, *The migrant cocoa farmers of southern Ghana: a study in rural capitalism*, in the press. The distinction between matrilineal and patrilineal lands is also drawn in a recent article by Miss Hill, "The migrant cocoa farmers of southern Ghana," *Africa*, 31 (1961), 209–30.

[7] J. M. Hunter, "Akotuakrom: a case-study of a devastated cocoa village in Ghana," *Transactions and Papers*, Institute of British Geographers, 29 (1961), 161–86.

[8] Figures 10, 11 and 12 indicate departures from the normal mosaic of the family system. Miss Hill also shows an Akropong family land which is unusual in the measured regularity of its lay-out, op. cit. (1961), Map VI.

[9] M. J. Field (op. cit.) shows how the Krobo system of migration by company was first developed for the food-farming migration which commenced in the mid-nineteenth century.

[10] The Adangbe word for a bargain-sealing ceremony is *ayibapom;* the Twi equivalent is *guaha.* Children may be selected to perform the ceremony since they are likely to live longer than adult witnesses to testify in case of dispute. See A. A. Opoku's description of *guaha* in *Across the Prah,* quoted in Polly Hill, *The migrant cocoa farmers of southern Ghana,* Appendix I(V) (in the press).

[11] The Adangbe word for fathom is *gugwe* and for rope *kpa;* the Twi equivalents are *abasa* and *hama.*

[12] The conventional boundary tree is *Dracaena arborea* known in Adangbe as *buna* and Twi as *ntome.*

[13] The Shai-Adangbe word for a company is *kakatopim,* for company settlement *huza* and for head of the settlement *huzache.*

Highland environments present specific problems of adjustment in the relationship between people and land. These may arise through altitudinal modifications of climate, which in Tropical Africa produce conditions ranging from warm and cool temperate to alpine. As elevation increases, non-tropical plants may be cultivated and dairy farming, which would be impossible or at least difficult at lower levels, can be introduced (Gleave and Thomas, 1968). Because highland areas are free from malaria and trypanosomiasis, they have attracted both African and European settlement (Dresch, 1952; Gourou, 1953; Papy, 1953; Richard-Molard, 1958). In the past, the highlands provided refuge for groups seeking protection from stronger marauding neighbors (Gleave, 1963). The settlers, finding agricultural land limited, frequently terraced steep slopes, changing marginally useful land to areas of intensive farming (Froelich, 1952; Netting, 1965).

Peaceful conditions during the colonial era removed the need for settling in highland areas, and in many parts of Africa, recent decades have seen the "downhill" movement of people, both spontaneous and organized (Gleave, 1966). Planned schemes of resettlement were introduced in some instances because spontaneous movement created problems. People from the highlands, who had once farmed intensively and with great care, were quick to adopt the extensive and wasteful systems of the lowlands (Mercier, 1949). But even with controlled change, administrative reorganization and the problems of providing basic amenities have been considerable (Chambers, 1970).

The Ingessana of Blue Nile Province in the Sudan illustrate many of the features outlined above. Both cultivators and pastoralists, the Ingessana now engage in a form of seasonal transhumance between higher and lower lands, depending upon the availability of pasture (see also Lebon and Robertson, 1961).

9. *A Study of Tribal Re-adjustment in the Nile Valley: The Experience of the Ingessana*

H. R. J. DAVIES

The need to adapt oneself to changing conditions has long been the lot of Africa's indigenous peoples. The object of this paper is to examine the response of the hill-dwelling Ingessana [1] to the peaceful, stable conditions in their part of the Nile Valley resulting from the establishment of the Anglo-Egyptian Condominium government in the Sudan in 1898. Today the Ingessana peoples number about 38,000 persons.[2] They are to be found in hilly country stretching some 50 kms. from east to west and from north to south between the

White and Blue Niles in approximately lat. 11° 30′ N and long. 34° E (Figs. 1 and 2). There they comprise at least 99 per cent of the population. The Ingessana are a distinctive people who have maintained their cohesion through many trials and difficulties more especially during the last 150 years. For want of a better description they are usually classed as one of the negroid Pre-Nilotic group. Incursions confined the Ingessana to their present area. The Nilotic Dinka and Nuer established themselves to the west and south. With the fall of the Christian Kingdom of Alwa about A.D. 1504, and its replacement by the Fung Kingdom, Moslem influence spread southwards. From the new capital at Sennar raids were made against the Pre-Nilotics for slaves, and from this time onwards Arab nomads became established between the Niles. The Fung Kingdom came to an end with the Turco-Egyptian invasion of the Sudan in 1821. The occupation of Sennar was quickly followed by raids against the negroid peoples

[1] The Ingessana peoples have no collective name to describe themselves. "Ingessana" is the name given to these people by the Arab nomads, who say it means "People without any thanks."

[2] The total number of Ingessana according to the First Sudan Census was 31,250 in December 1955. The estimated annual increase in population of Southern Fung Census Area, in which the Ingessana Hills lie, is 2.86 per cent per annum, which gives a figure of something over 38,000 for the end of 1962.

From *The Geographical Journal, 130,* 1964, pp. 380–389.
Reprinted by permission of the Royal Geographical Society.

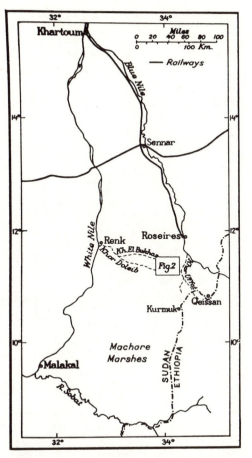

Figure 1.—General position of the Ingessana country.

toral Dinka and Nuer occupying the plain lands to the north, west and south. That these influences, but especially those of the slave trader, pressed hard upon the Ingessana can be gleaned from the Gleichen report of 1905 (Gleichen, 1905) which states that the Ingessana welcomed the arrival of the British authorities to their area because they were convinced that it would mean the end of slave raiding. Not all their Pre-Nilotic neighbours were as successful in resisting these outside influences as the Ingessana. The Koma, for example, had been so harried by the end of the nineteenth century that those on the Sudan side of the Ethiopian frontier could only be found taking refuge in the villages of the warlike Nuer. It was not until after 1924 that they seem to have been able to re-assert some form of separate existence.

In the past the Ingessana success in resisting outside influences has been in part a result of a sturdy independence. This may be illustrated today by the strength and vitality of the Ingessana language (Murdock, 1959) and the singular failure of Islam to penetrate the area. Some Ingessana, it is true, claim to be Moslems, but this is only when it is to their advantage in dealing with the agents of government. They were courageous fighters, inflicting reverses on the first Turco-Egyptian slave-raiding and gold-seeking expedition in 1821 (Cailliand, 1826–7). Their epic songs are about the defeats they inflicted in battle upon the Turco-Egyptian forces, the Dinka, the Hill Barun and their other neighbours. Today the young Ingessana male is not fully dressed unless he has his axe and his spear with him.

Yet it seems likely that all these qualities would have been of little avail if the physical environment had not been favourable to them. The Ingessana Hills consist of two large and several smaller basins. Most of the hills are composed of serpentines and in many cases are synclinal remains of an ancient system of folding. Some of the basins may be partly associated with the

of the south with the object of procuring slaves and gold. Raids continued throughout the Turco-Egyptian period and during the succeeding Mahdiya (1885–98). These raids were of much more serious consequence for the Ingessana and their neighbours as now the raiders had firearms to use against them. The nineteenth century also saw occasional slave-raiding incursions from Ethiopia. Thus at the establishment of the Anglo-Egyptian Condominium in 1898 the Ingessana were subject to slave raiding from the north and east, and constant conflict with Arab nomads and pas-

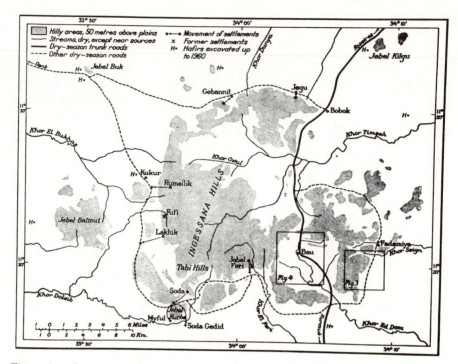

Figure 2.—The Ingessana Hills.

denuded anticlines of these old fold systems, but the geological structures are masked by considerable quantities of alluvium. The Bau basin is, however, different, being underlain by granites (Kabesh, 1961). The hills rise to over 300 metres above the surrounding clay plains and provide excellent hilltop refuge spots and defiles where ambushes could be set against the intruder. The Ingessana Hills are surrounded by a vast, flat, clay plain. The Ingessana is by far the largest hill mass between the Niles in the Sudan, so that the Ingessana people were better able to defend themselves from attack than were their neighbours.

The climate and vegetation were also to their advantage. Bau's average annual rainfall is of the order of 900 mms p.a. falling between the end of April and the end of October. It is thus situated at about the southern limit of the seasonal migration of the camel-owning nomads. This, plus the fact that the clay plains are virtually waterless during the dry season, has meant that neither the Arab nomads nor the Nilotic pastoralists have found it convenient to stay in the vicinity of the Ingessana Hills for long periods. The vegetation of the clay plains is a "fire climax" of acacias and *heglig* (Balanites aegyptiaca). On approaching the hills the annual fires that rage across the plains are soon broken up by the rocks and a more abundant vegetation, including tree species not so resistant to fire, is to be found, making ambush and defense a little easier.

The unsettled nature of life on the clay plains during the nineteenth century forced the Ingessana to confine more of their activities to the hills than they would otherwise have done. The Anglo-Egyptian Condominium provided settled conditions so that the Ingessana are now in a state of transition and adjustment, and it is only in these terms that developments in this century can be understood. This is clearly illustrated by a study of the settlement pattern and way of life.

Until recent years nearly all the Ingessana settlements have been situated upon the tops or upper slopes of the hills (Figs. 3 and 4). Such sites were remote from the plains and easily defended. The advantages during periods of unrest on the plains are positive disadvantages today. The soils of the hills are thin and infertile, whereas the clays of the plain are much better. The hilltop sites are remote from these better lands. Further, during the dry season water is available today from several sources: from the streams flowing out of the hills of which the larger are perennial; from the sandy deposits in the stream beds; from shallow wells dug in the hillfoot pediments and, more recently, from the surface reservoirs (hafirs) dug by the Department of Land Use and Rural Water Development in the impervious clays to collect run-off (Fig. 2). All these factors would encourage the Ingessana to abandon their homes on the heights and come down to the plains. This

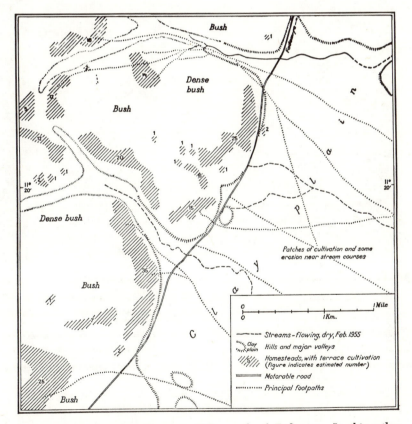

Figure 3.—South-eastern Ingessana Hills, south of Fadamiya. In this rather remote area the traditional hill slope for the Ingessana homesteads with their attendant terraces are in evidence. (Based on Sudan Government air photographs, February 1955).

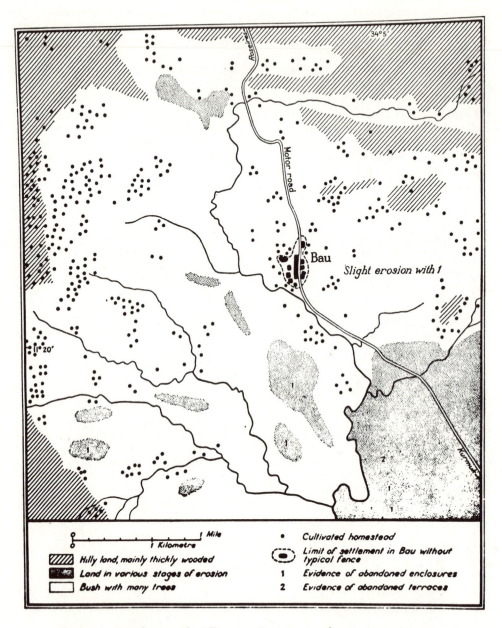

Figure 4.—Bau basin. This illustrates Ingessana settlement pattern in part of the area most affected by outside influences. Many of the homesteads have forsaken the hills for the flatter land of the basin. Bau is an administrative centre and trading post. (Based on Sudan Government air photographs, February 1955).

process is now taking place and new settlements are being established near the hillfoot. The clays themselves are avoided because they become a sticky quagmire during the rainy season, difficult for both people and animals. This movement began during the thirties as the Ingessana gained confidence in the revised conditions of the plains where the movements of the nomads have been brought under government control. On old maps the settlements of Rumeilik, Lakluk and Fufi are indicated as having hilltop sites. Now Rumeilik and Lakluk are to be found beside the track running near the foot of the western hills, while Fufi has disappeared. Soda illustrates a progressive approach towards the plains. Originally the settlement was to be found on the slopes of the Tabi Hills. The Condominium authorities established an administrative post here, which was removed to Bau in 1922. This established confidence in the people from an early date and the present hillfoot site of Soda was chosen. The settlement began to split up as new offshoots were established even better situated for cultivating the plains, such as Soda Gedid and Myful on the southern side of Jebel Kurba, so that by 1952 the hillfoot Soda was itself almost deserted. Other large settlements which have completed their move to the hillfoot include Jegu (1945) and Gebannit (1950), both on the north side of the hills.

These movements towards the plains have misled many observers into believing that the Ingessana are forever moving their settlements. This is far from true; many of the hilltop sites had been occupied continuously for very many years. The Ingessana do move the position of the homestead when the father of the family dies, but this has in the past meant a movement of only a few yards. In recent years it has been the signal for the family to move nearer to the plains. One result is that settlement names are frequently applied today to a whole hillside rather than to a single collection of homesteads. At Jebel Feri, for example, three hamlets are included within the one settlement; the old one on the hilltop, a second one near the perennial stream in the valley, and a third one near the hillfoot track to Soda.

The Ingessana farmland normally falls into three distinct portions: around the huts themselves; on the nearby hill slopes; and out on the clay plains (Fig. 3). The immediate vicinity of the hills is rarely cultivated because the soil is usually stony and the area provides useful grazing lands within reach of the homesteads, so that crops grown here would be susceptible to damage by straying animals. Before stable and peaceful conditions prevailed on the plains the Ingessana cultivator could not be sure of harvesting the crops he planted there, so that he was forced to develop the hillsides to provide his needs. This implied the construction of terraces to preserve the soil from erosion and to make the most of the rain falling on the hills. As conditions became settled so the Ingessana have been able to rely less on the hillsides and more on the plains so that today, apart from some of the more remote portions of the basins, the clay plain farm is the most important part of the cultivated land. Terrace cultivation is declining and abandoned terraces can be seen in many parts. Yet there is a very wide range of variation. In the case of the hilltop hamlet of Jebel Feri, where the clay plain farms are more than two and a half hour's walk away, the terrace and homestead cultivation are still of considerable significance. At the other extreme are Bobok and the new offshoots of Soda, from where the plains farm is no more than half an hour's walk away. Here there is hardly a terrace to be seen. However, the size of the clay plain farm does not depend solely on the distance from the homestead. Bride-service on the part of the prospective husband's family is required to supplement the work of the family. The Ingessana have no land measurements and it is therefore almost impossible to say how much land an average family might cultivate on the clays, but it is unlikely to exceed five acres, for the clays yield well and, because of their heaviness, are not easy to cultivate.

The rainfall of the Ingessana area falls during the six months from May to October. It is not only quite high but also relatively reliable. The annual total can be relied upon to fall within the range of 800 to 1000 mms. more often than not. Furthermore it is always warm and during the months preceding the rains can be unpleasantly hot. August at the height of the rainy season has the lowest monthly mean (30° C) and April, just before the rains begin, the highest (32° C). During the dry season (November to end of April) the diurnal temperature ranges are much greater than during the rains so that day temperatures of over 40° C can be expected for four months of the year, while during occasional cold spells in January the night temperature may fall to below 15° C. Under these conditions it is availability of moisture in the soil rather than temperature that restricts plant growth, and a wide variety of quick growing tropical crops can be cultivated. The most important ones to the Ingessana are various varieties of dura (or Great Millet (Sorghum vulgare)), sesame, spices, cotton, gourds, vegetables, maize and tobacco. Furthermore, famine due to the failure of the rains is rare. Some of these crops are more suited to plains cultivation, and some are better cultivated close to the household. For this reason homestead and/or terrace cultivation is never completely abandoned, so that each play a necessary role in the Ingessana economy.

The exact form of the homestead varies somewhat from one part of the Ingessana country to another, but commonly each hut or group of huts belonging to one family (in the limited sense of mother, father and unmarried children) is enclosed by a thorn or rough wooden fence. Besides the living huts there is very often a *suweiba* (conical hut raised slightly off the ground in which grain is stored), a guest house and tiny huts

for pigs and chickens. The rest of the enclosure is often about a third of an acre. The most important crops grown here are quick maturing dura, maize, gourds and some sesame. The dura is usually sown in May-June and harvested in August-September. It is of vital importance as it brings to an end the reliance on the previous harvest, and very often the last month or so before it ripens has been a rather lean time for the cultivator and his family. The sweet gourds are grown for eating and the sour for household utensils. These enclosures are cultivated year after year and it is the tethering of animals within them which appears to account for their continued fertility. Several of these enclosures are frequently found linked together forming an extended family group. When the homesteads are upon hillsides the terrace cultivation, also frequently enclosed, is close by. Here the same crops are sown together with such additions as tobacco for snuff, chillies, and various spices. When however there are no terraces then these crops are to be found in the homestead enclosure. The selection of crops grown both within the homestead and on the nearby terraces is of great interest. The cultivation in both cases is largely the responsibility of the womenfolk who are also responsible for preparing the food, hence the concentration on the early crops and on items to improve the flavour of the diet and on gourds for household utensils. However other factors also play a part. The Ingessana believe that chillies and other spices will not be so effective in flavouring food unless picked at dawn. Chillies too are always grown by them in the shade. Again the tobacco, chillies and some other spices require good drainage. It is interesting to note here that Gebannit used to have a high reputation as a chilli producing settlement, but its production has considerably declined since the homesteads descended towards the plain and the terraces became abandoned.

The clay plains farm also provides evidence for this theme of transition in the method of cultivation. At first the Ingessana began to cultivate the plain continuously with the same crop until the land was exhausted and had to be abandoned (Fig. 4). Though the plains are flat this has led to a certain amount of soil erosion, especially near some of the major watercourses, and has also caused some Ingessana to have to go further out on the plains to find suitable land. The Government agricultural inspectors have tried to persuade the Ingessana to adopt a rotation system. They attempted to introduce an arrangement of dura, sesame, dura, followed by two years fallow. Though the Ingessana have refused to take much notice, they are an intelligent people and seem to have realized that some form of land management is required. In recent years they have introduced some simple systems of their own, which vary considerably from place to place in respect of the relative importance of the two chief crops grown, dura and sesame. A piece of land is brought under cultivation by the *hariq* method. Under this the grass is burnt off at the beginning of the rainy season as soon as the new shoots have sprouted, so that old and new season grass is thus destroyed at once and weeds are minimized. Each man's clay plain farm is divided up into several parts, usually one for each year's *hariq*. Single crops are rarely planted, some sort of intercropping being universal. Hyacinth bean, for example, can be found in almost every field. However, one crop is usually dominant. This is clearly illustrated by the system at Jegu.

1st year.
Tilngak mixed with *look*.

Tilngak is a variety of dura with a white grain. Sown in August on *hariq* and harvested in February. *Look* is a black variety of sesame grown for use in the social life of the community on special occasions such as marriages. It is not sold.

2nd and 3rd years.
Sesame and *kourgi*

Kourgi is a heavy yielding "head-hanging" variety of dura. Sown in June and harvested in February. Sesame for sale is sown before rains in April and harvested in September or October.

3rd and 4th years.
Kourgi mixed with *bedelik*.

The *bedelik* variety of dura is sown in June and harvested in October. Medium white grain.

Leave fallow for the next five years.

The relative importance of sesame and dura in the rotation system [3] adopted gives a general indication of the degree to which peaceful commerce has penetrated the area. Broadly, the remote areas give less consideration to sesame and more to the subsistence crop, dura. Conversely the more accessible areas, particularly where traders have established themselves, give more consideration to the growing of sesame for cash. At Jegu sesame for sale occurs only once in the rotation. By comparison Kukur, with a number of Arab traders, has the first and fourth years of the rotation mainly given over to sesame. At the other extreme lies Fadamiya, a rather remote village in the eastern part of the mountains, where sesame is not always included anywhere in the rotation, but when grown it usually appears in the third year, which at Fadamiya is the last year before leaving the ground fallow for three years.

A cash economy was first introduced into the Ingessana Hills by the advent of the

[3] To the extent that the Ingessana do not understand "crop rotation" as a concept then the word "rotation" is a little misleading. Perhaps "pseudorotation" is better; it is used by de Schlippe and Batwell to describe a somewhat analagous situation in Sudan (de Schlippe and Batwell, 1955).

motor lorry from about 1935 onwards. The chief articles exported today are, in order of importance, sesame, dura, *talh* gum, together with a few ground nuts grown on sandy patches and some *wekr*.[4] *Talh* is the second-grade gum produced by the red-barked Acacia seyal. Unlike the high grade Acacia senegal, the true gum arabic tree, the bark does not require cutting, and the gum simply oozes out and is picked off the tree. There is an especially important area of gum "gardens" to be found to the north and west of the Ingessana Hills. Gum gathering is an occupation carried on during the closed agricultural season. There are three main Ingessana harvests. In September/October both the homestead and terrace dura is harvested. A harvest festival to celebrate this is held in October for the adults and lasts for two to three days. A second one is held, for the children, only in November. From the clay plains farm there are two harvests, the first in October and the second in February. These two are celebrated by an event lasting about seven days in December which is the highlight of the year with much feasting and drinking. Most of the gathering of *talh* takes place in January, March and May. January is the month between the first and second harvests on the clay plains farm; March lies between the February harvest and the April marriage season; whilst May is the month before preparations are required for the new agricultural year.

The Ingessana are not only agriculturalists but also enthusiastic pastoralists. Cattle and goats are of greatest significance though pigs, a few sheep, donkeys and even camels are owned by the Ingessana peoples. All families have one cow and most seem to have at least ten goats. The goat has considerable advantages over the sheep, being easier to keep and costing less in taxes. Most of the camels are owned by Ingessana

living on the north and east sides of the hills where there has been greatest contact with the camel owning Arab nomads. The settled conditions of the plains have allowed the Ingessana to own more animals than was possible in the past, for then the plains grazing was not at their disposal and cattle and goats were likely to be driven off by the slave raiding marauders as part of their booty.

Animals play a most important part in the Ingessana community. A bride price payable in animals is usually required from the prospective husband's family as well as bride service. For these purposes a reasonable sized cow is considered equivalent to fifteen goats. The cattle and goats also provide milk. Domestic animals are rarely killed for meat except for certain festivals when a wealthy man would be expected to provide an ox and the less wealthy a goat. Animals are also sometimes killed or sold to strangers to help pay for weeding or for tribute money. Most of the work on the clay plains farm is the responsibility of the family, though weeding is an exception. Occasionally, however, some of the more wealthy will employ people to help with sowing or even harvesting. This is usually paid for by providing large quantities of native beer brewed from dura, though sometimes meat may also be provided.

During the rainy season the animals are grazed on the hill slopes away from the sticky clays of the plain. At night the animals are herded into thorn enclosures to protect them from wild animals, and fires are lit to keep the biting insects at bay. At this season the goats are often herded within the homestead enclosure and herein lies the clue to the continued fertility of the homestead land. During the dry season the goats are still kept in enclosures at night but the cattle are allowed greater freedom as most of the wild animals likely to attack them have migrated to the south.

Most of the cattle and some of the goats are taken away from the hills during the dry season so as to reduce the pressure on

<hr />

[4] Dried lady's fingers. Rarely cultivated by the Ingessana who rely on its occurrence in the wild state.

the local supplies of water and grazing. The movement outwards from the hills begins in December or January. On the west the herds move towards Khor Dolieb and Khor el Bukhas; to the east they converge on Khor Uffat (Fig. 1). By February and March the herds have moved beyond, to the northern fringes of the Machare Marshes in the south and to the Blue Nile-Ethiopian border region between Khor Uffat and Qeissan. In bad years the Ingessana herdsmen find it necessary to leave the hills earlier. The year 1957 had a poor rainy season so that by the following January the first Ingessana herdsmen had already reached the Qeissan area. As a result of a series of dry years between 1940 and 1945 the Machare Marshes shrank considerably in size and Ingessana herdsmen made their appearance on the River Sobat. Many families have only a few cattle and herding is often done on a communal basis.

On their journeys with their animals the Ingessana come into contact with the Arab nomads, especially the Rufa'a el Hoi. These two groups can often be seen grazing their animals together and watering them at the same hole. This spirit of cooperation is a far cry from the old animosities and is a change made possible by Government control of nomadic movement so that the Arabs' animals no longer destroy the Ingessana people's crops. Another example of this new-found spirit of cooperation concerns the movement of camels. In contrast with the cattle the camels spend the dry season at home with their owners but are sent off northwards with the Arabs during the rainy season.

The Ingessana peoples engage in a number of handicrafts during the closed agricultural season. These include rope making from the bark of the *tebeldi* (Adansonia digitata), mat-making using leaves from the Palmyra and Fan palm trees, cotton cloth making, pottery and iron work. There is considerable specialization among the villages so that one makes mats but does not make cloth, or makes rope but not mats,

etc. Generally speaking, however, the major centres of handicraft production are Soda, Bau and Kukur. Cotton spinning and weaving is probably the most widespread of the crafts. The cotton is grown on its own special piece of *hariq* land. It is spun into thread by the womenfolk, while the men do the weaving. The chief centre for iron work and pottery making is Soda where spears and swords are made with their traditional patterns and styles. All these crafts are tending to decline to some extent. Cloth from Egypt or the Far East has made its appearance together with pots and pans of aluminum made near Khartoum and also with knives and axes imported from abroad.

The Ingessana peoples are thus in the process of adjustment and transition made necessary by the establishment of peaceful conditions within their area. Under discussion at the moment are three new projects which may seriously affect the area and may force on the Ingessana peoples a further agonizing period of re-adjustment. To the north-east of the hills there are projects for the expansion of mechanized agriculture and for the expansion of irrigation in the form of a 1.2 million acre irrigation scheme based on the Roseires Dam which is at present under construction. Furthermore there is a suggestion for the extension of the railway from Roseires west across the clay plains towards Malakal (Fig. 1). This new line would pass fairly close to the south side of the Ingessana Hills area. These new projects are bound to bring the Ingessana into much closer contact with a cash economy than they have been hitherto. Some may be drawn into these new projects as labourers or in the case of the agricultural projects may be gathered in as tenants. It seems that it will be increasingly difficult for the Ingessana to maintain their old way of life and the tribal distinctiveness which is theirs today. So far, civilizing influences have enabled the Ingessana to make a fuller use of their environment and to engage to a limited extent in commerce. In the future it may well be that the insidious pressures generated by modern technological civilization may succeed in bringing to an end the tribal distinctiveness of the Ingessana where the cruder brute force of the past failed.

REFERENCES

Cailliaud, F. 1826–7. *Voyage à Méroé* etc. . . . (4 vols.). Paris. See vol. 2, chaps. 37–9 and vol. 3, chaps. 40–3 for the experiences of the first expedition of Mohammed Ali's troops, south-west from Sennar.

Davies, H. R. J. 1960. Some tribes of the Ethiopian borderland between the Blue Nile and Sobat rivers. *Sudan Notes* 41: 21–34.

Evans-Pritchard, E. E. 1927. A preliminary account of the Ingessana. *Sudan Notes* 10: 69–83. 1932 Ethnological observations in Darfung. *Sudan Notes* 15: 1–61.

Gleichen, Count. 1905. *The Anglo-Egyptian Sudan: a compendium prepared by officers of the Sudan Government.* Vol. 1: p. 22.

Grottanelli, V. L. 1948. I Pre-Niloti: un'arcaica provincia culturale in Africa. *Ann. lateran.* 12: 282–386.

Kabesh, M. L. 1961. The geology and economic minerals and rocks of the Ingessana Hills. *Geol. Surv. Bull., Khartm.* No. 11.

Murdock, G. P. 1959. *Africa: its peoples and their culture history,* New York, McGraw Hill, p. 172, where it is stated that the Ingessana language is the sole representative of a distinct branch of the eastern Sudanese language sub-family.

Robertson, J. W. 1934. Further notes on the Ingessana tribe. *Sudan Notes* 17: 118–24.

Schlippe, P. de, and B. L. Batwell 1955. A preliminary study of the Nyangwara system of agriculture. *Africa* 25: 321–51.

Seligman, C. G. and B. Z. 1932. *Pagan tribes of the Nilotic Sudan.* Ethnology of Africa series, Routledge and Kegan Paul. Chap. 12: Darfung.

Verri, S. 1955. Il linguaggio degli Ingessana nell'Africa Orientale. *Anthropos.* 50: 282–318.

There is little indigenous irrigated agriculture in Africa south of the Sahara. Areas with insufficient rainfall for cultivation are extensive, but only a few groups, such as the Sonjo in Tanzania, have established economies based on irrigation (Gray, 1963). Also irrigated by indigenous systems are small areas in the zone of low rainfall in West Africa, but their contribution to total production is small, and their potential is limited (Prothero, 1962).

Traditionally, Africa's main areas of irrigation were located in the North, associated in particular with the great hydraulic civilizations in lower Egypt. These areas of gross rainfall deficiency depended on the waters of the Nile basin, which derive from the high rainfall areas and natural lake storage of East Africa and Ethiopia (Lebon, 1960). Within the past century, the sources of the Nile have been progressively harnessed to increase the amount and availability of water in dry areas, with the recently completed Aswan High Dam in Egypt the major project (Frood, 1967).

The use of water in Egypt and in the Sudan is governed by international agreement and is controlled by coordinated works (Barbour, 1961). In the Sudan, a consortium of government, public, and other interests control the vast Gezira scheme, which is irrigated by gravity flow from the Sennar dam on the Blue Nile (Barbour, 1961; Hance, 1968). But as the following paper indicates, important though small developments have taken place in areas farther south. Water pumped from the Blue and White Niles supply these schemes, which are significant as products of private enterprise and stand in direct contrast with interests involved in the Sudan Gezira. Yet both methods of organization have been successful, and they demonstrate the possibilities for changing the relationships between people and land through the exploitation of resources in an unfavorable environment. Transformation is manifest not only in the number of people supported but also in the major contribution that large-scale schemes have made to the Sudanese economy.

Success has not been achieved without problems, some of which must be solved in the future (McLoughlin, 1962; Davies, 1964b). But the difficulties are minor compared with those that bedevil the development of irrigation in other parts of tropical Africa, particularly in West Africa (Church, 1961). Nothing comparable to the Sudan Gezira has been achieved on the Niger (Mali) or on the Senegal, and prospects are still unknown for the success of schemes recently underway or planned for the Volta (Steel, 1968), the Niger in Nigeria (Ledger, 1963), the Zambesi, the Limpopo (Pollock, 1968), and various rivers in Tanzania. Major schemes for European-controlled irrigated agriculture are also being undertaken in South Africa (Fair and Shaffer, 1964).

10. *Irrigation in the Sudan: Its Growth, Distribution and Potential Extension*

K. M. BARBOUR

Probably the most durable and significant results of the period of British administration in the Sudan (1898–1955) were the development of the limited railway network in the early years and the inauguration of a modern system of irrigation from the Nile. The greatest single irrigation work was the Gezira scheme, established in 1925 and now covering an area of about 1500 square miles; yet irrigation was not a wholly governmental affair, for from the earliest days of British rule private capital played an important part in setting up irrigation schemes and discovering the best crops to grow in them.

At the present time there is a total of

From *Transactions*, Institute of British Geographers, *26*, 1959, pp. 243–263. Reprinted by permission.

about 2.4 million feddans of land commanded by pump or gravity irrigation schemes in the Sudan (the unit of area employed in all official statistics concerning Egypt and the Sudan is the feddan, which equals 1.038 acres). Of this total the Gezira and other Government-run schemes within the Basin (including the Manaqil extension) account for 1.3 million feddans, and private schemes on the banks of the Nile total more than 1 million feddans; the balance is made up of one minor and two major schemes of flush irrigation, where the area irrigated varies considerably from year to year.

It is not intended to discuss the Gezira scheme or the areas of flush irrigation, for being under Government control these present few problems of growth or location that are not dealt with in official publications.[1] Attention will be devoted to the nature and distribution of the pump schemes, whose development has attracted less publicity.[2] An outline will then be given of various schemes at present under consideration for the extension of irrigated agriculture of all kinds in the country. It is the very large area available for such expansion that makes the Sudanese so determined to obtain Egyptian recognition of their rightful claim to a larger share of the Nile waters in the future.[3]

The importance of irrigation to the Sudan can hardly be questioned, if the country is ever to rise from its present poverty, with a chiefly subsistence economy based on uncertain tropical rains, to a more satisfactory and secure financial position. Stretching from latitude 4° North in the south almost to the tropic of Cancer in the north, the Sudan is a desert or a semi-arid country with a restricted rainy season, and so the need for irrigation springs primarily from the inadequacy and unreliability of the rains. North of Khartoum, unirrigated agriculture is virtually impossible, and in the central Sudan the fertile clay plains, at least in the part north of Singa and Kosti where most of the population now lives,

receive annual totals of 600 millimetres of precipitation or less. Such conditions are barely adequate for the cultivation of drought-resisting crops like millet (*Sorghum vulgare*), "bamia" (*Hibiscus esculentus*) or sesame (*Sesamum indicum*), and are quite unsuited to more valuable cash crops, particularly cotton (Fig. 1). Even in the southern provinces, with rainfall totals of 1000 millimetres or more, irrigation could afford a useful supplement to rain cultivation, but this is not yet a live issue.

In the central and northern Sudan irrigation is fairly easy to establish, and once established is very profitable. The areas where modern works have been set up consist either of alluvial terraces beside the main Nile, essentially similar in origin to the cultivated lands of upper Egypt, or else of the central plain of the Sudan, with its dark, heavy, cracking clay soil. In the arid climate prevailing, these soils appear to retain their fertility well, and to be capable of prolonged cultivation, provided that suitable crop rotations are adopted with ample fallow periods.[4] In compensation for the high water losses experienced through evaporation and transpiration, the clays are remarkably impermeable when wetted, and so losses through percolation are slight.

Yet these favourable conditions alone would not have sufficed to account for the striking increase of irrigated cultivation that has taken place in the country, particularly in the last twelve years, were it not for the absence of many alternative lines of equally profitable investment. In fact the Sudan lacks extensive workable minerals or other obvious opportunities of industrial development, and so the demand for licenses to establish pump schemes has come not merely from the inhabitants of the areas concerned, who have hitherto enjoyed grazing and cultivation rights on a tribal basis, but rather from the more educated and enlightened of the townspeople such as merchants, professional men and retired Government officials.

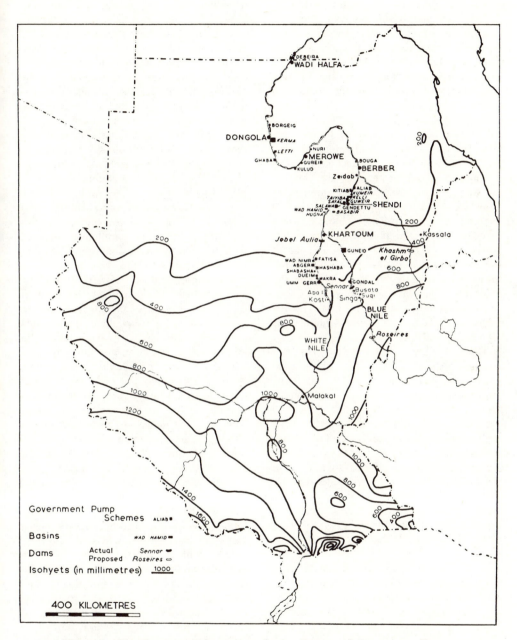

Figure 1.—Location map with certain isohyets. Basins and Government Pump Schemes, with symbols approximately indicating their relative sizes, are taken from *Sudan irrigation* (1957), 13 .

The participation of private capital in irrigation schemes in the country is accepted as a normal arrangement, and tradition lays down the share of the crop appropriate to those who have contributed to produce it. The precise shares may vary, but in general it is recognized that the man who provides the water and the land should receive 50 or 60 per cent of the crop. This was taken as the basis of the original allocation of the proceeds of cotton-growing in the Gezira, when it was decided that the tenants should get 40 per cent, the Government 40 per cent and the managing company 20 per cent, and a similar system is adopted on the private cotton-growing schemes, where the pump-owner takes 50 per cent of the profits on cotton and shares the rest between his tenants, each being rewarded according to the yield on the fields for which he is responsible. When additional crops, millet or "lubia" beans (*Dolichos lablab*), are grown, the tenants take 100 per cent.

The suitability of such systems of share cropping depends on the value of the crop produced. Where it is too low, peasants are disinclined to come forward as tenants, though they may be forced to do so by economic circumstances; but where it is high, both tenants and capitalists are pleased, and there is steady pressure to increase the area under cultivation. In the Sudan cotton has until quite recently proved very successful, and the arrangement has worked well: the Government has made a handsome profit on the estimated £20,000,000 that it invested in the Gezira, and this and other irrigation schemes have gone to swell the state revenues, while private scheme owners have received their money back so quickly that the normal period for the repayment of loans to set up pump schemes has been three years.

In consequence the Government of the Sudan has commissioned several investigations into the possibilities of further irrigation. The results of these investigations have been most promising, and have confirmed that there is still a large additional area in the Northern Province capable of being irrigated; that within the clay plain stretching from Khartoum to the Ethiopian border there are nearly two million feddans of bush suitable for the setting up of irrigation schemes; and that a large scheme can be set up beside the Atbara river.

Work is going ahead rapidly to convert these potentialities into actual schemes, and 200,000 feddans in the Manaqil extension of the Gezira were brought into use in July 1958.[5] Even more rapid extension might be expected if more capital were available, for the Sudanese are not allowing development to be completely held up pending a revision of the Anglo-Egyptian Nile Waters Agreement.

That agreement was signed in 1929, at a time when the demand for irrigation in the Sudan was very much less than it is today, and there is no doubt that a new agreement will have to be signed if the High Dam at Aswan or any other new conservation works are undertaken on the Nile. When this happens the Sudanese will certainly insist on more water for themselves, particularly in the first half of the year, when water is scarce. In the meantime, the effect of the agreement is that all water used in the Sudan between January 1st and July 1st each year has to be debited against the Sudan Water Account, i.e. the amount stored in the Sennar Dam (plus a small amount allowed from that stored in the Jebel Aulia Dam), and the schemes now in operation consume the whole of the water credit available. Temporarily, therefore, the issue of licenses to pump water during the first half of the year has almost come to an end, and the Manaqil extension has had to depend on economies in the use of water in the existing Gezira scheme to make water available for a rather reduced cultivation period.[6]

The story of the growth of irrigation in the Sudan, and of its value to the country, may be studied from several angles. First, there are accounts and statistics in official publications, including *Agriculture in the Sudan,* departmental bulletins on the Gash Delta,[7] the White Nile schemes,[8] pump irrigation,[9] and Sudan irrigation in general.[10] These may be supplemented from the annual reports of the Gezira and Gash Boards, the White Nile Schemes Board (this deals only with the governmental schemes along the White Nile), and the Ministry of Irrigation and Hydro-Electric Power.[11]

Secondly, in order to obtain a more detailed picture of pump irrigation in particular, use may be made of the register kept by the former Department of Irrigation, now the Ministry of Irrigation and Hydro-Electric Power, wherein details are recorded of every pump in the Nile Basin that draws water for irrigation. Other pumps, for instance those supplying drinking water in the riverain towns, or those in the irrigated land near Kassala, are not included, since the water they consume is not debited to the Sudan's Water Account. The pumps register allots a sheet to each pump, and records its location (by latitude, river and bank), the name of the licensee, the type of license (i.e. whether pumping is permitted at all seasons or for a limited period only),[12] the size of the pump intake, the date at which pumping was permitted to begin, and the approximate total area commanded. Read in conjunction with the Water Account Book, wherein the volume of water drawn into the Gezira main canal is recorded, the register gives a complete picture of the distribution of modern, though not of traditional, irrigation throughout the Nile Basin in the Sudan. Since it includes the names of the license-holders, moreover, it might form the basis of some interesting research into the way in which the leading families and politicians of the country, of whatever party, have been securing for themselves dependable sources of income that are immune from the results of elections or *coups d'état*. In fact since the summer of 1957 it has become much

more difficult to obtain permission to consult the register, but this is thought to be the result of a scandal in the Ministry over another matter.

The page in the pumps register is nominally inserted at the time when the work of setting up the pump scheme is completed and before pumping begins. In fact the register is usually rather behind-hand with the latest schemes, and so in compiling the graphs and maps that accompany this article use has also been made of the minutes of the Pump License Allocation Committee, known officially as the Advisory Committee of the Nile Pumps Control Board, which grants the licenses that enable capitalists to proceed with the work of setting up schemes. The latest meetings for which information is available are those of July 3rd, 1957, and November 11th, 1957; it is likely that most of the schemes approved at the earlier meeting were in operation by the time that irrigation started in August or September 1958. Experience has shown that less than 5 per cent of licenses issued are subsequently cancelled, for if by any mischance one man fails to find the necessary capital or changes his mind, he can always dispose of his license very easily rather than allow it to lapse. To have omitted the schemes that have not yet reached the register would have been to disregard the very striking increase in the rate of establishment of pump schemes on restricted license that has been a feature of the last three years.

Before 1950 the procedure for keeping the pumps register was less precise than it is today, and the records of earlier pumps record the locations but not the dates of inauguration. Government pump schemes are adequately dated and documented in *Agriculture in the Sudan* and *Sudan irrigation,* but the only way to obtain figures for the growth of private pump irrigation has been by inference from the volume of water debited to the annual Water Account, with occasional rays of light thrown by the publications just named. This accounts for the measure of uncertainty to be seen in Figure 2 in the curve representing the growth of private pump schemes. Fortunately, the recent and most rapid growth has been ascertainable from the annual reports of the Ministry of Irrigation and Hydro-Electric Power, and from private communications.

There is no way of gauging the growing importance of irrigation from investigating the areas or totals of different crops produced in various parts of the country, since reliable statistics of production are not kept. For long staple (Sakel) cotton, however, which is grown in the pump schemes of the Blue and White Niles as well as in the Gezira scheme, statistics of areas and yields can be obtained from the Foreign Trade Report, with some Internal Statistics, which is published monthly and annually by the Government of Sudan (Fig. 3). This clearly shows how pump scheme cotton production, which was negligible before the Sec-

ond World War in comparison with the Gezira crop, has in the last few years come to be of almost equal importance. The deltas of the east also grow Sakel, but their yields, always much less than those of the perennially irrigated areas, are extremely variable, and they are of relatively little importance.

These statistical investigations may be supplemented by a geographical analysis of how irrigation has affected the visible landscape of the Sudan. On a large scale the contrast between irrigated lands on the one hand, and desert or unirrigated fields on the other, is most striking. On a small-scale map, however, only the great Gezira scheme can be fairly represented. The areas of almost all the pump schemes are relatively insignificant, and indeed for many of them details of their lay-out have never been incorporated in the Sudan's topographical maps. Similarly, the villages of cultivators belonging to the irrigation schemes are

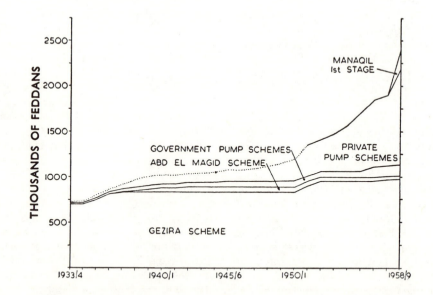

Figure 2.—The growth of the irrigated area in the Sudan, 1933–59. This graph pays no heed to traditional methods of irrigation, which have remained fairly constant, nor to the Gash and Tokar deltas, where the area irrigated varies widely from year to year according to the flood. Totals for private pumps are conjectural before 1951, except for 1933 and 1944.

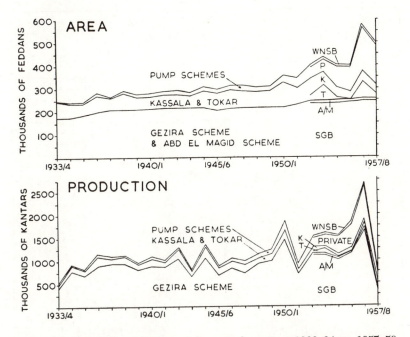

Figure 3.—Area and production of long-staple cotton, 1933–34 to 1957–58. In 1951 the administration of the Gezira scheme was taken over from the Sudan Plantations Syndicate by Governmental Sudan Gezira Board. W.N.S.B. stands for the White Nile Schemes Board which runs the Government Pump Schemes along the White Nile. One kantar of ginned cotton = 100 *rotls* = 99.05 lb.

often not mapped, nor have there been roads, railways or even telegraph lines established to serve them that might give an impression of their growing wealth.

Certain inferences concerning the results of irrigation in the Sudan may be drawn from a study of the map of the distribution of the population as revealed by the 1955–56 census. This approach unfortunately gives no opportunity for comparison with the distribution at an earlier date, since only one census has been taken in the Sudan, while of the other two population maps that have been drawn of the country the former gives a rough picture only, while the latter was produced too recently to differ significantly.[13]

GRAVITY IRRIGATION AND PUMPING SCHEMES

When a map is drawn to show the distribution of irrigation throughout the country (Fig. 4), the contrast is made apparent not only between different systems of irrigation but also between the information available concerning them. For the great Gezira scheme the limits of the canalization can readily be shown, and can be taken with complete accuracy from the 1:250,000 sheets published for the northern and southern Gezira. For the pumping schemes, on the other hand, even the original large-scale maps that should by statute be deposited when a license is issued are in many in-

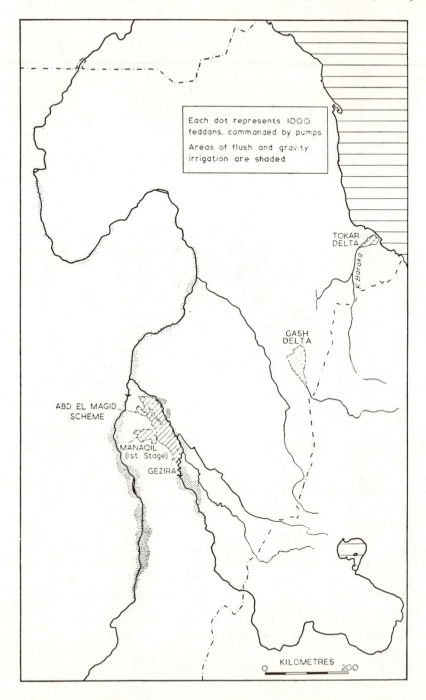

Figure 4.—The distribution of gravity irrigation and pump schemes, 1958.

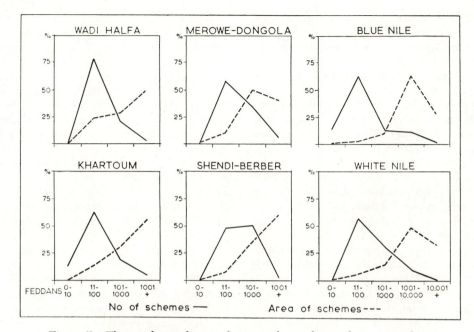

Figure 5.—The number and area of pump schemes by reaches, arranged according to size-groups. The number and area in each size-group have been expressed as percentages of the total in each reach.

stances not available, just because the surveyors needed to prepare them cannot be found.[14] If such maps had been prepared, moreover, it would not be possible to show the limits even of schemes of 100 feddans or more, when working on a scale of 1:2,000,000, as was used by the writer in the map accompanying the pamphlet referred to in footnote 2. At any smaller scale the use of some conventional representation becomes inevitable. Similarly, there is no means of representing every scheme separately, since these vary in size from 10 feddans or even less to a maximum of more than 30,000 feddans. The map printed here shows instead the area commanded by pumps, each dot having a value of 1000 feddans, which may represent a part of a large scheme or a number of small ones grouped together. To indicate the differences between the typical sizes of schemes in the different reaches of the Nile,

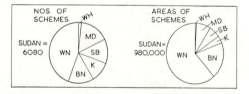

Figure 6.—Relative numbers and total areas of schemes by reaches. These graphs stress the fact that both in number and area the "new" irrigation areas beside the Blue and White Niles quite over-shadow the traditional reaches beside the Main Nile.

Figures 5 and 6 have been drawn to show the percentage, by number and area, of schemes within selected sizes in each reach, and the relative importance of the reaches, both numerically and areally.

Taken together the map and diagrams pose a number of problems, to which it will be attempted to provide answers in the following pages. First, how can the contrasts between the different methods of irrigation adopted in various parts of the country be explained? Secondly, why has irrigation more nearly occupied all the country suitable to it in one part of the country than in another? Thirdly, why do the average sizes of schemes differ, as is particularly noticeable between Khartoum Province and the lands along the White Nile?

The solution to the first problem is primarily physical. There is an immediate contrast between two major zones, the riverine below Khartoum and the clay plain of the central Sudan. In the former area the Nile is incised into a rocky or stony desert, and the only pieces of land suitable for irrigation are the alluvial terraces beside the river. These are not continuous, as is the case in middle Egypt, since the Nile crosses several distinct geological formations. Where its path lies across the sandstones of the Nubian Series the banks are fairly open, and the terraces have a mean width of about two kilometres, but where it traverses the igneous rocks of the Basement Complex the alluvial terraces are scarce and discontinuous, and there can be very little cultivation. South of Khartoum, on the other hand, most of the clay plain is suitable for irrigation if water can be brought to it, but a significant contrast is afforded by the fact that while the Blue Nile is deeply incised, the White Nile occupies a broad shallow depression with few marked banks on either side (Fig. 7).

North of Khartoum there is a number of alluvial basins beside the Nile which receive natural flooding when the level of the river is at its highest; these are gradually being converted to perennial pump irrigation, which is at once more profitable and more secure. Traditional systems of irrigation are also in operation, employing simple lifting devices, either the *saqia* (the ox-turned water-wheel) or the *shaduf* (the hand-operated lever). These are today being replaced or supplemented by diesel-driven pumps, but the area available in one block of land is rarely more than a few thousand feddans. There has, therefore, been no question of undertaking the great expense of constructing barrages across the river to command canals, as is the practice in Egypt. On the contrary, the private ownership of land has been a bar to co-operation, and many pumps might well have commanded larger areas had not obstructive individuals refused to participate in the new schemes. The area under pumps would be very much less than it actually is had not the greater lifting power of the diesel pump made it possible to incorporate many tracts of land hitherto too high to be irrigated by primitive means.

South of Khartoum a large proportion of the plain between the Blue and White Niles is suitable for irrigation, and the most economical way to bring water to large tracts of it would be to construct a number of barrages along the Blue Nile, each commanding a system of canals to carry water down the general tilt of the plain towards the White Nile. This is what the existing Sennar Dam and Gezira canalization do, and what the projected Roseires Dam is intended to do in the future. Such works, however, are extremely expensive to construct and take a long time to pay for themselves; they afford, moreover, few opportunities for private investment, and they bring their chief benefits to the state and to the individuals who are fortunate enough to be awarded tenancies upon them.

Since the Second World War, when the cultivation of cotton, the crop best suited to the physical conditions of the central Sudan, has been particularly profitable, the Government of the Sudan has been fairly fully occupied in carrying out developments over a wide range of fields. It has, therefore, been fortunate that private capitalists have come forward to invest sums in irrigation, since these have brought a great deal of wealth to the country. For the man with £5000 to £50,000 or more to invest, a pump scheme has afforded a safe and extremely profitable venture that does not

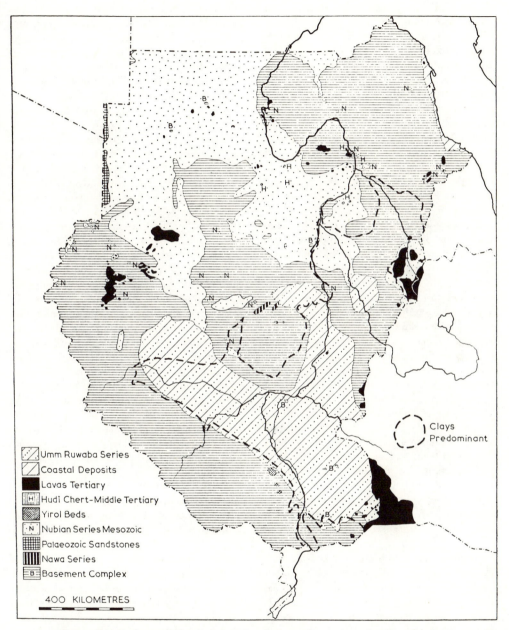

Umm Ruwaba Series
Coastal Deposits
Lavas Tertiary
Hudi Chert-Middle Tertiary
Yirol Beds
Nubian Series Mesozoic
Palaeozoic Sandstones
Nawa Series
Basement Complex

400 KILOMETRES

Figure 7.—Geology of the Sudan. The deep cracking clay which masks the solid geology south and east of Khartoum is generally well suited to irrigation.

involve too great a delay, the capital laid out being normally regained within three or four years, and sometimes even more quickly. While it might be argued that once the great profitability of cotton growing had been established, the state should have imposed very stiff licence fees to secure to itself some portion of the element of increased land value involved in the setting up of a pump scheme, this has not occurred. The licence-holders pay the normal rate of business profits tax appropriate to all kinds of commercial enterprise; their licences are normally of a nominal ten years' duration, but in fact when these lapse they are renewed as a matter of course.

The physical conditions favourable to the setting up of a pumping station are discussed in the Ministry of Irrigation's pamphlet; [2] they include such topics as proximity to the river channel, the ease of construction of the main canal to the fields, and the lift required at low Nile. The latter point has an important effect on running expenses, since one of the major recurrent charges to the scheme owner is the cost of fuel to raise water. In this connection considerable benefit has been obtained from the presence of the Sennar and Jebel Aulia Dams; these make pumping much easier for the schemes that lie upstream of them, since they keep up the levels of the Blue and White Niles during most of the season (September-March) when water is required for irrigation. The level in the Sennar Reservoir (whose effect is appreciable for 80 kilometres upstream of the dam) is that required to command the Gezira canalization, and naturally lasts throughout the cotton-growing season; that in the Jebel Aulia Reservoir is controlled by the manner of operation of the dam for the benefit of irrigation in Egypt, and is therefore less assured, but in practice it usually lasts until some date in February, and certainly assists pump owners as far upstream as Kosti.

A second major contrast between areas north and south of Khartoum is that the irrigable areas beside the main Nile, like those in Egypt which they in many ways resemble, are long-settled and over-populated. The Gezira, on the other hand, may be looked on as merely the least underpopulated portion of the great clay plain that stretches from Khartoum to Juba, one of the largest areas of fertile soil in the whole continent of Africa that have yet to be effectively settled and brought into cultivation. From all the northern Sudan there is a constant flow of men seeking work, not only in Khartoum and other parts of the Sudan but also in Egypt, and so it is not to be expected that any very extensive areas still undeveloped should exist beside the main Nile. This was made apparent when the Government carried out a survey of potentially irrigable areas in the northern Sudan in 1954. It was assumed for the purposes of this survey that the greatest lift of water economically practicable was 15 metres, a height which incidentally embraces almost all the terraces of alluvial land (except for the most ancient) that are to be found beside the river. The only areas of any considerable size still undeveloped proved to lie in the Kerma Basin, south of Borgeig pump scheme, and on the west bank of the main Nile opposite, i.e. just north of Dongola town. Elsewhere the pattern of undeveloped but potentially irrigable land closely reflected that of existing schemes.

In the clay plain, on the other hand, the obstacles to the extension of irrigation have hitherto consisted not of the scarcity of suitable soil, but chiefly of the lack of capital, as discussed above, and the lack of water. South of the latitude of Kosti or Singa, moreover, there has until recently been a small population only, so that there has been no pressing need to increase food supplies. The lack of water has not been due to any shortage in the rivers themselves, for pumping from the White Nile does not consume very much, and the total volume of water consumed in the Sudan between January 1st and March 31st in any year is less than two days' flow at the height of the Blue Nile flood. The difficulty has stemmed from the fact that when the Sennar Dam was built the Sudan was being ruled by the British, who had only just granted independence to the Egyptians and still had important naval and military bases in lower Egypt. The Egyptians were fearful that the extension or irrigation in the Sudan might one day lead to a shortage of water in the vital Timely [15] season, when they already needed, and had established their right to, the whole of the Nile flow. To set their fears at rest the British negotiated with them in 1929 the Anglo-Egyptian Nile Waters Agreement, which accepted the established Egyptian rights, and hence severely restricted the amount of water that the Sudanese might draw from the Nile. While adequate for Sudanese needs at the time, this agreement now needs revision, but neither the British before 1955 nor the Sudanese since that date have been able to arrive at an agreement which both Sudanese and Egyptians regard as satisfactory.

Today, with the Sudan independent, the dispute about water is not yet settled, though investigation has revealed that there are vast areas in the Sudan well suited to irrigation. In terms of irrigation practice, the restrictions on the Sudan's use of water have meant that crop rotations have been devised to give the maximum return per unit of water, rather than the maximum per unit of land. The rotation adopted in the Gezira has thus produced three crops only in a period of eight years, as contrasted with the normal three crops in two years in Egypt; while this has in part been due to the character of the Gezira soils, and to the need to maintain their fertility by lengthy fallows, it can principally be explained by the fact that land shortage is not a factor of any importance in the central Sudan. The private cotton schemes normally grow one crop of cotton and one of millet in a three-year rotation. Away from the rivers settlement in the Gezira plain is closely restricted by the lack of permanent water supplies, but even along the rivers the population is not at all dense south of latitude 12° North.

To understand the differences in size of pump schemes in the Sudan, it may be convenient to make a rather more detailed subdivision of areas or reaches of irrigation. Six of these may readily be distinguished:

(a) In Wadi Halfa district there are only 30 schemes in all, with half the area in one Government scheme at Debeira. There is now no scheme in the smallest category, 1–10 feddans.

(b) In the Merowe-Dongola reach there are more than 300 schemes. More than half numerically are of 11–100 feddans, but in area the largest class is that between 100–1000 feddans. The area involved in large schemes (1001–10,000 feddans) is swollen by the Government's schemes at Borgeig, Ghaba, Kulud, Gureir and Nuri, which amount to almost half this category by area. For this reach and for Shendi-Berber no figures are available since the end of 1955.

(c) In the 250 schemes of the Shendi-Berber reach the situation is similar, except that in terms of area the largest class is more important, being swollen by Government schemes at Bouga, Aliab, Kitiab and Gendettu; there is also the large private scheme at Zeidab, of more than 17,000 feddans, which is being enlarged to 25,000 feddans.

(d) In Khartoum Province nearly three-quarters of the 212 schemes are of less than 100 feddans, being fruit and vegetable gardens and pleasure gardens in the capital. There are also several large private farms engaged in dairying and in growing lucerne; in fact nearly 60 per cent of the irrigated area is in schemes of more than 1000 feddans.

(e) In the Blue Nile area there are 275 schemes. As in Khartoum Province, there is a numerical preponderance of schemes of less than 100 feddans, but these occupy less than 4 per cent of the whole irrigated area excluding the Gezira. Even discounting Guneid, which is quite exceptional with 30,000 feddans, nearly four-fifths of the irrigated area lies in schemes of over 1000 feddans.

(f) Along the White Nile there are 864 schemes. The percentage of very small schemes is extremely low, and the area that they occupy is negligible. Over 90 per cent of the irrigated area is in schemes of more than 100 feddans, there being some very large schemes of more than 10,000 feddans. The Government schemes controlled by the White Nile Pumps Board used, as recently as 1955, to control almost a quarter of the whole area, but the very rapid increase in the last three years in the number of large private schemes issued on Flood or Restricted Licence has diminished the relative importance of the Board's activities.

The conclusions to be drawn from these figures are several. Government schemes tend to be large, since it is not considered worth officials' time to visit and control small ones; limitations on the irrigable area, together with the obstructions caused by private land ownership, tend to restrict the number of large schemes in the Northern Province; near the capital the large market for fruit and vegetables has encouraged the establishment of numerous small gardens, and at the same time the common practice of keeping a goat in Sudanese homes to give milk means that there is a steady demand for animal fodder; along the Blue Nile the areas of silty soils where gardens may be established are very limited, while the clay areas where large cotton-growing plantations can flourish are most extensive; finally, along the White Nile, whose width may vary by a kilometre or more according to the level of the water, there are very few small schemes at all, and conditions lend themselves readily to the establishment of large cotton plantations.

THE GROWTH OF IRRIGATION

The present distribution of irrigation in the Sudan has not come about in a few years only but is the result of an intermittent growth throughout many centuries; the adoption of modern mechanical devices for lifting water, however, has taken place entirely in the twentieth century, during and since the period of British rule.

The expansion of the Gezira scheme since its inauguration in 1925 has been a steady process, for which provision was made from the start when the dimensions of the reservoir and the main canal were determined. The Abd el Magid scheme, which is physically an extension of the Gezira, is recorded separately because its administration, manner of allocating tenancies, and cropping system have always been distinct from the Gezira scheme. Until the latest extension towards Manaqil, the land irrigated from the Blue Nile was kept to the eastern side of the Gezira plain, with its main canal running along the watershed between the Blue and the White Niles. In addition to providing the capital for its own extensions the Gezira scheme has proved a major source of Government revenues, and has thus financed numerous development schemes throughout the whole country.

The graph (Fig. 2) showing the relative areas of pump and gravity irrigation in the Sudan from 1933 to 1959 differs principally from Figure 3, not only in total but also in pattern, because it shows the total area irrigated by pumps, and not merely that part of it which is devoted to cotton growing. Along the White Nile there is virtually no irrigated land that is not used for cotton, but along the Blue Nile there is a number of small fruit gardens quite separate from the cotton fields, while in the Khartoum and Northern Provinces there is virtually no cotton grown except in the large private scheme at Zeidab producing American Upland cotton. In the Northern Province much of the land brought under pumps was previously commanded by saqia, while other areas were waste because they lay too high to be reached by primitive lifting devices. Rather surprisingly, the growth of pump irrigation has not led to a decline in the number of *saqias*, since many of these are now set up on islands and small pockets of land not formerly thought worth cultivating.

The record of ownership of the pumps reveals the early part played by the Government in the development of irrigation. The schemes established in the Northern Province during the two world wars were intended to improve food supplies in the Middle East theatre of war and to serve as examples to the inhabitants of the surrounding areas of the advantages of modern techniques in agriculture. The schemes beside the White Nile, on the other hand, provided alternative livelihoods for the tribesmen displaced from their traditional lands by the construction of the Jebel Aulia Dam in 1935. The Zeidab scheme, opposite the confluence of the Atbara river with the main Nile, was first set up as a colony for the resettlement of freed slaves from North America; when that failed, it became the home of the Sudan Plantations Syndicate, a British company which subsequently took over the management of the Geizra scheme from the time of its inception until its nationalization in 1950.[16] The Government pump schemes, while small by comparison with the great Gezira scheme, were of particular importance in that they showed how private individuals, with more limited resources, could profitably take part in the development of irrigation (Fig. 1).

In the period between the two wars the development of pumps was mainly the work of a number of enterprising individuals, including such distinguished personalities as Dr. Malouf, head of the Syrian community in Khartoum, Messrs. Kfouri, who run a highly efficient dairy farm in Khartoum North, Sayed Surur er Ramli and a number of others. A significant feature of this period was the establishment of pumping schemes by the leaders of the main religious sects in the Sudan. These are Sherif Yousif el Hindi, leader of the sect that bears his name, who has a large scheme on the Blue Nile; Sayed Ali Mirghani, leader of the Mirghaniyya sect which includes many of the educated riverain Suda-

nese, who owns a pump scheme in the Merowe reach; and outstandingly the late Sayed Abd er Rahman el Mahdi, son of Muhammad Ahmed el Mahdi, whose chief following is in the western Sudan, and whose cultivations at Aba Island and elsewhere on the White Nile support many of his followers. Since the Second World War many of the leading notables and politicians of all parties have become scheme owners, following the lead of the 20,000 feddan Busata scheme set up by the Abu el Ela family near Suqi on the Blue Nile in 1948. Subsequently it has been the practice of several of the wealthiest Sudanese capitalists to lend money to responsible persons who have secured pump licenses, so as to enable them to buy pumps and set up irrigation works in suitable areas. The traditional Islamic prohibition on usury has usually been circumvented by requiring the repayment of the sum lent in three annual instalments, whose total would be appreciably higher than the original loan.

Clearly, such a steady growth of irrigation could only have taken place if the schemes established had generally proved profitable, and, indeed, much of the most recent development has clearly been financed by the profits earned in cotton growing in the years immediately after the Second World War. Nevertheless, a proviso should perhaps be made in respect of some of the schemes established in the Northern Province. In the Dongola area, particularly, there has been a practice of setting up co-operative schemes, whose capital has been subscribed by persons born in the area who have gone away to find employment elsewhere; in such instances the investors might be as much influenced by the desire to do something to relieve poverty in their home villages as by the prospect of a good return on their capital. Throughout the Northern Province, moreover, the Government schemes are run year after year at a loss to the Treasury of several thousands of pounds. There has been protracted debate whether these losses are to be ascribed to maladministration, to undercharging for

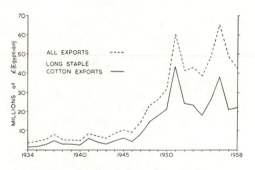

Figure 8.—Graph of the value of all exports, 1934–58, with the share of the total due to long-staple cotton. If the value of cotton seed and of medium-staple cotton were added, the relative importance of the corp would be even more marked, but this would not be a fair reflection of the effect of irrigation on the national economy. Since 1956 the Sudan has adopted as its currency the £ Sudanese, having the same value as the £ Egyptian.

development of irrigation has brought the most marked break with the past, and it is there that we have the best prospect of estimating the value of agricultural production, whether from direct returns, as in the Gezira scheme, or from studying the figures for the export of cotton from the country. When the value of long-staple cotton exports from the Sudan over the last twenty-five years is compared with those for all exports, it will be apparent that cotton production has been a major factor responsible for the country's present measure of prosperity, while without irrigation this total of cotton production would have been quite impossible (Fig. 8).[17]

The further extension of irrigation in the Sudan is likely to follow fairly closely the pattern already established by existing schemes, whether in terms of the crops to be grown or of the manner of organizing the work and sharing the profits.

North of Khartoum the prospects are necessarily limited, both by soil conditions and by the lift that would be needed to bring water to higher areas. In 1950, when the negotiation of a new Nile Waters Agreement was under consideration, a combined soil and contour survey was carried out in the Northern Province to determine the area capable of being irrigated, it being assumed for this purpose that the maximum economic lift was 15 metres above mean low Nile, while the soil requirements were a clay content of 35 per cent or more and not too high a sodium value. The results of the survey may be summarized by saying that approximately 715,000 feddans were found to be commandable from the river, while of this total about 22 per cent, approximately 160,000 feddans, consisted of suitable soil.[18]

water, or to other causes, but in view of the general poverty of the area it has been felt that the element of public subsidy involved in maintaining these schemes is not unwarranted. The difficulties spring fundamentally from the failure to develop suitable high-priced cash crops in this area of poor communications. Cotton, surprisingly, has been a disappointing failure everywhere in the northern Sudan except at Zeidab; this has been due not so much to technical problems as to the difficulty of imposing the necessary discipline, both in the careful preparation of the ground and in avoiding the cultivation in fields nearby of crops that harbour the pests of cotton.

On the whole, there is no doubt that irrigation schemes are reasonably profitable in the Northern Province, for there is a continued demand for perennial licenses. In Khartoum Province conditions are more favourable still; yet, as has been indicated already, there are virtually no statistics of production available for either province, apart from the official schemes and the American cotton production at Zeidab.

It is in the Blue Nile Province that the

South of Khartoum the areas available for further irrigation are much more extensive. The physical conditions make the Blue Nile well suited to the establishment of reservoirs and gravity irrigation, while close to the White Nile there will always be areas best reached by pumps (on the left bank necessarily so); and the existing pattern is likely, therefore, to be followed in the future. By now most of the possibilities of small- or medium-scale schemes north of Kosti or Singa have been exploited, and irrigation began in 1958 in the most obvious extension, that of the Gezira canalization towards the Manaqil area.

In 1950 Sir Alexander Gibb & Partners were invited to carry out a survey of irrigation prospects in the whole area between Khartoum and the Ethiopian border, stretching as far south as Malakal; the area has a higher rainfall than the northern Gezira plain, and is much more densely wooded. The engineers recommended that a reservoir be constructed at Roseires on the Blue Nile, to be operated in much the same manner as the Sennar Dam, to irrigate a large area between the two Niles, and also drew attention to a large number of sites beside the rivers where soil, drainage and other conditions were suitable for the setting up of pump schemes. The total area recommended was 1,771,000 feddans, which, if cropped in much the same way as the existing schemes (cotton one year in three), would require a total of 4–5 milliards of cubic metres of water per annum.[19]

It has also been recognized for some years that the Atbara river, though much further incised into the clay plain than the Blue Nile, could similarly be dammed to feed a gravity irrigation scheme. Investigation by Government departments[20] has revealed a promising dam site at Khashm el Girba, and an area of favourable soil has been found 30 kilometres away, where a total of 500,000 feddans could be brought under irrigation. The possibility of using the dam to improve the irrigation of the Gash Delta was also investigated, but was found to be less practicable (Fig. 9).

The potential schemes listed above by no means represent the whole of the Sudan's future prospects of extending the irrigated area, though it will certainly be many years before all the schemes contemplated can be brought into operation. As irrigation proceeds farther towards the south difficulties of drainage become important, since the annual rainfall increases steeply. This may mean that the most suitable crop will prove to be rice rather than cotton, but no early shift is to be expected, since rice cultivation, whether as a peasant or a plantation crop, would raise major problems of labour supply whose solution cannot easily be envisaged.

The other major factors that will influence further developments are the price of cotton and the availability of water. In the past thirteen years cotton prices have fluctuated wildly, but have at no time fallen so low as to make production in the Sudan unprofitable; their levels must have a major

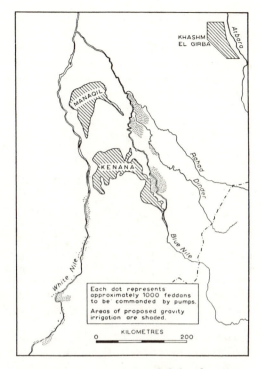

Figure 9.—Areas recommended for the extension of irrigation by Sir Alexander Gibb & Partners, 1954, and the proposed Khashm el Girba scheme.

effect on the rate of development and on the willingness and ability of the Government to undertake major schemes. When low yields coincided with the low prices of the 1931 depression the Gezira scheme came near to foundering, and the even lower yields of 1957–58 were almost equally harmful to the national economy, since they came at a time when the price of cotton was falling, and disposal of that crop and that of the previous year, which had been exceptionally high, proved extremely difficult.

The negotiation of a new Nile Waters Agreement has still to be successfully accomplished. Whatever solution is finally arrived at, it seems likely that the Sudanese will continue to have to be economical in their use of water, since their potentially irrigable area will probably always be greater than they can irrigate from their share of the Nile waters. They have the comfort of knowing that their position farther upstream on the Nile than the Egyptians ensures that their claim to a reasonable proportion cannot be denied.[21]

ACKNOWLEDGMENTS

The author thanks the following for their help in various stages of the work: Mr. H. A. W. Morrice, c.m.g., Musa Effendi Awad Billal, Ustaz Isam Ahmed Hassoun, and Mr. Michael Watts. He also acknowledges a grant from the Central Research Fund of the University of London, which made it possible to visit the Sudan in 1957 and so to finish the paper.

NOTES

[1] Several of the chapters in J. D. Tothill (editor), Agriculture in the Sudan (1948), discuss the Gezira scheme and the Gash and Tokar Deltas, particularly the chapters concerned with crops, crop production, irrigation, experimental work and the Blue Nile and Kassala Provinces. Up-to-date statistics concerning the former, together with an account of recent developments and changes of policy, may be found in the annual reports of the Sudan Gezira Board, beginning with no. 1 in 1951. For the Flush Irri-

gation schemes reference may also be made to C. H. Richards, The Gash Delta, Ministry of Agriculture Bulletin no. 3 (Khartoum, 1950), and F. W. C. Roberts, Report on Tokar, with proposals for the more efficient utilization of the Khor Baraka and its flood waters, Government Publications, Ministry of Finance (Cairo, 1923). A convenient summary of Gezira material is provided by W. A. Hance, "Gezira: an example in development," Geographical Review, 44 (1954), 253–70.

[2] Technical aspects of pump irrigation are discussed in Irrigation by pumps from the Nile in the Sudan, a pamphlet published by the Sudan Ministry of Irrigation and Hydro-Electric Power in 1955. This includes a map by K. M. Barbour and M. A. Billal showing the distribution of irrigation at that date.

[3] The dispute between Egypt and the Sudan concerning the allocation of Nile waters may be studied in The Nile waters question, a pamphlet published in Khartoum by the Ministry of Irrigation in 1955 which prints both Egyptian and Sudanese official presentations of their attitudes, and attempts to refute the former. See also K. M. Barbour, "A new approach to the Nile waters problem," International Affairs, 33 (1957), 319–30.

[4] T. N. Jewitt, Gezira soil, Bulletin No. 12, Ministry of Agriculture (Khartoum, 1955).

[5] H. R. J. Davies, "Irrigation developments in Sudan," Geography, 43 (1958), 271–3.

[6] The technique required to irrigate the extra area of the Manaqil extension while observing the Nile Waters Agreement is discussed by H. A. W. Morrice in "The use of stored water in the Sudan with particular reference to the Manaqil extension and the Roseires Dam," which was issued as Technical Note No. 4 (1955) by the Ministry of Irrigation.

[7] C. H. Richards, see note 1.

[8] J. R. Thomson, Pump scheme management on the White Nile, Ministry of Agriculture Bulletin no. 7 (1952).

[9] See note 2.

[10] Sudan irrigation, Ministry of Irrigation (Khartoum, 1957).

[11] The publication of these annual reports is often irregular, and it may prove necessary to visit the Ministries concerned to consult them.

[12] There are in fact three types of licence: the perennial, which allows pumping at all seasons, and is applicable to irrigation in the Northern Province and in fruit and vegetable

gardens elsewhere; the flood, which allows pumping between July 1st and March 31st, i.e. during the whole cotton-growing season; and the restricted, which allows pumping from July 1st to December 31st only.

[13] The first population map of the Sudan was printed as Appendix XXIV to the Report of the Soil Conservation Committee of the Sudan Government, 1944, at a scale of 1:8,000,000. The second, at 1:3,000,000, was drawn in 1951 by Dr. E. J. Howell, then head of the Department of Geography in the University College of Khartoum, on the basis of administrative reports: this map was issued privately by the College. The third has been drawn by K. M. Barbour to accompany the reports of the First Population Census of Sudan, 1955–56, and may be found in K. J. Krotki, *Twenty-one facts about the Sudanese* (Khartoum, 1958).

[14] The recent resignation of the first Sudanese Director of Surveys, who found it more profitable to work as a private surveyor than to be the head of a Government department, illustrates very vividly how great is the shortage of trained technicians.

[15] In Egypt the Timely season, when any increase of the Nile flow would be very welcome, is from February 1st to July 31st. *See* H. E. Hurst, R. P. Black and Y. M. Simaika, *The Nile Basin*, VII (1946), 118.

[16] C. B. Tracey, "The Zeidab scheme," in *Agriculture in the Sudan* (1948).

[17] An interesting analysis of the relation between cotton yields and prices, and of the effect of both on schemes of development in the country, is to be found in R. H. B. Condie, "Cotton exports and economic development in the Sudan," *Sudan notes and records*, 37 (1956), 70–8.

[18] This information was obtained from a report prepared in the Soil Research Section of the Research Division of the Ministry of Agriculture dated 23.10.1954.

[19] Sir Alexander Gibb & Partners, *Estimation of irrigable areas in the Sudan, 1951–53*, Report submitted to the Government of Sudan, 1954.

[20] H. Bell, *Irrigation by gravity from the River Atbara*, Ministry of Irrigation and Hydro-Electro Power, Khartoum (undated, but *c.* 1956).

[21] Just before the publication of this paper it was announced that in November 1959 the Egyptians and Sudanese had signed a new Nile Waters Agreement. This gives the Sudanese the right to use up to 17,000,000,000 cubic metres of water per annum, as compared with their present consumption of 4,000,000,000. In consequence shortage of water is not likely to prove a bar to the extension of irrigation in the Sudan, whether by government or by private individuals, for many years to come.

III. POPULATION-LAND RELATIONSHIPS: MALADJUSTMENT

It is difficult to distinguish readily between population-land relationships in a state of adjustment and those which are maladjusted. There are unsatisfactory as well as satisfactory features to be discerned in the examples given in the previous section. The situations presented thus far are not without problems, but the contrast with production systems that are strained to provide people's essential needs is evident.

When relationships are maladjusted, pressure is exerted on human and environmental resources, causing the quality of both to deteriorate. Repercussions may be considerable, but perhaps only temporary, for strains can become the stimuli that lead to economic improvements. But a major problem in identifying and studying maladjustment is the lack of sufficient historical information from which to determine the origin of relationships and how they evolved.

Manifestations of maladjustment are land shortages, soil erosion, reduced fertility, decreased yields, restricted production with recurrent food shortages, and limited cultivation of cash crops (Prothero, 1962; Grove, 1951; Floyd, 1965). People subjected to these pressures may migrate to other areas, either seasonally or permanently (Prothero, 1957c, 1964; Udo, 1964). Migration is selective and results in sex and age imbalance through the absence of at least the younger male adults of the population (Hunter, 1965; Kay, 1967b), with consequent social and economic repercussions. Within age and sex groups, there is frequently further selection, with the more active and dynamic persons being the least satisfied and in the van of those seeking new opportunities.

Cause and effect in maladjusted relationships are extremely difficult to distinguish clearly. Migration, for example, may be caused by a deterioration of the economy arising from pressure upon resources, and its effect may be to alleviate pressure by reducing demand. But this alleviation may be only temporary, since migration could cause further economic degeneration by removing the more physically and mentally active members of a community.

The papers which follow describe and discuss a variety of factors contributing to maladjustment and illustrate the problems of imbalance. The examples represent different environmental conditions and involve varying numbers of people. In all but one example population mobility occurs.

Much of central Ghana is characterized by water shortage, sparse population, and low productivity—problems common to the so-called "Middle Belt" of West Africa (Church, 1969; Gleave and White, 1968), but particularly acute in Nigeria (Agboola, 1961, 1968). Manshard comments on this poorly developed zone as being too dry for the crops of the forest belt and too wet for those of the savanna. In fact, forest and savanna crops overlap in the Middle Belt, suggesting the area's potential as a major food source for the higher concentrations of population to both the north and the south.

The agricultural migrations discussed here involve the extensive and wasteful use of previously unpopulated land being farmed for the first time, which is comparable to what happens when highland environments are deserted for lower-lying areas (Gleave, 1966; Prothero, 1964). As long as land is available, the migrants are able to abandon over-farmed areas for new ones, and instability perhaps more than maladjustment becomes the basic characteristic of population-land relationships. This fluid situation continues until no unoccupied areas remain; maladjustment will follow if there is no complementary increase in the intensity and frequency of land use.

11. Land Use Patterns and Agricultural Migration in Central Ghana (Western Gonja)

W. MANSHARD

INTRODUCTION

This article attempts to throw some light on the patterns of land-use and settlement in a sparsely populated, rather unproductive part of central Ghana. Apart from some agricultural survey reports [1] and the work of the Gonja Development Corporation,[2] very little research on land-use and migration has been conducted in Western Gonja.

The region under investigation is bordered on the west and south by the Black Volta, which serves both as an international frontier between the Ivory Coast and Ghana, and as a boundary between the Brong-Ahafo and Northern Regions. As dividing lines in the East the Konkore-Scarp, which fringes the Volta Basin was chosen; and in the North the administrative boundary of the Lawra-Wa district (about 9° 40′ N.) where there is some increase in density of population (Fig. 1).

The most striking feature of Gonja is its *emptiness*: many parts of it have less than one inhabitant per square kilometer. The explanation often given for this are the activities, at the end of the 19th century, of slave-raiders like Samory and Babatu. Later British rule brought peace and increased trade along the Black Volta: the danger now was the spread of sleeping sickness from the North, river blindness (onchocerciasis) and other epidemics— there were, for instances, severe outbreaks of cerebro-spinal meningitis in the early 1940's.

These factors, however, offer a partial explanation only of why so few people inhabit this "Middle Belt," for they oper-

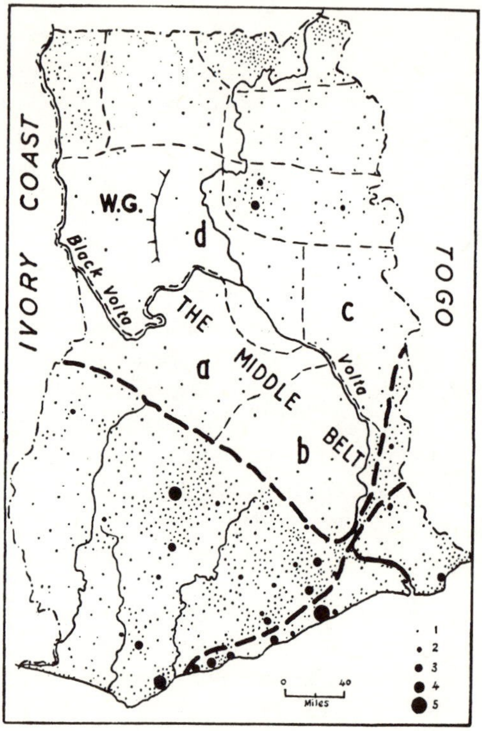

Figure 1.—Ghana's Population and the Regional Division of the "Middle Belt."

Rural population   1 =   2.000 inhabitants
Urban population   2 =   5–10.000   "
                 3 =   10–20.000   "
                 4 =   20–50.000   "
                 5 = over 50.000   "   (1948 Census)

—————— *Boundary of Forest Belt*
Regional division of Ghana's "Middle Belt":
   a. *Brong (Northwest Ashanti)*
   b. *Afram Plains*
   c. *Krachi and South Dagomba*
   d. *Gonja*
       W.G. *Western Gonja*
       Konkore Scarp

Source. White, H. P. and Varley, W. J., The Geography of Ghana, London 1958.

From *Tijdschrift voor Economische en Sociale Geographie*, 52, 1961, pp. 225–230. Reprinted by permission. This article, which is based on a paper read to the I.G.U. Commission for the "Humid Tropics" in Stockholm (August 1960), is dedicated to *Professor Gottfried Pfeifer,* Heidelberg, on the occasion of his 60th birthday.

ated also in areas which, by contrast, are today thickly populated. It is true that the decrease of population resulting from slave-raids and epidemics reduced the area under cultivation, and that as land previously farmed reverted to "bush," the number of wild animals—all potential carriers of sleeping-sickness—increased. This phenomenon is not, of course, peculiar to Ghana. It is to be observed in many other parts of Africa also, *Gillman*, for example, has shown that in Tanganyika it was not the tse-tse which drove out the population but rather man who surrendered his land to them.[3]

In respect of Central Ghana, tse-tse and slave-raider had a real but limited significance, and "physical" factors such as *water-supply* and *poor soils* (as controlled by a variable climate and hydrology) had a more marked effect on population distribution than has been assumed hitherto. For they limited the possibilities of cultivation in a region which often proved either *too dry* for forest crops or *too wet* for typical savannah products. As a kind of "no man's land" between South and North, the "Middle Belt"—here, as in Nigeria[4]—combines most climatic disadvantages with no compensating advantages: It thus experiences the worst of two worlds. Exposed as it is to the aridity, of the Harmattan, as well as the heavy precipitation of disturbance lines and the so called monsoonal rain this central zone seems, in fact, to have one of the severest "agricultural climates" in all West Africa.

The *climate* of the Southern Guinea Savannah is characterized by sharp seasonal fluctuations of rainfall, mostly of the "line squall" type. *Bole* is the only meteorological station in the area (Fig. 2). Because of this great variation in rainfall, water supply is a major problem affecting further development schemes.

There are very few permanent streams besides the Black Volta, and even the bigger tributaries dry up for several months of the year. Only further east, on the Upper Voltaian, are to be found more or less permanent streams. Most of the people have to rely on water holes that are often polluted. This water shortage is one of the chief reasons for scattered and small settlement. Otherwise conditions are often not unfavourable for life: for the most part, even those soils which were formerly cultivated, have been under "bush" fallows for a long time. Wide areas have hardly ever been touched.

The *vegetation* comprises tree savannah on uplands and merges into savannah woodlands to the South. These woodlands are open on ill drained soils and thicken to riverine forests along the water-courses. This contrast in vegetation between valleys and uplands is accentuated, as elsewhere, by the fact that the peasant farmer tended to work the lighter and poorer soils on the upper slopes near the water-sheds, and to neglect the swampy, heavier soils in the valleys. With limited agricultural techniques at his disposal, the peasant found the latter harder to work; but in fact they offer a better long-term prospect.

Except for the fairly steep scarp leading up to the edge of the Upper Voltaian (350–500m) below Larabanga, most of the *relief* is gentle and even flat. The crystalline rocks (Birrimian and Granites) show a slightly rolling landscape; only where quartz veins occur are there steeper slopes.

Though the Northern Savannah covers ⅔ of the country much research remains to be done on its *soils*. Work undertaken so far has been mainly confined to the Voltaian sediments, and much less is known about the granites and the soils found on Birrimian rocks.

Brammer, in referring to Northern Ghana, distinguishes Savannah Ochrosols in the south.[5] These merge, south of Bole, into a wide zone of Groundwater-Laterites and Groundwater-Laterite-Ochrosol intergrades. There is one interesting point: Savannah Ochrosols of the "red-earth" type develop over Voltaian sandstone as well as over Lower Birrimian rocks and over certain granites in the southwest. Thus, parent

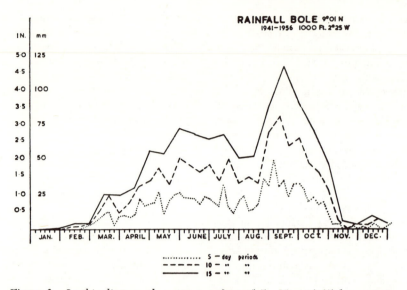

Figure 2.—In this diagram the average values of 5-, 10- and 15-day periods for Bole are represented. This method was chosen since monthly totals of rainfall present too broad and daily falls too fine a picture for easy intepretation. *Annual percentages of precipitation were as follows:*

30%:   30–40 inches (750–1000 mm).
40%:   40–50 inches (1000–1250 mm).
20%:   50–60 inches (1250–1500 mm).
10%:   over 60 inches (over 1500 mm).

Source. Walter, M. W., Ghana Met. Dept., Note No. 10, Accra 1958.

rocks are not as important for soil formation as some of the soil maps of West Africa, which are mainly based on geological data, tend to suggest. Most of the Ochrosols occupy the gently undulating savannah areas with an average annual rainfall of 1,000–1,375 mm in a single wet season. They are fairly heavily farmed in the north-east and around Tamale, but only very sparsely populated in Western Gonja.

The Groundwater-Laterites and Ochrosol-Groundwater-Laterites intergrades cover extensive areas over Voltaian shales as well as over granites. Their origin is due to poor internal drainage.[6] Over the shales drainage is impeded by horizontal layers of imprevious bed-rock, while over granites it is hampered by the clayey nature of the weathered rock. The unfavourable water

balance of these soils, which are generally recognized as belonging to the poorest soils in the humid tropics, allows for very little farming.[7] They have hardly any potential for agricultural development and could best be used for rough grazing or game-reserves.

TRIBAL GROUPS

Figures 3 and 4 showing the tribal distribution of settlements, suggest a rather more complex picture than one is led to expect by reading the usual small scale maps,[8] which explain the tribal distribution of Ghana's population. Various cultural groups exist which can be classified according to language and cultural heritage. Early in the 17th century Gonja was overrun by invaders from the Mande country in the

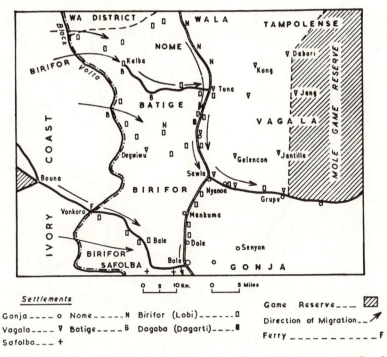

Figure 3.—Tribal distribution of settlements and recent tends in agricultural migration in the northern part of Western Gonja.

west. The newcomers, under their leader Jakpa, appointed their own chiefs and founded an "empire," which at one time stretched from Bole to Salaga and Bassari. In the 18th century they were defeated, in turn, by the Dagoma and by the powerful Ashanti, to whose king they became subject.

When the present "rulers," the Gonja, first invaded the country, they took over the language of the Guang speaking natives. The Grusi speaking groups (Degha or Mo, Tampolense and Vagala) and the Senufo speaking people (Banda or Nafana) arrived before the Gonja, while most of the Mossi speaking inhabitants came later. It is the fact, therefore, that a Gonja chief often rules over people who have been settled in the country much longer than his own group, and that while the chief is a Gonja, the village population may be Batige or Birifor.

From a geographical standpoint the most interesting groups for study are the Dagaba, Lo Dagaba, Lo Wiili and Birifor, which are popularly known by the Administration as *Lobi* and *Dagarti*. They moved into Gonja comparatively recently. An entry in the West Gonja District Record Book (1919) refers to 12 Lobi compounds; the 1948-Census, on the other hand, puts the Lobi population of Gonja at over 7,000.[9] Figures 3 and 4 show some of the recent migratory movements in the region.

Examples of recent Dagarti movements south of Bole are set out in Table 1.

These groups—described by *Labouret*[10] as early as 1931 as "très mobile"—have moved into Ghana mainly from the Ivory Coast, during the last 20–30 years. The vast majority are farming communities.

The contrast between the old established people like the Mo, Safalbo, Vagala, and

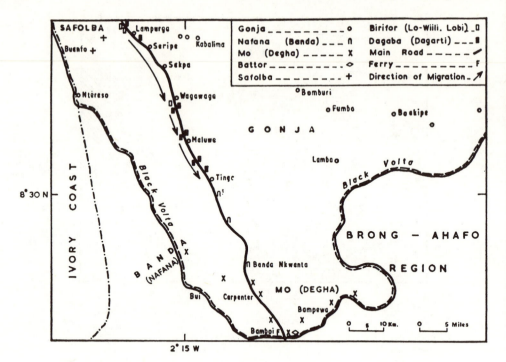

Figure 4.—Tribal distribution of settlements and recent trends in agricultural migration in the southern part of Western Gonja.

Table 1

DAGARTI MIGRATION SOUTH
OF BOLE, 1957

Settlement on Bamboi-Bole Road

Mileage from Bamboi	Time of Arrival	Migrating from:
35	1950	Lawra Area
37	1955	Jirapa
43	1957	Tuna
48	1956	Jirapa & Gbari
49	1957	Tuna
64	1950-51	Babile, Duri
69	1940	Tuna & Ivory Coast

Gonja and these more recent arrivals is reflected not only in settlement and land-use, but also in their general *social* organisation. While the Gonja possess a well defined political structure, there is relatively little organised chieftaincy among the Birifor or Lobi: their tribal organsation revolves round the family and the "clan"; here kinship ties are of paramount importance.[11]

PATTERNS OF LAND-USE

The old established *Gonja* farmers generally practise land rotation with bush fallowing (Fig. 5). After the land has been cleared it is farmed for 2–5 years (average 3 years). The shortest farming periods (2 years) and the longest fallows are practised in the south-west of Gonja. *Yams* is generally planted on the best virgin soils. Millet is often interplanted with beans or

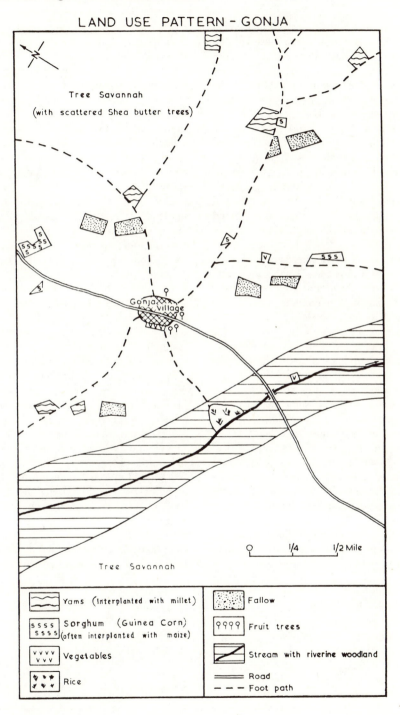

LAND USE PATTERN – GONJA

Tree Savannah
(with scattered Shea butter trees)

Gonja Village

1/4   1/2 Mile

Tree Savannah

Yams (Interplanted with millet)

Sorghum (Guinea Corn) (often interplanted with maize)

Vegetables

Rice

Fallow

Fruit trees

Stream with riverine woodland

Road

Foot path

Figure 5.

maize and only sometimes with cassava (manioc). Beans are interplanted with all crops except groundnuts, which are not planted widely. Gonja farms are scattered within a radius of several kilometers of the villages. The main crops is *yams*, which in recent years has become increasingly important as an "export crop" to the south. Sorghum (Guineacorn), millet, maize, and hill rice are also widely grown. Swamp rice is occasionally found along riverine wood-lands or thickets. Vegetables (e.g. garden eggs, beans, and tomatoes) are planted near the villages, Shea-nuts are collected from trees growing wild in the open savan-nah. Small herds of cattle, mostly under the supervision of *Fulani* herdsmen, are also kept. There are cattle "kraals" in many villages. Goats, sheep and poultry are used more for marriage payments, feasts and sacrifices than for cash-sales.

The farming practice of the *Lobi – Birifor* groups follows a different pattern (Fig. 6). They have a small farm with a few yards of their houses ("compound-" or "house-farm"), mainly given over to the growing of vegetables, but with some cereals such as maize and sorghum also. These "farms," which are in fact more like gardens or allotments in our sense, are kept under *permanent* cultivation. As long as the house stands the fertility of these patches is main-tained by the use of "night soil." In addi-tion these groups establish quite extensive "family-fields" in the immediate neighbour-hood of their settlements. These fields are cleared completely of vegetation—a prac-tise with the obvious danger of soil-erosion. Further away from the settlement there are also a number of "bush farms," but the crops which they yield are used rather more for cash sales by individuals than for the supply of the family-farming units. Their main crops are cereals such as sor-ghum and millet. There is, however, an increasing tendency among the older and more experienced Lobi farming units to establish yam cultivation, because of the attractive prices on the internal Ghana market. The Lobi-Birifor do not employ Fulani help, but look after their livestock themselves.

The *Lobi* and *Dagarti* farming-groups, particularly those further north, offer an in-teresting contrast in land-utilisation. The emphasis of Dagarti land-use is on rota-tional "bush-farms" often far outside their villages. The Lobi, on the other hand, tend to concentrate much more on their more or less permanent "compound and house-farms."

One possible explanation of this phe-nomenon is related to geological structure and resulting soil distribution.[12] While the Dagarti, for the most part, occupy fairly homogenous soils on granites which are suitable for large "bush farms," the Lobi have tended to settle on poorer quality soils of the Birrimian, where there are only few granite outcrops. The latter soils then tend to be cultivated more intensively by using the "compound farming" system.

This is an oversimplification of a much more complex relationship. Agricultural officers tend to praise the "compound farming" system, characterized by small areas under permanent cultivation and to assume that these farmers have reached a higher standard of agricultural technique. When, however, a peasant practising the "compound system" moves into the empty areas of the "Middle Belt," he ceases, in-variably, to rely solely on "compound farming" and quickly returns to a fairly extensive land-rotation. This change-over suggests that the practice of "compound farming" in the north-east and north-west of Ghana does not really represent a con-spicuous agricultural advance from "shifting cultivation" to "fixed cultivation." It is significant that wherever there is abundant unused land these African farmers go straight back to field shifting.

MIGRATION AND SETTLEMENT

Besides ethnic differences, two other main factors have played an important role in

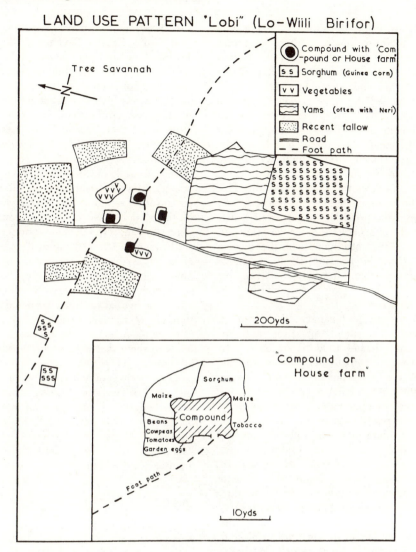

LAND USE PATTERN 'Lobi" (Lo–Wiili Birifor)

Tree Savannah

Compound with 'Com-pound or House farm'
S S Sorghum (Guinea Corn)
V V Vegetables
Yams (often with Neri)
Recent fallow
Road
Foot path

200yds

"Compound or House farm"

Sorghum

Maize   Maize

Beans
Cowpeas
Tomatoes   Compound   Tobacco
Garden eggs

Foot path

10yds

Figure 6.

the more recent development of *settlements*: firstly, the availability of *water*, mentioned earlier, which is no doubt a very limiting factor in this region; secondly, the opening up of the country to road transport within the last 10–20 years. It has become a common feature for settlements to move to lorry roads—sometimes without adequate regard to the supply of water in the neighbourhood, (1960 over 28,000 sq/km were served by little more than 500 km all-season-roads).

Central and Northern Ghana is not yet characterised by that permanence of settlements which is to be observed in the cocoa growing areas of the Closed Forest Belt.

In Western Gonja the situation is kept fluid by the influx of new agricultural migrants.

Some tribal groups (e.g. the Lobi, Birifor, Dagarti) have a greater mobility than others —the Gonja and Dagomba, for example, have occupied the same region for several centuries. Today, however, even in the more remote areas, there is a tendency for the settlements of groups which, in the past, have shown a fairly high agricultural mobility to become more stationary.

One reason for this is the rapid development of communications in recent years; another is the provision of improved amenities such as schools and dispensaries. In particular, the introduction of the bicycle has enabled the peasant farmer, to move more freely than formerly between his village and farms, which may well be several miles apart.

With regard to Ghanaian development, an observation about migration and resettlement schemes may be in order. In past years, principally as part of the ill-fated Gonja Development Scheme, Government has tried to move a number of Frafra from the overpopulated Bolga-Zuarungu area and resettle them at Damongo in Gonja. To-date, however, only a comparatively small number of Frafra families (1960: about 400 families) have moved and the resettlement scheme has met with limited success.[13] It is unwise to attempt in this way, to move a group whose preference is to seek employment in the towns of the South, and to retain traditional land ties by returning home at periodic intervals.

Why does the Ghana Government not assist the hard-working Lobi-Dagarti groups (or in the same way, the Konkomba in the Eastern Gonja and Krachi Districts) which have a live interest in agriculture? Why are those farming communities, who have already begun to move into this region not channelled into areas that require and can also carry additional population?

The broad zonation of Ghana's agricultural pattern seems to be determined chiefly by physical factors. It is allied closely to the three main climatic vegetation formations: the Coastal Savannah, the Closed Forest Zone and the Northern Savannah, which merge into one another along transitional belt of contact.[14] It must be emphasised, however, that remarkable differences of land-use, differences based on social structure, tribal tradition and agricultural technique, exist within this wider zonal framework.

It is a well known fact that in African communities the emphasis is often more on kinship ties than on the spatial coherency of their lands. We cannot, of course, explain human responses in agriculture and settlements in terms of physical background alone. It is the authors opinion that social phenomena must, increasingly, be taken into account in this field if we as geographers are to arrive at a fuller regional understanding of tropical Africa.[15] The analysis of these phenomena both in time and space tends to show that it is often the difference in mobility of social groups and the expansion and contraction of their typical "mosaics" of land-use patterns, which allow us to see the whole question in proper perspective. Only then shall we be in a position to press for more enlightened assistance to be given to agricultural communities in the humid tropics.

NOTES

[1] Schwencke, F. P., Agricultural Extension Program, Western Gonja. Accra 1959.

[2] Report of the Second Advisory Committee on the Gonja Development Corporation Ltd. Accra 1955.

[3] Gillman, C. G., A Population Map of Tanganyika Territory. Geogr. Rev. 1936, p. 354.

[4] Harrison-Church, R. J., West Africa, London 1957.

Buchanan, K. M., The Northern Region of Nigeria. Geogr. Rev. 1953, pp. 451–73.

[5] Brammer, H., The Soils of Ghana. S.L.U.S. Departmental Paper No. 17, Kumasi 1957.

Agriculture and Land Use of Ghana (Editor: Wills, J. B.) Oxford Univ. Press 1961 (in Press).

[6] Purnell, M. F., Report on the Area Adjoining

the Sawla-Yapei Road. Ms. S.L.U.S.: Kumasi 1956 and: Brammer, H., *op. cit.*

[7] Kellog, G. E. and Davol, F. D., An Exploratory Study of Soils Groups in the Belgian Congo. Brussels. Série Scientifique no. 46, 1949, and: Brammer, H., *op. cit.*

[8] Gold Coast Atlas, Accra 1959.

[9] At the time of writing detailed figures of the 1960-Census were not yet available. Preliminary figures indicate that population in the whole of Western Gonja has increased from about 20,000 (1948) to 60,000 (1960) inhabitants.

[10] Labouret, H., Le Tribus du Rameau Lobi. Paris 1931.

Labouret, H., Nouvelles Notes sur le Tribus du Rameau Lobi. I.F.A.N. No. 54, Dakar 1958.

[11] Goody, J. R., The Ethnology of the Northern Territories of the Gold Coast, West of the White Volta. Col. Office. London, 1954.

Goody, J. R., The Social Organisation of the LoWiili. H.M.S.O. London, 1956.

Goody, J. R., Fields of Social Control among the Lo-Dagaba. *Journ. Royal Anthropol. Inst.*, 87/1 1957.

Goody, J. R., Fission of Domestic Groups among the Lo Dagaba, *in:* Cambridge Papers in Social Anthropology, Cambridge Univ. Press 1958.

[12] Hinds, J. H., Agricultural Survey of the Wa-Lawra District. *Bull. Dept. of Agric.*, Accra 1951.

Davies, O., Soil and Water. *Universitas,* Accra June 1960, pp. 80–81.

[13] Hilton, T. E., Land Planning and Resettlement in Northern Ghana. *Geography*, 1959, pp. 227–240.

Hilton, T. E., Frafra Resettlement, *Universitas* Vol. III/5, Accra 1959.

Damongo, C. L. A., The Frafra Farmer Moves South. *The Ghana Farmer,* III. No. 3 (1959).

[14] Wills, J. B., The General Pattern of Land Use. S.L.U.S. Kumasi 1957.

[15] Manshard, W., Die geographischen Grundlagen der Eingeborenenwirtschaft Ghanas in ihren natürlichen, historischen und sozialen Zusammenhängen. Ms. Köln 1959.

Morgan, W. B., The Approach to Regional Studies in Nigeria. Research Notes No. 6 Univ. Coll., Ibadan, 1954.

Population pressure occurs in the northeast corner of Ghana, where the number of inhabitants is estimated to be several times the supporting capacity of the land, densities are high, and settlement is completely dispersed (Hunter, 1967b). Concentrations of population have built up because diseases such as sleeping sickness and river blindness inhibit, if they do not prevent, the occupation of nearly 40 per cent of the total area (Hunter, 1966a).

Social and economic conditions are unsatisfactory and stand in stark contrast to those in more developed areas to the south (Boateng, 1966). All the characteristics of maladjusted population-land relationships are exhibited; migration has provided the only important outlet (Hilton, 1960; Rouch, 1957). Various schemes of land-planning and re-settlement have been tried (Hilton, (1959b), including state farms on the Soviet model, but all have failed to contribute significantly to solving the problems of the area (Dickson, 1969). It seems probable that migration will continue as the major means of alleviating population pressure, with seasonal absences tending to develop into permanent displacements (Engmann, 1965).

12. *Population Pressure in a Part of the West African Savanna: A Study of Nangodi, Northeast Ghana*

JOHN M. HUNTER

Abstract. The hard environmental conditions of the African savanna, particularly during the long dry season, at best allow a accumulation of foodstuffs beyond normal requirements. Indigenous groups who traditionally rely upon cereal cultivation for their sustenance are often sorely pressed, particularly so when population is increasing. The concept of population carrying-capacity of an indigenous agricultural system is examined in Nangodi, which may be regarded as representative of northeast Ghana and, to some extent, of other parts of the West African savanna zone. It is suggested that approximately 280 persons per square mile is the maximum possible population load, whereas a density of over 1,000 is found in parts of Nangodi with resultant soil exhaustion and erosion. River blindness adds to the problem of population pressure by rendering two-fifths of the land uncultivable. Emigration, estimated at four percent per annum, is the only outlet. The residue population is structurally unbalanced, sex ratio in the 15–44 age group being 52 males per 100 females.

Observers of the African scene have remarked upon the low population density of that continent. It has been suggested that there is a basic problem of under-population; but, as Steel has recently pointed out, population distribution is patchy and includes limited areas of serious overcrowding where the question of population/food relationships requires urgent attention.[1] Study of such problem areas,

it is felt, should assist the present and future planning considerations of African states for, undoubtedly, with declining death rates and a continuance of traditionally high birthrates (the latter for some time at least), Africa will have to face increasingly acute population problems in the future.

The small traditional state of Nangodi lies on the right bank of the Red Volta, some 378 miles due north of the Gulf of Guinea. It covers an area of sixty square miles and contained an enumerated population of nearly 14,020 in 1960. In much of its human geography, it may be considered typical of northeast Ghana, an area of 3,400 square miles with a population of 469,000 (boundary indicated, Fig. 1).

Nangodi is underlain by phyllites and schists, except for the two sections of Pelungu and Dusobilogo (areal units 20, 21, and 9 on Fig. 2) where granodiorites occur. A central range of hills, reaching a maximum height of 1,250 feet above sea level, strikes NNE from Tindongo to Zoa (areal units 22, 23, 10, and 11 on Fig. 2), with land on either side generally averaging 700–800 feet. Annual rainfall is in the order of forty inches, nine-tenths of which falls in a six-month rainy season from May to October. Low humidity and drought characterize the remainder of the year. Natural vegetation is Sudan-Guinea savanna woodland (Fig. 1), but the occupied areas (Fig. 2) actually resemble open parkland since only trees of economic value have escaped clearance. These are notably *shea* (*Butyrosperum parkii*) and *dawa dawa* (*Parkia filicoidea*) shown in Figure 12. Apart from deserted riverside lands, which are discussed below, the only areas free of cultivation and farming, and therefore likely to develop near-climax woodland,

[1] R. W. Steel, "Population Increases and Food Production in Tropical Africa," *African Affairs,* Special Issue, no volume number (Spring, 1965), pp. 55–68.

Reproduced from the *Annals of the Association of American Geographers,* Vol. 57, 1967, pp. 101–114. Reprinted by permission.

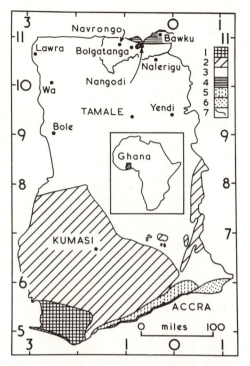

Figure 1.—Position of Nangodi, N.E. Ghana. 1) rain forest; 2) moist semi-deciduous forest; 3) Guinea savanna woodland; 4) Sudan savanna woodland; 5) coastal savanna and thicket; 6) strand and mangrove; 7) boundary of northeast.

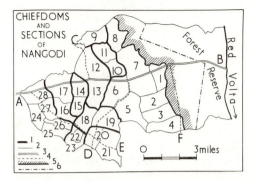

Figure 2.—Chiefdoms and sections of Nangodi. 1) chiefdom boundary; 2) section boundary (names listed in Table 1); 3) road to A: Bolgatanga and B: Bawku (see Fig. 1); 4) motorable track to C: Kumbusig, D: Dusi and Shiega, E and F: Sakoti; 5) eastern limit of settled area, western limit of abandoned zone; 6) boundary of forest reserve, demarcated to include already abandoned area. Boundaries approximately surveyed by author.

are the sacred groves which feature conspicuously in the landscape.

Like the rest of northeast Ghana, Nangodi is characterized by a remarkable absence of nucleated settlement. Each house is set amidst its home farm; hence, even in densely populated areas, the pattern of complete dispersal is maintained. (Fig. 3). The system of farming is highly distinctive in that each farmer intensively cultivates the same parcel of land around his house year in and year out. Production from these fixed home farms is supported by crops taken from inherited farms and also from bush farms in unsettled areas, where normal fallow rotation (shifting cultivation) is practiced. The most common crops are early millet (*Pennisetum typhoideum*), late millet (*P. spicatum* var.), Guinea corn

(*Sorghum vulgare*), and ground nuts (*Arachis hypogea*). No irrigation is practiced, although there are a few small gardens for the raising of commercial vegetables, mainly tomatoes, in the dry season. Cattle are reared for sacrificial purposes and for payment of bride price. They supply man-

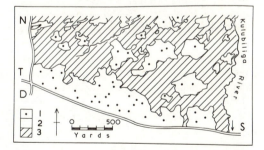

Figure 3.—Settlement in Central Pelungu. 1) house; 2) area cultivated annually; 3) rough grazing and fallow. Road N to Nangodi Soliga, T to Tindongo, D to Dusi, and S to Sakoti. In the large area of fixed cultivation north of the road, a density of about 1,100 persons per square mile obtains. Based on air photos taken in 1949, and Census data of 1948; see Table 3.

ure, which is vital for the maintenance of the agricultural system, but no cattle are ever sold, except in time of dire extremity, such as famine, and none are eaten in the normal course of domestic events.

The Nangodi politico-military traditional area, which is ruled by the paramount chief, the Nangodi-Naba, is divided into ten chiefdoms and twenty-eight sections (Fig. 2, names in Table 1). The boundaries of these areas were sketched in the field by the author, with the aid of air photos, and are used here as convenient units for population study. Problems of handling the Census data are briefly touched upon in the notes following Table 1. Discussion below focuses upon the problem of population density in relation to the carrying capacity of the indigenous agricultural system. Details of the settlement pattern, social organization in relation to agriculture, and periodic migration are not discussed.

Mean population density in Nangodi is 228 persons per square mile (hereafter psm) but, in fact, no less than thirty-eight percent of the traditional area is unoccupied and unfarmed because of the disease river blindness.[2] River blindness (onchocerciasis) is hyperendemic in Ghana, north of latitude 10° 30' N. The frontier of settlement in Nangodi, as plotted from air photos taken in 1960, is indicated in Figure 2 (areas are given in Table 2). Evidence collected in 1963 shows that blindness is still spreading westwards, away from vector breeding sites in the Red Volta. As settlements along this retreating frontier (Figs. 4–7) gradually die out, advancing bush recolonizes the abandoned farmland. The grave consequence of land falling out of production, in a

---

[2] River blindness (onchocerciasis) is transmitted by a small, black-fly vector (*Simulium damnosum* in Ghana) which oviposits in fast-flowing streams. Heavy infestation renders extensive riverine areas uninhabitable. See J. M. Hunter, "River Blindness in Nangodi, Northern Ghana: an Hypothesis of Cyclical Advance and Retreat," *Geographical Review,* Vol. 56 (1966), pp. 398–416.

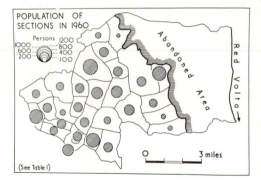

Figure 4.—Population of sections, 1960.

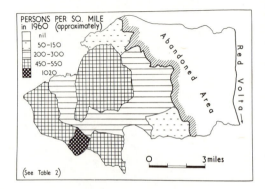

Figure 5.—Persons per square mile, 1960.

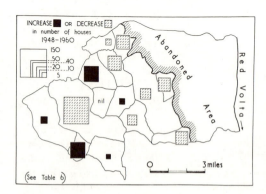

Figure 6.—Change in number of houses, 1948–1960.

TABLE 1. POPULATIONS OF CHIEFDOMS
AND SECTIONS OF NANGODI, 1960

Chiefdom	Population	Section	Population
Nangodi	3,364	1 Kalini	971
		2 Guosi	313
		3 Nkunzesi	105
		4 Nyaboka	102
		5 Yakoti	600
		6 Soliga	734
		7 Nakpaliga	445
		8 Gongo	94
Dusobilogo	170	9 Dusobilogo	170
Zoa	854	10 Zoa Nayiri	389
		11 Bariyambisi	465
Kongo	1,888	12 Adusabisi	1,134
		13 Asinabisi	754
		14 Logri Nayiri	475
		15 Aringon	389
Dagliga	611	16 Dagliga Nayiri	234
		17 Gaagin	377
Damologo	716	18 Damologo Nayiri	456
		19 Zook	260
Pelungu	1,491	20 Pelungu Nayiri	994
		21 Vea Dabok	497
Tindongo	1,145	22 Tindongo Nayiri	504
		23 Ntook	641
Zanlerigu	2,530	24 Zanlerigu Nayiri	957
		25 Namoog	357
		26 Zoagin	478
		27 Gani	427
		28 Asongo	311
Totals	13,633		13,633

Note: Compiled by author. Boundaries of
chiefdoms and sections (see Fig. 2) were sketched
in the field by the author, with the aid of air
photos taken in 1960, during a survey in 1963.
Population data (see Fig. 4) are taken from the
1960 Census, Vols. 1 and 2, and the Census Map of
Enumeration Areas of the Northern Region,
1:250,000 scale, designed by the author. Since
section and Census boundaries do not coincide,
some proportionate estimates have been made,
within the overall Census total of 13,633. Lists of
rateable adults, kindly supplied by the Nabdam
Local Council, were useful in this respect.

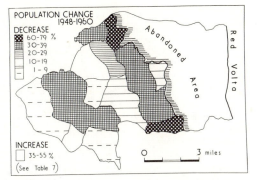

Figure 7.—Population change, 1948–1960.

purely agrarian society, does not need to be
stressed here.

Sections are small in population size
along the edge of the abandoned zone (e.g.,
Nyaboka, 102, Gongo, 94) and much larger
in the interior, three being over 900 (Adu-
sabisi, Pelungu Nayiri, and Zanlerigu Nayiri, Table 1, Fig. 4). Similarly, population
density, which averages 366 psm in the
settled area, is highest in the interior and
lowest on the frontier (Table 2, Fig. 5).
Kalini is the major exception in this pattern.
As the seat of the paramount chief, its institutional status and functions enable it
to attract population in a general area of
decline. Compared with about 100 psm on
the frontier, most of the interior sections
have densities in excess of 450. Pelungu,
Tindongo, and Zanlerigu, lying the greatest
distance from the river, have the highest
densities, ranging from 536 to 1,020 psm.
For agricultural areas, these densities may
be the highest in Ghana, although other
parts of the northeast also have very high
densities.

It is clear from field observation that,
under the present system of agriculture and
settlement, the land is overcrowded and
over-worked. There is insufficient land for
adequate bush fallow, and many areas have

TABLE 2. POPULATION DENSITY, 1960

	Square miles	Popula-tion	Density	
			Persons per sq. ml. (psm)	Acres per person (app)
Gongo	1.43	94	66	9.7
Nyaboka	1.36	102	75	8.5
Nkunzesi	1.28	105	82	7.8
Dusobilogo	1.20	170	142	4.5
Dagliga	3.14	611	194	3.3
Guosi	1.44	313	217	2.9
Yakoti	2.33	600	258	2.5
Damologo	2.54	716	282	2.3
Kalini, Nakpaliga	4.62	1,416	307	2.1
Soliga	1.69	734	448	1.4
Zoa	1.93	854	454	1.4
Kongo	3.99	1,888	473	1.4
Logri	1.75	864	494	1.3
Pelungu	2.78	1,491	536	1.2
Zanlerigu	4.62	2,530	548	1.2
Tindongo	1.12	1,145	1,020	0.6
Occuped area	37.22	13,633	366	1.7
Abandoned area				
(i) now reserved	11.9	nil	nil	nil
(ii) other	10.7	nil	nil	nil
TOTAL	59.8	13,633	228	2.8

Note: Compiled by author. See Figure 5.

already been stripped of their topsoil. Sheet-wash erosion is common, and gullying is not infrequent. Nutritional levels are at best precarious, and before each harvest there is an estimated forty to sixty percent deficiency in calorie intake.[3] Seasonal hunger is faced with equanimity, and seasonal loss of body weight accepted as part of the

[3] B. S. Platt and J. Mayer, "Report of Joint FAO/WHO Mission to Ghana, 1959," FAO/59/5/3880, Accra, 44 p. (cyclostyled).

normal pattern of events. During the 1963–1964 hunger season, a sample consisting of 265 individuals in Nangodi, many already bodily underweight, lost an average of 6.5 percent of their body weight.[4]

The problem of overcrowding is most acute in the central areas of fixed cultivation in each section where densities in the order of 1,000-1,200 psm obtain, to the exclusion of all fallow and grazing (Table 3, Fig. 3). Even where the whole area of a section is considered, as in the case of Zoagin, in Zanlerigu chiefdom, mean density, including such bush farms and areas of rough grazing as there are, can be as high as 956 psm, with a central density of 1,420 psm (Table 4, Fig. 2).

An interesting question arising here is how to ascertain the degree of overcrowding. How can optimum density be determined? What constitutes a reasonable

TABLE 3. POPULATION DENSITY IN SELECTED DENTRAL AREAS OF FIXED CULTIVATION, 1948

	Part of Tindongo	Part of Pelungu	Part of Sakoti
Area cultivated annually (acres)	337	122	83
Number of houses (1949)	87	27	18
Total population (1948)	644	211	135
Persons per house	7.4	7.8	7.5
Acres per house	3.87	4.5	4.6
Acres per person	0.523	0.578	0.612
Persons per square mile	1,223	1,107	1,046

Note: Compiled by author. Air photos and census data are nearly contemporaneous, a rare coincidence, thus permitting accurate calculation of density. Areas calculated from air photos of 1949; population data calculated from 1948 Census tables. Densities relate only to land around houses cultivated annually, not to areas of bush farms and rough grazing. Sakoti, just east of Pelungu, lies outside Nangodi traditional area. See Figures 2 and 3.

[4] Author's survey of body weights.

TABLE 4. POPULATION DENSITY IN THE
ZOAGIN SECTION OF ZANLERIGU
CHIEFDOM, 1960

	Whole section	Central part of section
Population	478	355
Area in acres	322	162
Area in square miles	0.50	0.25
Number of houses	62	46
Persons per house	7.7	7.7
Acres per house	5.2	3.5
Acres per person	0.67	0.46
Persons per square mile	956	1,420

Source: Compiled by author. Number of houses and section boundary surveyed by author in 1963. Population estimated from 1960 Census; see Table 1. Whole area of section includes two sacred groves, waste- and grazing-land. All bush farms and fallow land lying beyond the section boundary are excluded from the table.

maximum density under the existing agricultural system? In the savanna areas under shifting cultivation in northern Ghana, another study has shown a strong correlation ($r = 0.778$) between migration trends and population density, but interpretation of the limited data is difficult.[5] In contrast the fixed farming system, with its highly individual characteristics, calls for a different approach. Fortunately, some relevant data exist. In an intensive survey of fifty-four houses in northeast Ghana in 1932-1936, Lynn, an agricultural officer, concluded that the average amount of land cultivated per head per annum was 0.66 acres, of which 78 percent was fixed (i.e., cultivated each year) and 22 percent in bush farm. The average farmer cultivated 2.49 acres which supported 3.7 persons including himself.[6] Conditions have not changed

[5] J. M. Hunter, "Ascertaining Population Carrying Capacity under Traditional Systems of Agriculture in Developing Countries: note on a method employed in Ghana," *Professional Geographer*, May, 1966, pp. 151–54.
[6] C. W. Lynn, *Agriculture in North Mamprusi* (Accra, Ghana: Dept. of Agriculture, Bulletin 34, 1937), 93 pp.

markedly since the 1930's and Lynn's data still are generally applicable.

Using Lynn's data, we may now attempt an evaluation of the population densities obtaining in Nangodi today, since the system of fixed cultivation is unchanged. In a hypothetical situation where all land is cultivated at a rate of 0.66 acres per person (hereafter "app") (0.515 fixed and 0.145 bush farm) the equivalent population density in Nangodi would be 970 psm. Hence where today densities of this order are found, it may be assumed that no space remains for fallow land. Under such pressure, erosion is inevitable, although it may be delayed by the working of bush farms at some distance from the settled area. In Nangodi, however, much land has been rendered uncultivable by river blindness, and the same is true of many other parts of northern Ghana.

In another hypothetical situation, let us assume that the bush farm is part of a seven-year rotation. Under these conditions, no erosion would develop on the bush farm. An amount of 1.53 app (0.515 fixed, 0.145 bush farm, and 0.87 fallow for bush farm) would be required, giving an equivalent population density of 418 psm. By this criterion, half of Nangodi is overpopulated.

However, the foregoing calculation assumes that all land in the settled area is utilizable, whereas in fact some allowance must be made, say fifteen percent (which is rather conservative) for sacred groves, rock outcrops (especially quartz), and other infertile land. Hardly any slope in Nangodi is too steep for cultivation under the system of crude stone terraces that are constructed. It is assumed here that cattle will graze on this land (excluding the sacred groves) and on the fallow bush farms. On the basis of fifteen percent waste or nonarable, an amount of 1.8 app would be required, giving a mean density of 356 psm. By this standard, the whole of Nangodi is overpopulated and parts of it are apparently carrying three times the possible load.

Implicit in all considerations so far is the

idea that productivity can be maintained indefinitely in the area of fixed cultivation around the house (0.515 app). But one sees in the field that, in areas of lower natural fertility, particularly where dressings of cattle manure have been meager for various reasons, some home farms not surprisingly become exhausted and have to be abandoned. An allowance for this factor of declining fertility among a proportion of home farms would, therefore, reduce still further the hypothetical carrying capacity of the land to an undetermined value significantly less than 356 psm, possibly in the order of 278 psm, if one allows for the equivalent of a reserve home farm to be developed in the event of advancing soil exhaustion.

By all accounts, therefore, Nangodi is patently overcrowded.[7] Quite apart from the inevitable concomitants of soil exhaustion and soil erosion, this means that no food is available to support the natural rate of population increase (i.e., births in excess of deaths) which is in the order of 2.5–3.0 percent per annum. At present the chronic imbalance is redressed by a continuous stream of emigration. Pressure would be relieved if the abandoned zone were to be resettled; in fact the mean density would fall to 228 psm. But this is not practicable in the immediately foreseeable future and, until the problem of river blindness is solved, it appears likely that the amount of available agricultural land will continue to contract.

Increased agricultural productivity would raise the carrying capacity of the land, but so far little headway has been made in this direction. Food production is strictly limited by the technique of hoe cultivation. On an average, a farmer supporting 3.7

persons, including himself, can cultivate only 2.49 acres. Any attempt to increase the acreage would not be worthwhile because of the lack of manure and, more importantly, because of the farmer's inability to keep down the rank growth of weeds in the rainy season. Weeding of Guinea corn and millet is backbreaking toil, often continuing from dawn to dusk. The techniques of the agricultural system therefore impose a strict physical limit on the amount of the land that can be cultivated. For survival in the dry season the farmer knows that he must reap an adequate harvest of cereals in the rainy season. He prefers, therefore, to cultivate, a fixed parcel of land around his home which he can manure annually, and on which ripening crops can be protected against birds and rodents. Because of the tendency for agnatically related families to live as close as possible to each other, and because of the system of fixed cultivation, the normal population density in settled areas tends to be higher than perhaps one might expect.

To summarize, it may be said that relatively high population densities are the norm under the fixed agricultural system but, by comparison with certain hypothetical situations, it seems clear that prevailing densities in Nangodi are three to four times in excess of the apparent carrying capacity of the system. Relief would be forthcoming if land abandoned because of river blindness could be resettled, or if a radical breakthrough in agricultural technique could be achieved, but immediate prospects are not bright. Land Planning [8] seems to offer possibilities for the implementation of changes in agriculture more or less within the existing social framework, but early promise of rapid development has not been fulfilled. More recently a start has been made with state farms which of course permit com-

---

[7] For purposes of comparison with the present study, reference may be made to A. T. Grove, "Population Densities and Agriculture in Northern Nigeria," in K. M. Barbour and R. M. Prothero (Eds.), *Essays on African Population*, 1961, pp. 115–36. The highest density Grove records is 307 psm for the Dan Yusufu District of northern Katsina, an area of 121 square miles, where problems of land impoverishment and emigration are very acute.

[8] T. E. Hilton, (1) "Land Planning and Resettlement in Northern Ghana," *Geography*, Vol. 44 (November, 1959), pp. 227–40, and (2) "Frafra Rettlement and the Population Problem in Zuarfungu," *Bull. Inst. Français Afrique Noire*, Series B, Vol. 22 (1960), pp. 426–42.

TABLE 5. SUMMARY OF POPULATION
DECLINE IN NANGODI, 1948-1960

| | 1948 | 1960 | Decline | |
			Absolute	%
Number of houses	2,147	1,936	211	9.8
Persons per house	7.45	7.04	0.41	5.5
Total population	16,004	13,633	2,371	14.8

Source: Based on Census Tables of 1948 and 1960.

plete severance with traditional practice. It is early to judge, but progress so far has been uncertain. This leaves emigration as the only effective outlet for overpopulation.

In an intercensal period of twelve years, between 1948 and 1960, the number of houses in Nangodi declined by 9.8 percent, house-size by 5.5 percent, and total population by 14.8 percent (Table 5). Unadorned, these figures tell a sorry tale.

With the exception of five interior areas, which show slight increases, every section suffered a reduction in the number of houses (Table 6, Fig. 6). The heaviest de-

TABLE 6. DESERTION OF HOUSES, 1948—1960

| | No. of houses | | | Persons per house | | |
	1948	1960	Change	1948	1960	Change
Kalini	155	123	−32	7.6	7.9	+0.3
Guosi		31				
Nkunzesi	136	20	−25	9.2	7.8	−1.4
Nakpaliga		60				
Nyaboka	62	28	−34	6.5	3.6	−2.9
Yakoti	114	94	−20	6.4	6.4	—
Soliga	110	117	+7	7.5	6.3	−1.2
Gongo	47	11	−36	6.1	8.5	+2.4
Dusobilogo	35	28	−7	7.8	6.1	−1.7
Zoa	177	142	−35	6.4	6.0	−0.4
Adusabisi	133	179	+46	6.4	6.3	−0.1
Asinabisi	116	116	—	7.0	6.5	−0.5
Logri	179					
Dagliga	121	322	−136	7.2	6.8	−0.4
Damologo	158					
Pelungu	192	196	+4	7.8	7.6	−0.2
Tindongo	100	148	+48	7.4	7.7	+0.3
Zanlerigu	312	321	+9	8.8	7.9	−0.9
Totals	2,147	1,936	−211	7.5	7.0	−0.5
Subtotals			−325			
			+114			

Source: Based on 1948 and 1960 Census tables. Intercensal change only is recorded, not actual numbers of houses built and abandoned in the intercensal period. Sections not separately listed in the Census tables are grouped together; see Figure 6.

cline occurs along the retreating frontier of settlement: Gongo, for example, fell from forty-seven to eleven houses. Population change, by sections, follows an almost identical distributional pattern (Table 7, Fig. 7). What emerges from a comparison of Figures 5, 6, and 7, is that, paradoxically, the areas of greatest population density have declined the least. Factors such as soil fertility and clan affiliation (interior core areas being most resistant to decline) are undoubtedly influential. The adjacent chiefdoms of Tindongo and Zanlerigu, both with high densities, occupy very hilly and presumably healthy areas farthest from the disease stricken abandoned zone.

The relative significance of these population figures may be best appreciated by comparison with intercensal trends in Ghana as a whole. Between 1948 and 1960, Ghana's population rose by sixty-three percent, and of the country's sixty-nine local councils existing at the time of the last census, only four failed to register an increase, and two of these lay in the northeast: Builsa, −0.6 percent, and Frafra, of which Nangodi is a part, −8.2 percent. In the other northeast councils, the 1960 populations fell short of natural increase over the period: Kassena-Nankani, +3 percent and Kusasi, +18 percent.[9]

In Nangodi, as in most parts of Africa, birthrates appear to be remaining at traditionally high levels, whereas certain former checks to population growth, such as interclan warfare, slave-raiding, famine, and major epidemics no longer apply. It may be noted here, as a subjective impression, that infant mortality does not appear to have been significantly reduced as yet. The law of survival of the fittest appears to operate harshly amongst infants with regard

TABLE 7. POPULATION CHANGE, 1948–1960

	Population		Change	
	1948	*1960*	*Nos.*	*Precent*
Kalini	1,172	971	−201	−17.2
Guosi		313		
Nkunzesi	1,248	105	−385	−30.8
Nakpaliga		445		
Nyaboka	405	102	−303	−74.8
Yakoti	733	600	−133	−18.1
Soliga	824	734	−90	−10.9
Gongo	288	94	−194	−67.4
Dusobilogo	274	170	−104	−38.0
Zoa	1,133	854	−279	−24.6
Adusabisi	850	1,134	+284	+33.4
Asinabisi	810	754	−56	−6.9
Logri	1,267	864	−403	−31.8
Dagliga	897	611	−286	−31.9
Damologo	1,113	716	−397	−35.7
Pelungu	1,500	1,491	−9	−0.6
Tindongo	740	1,145	+405	+54.7
Zanlerigu	2,750	2,530	−220	−8.0
Totals	16,004	13,633	−2,371	−14.8
Subtotals			−3,004	
			+633	

Source: Based on 1948 and 1960 Census tables. Sections grouped together, above, are not separately listed in the Census tables; see Figure 7.

to endemic diseases. Nevertheless, on balance, one may reasonably expect an expansion rather than a decline of population, and more so, in fact, as health services improve. A very useful indication is given in Fortes' pioneer survey of fertility among the neighboring Tallensi which showed, on the basis of data collected in 1934 and 1943, that population had been increasing moderately.[10]

Intercensal population decline in Nangodi is caused by heavy emigration (Table 7). This results from the combined effects

[9] J. M. Hunter, "Regional Patterns of Population Growth in Ghana, 1948–1960," in J. B. Whittow and P. D. Wood (Eds.), *Essays in Geography for Austin Miller* (Reading, England: University of Reading, 1965), Table 3, p. 277, Fig. 65.10, p. 290.

[10] M. Fortes, "A Note on Fertility among the Tallensi of the Gold Coast," *Sociological Review*, Vol. 35 (1943), pp. 99–113.

of local population pressure and the ever-present lure of money and adventure in the south of Ghana. An attempt is made in Table 8 to estimate the mean rate of net emigration from Nangodi between 1948 and 1960. On the basis of certain assumptions, explained in the table, one may conclude that, in the twelve-year intercensal period, total net emigration amounted to about fifty-two percent of the 1948 population, a staggering figure. The mean annual rate appears to have been about four percent. Nangodi is running down, and, overcrowded as it still is, it already faces a serious man-power problem because those

who emigrate are generally males of the most active age-group.

As a result of emigration, structural imbalance of the population is best illustrated by comparing the number of males to every 100 females in the economically active age-group of 15–44 years (Table 9, Fig. 8). As compared with the Ghana mean of 98, Nangodi's mean was only 52. The most balanced parts of Nangodi are Nkunzesi and Nyaboka, but these areas have declined so much through blindness that they are not numerically significant when compared with other areas. Even though Nangodi's sex ratio is so low, it is not untypical of north-

TABLE 8. ESTIMATES OF NET EMIGRATION FROM NANGODI, 1948–1960

		(a)	(b)
1. 1948 Census population		16,004	
2. 1960 Census population		13,633	
3. Intercensal decline		−2,371	
4. % Intercensal decline		−14.8%	
5. 1960 hypothetical population based upon assumed rates of natural increase (1948–1960) of (a) 2.5% per annum and (b) 2.88% p.a.		21,522	22,501
6. Hypothetical natural increase (5−1)		+5,518	+6,479
7. % Hypothetical natural increase (i.e., of 1948 pop.)		+34.5%	+40.6%
8. Net emigration (5−2)		−7,889	−8,868
9. % Net emigration (i.e., of 1948 pop.)		−49.3%	−55.4%
10. Rate of intercensal decline, percent per annum		−1.326%	−1.326%
11. Assumed rate of natural increase percent per annum		+2.500%	+2.875%
12. Deduced net emigration rate percent per annum		−3.826%	−4.201%

Calculated by author. The estimates of mean rate of natural increase which are used above apply to the whole of northern Ghana (Northern and Upper Regions) and are kindly supplied by Dr. J. C. Caldwell, Associate Professor of Demography, University of Ghana. Using age-structure data, various hypothetical life tables and hypothetical lengths of a generation (42.5 years in 1960 37.5 years in 1948), to develop approximate replacement indices, Dr. Caldwell arrived at provisional figures of 3% p.a. for 1960 and 2.75% p.a. for 1948; the mean for the period being 2.875%. But he considers it probable that overstatement of age among the older women has inflated the rates, and he therefore suggests values of 2.5–2.75% for 1960 and 2.25–2.50% for 1948; the mean being 2.50%. In the above table on Nangodi both means have been employed. Dr. Caldwell estimates that birthrates in northern Ghana are about 50 per thousand per annum and death rates 20–25.

TABLE 9. SEX RATIO IN 1960 AS AN
INDEX OF EMIGRATION

	Males per 100 females in age-group 15–44 yrs.		Males per 100 females in age-group 15–44 yrs.
Kalini	65	Adusabisi	53
Guosi	60	Asinabisi	51
Nkunzesi		Logri	54
	81		
Nyaboka		Dagliga	35
Yakoti	59	Damologo	57
Soliga	48	Pelungu	60
Nakpaliga	43	Tindongo	29
Gongo		Zanlerigu	57
	45		
Dusobilogo		All Nangodi	52
Zoa	38	Ghana	98

Calculated by author from 1960 Census tables; see Figure 8.

east Ghana generally, which has the lowest ratios in the country: Frafra 59, Kassena-Nankani 66, and Kusasi 74.[11]

The local and regional implications of this very heavy emigration from northeast Ghana are far-reaching. The crisis of over-population needs to be solved, whereas at the same time, the present high rate of emi-gration must be arrested, or at least bal-anced to some extent. The present residue

[11] Hunter, *op. cit.*, footnote 9, Table 3, Fig. 65.8.

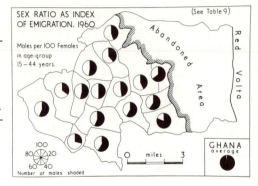

Figure 8.—Sex ratio as index of emigration, 1960.

population is lopsided in its sex balance and age-structure, which is highly undesirable from both economic and social viewpoints. Furthermore, whereas it can be suggested (and this is a topic calling for further inves-tigation) that emigration is to an important extent seasonal, it is apparent from the population record that much of it soon be-comes permanent. If it is accepted that the impoverished northern savanna of Ghana, and particularly its overcrowded northeast, should receive a share of the nation's devel-opment capital, then it is clear that only a coordinated, interdisciplinary plan, drawn up on broad regional lines, would have any chance of success when confronted with an array of interrelated problems as intransi-gent as population pressure, overcultivation, soil erosion, seasonal hunger, emigration, and hyperendemic disease.

The remoteness and inaccessibility of northeast Ghana only exa-cerbate its population-land problems (Taafe *et al.*, 1963). In the West Nile District of Uganda, the situation is similar, although socio-cultural systems, agricultural practices, and population num-bers differ markedly throughout the district (McMaster, 1962a).

The Lugbara illustrate problems that arise from population fixation: before achievement of political stability under colonial government, these people acquired land as they needed it, and at the expense of weaker neighboring groups. Similar examples of the effects of colonial rule upon population-land relationships are to be found in other parts of Africa (Schlippe, 1956). Population in the West Nile District is not distributed in relation to potential carrying capacity, and evidence from different parts of the district illustrates the environmental and social consequences which may ensue. Land shortages have seriously impaired the environmental base, particularly soil fertility, and it is possible that labor migration, which has developed in response to these shortages, may destroy the social organization of the district. Yet the latter consequence is not inevitable, for there are examples of traditional societies in Africa that have adjusted socially and economically to the absence of a large proportion of the male labor force at any one time (Van Velsen, 1960; Watson, 1958).

13. *Land and Population in West Nile District, Uganda*

J. F. M. MIDDLETON AND D. J. GREENLAND

The West Nile District of Uganda is one of the most remote areas of the Protectorate: it is also one of the most densely populated. The economy of the District is very considerably affected by shortage of land and by pressure of population. The analysis of the relationship between these factors was the central problem of research of the Oxford University Expedition to Uganda, which spent three months in the District in the summer of 1953.[1] The expedition made comparative surveys of four small village areas—"village" is here used to refer to the scattered settlement of a small lineage or sub-clan selected from different geographical zones and tribal groups. Study was made of land use, the effects of over-population, labour migration to the

[1] The expedition consisted of a botanist, a geographer, a soil scientist (Greenland) and a social anthropologist (Middleton). For a time it was joined by an ecologist from the East African Agriculture and Forestry Research Organization. Acknowledgement is made for financial and other assistance to the Royal Geographical Society, the late Mr. H. N. Spalding, various colleges and trusts of the University of Oxford, the Colonial Office and the Government of Uganda. The anthropologist had earlier spent two years in the area, with assistance from the Worshipful Company of Goldsmiths, the Colonial Office and the Wenner-Gren Foundation for Anthropological Research, New York. D. J. Greenland acknowledges permission to take part in this work during tenure of an award from the Agricultural Research Council.

From *The Geographical Journal, 120*, 1954, pp. 446–455.
Reprinted by permission of the Royal Geographical Society.

wealthier parts of southern Uganda, the introduction of new crops (especially cash crops) and the general economy of these groups, as far as was possible in three months. This is far too short a time to make anything but a cursory study of such problems, but the fact that the anthropologist had already collected a certain amount of background material partially overcame objections to such an ambitious programme. General botanical and pedological surveys of the area were also made, as far as was practicable.

The West Nile District of the Northern Province of Uganda is separated from the remainder of the Protectorate by the Albert Nile. It is geographically part of the Nile-Congo divide and has more in common with the neighbouring areas of the Belgian Congo than with the rest of Uganda. On its eastern border the valley of the Nile is some 2000 feet above sea level, but the line of the divide, which forms the international boundary on its west, is between 4000 feet in the north of the District, where the Uganda, Congo and Sudan borders meet, and 6000 feet in the south. Most of the population is clustered in the highland zone near the divide. Much of the low-lying country along the Nile, to the east of the Madi escarpment which marks the edge of the highlands, is virtually empty of population and is thick bush, with low rainfall, and infested with game and tsetse. The highland zone however, an open and almost treeless plateau, has a well-distributed rainfall of some 50 inches a year, with everywhere abundant permanent streams and a fertility able to support a population of up to 250 persons a square mile in some areas, a comparatively high figure for a simple African agricultural economy.

There are four main tribal groups in the District: the Lugbara (183,000) and Madi (63,000) both Sudanic-speaking, the Nilotic-speaking Alur and Jonam (together 81,000) and the Nilo-Hamitic-speaking Kakwa (17,000). These figures are for those living in Uganda only: all of them extend across the international boundaries into the Congo or the Sudan. Two villages were selected from Lugbara, one (Maraca) in the most thickly populated area of the highland plateau and the other (Omugo) near the lowland region of the Nile Valley; one from Alur (Paidha) in the southern highlands, and one from Madi (Metu) in the isolated massif in the north-east corner of the District. In this short article most attention is given to the situation in Maraca, since longer was spent there than at the other villages.

The central feature of the surveys was the study of land shortage and over-population. Critical land shortage for a peasant community can be defined as inability of the land to produce sufficient to support the people living on it, both as food and as a means to acquire consumer goods; it also exists when the community is able to support itself only by ruining the soil on which it depends, although in this case the effects on the community may not be immediately obvious. It is often said that land shortage in an area such as this is merely the result of the breakdown of indigenous systems of agriculture under modern conditions, with increase of population and the introduction of a cash economy and new crops, without proportionate development of agricultural methods and techniques. It is implied that if different methods of agriculture were introduced land shortage would cease. Although there is considerable truth in this view, it takes into account only the purely agricultural aspect of the problem and ignores the sociological one. The insufficiency of land to a population may be studied from these two aspects, which are significant in different situations. We use the term "land shortage" to refer to the lack of sufficient land as far as purely agricultural needs are concerned, and the term "land pressure" where the criterion for assessing insufficiency of land is a social one rather than a purely agricultural one.

The soils and climate of West Nile District are such that over-use of the soil will

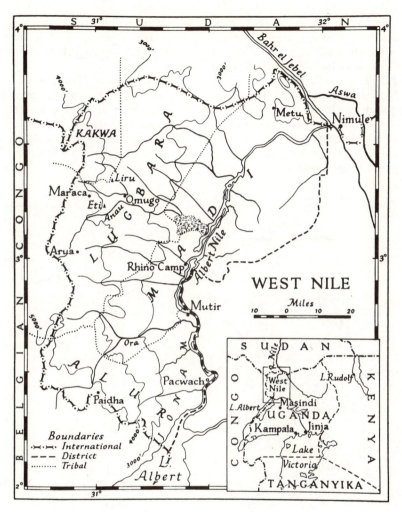

Figure 1.

lead to accelerated soil degradation and erosion. The central part of the district is a maturely eroded plateau, divided into low convex hills by the many small streams that thread their way across it. The tops of these hills are often denuded of soil, exposing the grey granitic gneiss of the African Basement Complex, the principal rock formation of the district. The soils on the hillsides consist of grey sandy loam overlying a heavy compact red subsoil. Near the outcrops the grey topsoil lies directly on the parent rock, and it seems probable that the composite profile has been formed by gradual drift of the sandy loam from higher ground to lower. The total soil depth is seldom greater than 4 feet. Unsatisfactory agricultural practices on such a soil would be expected to lead to serious sheet erosion. At Maraca the indigenous agricultural practices combine to satisfy all the essential requirements for preventing serious erosion. The cropping period is short so that soil structure is never completely lost and is regained by the end of three or four years' fallow; a system of sowing crops in mixed stand and use of weeds as a mulch keep a vegetative cover on the soil for much of the year; and the field size is usually so small—two-thirds of the total cultivated area is in fields of less than a quarter of an acre (see Table I)—that it is impossible for surface run-off to attain much size, as the field boundaries serve as bunds. It is a system of low productivity agriculture, but with

our present limited knowledge of tropical management it is doubtful whether any other would maintain the soil fertility so well.

The facts about Maraca are the more significant when comparisons are made with the situations at Omugo and Paidha. At both places the physical features are such that accelerated erosion is more likely to occur than at Maraca. Pavement *murram*, or sheet ironstone, is found over large areas

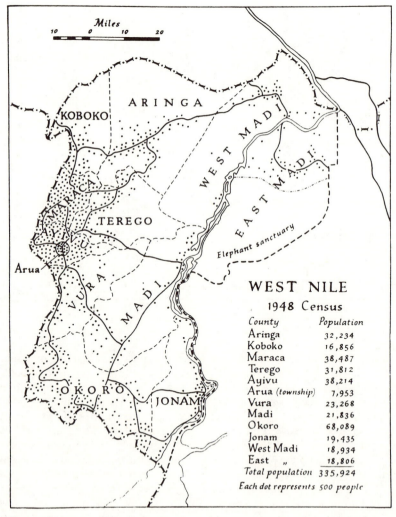

Figure 2.

at Omugo, frequently very near the surface. It is highly impermeable, so that during rainstorms the soil soon becomes saturated and the amount of run-off is considerable, even from a well-structured soil. This has led to the exposure of the pavement *murram* in some areas. This naturally great liability to erosion is accompanied by an unsuitable agricultural system, in which variations of practice are more extreme than at Maraca. The chief differences from Maraca are longer cropping periods between fallows and larger field sizes. Tobacco is grown as a cash crop, but it has not been grown for a sufficiently long period for any faults in the agricultural system to be attributed to its cultivation. It is grown rather haphazardly and its place in the rotations seems to vary according to individual whim.

At Paidha there are very pronounced topographical differences from Maraca and Omugo. In place of the open plain intersected by many small water-courses there are steep grassy hillsides and sharp valleys containing large trees. Many of the ridges and valleys have deep soils, but on the hillsides which comprise by far the greatest proportion of the land surface of this region the soil is only about a foot deep and where erosion has occurred the fragmentary quartzite, which the soil normally overlies, is found at the surface. These steep hillsides are very frequently cultivated and the existence of only occasional and then very inadequate anti-erosion measures allows erosion on them to proceed rapidly. This erosion is aggravated by the fact that cropping is usually continued until the soil structure is completely lost, causing a greater loss of soil during run-off and making recolonization by grasses after cropping slow, so that the soil is directly exposed to the destructive effects of the sun and rain for a longer period.

At Omugo and Paidha, and also at Metu, land is said by the people to be plentiful. This may partly account for the very lax agriculture practised at the former places, but at Metu there is as well organized a

system as at Maraca. Erosion is less likely to occur at Metu since almost all the cultivated land lies along a flat plain. Cotton is grown as a cash crop, but it has taken its place within the agricultural system and so far there are no signs of any ill effects.

Maintenance of soil fertility in the tropics requires primarily the maintenance of stability of the soil to erosion. Nutrient status is usually of secondary importance. The results of analyses of soil samples collected at Maraca, Omugo and Metu have however shown that they are unusually poor in nutrients; at Paidha they are somewhat better in this respect. Results of experiments conducted by the Uganda Agriculture Department have shown that the soils at Maraca are not suited to the production of high value cash crops.[2]

Land shortage is a relationship between man and the soil he cultivates; land pressure is a relationship either between persons or groups of the men who live on the soil, this essentially social relationship being expressed by the persons in it in terms of land. Land pressure is thus a concomitant of certain critical stages reached in changes in social organization. These stages may be seen in terms of availability of land, livestock or other resources which have high social value for the society. For the people of West Nile District, who although they possess livestock are primarily cultivators and who have little of the emotional relationship with livestock found among some other East African peoples, land has such a value. Lugbara say that it is at Maraca that there is the highest degree of land pressure in their country. They say "here there are no fields, people crowd together, the territory is destroyed". Land pressure

---

[2] Our attention has been drawn to this by Dr. A. S. Thomas, formerly Economic Botanist to the Uganda Government. We are grateful to the Department of Agriculture Research Station, Kawanda, Uganda, and the East African Agriculture and Forestry Research Organization, Kikuyu, Kenya, for carrying out analyses of soil samples.

is a continuous topic of conversation and is the focus of local complaints and of local opposition to change. For the people of Maraca indeed increasing land pressure and social change are almost synonymous.

Lugbara live in extended family groups, each based on a lineage of three or four generations. A typical group includes a man, his sons and grandsons and their wives and children, and there are frequently attached uterine and affinal kin also. These groups are units of a wider system of territorial sections based on lineages and clans, the largest of which average 4000 people. There are no larger indigenous groups. Formerly each clan group lived in the centre of its own territory, which might be some 20 square miles or more, and around its homesteads was a stretch of unsettled land, on which were farms and grazing areas. Each homestead—occupied by a

single wife—had, and Lugbara say still should have, three main types of field, the *amvu akua*, the fields at home, the *amvu amve*, the fields outside, and the *yimile*, the riverine fields.[3] Riverine fields have high fertility and are used for crops such as sweet potatoes, maize, sugar and bananas, and are given at most very short fallow periods. Home fields are fertilized with ashes or manure and are used for the more demanding crops. Outside fields are not fertilized and are used for the staple, eleusine, grown in mixed stand with sorghums, simsim and pigeon pea. The rotation cycles are traditionally different for each type of field, and only the outside fields can be said ever to be under a system of shifting

[3] The names vary in different parts of Lugbara. Similar systems are found in the other tribes of the district.

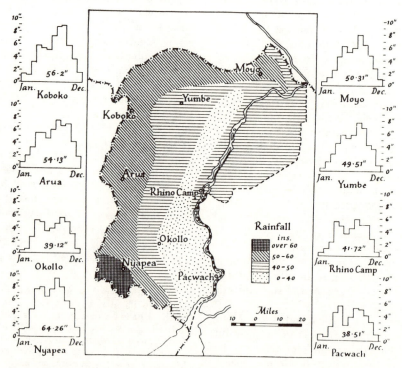

Figure 3.

agriculture; the others are under a system of permanent farming. Outside fields are traditionally either cultivated for two or three years and then revert to bush, or reopened after three years' fallow. Home fields have a higher proportion of cultivation to fallow. These figures are for Maraca. Elsewhere they differ according to soil type: fallow is often as long as fifteen years after two years of cultivation. Some crops are also grown on the rubbish heaps outside the compounds, but these are outside the main agricultural system. Fallow is used for grazing, and there are also specific grazing areas, usually where the soil is known to be too thin for permanent cultivation. The use of indicator plants to show when a field is ready for fallow or ready to be opened after fallow means that the proportion of cultivation to fallow varies from area to area according to soil potentialities.[4]

Traditionally each clan territory contained more or less sufficient land for cultivation, fallow and grazing, and sufficient of each type of land, riverine and dry fields, for its population. Amongst the Lugbara there has always been a considerable degree of individual mobility, a man being able to attach himself to his mother's or his wife's kin—both these categories live in different clan areas, by the rule of clan exogamy. Such a tenant is given sufficient land for his needs so long as he and his descendants stay. By this means it has always been possible for individual adjustments to take place in land distribution; often a man merely acquires cultivation rights in one or two fields in this way, if his village is short of land of a particular type.

Traditionally the distribution of Lugbara settlements was always in a state of slow

[4] Details of agricultural methods, rotations, seed mixtures and so on are not given in this paper. They vary throughout the area with local differences in soil, rainfall and other factors. They are generalized in "Agriculture in Uganda," by J. D. Tothill and others (London, 1940).

change. The whole tribe came from the north, and when the Europeans entered the country seems to have been still drifting slowly southwards. There were no stable boundaries between clans and lineages, but the entire society was in a permanent state of territorial adjustment. Expanding groups could thus acquire control over an area at the expense of a decreasing group.

Today there are many changes from this traditional pattern. The Administration has fixed boundaries between tribes, clans and villages at the places where these were when it created chiefs and tried to stabilize this fluid system of social organization. Effective administration dates from 1915 or so—although the area has been administered nominally since 1900—and men can show where the fields, grazing grounds and former village areas used to be. There has also been considerable increase in population. One consequence of these factors has been an ever-increasing disparity between the distribution of population and that of land, so that instead of the density of population varying according to the carrying capacity of the land, there is now serious maldistribution of population to land. The people of one village may be living at a far higher density than those of a neighbouring one. Boundaries are fixed and anyone who attempts to farm across them is haled before a Government chief as a troublemaker.

The distribution of types of field has altered radically in Maraca, though not in Omugo. In the former there are no longer any outside fields. The staple millet mixture, traditionally grown on them, is now grown on home fields only. Outside field areas today are occupied by family groups which have built their homesteads and opened their home fields there; they are almost invariably groups with a kinship tie with the owners of the territory and so their tenants. There are still grazing areas, although people say they are inadequate, but they are found only in places of poor soil that are unfit for intensive farming.

However it is significant that at Maraca

the average total area of cultivated fields per head is the same as at Omugo, where the traditional field types are still found (see Table I). At Maraca there has been

TABLE 1. PERCENTAGE OF CULTIVATED LAND USED IN FIELDS OF DIFFERENT SIZES IN SQUARE YARDS

Group	0–1200	1200–2400	2400–3600	3600–4800	over 4800
Maraca	65.3	29.9	4.8	0	0
Omugo	18.9	17.6	19.3	2.7	41.5
Paidha	26.5	37.2	18.6	7.1	10.6
Metu	34.7	22.9	27.6	6.7	8.1

little or no radical change in the crop rotations themselves, although change might have been expected. It might have been expected also that the proportion of cassava grown would be greatest where land shortage is most pronounced, since this crop is far higher yielding, though of lower nutritional value, than any other known in the district. Maraca in fact was found to be using a smaller proportion of its land for cassava than the other three groups (see Table II). Also three years is still the minimum for fallow at Maraca. It is at Omugo and Paidha, in both of which areas

TABLE 2. CULTIVATION OF LAND AT FOUR SELECTED VILLAGE AREAS

Group	Members	Total cultivated land, square yards	Percentage in cassava	Percentage in cash crops	Average amount of land cultivated per head, square yards
Maraca	34	85,020	25.2	0.9	2500
Omugo	48	117,730	36.4	2.4	2450
Paidha	99	239,760	52.7	3.2	2380
Metu	52	123,760	42.1	9.4	2420

there is said by the inhabitants to be little land pressure (but where there is considerable soil erosion) that rotations are not followed.

The people of Maraca however are adamant in stating that they are suffering from serious overcrowding. The factor that is most important here is the migration of men to work as labourers outside the West Nile District: it is perhaps the most obvious social feature of Maraca today. Over a quarter of its adult men are absent at any one time, the highest rate for any Lugbara area, either in Uganda or the Congo. The basic factor is the inability of the highland areas of the district to grow cash crops or provide any other form of cash income, but land scarcity is also important. The 1948 census figures show that the higher the density of population of a Lugbara county (the largest administrative unit) the higher is the rate of labour migration (see Table III). The migration is of two types:

TABLE 3. POPULATION DENSITY AND MIGRATION RATES, LUGBARA COUNTIES

County	Density per square mile	Percentage of adult males away	Percentage of total population away
Maraca	240	26.5	7.8
Ayivu	239	20.9	7.5
Terego	80	17.8	5.2
Vura	65	13.7	5.8
Aringa	16	12.4	5.2

Note: The figures for Terego, Vura and Aringa counties are deceptive, since they contain large tracts of empty or almost empty bush. The centre of Terego has a density of about 150 per square mile, and that of Vura some 140.

Maraca supplies mainly contract labourers, young unmarried men for the most part, who go south on contract to the Indian sugar plantations for comparatively short periods and who in their lifetime make on the average three or four trips south, whereas Omugo supplies mostly migrants who go south to work in the cotton and tobacco fields, stay longer and make on the average only one trip.

The people of Maraca say that they have the highest rate of labour migration in the area because the young men have no land on which to farm or to grow cash crops to earn money: their contention seems to be correct. They say that there is witchcraft everywhere—Lugbara witchcraft is a result of arousing envy, and no man likes his home to be too close to another, nor his fields too fertile nor his cattle too many and fat, lest he be bewitched. They say that people are always quarrelling and taking land disputes to court because they are so overcrowded. These expressions of discontent with the general land position are far more marked at Maraca than anywhere else in the District. The village area surveyed has some quarter of its total territory occupied by fields loaned to sisters' sons and other kin, and the group has recently had to split up and two component segments move a mile or two away to another clan territory of poorer but emptier land, due to lack of spare bush land and long fallow for grazing and to repeated quarrelling over what resources there are.

From an agricultural viewpoint Omugo is in a much poorer state than Maraca. A shallow soil is eroding rapidly, and probably because of the present poverty of the soil the traditional agricultural system has almost completely broken down. Yet here outside fields are still available, and to the north of Omugo there are many square miles of little used land in which people open fields and let them revert to bush after a couple of years' cultivation. These fields are often as much as 7 or 8 miles from the homesteads. Because people do not yet have to live in too close proximity the symptoms of land pressure are not observed.

In Maraca, on the other hand, a balance has been struck between the factors of fixation of boundaries, increasing population and soil potentialities. This equilibrium could be upset by any large increase in effective farming population, that is, the population wholly or mainly dependent upon the land for its livelihood, but at present this is prevented by the high rate of labour migration. By men being absent the effective population is kept static; but the social population, the full membership of the area whether at home or temporarily away on migration, increases every year. A critical stage seems to have been reached in that the proportion that must necessarily be absent due to land shortage is so large as to threaten the smooth functioning of the social organization; this is seen by the people in terms of land pressure, of which they complain continually. The unsuitability of the soil at Maraca for cash crops is an important factor in determining the number of young men leaving the area to work in southern Uganda, but it is not the only cause. The rate of migration might be considerably reduced if the people were to modify their agricultural system, reduce their fallow period and grow tobacco, which will grow there, though not well. In all cases of land shortage there are three possible methods of relief: a decrease in population, an increase in soil fertility or a change to a more intensive agricultural system. It is often the last measure which has to be adopted, usually at the expense of the soil, being followed by disastrous soil erosion, and the community finds itself in a worse position than that in which it started. At Maraca however the agricultural system has not been changed. By migrating temporarily to Bunyoro and Buganda, in southern Uganda, the Lugbara have been able to borrow on the soil fertility of those areas, their absence from West Nile District at the same time relieving the population pressure there. Thus labour migration may be regarded as a symptom of land shortage, replacing the more usual symptoms of over-use of the soil. When land shortage leads to over-use of the soil, the soil is destroyed, when it leads to labour migration, the social structure may be destroyed.

Even where there are adjusted relationships between people and land, the balance between sufficiency and insufficiency to meet essential needs is delicate. These terms are highly relative—sufficiency, for example, may mean that life is maintained at subsistence levels only (Clark and Haswell, 1964). Sufficiency may also be subject to seasonal variations. The concept of "seasonal hunger" has been challenged as vague and inadequately supported (Miracle, 1961), but there is evidence that it can and does occur (Prothero, 1957c) and that its influence can be measured in terms of the physique of the people affected (Hunter, 1967c).

The period of seasonal hunger usually extends from the latter part of the dry season until the harvesting of the first crops in the wet season following. Shortages may be exaggerated by unusual climatic conditions (severe drought, torrential rains, etc.) or by political or social disruption. Seasonal hunger may be mitigated by the storage of local food surpluses (McMaster 1962b; Morgan 1959a), but more so by contributions of food from neighboring areas and other nations. On the whole, disruption through human agency has been reduced during the present century, but in recent times warfare has been responsible for food shortages in the Congo (Kinshasa) and Nigeria.

It has been possible to trace partially the history of food shortages in Tanzania, to indicate their nature, to identify the factors causing them, to outline human responses to them. Extreme shortage may produce apathy or even physical inability to do anything. But moderate shortages may motivate improvement. Reaction may depend on local tradition, with some groups complacently accepting what they consider to be inevitable. Changes in such long-established attitudes are likely to come about only if and when levels of expectation are raised, providing people with an incentive for improvement.

14. *Types of Food Shortages in Tanzania*

CLARKE BROOKE

The diversity of the problems of food supply in mainland Tanzania (Tanganyika) (Fig. 1), in location, cause, and effect, presents opportunities for analysis and classification. Where cash reserves are small and communications poor, as in much of the country, a single bad harvest frequently results in reduced food consumption; for the amounts of stored foodstuffs are rarely adequate to maintain rural populations much longer than from one year's harvest to the next. In a series of lean years the effects become cumulative. In many parts of the country two consecutive seasons of crop failure bring near-famine conditions to the stricken area, and a sequence of three years of poor harvests is usually catastrophic in its impact.

In most of the country physical conditions (Fig. 2) make agriculture and herding difficult. Two-thirds of Tanzania, including most of the Western, West Lake, Eastern, and Southern Regions,[1] is tsetse-infested woodland, bushland, and thicket. About 90 percent of the country has no permanent streams. A little more than half receives at least thirty inches of rainfall annually in four years out of five,[2] but only one-tenth receives more than forty inches with 80 percent probability (Figs. 3 and 4).

The distribution of mainland Tanzania's ten million people is shown in Figures 3 and 4. Gillman's study published in 1936 indicated that about two-thirds of the population were settled on one-tenth of the land area, and that almost two-thirds of the country was virtually uninhabited. This pattern has not changed greatly in thirty years, though the population has more than doubled.[3] Five general types of food shortages (one of which comprises three subtypes) have been determined, based on a combination of physical, social, and economic characteristics. These type categories are delineated in Figures 3 and 4 and summarized in Table I.

THE HIGHLAND (TYPE A)

About two million people, 20 percent of the population, live in the parts of the moist highlands that make up a little less than 2 percent of the total area of the country. These population clusters are in the northeast (Usambara and Pare Mountains and the lower slopes of Kilimanjaro and Meru), in the Uluguru Mountains near Morogoro, in small, widely separated parts of east-central Tanzania from Kilosa southwest to Iringa, in the Poroto Mountains north of Lake Malawi, in the west (northeast shore of Lake Tanganyika adjoining

[1] In 1962 the nine largest administrative units, formerly called "Provinces," became "Regions." Additional changes in 1963 created seventeen Regions from the nine. In this paper the pre-1963 names and boundaries of provinces are used.

[2] J. F. Griffiths: The Climate of East Africa, *in* The Natural Resources of East Africa (edited by E. W. Russell; Nairobi, 1962), pp.77–87; reference on p. 79.

[3] Clement Gillman: A Population Map of Tanganiyika Territory, *Geogr. Rev.*, Vol. 26, 1936, pp. 353–375; reference on p. 357. Compare with Philip W. Porter: East Africa—Population Distribution—As of August 1962, *Annals Assn. of Amer. Geogrs.*, Vol. 56, 1966, Map Supplement No. 6 (with accompanying text, p. 180).

Reprinted from *The Geographical Review*, Vol. 57, 1967, pp. 333–357. Copyright © 1967 by the American Geographical Society of New York. This study was supported by a grant from the National Science Foundation. The writer thanks Mr. Murray Lunan, formerly the director of the Tanzania Department of Agriculture, and many other residents of Tanzania for their cooperation and hospitality. Of special value were historical data on food shortages in the country provided by 127 mission stations, Catholic, Anglican, and Lutheran.

Figure 1.

the borders of Burundi and southeastern Rwanda), and in the Bukoba District west of Lake Victoria. These are the most densely settled rural parts of the country, with more than 200 people per square mile.[4] Land use is marked by its sedentary character and by the emphasis given to garden crops and bananas. Some cultivators gain cash income from coffee and other tree crops, and in several places there is an incipient system of individual land tenure.

Although rainfall reliability is a basic limitation to productivity, its relationship

to famine is not simple. In the highlands the probable minimum annual rainfall over a five-year period is 40 inches or more. Yet food shortages in these "most favored" parts are by no means rare. Some shortages are attributed to "too much rain," others to political and administrative causes, but most of the famines on record have been due to the failure or partial failure of the rains during critical periods of crop growth.

In several parts of the Bukoba District population pressure on the land is a serious problem, especially on the lake coastal ridges.[5] Corn, millets, and bananas are

[4] Estimates of population density by Areas (Districts) and smaller administrative units of Tanzania in 1962 are given in Porter, *op. cit.* [see footnote 3 above].

[5] See D. N. McMaster: Change of Regional Balance in the Bukoba District of Tanganyika, *Geogr. Rev.*, Vol. 50, 1960, pp. 73–88; reference on pp. 85–87.

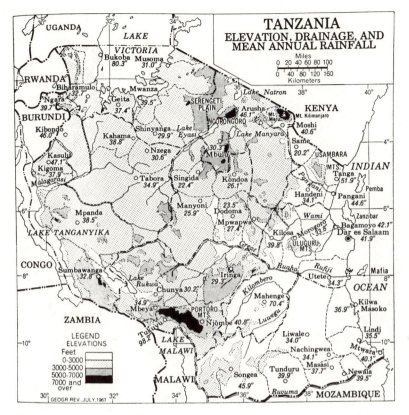

Figure 2.

staple foods for the 400,000 inhabitants, and robusta coffee is a cash crop. In the north, Bambara groundnuts are cultivated as the traditional catch crop as soon as drought ends. From time to time food shortages have occurred when the local chiefs have forbidden the cultivation of this crop for disciplinary reasons or as an act of penitence.

There is little movement of people in the Bukoba District during periods of famine or food shortage,[6] but in the Biharamulo Dis-

trict, which adjoins Bukoba on the south, many people—not infrequently entire families—move to more favored parts of the Bukoba and Geita Districts during such times. There they may clear a small plot for planting to a catch crop or, more often, work in the field of another man in order to receive a share of his food crops for their labor. Nearly all return to their home areas before the next season's planting. Tem-

[6] One of the most disastrous famines occurred in 1928–1929, when some five hundred died of starvation in the Bugufi area of the Bukoba District. A full account is given in "Report by His Majesty's Government . . . to the Council of the League of Nations on the Administration of

Tanganyika Territory for the Year 1930," *Colonial No. 60*, London, 1931, pp. 112–116. Many of the casualties were refugees from drought-stricken Urundi, where famines were commonplace; see H. Scaëtta: Les famines périodiques dans le Ruanda, *Mémoires Inst. Colonial Belge, Sect. des Sci. Nat. et Médicales*, Vol. 1, Part 4, Brussels, 1932.

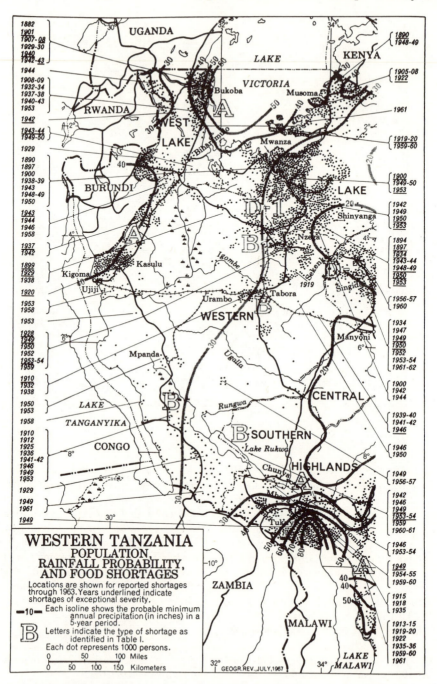

Figure 3.—Base map adapted from Plate 13 of the "Atlas of Tanganyika" (3rd edit., Dar es Salaam, 1956), with data for the European and Asian population deleted.

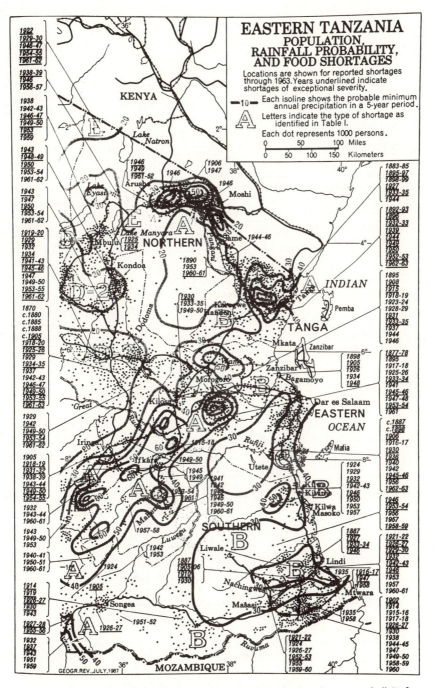

Figure 4.—Base map adapated from Plate 13 of the "Atlas of Tanganyika" (3rd edit., Dar es Salaam, 1956), with data for the European and Asian population deleted.

TABLE 1. CHARACTERISTICS OF FOOD

Type (Figs. 3 & 4)	Sub-Type	Principal Locations	Frequency and Intensity of Shortages	Population Characteristics	Precipitation Characteristics
A		Highlands Bukoba District Njombe District Usambara Mts. Uluguru Mts.	Sporadic, small-scale shortages, Severe, prolonged scarcity rare.	Density 200 to 700 per sq. mi., settled mainly in rural villages.	Mean annual > 50 in.; 80% probability > 40 in. Short droughts interspersed through the rainy season are not unusual.
B		Subhumid woodland and wooded grassland The locations of recurrent shortages are widely scattered in Handeni District and Eastern and Southern Regions; they occur in a few places in Western Region.	Local shortages occur annually. Acute dearth requiring famine-relief measures occurs at intervals of five to seven years.	Density; in the east, 15 to 45 per sq. mi.; in the west, < 1 to 10 per sq. mi. Some single homesteads, but mostly widely dispersed hamlets; a few "sleeping sickness settlements" in Western Region.	Mean annual 35 to 50 in.; 80% probability 28 to 30 in. Irregular seasonal distribution with both droughts and destructively heavy rains is common.
C		Flood plains Rufiji Valley Kilombero Valley	Severe shortages occur about one year in six.	Density 10 to 150 per sq. mi. Near the coast most live in rural villages; inland, single or two- to three-house hamlets are commonest.	Mean annual 32 to 50 in.; 80% probability 29 to 40 in.
D	D—1	Interior plains and plateaus Northeastern plain (Sukumaland)	Since 1954, local shortages only	Density 40 to 350 per sq. mi., settled mainly in rural villages.	Mean annual 29 to 40 in.; 80% probability 20 to 30 in.
	D—2	North-central plateau Mbulu District Kondoa District	In D—2 and D—3 local shortages occur almost every year.	Density 20 to 295 per sq. mi., about equally in single homesteads and rural villages.	D—2; mean annual 26 to 34 in.; D—3; 23 to 28 in.; 80% probability 18 to 25 in. in D—2; < 20 in. in all D—3.
	D—3	Central steppe Manyoni, Dodoma, Mpwapwa Districts (Gogoland)	About one year in six or seven there is a severe shortage requiring famine-relief measures.	Density 1 to 110 per sq. mi. Dispersed homesteads are commonest; there are few rural villages.	
E		Rift Valley	Nomadic herders experience shortages about one year in seven; agricultural peoples in the valley about one year in five or six.	Density 1 to 5 per sq. mi. in Masai grazing areas; 17 to 21 per sq. mi. in agricultural Sonjo and Mbugwe areas.	Mean annual 18 to 32 in.; 80% probability 17 in.

Crop Complex	Livestock and Animal Products	Population Movement During Food Shortages	Utilization of "Bush Foods" During Periods of Scarcity
Staples; bananas, millets, corn. Cash crops; coffee, tea, wattle, pyrethrum.	Mixed agricultural economy. Livestock and their by-products are important, but secondary to agricultural production.	Some *hemea* (p.000), but in most areas there is not much migration during times of scarcity.	No significant change in activities during food shortages.
Staples; corn (preferred), cowpeas, pigeonpeas, manioc. Cash crops; a little corn and cotton; cashew nuts in the southeast. The economy is not much above the subsistence level.	Livestock are of slight importance. Trypanosomiasis; and East Coast fever are endemic in almost all areas. Milk and milk products are not traditional foods of most peoples in the eastern and southern woodlands. Chickens are kept, but eggs are not accepted in the diet.	Migration is common especially in eastern Tanzania, where large numbers of men move from the affected villages to sisal estates.	The collection of "wild" foods is essential to the survival of small, isolated hamlets when staple crops fail or are destroyed by animals. Edible roots and honey are the main materials sought.
Staples; rice (preferred), corn, manioc. Cash crop; cotton, bananas.	As in Type B, livestock occupy a minor position in the economy.	Temporary movement, except during the worst famines, is rare. A small, steady migration is attributed in part to recurrent death.	Intensive efforts are made to collect bush foods during times of shortage.
Staples; in D–1 and D–2 millets and grain sorghums are the leading food plants. Beans, corn, and rice are secondary; in D–2 corn preferred. Cash crops are important only in D–1, where cotton has transformed the economy. Coffee (D–2) and castor beans (D–3) are relatively unimportant.	The northeastern plain has the greatest concentration of cattle in Tanzania, but economically, livestock are subordinate to cash-crop production. In D–2 and D–3 the economy is virtually at the subsistence level, and milk is a major food. Serious soil erosion, including widespread active gullying, has resulted from overgrazing. In all D areas the sale of livestock, especially cattle, is a major source of income for the purchase of food during periods of severe shortage.	*Hemea* is traditional and frequent in the D areas. There is a more nearly permanent type of movement by families in some parts of D–1. During acute shortages there is large-scale temporary migration of men from D–3 to sisal estates.	Uncultivated edible plants and fruits are gathered on a small scale throughout the year, but this activity is much intensified during food shortages. Honey and wax from "wild" hives are important sources of food and cash income in some areas.
The Masai do not cultivate. Staple food of Sonio and Mbugwe is grain sorghum. Although cash crops are not typical, in some years the Mbugwe grow and sell a little cotton.	The Masai are completely dependent on their cattle, goats, and donkeys. Cow's milk is the main food. During prolonged drought, when milk is in short supply and famine threatens, livestock or their hides are sold for cash to purchase food. Domesticated animals are subordinate to crops in the economic life of the Sonjo and the Mbugwe.	During severe, prolonged droughts there is mass movement by the Masai with their herds to Ngorogoro Crater and to the Serengeti Plain. The Sonjo and the Mbugwe do not migrate.	No significant change from normal collecting activities during food shortages.

porary movement of this kind (in Swahili, *hemea*) is widespread in East Africa. No man can know when misfortune in the form of successive crop failures and resulting famine may strike his fields and family, and consequently there is a high regard for mutual help in times of trouble.

In the Usambara Mountains of the Lushoto District population growth during the past half century [7] has reduced the cultivated area per family to less than three acres. The need for additional cropland, and for firewood and strucutral timber, brought about extensive devastation of forest and woodland, and by the mid-1930's soil erosin had become a major problem.[8] In the older cultivated parts it is no longer possible to fallow cropland. It has been officially proposed that population pressure in the Usambaras be relieved by emigration to the plains below, where swamp rice could be grown. However, as in many other highland regions of Africa, the inhabitants feel a strong aversion to resettlement in the lowlands, and the people of the Usambaras have consistently resisted the government's efforts toward this end.[9]

[7] The rate of population growth in the northeastern mountains is about twice that for the country as a whole (A. W. Southall: Population Movements in East Africa, *in* Essays on African Population [edited by K. M. Barbour and R. M. Prothero; London, 1961; New York, 1962], pp. 157–192; reference on p. 161).

[8] E. C. Baker: A Report by Mr. E. C. Baker on the Social and Economic Conditions in the Tanga Province (Dar es Salaam, 1936), p. 42. Baker held that deforestation of the Usambaras was chiefly the result of careless use of fire by farmers in burning their cutover fields and by honey hunters in smoking out wild bees from forest trees.

[9] Some other problems encountered in the Usambara Development Scheme and the Uluguru Land Usage Scheme, which in the mid-1950's were to draw excess population and livestock from the highlands to prepared lowland areas, are discussed in N. R. Fuggles-Couchman: Agricultural Change in Tanganyika: 1945–1960 (Studies in Tropical Development; Food Research Institute, Stanford, Calif., 1964), pp. 79–80.

Intertribal warfare in combination with drought was a contributory cause of two great famines in the Usambara Mountains in the late nineteenth century (1883–1885 and 1898–1899). But during the historical period swarms of migratory locusts have been the most destructive and frequent agency of famines. Partial food shortages in 1896 were caused by locusts. In 1898 both the "greater" and "lesser" rains failed. At the end of the year the rain were ample, but early in 1899 locusts returned to destroy the crops, and a major famine followed. The migratory locust was responsible for acute food shortages in parts of the Usambara Mountains in 1927, 1933, and 1944. Locusts returned again in 1948, but none have appeared since, thanks to control efforts in the breeding areas.

THE SUBHUMID WOODLAND AND WOODED GRASSLAND (TYPE B)

Subhumid woodland and wooded grassland extend over about two-thirds of Tanzania, including the greater part of the Eastern and Southern Regions and about 80 per cent of the vast Western Region. Precipitation characteristics are remarkably uniform from east to west, with mean annual rainfall greater than 35 inches but less than 50 inches. The records for most stations indicate that the minimum annual rainfall in a five-year period is more than 30 inches. But these figures conceal the fact that irregularities in seasonal distribution are common. With respect to food shortages, the eastern and western woodlands have much in common, but tens of thousands of square miles in the west are without permanent population. Food shortages are therefore more numerous in the east, and the discussion that follows deals chiefly with scarcity in the eastern woodland and wooded grassland.

The eastern third of Tanzania (the Handeni District of the Tanga Region, the Eastern Region, and all but the westernmost part of the Southern Region) is broken country ranging in elevation from sea level to about 3000 feet; a few isolated mountain blocks are much higher. This vast extent of hills, uplands, and coastal plain supports a cover of open woodland and wooded grassland—associations clearly fire-conditioned by the slash-and-burn agriculture practiced by almost all the cultivating peoples of eastern Tanzania. In addition to the population in the highlands and the flood-plains, about one million people of some twenty-two different tribal affiliations are settled in small hamlets (six to ten houses on the average) scattered throughout the countryside. Population density in the woodland ranges from 2 to 185 per square mile, but between 15 and 45 per square mile is most common.

The Germans, and later the British, considered the dispersed pattern of habitation a serious obstacle to economic development and effective bureaucratic control. Both governments made attempts to cluster the population into what were usually called "sleeping sickness settlements"—rural villages in tsetse-free clearings in the woodland. Most of these schemes failed for lack of popular support. Many resettlement projects were inadequately planned and poorly administered, and food shortages were common in the newly settled areas.[10]

[10] One of the most ambitious projects was an effort made between 1945 and 1948 to move the entire population of northern and central Nachingwea—some 30,000 people—to new settlements in western Kilwa. The region to be evacuated, the de facto Liwale District, was to become part of a game reserve permanently closed to settlement. Officially, resettlement was deemed necessary because of the presence of sleeping sickness in the vicinity of Liwale. Actually, the scheme was an exercise of arbitrary power by the Provincial Commissioner, who believed that Liwale, a remote and dreary place, was not suitable as a residency for British District Officers. It was planned to abolish all administrative positions as soon as the population was removed from Liwale. From the beginning the scheme encountered grave difficulties, including famines and severe shortages in the new areas. The transport provided by

Throughout most of the eastern and western woodlands corn is the staple crop, and the irregular seasonal distribution of rainfall explains in part the recurrent crises of food supply. The Handeni District, for example, is dependent on the corn harvest, and famine relief is required there on an average of one year in five. But the fact that corn is drought-sensitive does not explain fully the frequency of dearth in this region of erratic rainfall and degraded woodland. The excessive selling of reserves of corn in response to intensive propaganda programs by the government is equally responsible. Until about 25 years ago grain sorghum was the principal food crop in the eastern part of the country, and corn, like cowpeas and pigeon peas, was of secondary importance. But corn gained rapidly in popularity, and in Handeni during the 1950's it became the chief cash crop.[11]

Manioc is grown to some extent in almost every settlement, but it is not universally popular, and only on the Makonde Plateau in southern Newala is it a major cash crop. Its cultivation in many areas is the result

the government was not adequate to carry all the food stored by the families moved from Liwale, and excess stocks were burned. Consequently, there was not enough food to sustain the people until their crops ripened in the new areas. Some 4095 families were evacuated from the Liwale area. Plans to remove 2000 more were abandoned in 1948 when the Groundnut Scheme was started in Nachingwea. After the resettlement project was terminated, about three-fourths of the evacuated families returned to their home areas.

[11] "The Senior Agricultural Assistant at Handeni 1946–49 started the "grow more maize" campaign, which due to opening of markets and the comparatively high prices paid (and not least to his autonomous manner) soon became the main cash crop. The previous cash crop of cotton dropped in production from 812 tons in 1942 to 18 tons in 1953, while maize export figures rose from nil to 3,000 tons in the same period. The immediate consequence of this big increase in maize growing was a succession of food shortages, and in some years, near famine conditions" (John Ainley, "Maize," Handeni District Book).

of years of effort by the government to force manioc into a prominent place in the cropping complex of the agricultural population of eastern Tanzania. Official interest in the expansion of manioc in the eastern woodland was not so much because the crop is drought-resistant as because it is unvulnerable to locusts. Swarms of locusts invaded the eastern woodland in most years of the 1930's, and their destruction of crops was a common cause of famines.[12]

Trypanosomiasis and East Coast fever are endemic in practically the whole of the eastern woodland. Consequently, the cattle population is small, and other domesticated animals, too, are of no great economic importance. Many families keep a few goats, but they are not milked.

A little more than 90 percent of Tanzania's sisal, the leading export, is grown in the eastern woodland on plantations owned and operated mainly by Greeks and Indians. During times of food shortages men move en masse from their villages to the plantations in search of work. The returns from village-grown cash crops are seldom adequate to support the cultivator and his family during prolonged scarcity. In addition to corn, cotton and tobacco are commercial crops of the peasantry in the northern part of the eastern woodland; in the southern part, cashew nuts and cotton lead in sales.

Food crops grown in the small settlements scattered through the woodland are attractive to wart hogs, baboons, monkeys, and porcupines, all of which abound. In some places the main threat to planted fields is elephants or hippopotami. Considerable quantities of crops are eaten or destroyed by all these animals, and occasionally their depredations result in near famine in isolated hamlets. Periodically in the eastern woodland heavy crop losses are caused by plagues of field rats, as in the Southern Region in 1951, or by army worms, as in the Eastern and Tanga Regions in 1961–1962.

Dependence on edible wild plants during times of scarcity is greater in the subhumid woodlands than in other parts of Tanzania.[13] No doubt this is partly due to the greater abundance and variety of natural food plants, but many of the survival techniques practiced today were learned and perfected in the bush during the nineteenth century, when most of the agricultural country of southern Tanganyika was repeatedly raided by Angoni warriors. Then the only recourse of thousands of peaceful agricultural people was to scatter into the woodlands, where their survival depended on the collection of bush foods for some months until their first crops could be harvested. The search for hives as a source of honey for food and of beeswax for cash is still carried on today, with peaks of activity during the years of serious food shortages.

THE FLOODPLAINS (TYPE C)

About 10 percent of the population of Tanzania are settled on alluvial plains that are widely distributed but of small extent. The principal alluvial lands are in the east—strips along the valleys of the Pangani, the Wami, the Ruvu, and the Rufiji-Kilombero system. Each valley is subject to disastrous floods, which make most parts unfit for permanent occupation. But some of the lower valleys and deltas are densely popu-

[12] Locust swarms invaded the Tanga, Eastern, Lindi, and Northern Regions in 1932 and 1934. Distress was most acute in the Handeni and Bagamoyo Districts. See "A Report on Local Famine and Food Shortages and on the Cost and Nature of Relief Measures Organized by Government," *Sessional Paper No. 3 of 1934*, Legislative Council of Tanganyika, Dar es Salaam, 1934.

[13] A full account of the importance of "bush foods" to the survival of an agricultural people living in a District (Nachingwea) of recurrent serious shortages of food is given in A. R. W. Crosse-Upcott: Ngindo Famine Subsistence, *Tanganyika Notes and Records*, No. 50, 1958, pp. 1–20.

lated, even though destructive floods are frequent.

The upper valley in the Kilombero and its tributaries in Ulanga experiences recurrent food shortages, most of which are relatively minor "pre-harvest hunger months," [14] but in some localities dearth is more prolonged and serious. However, famines have occurred most frequently in the Rufiji Basin. About 70,000 people live in the valley and delta of the Rufiji River. In the west, settlements are thinly scattered and are not farther than several hundred yards from the riverbanks. Population density increases, and the area of settlement widens, from about sixty miles inland to the delta. The inner part of the delta is densely populated, with fairly even distribution. The outer delta is uninhabited grassland, bush, and mangrove swamps. Population is concentrated along the coastal strip in the few places favorable for settlement. It is believed that the Rufiji Basin was more densely populated in the past than it is now, but famine, disease, slave raiding, and political unrest have contributed to the decrease in population during the past century.

In the early 1880's a great famine followed the destruction of the crops by a plague of locusts.[15] About 1890 the area was afflicted by another famine, attributed to severe flooding of the Rufiji. The only food available was near the coastal town of

Lindi, 150 miles to the south. Great numbers died on the way to Lindi, but many of the survivors settled there. Again in 1906 famine occurred, in part as a result of crop damage by the Rufiji in flood, but the major cause was the Maji Maji Rebellion and its aftermath. Thousands fled in panic before the advance of the German troops and settled in other places. In 1914 bubonic plague swept through the valley, and in 1916 many lost their lives in an epidemic of cerebrospinal meningitis. Furthermore, although more than 15,000 porters from the Rufiji District were conscripted by the Germans during World War I, only 3000 returned. These are the main reasons for the decrease in the population. But even in recent years there has been a steady flow of emigrants from the Rufiji District. District officers explain the exodus chiefly as reaction to the government's close supervision to prevent evasion of taxes, but undoubtedly the frequent recurrence of food shortages is an important reason. Zanzibar is favored by many of the emigrants, and the Rufiji District Book records that in 1948 there were six villages on the island with a total of some 3000 persons from the Rufiji District.

Rice is planted in December and early January in lowlands that, hopefully, will be lightly flooded while the moisture requirements is high. Smaller quantities of corn and grain sorghum are also grown on the floodplain and, with manioc and bananas, on higher ground. If the rice crop fails because of destructive floods, the peasant replants with cotton and maize—as catch crops—on the floodplain as soon as the water recedes. But rice is preferred both as a food and as a cash crop. Cotton is not popular, and if the rice harvest is satisfactory, only a small amount of cotton is planted. This traditional cropping system is precariously dependent on the river's regime, and especially on the duration of the flood. If water levels remain high for two weeks or more in January and February, the main fields of rice and the early-

---

[14] The Ulanga District Book contains a graph prepared by A. T. Culwick that compares seasonal-shortage curves for cereals, fish, and cash with monthly heights of the Kilombero River and rainfall. Marvin P. Miracle has presented several hypotheses to account for preharvest shortages and "hungry seasons" in Africa ("Seasonal Hunger": A Vague Concept and an Unexplored Problem, *Bull. Inst. Français d'Afrique Noire*, Ser. B, Vol. 23, 1961, pp. 273–283).

[15] "Not a thing was harvested. Even the grass was eaten, and as a result many died. Fathers sold children into slavery for as little as five pounds of rice. The number of deaths is unknown, but must have been thousands" ("Population Distribution," Rufiji District Book, p. 1).

season plantings of maize are destroyed. Late heavy floods in April and May damage or destroy cotton and maize.

The Rufiji District has experienced at least partial crop failures for about one-third of the years of record since the mid-1930's. Before 1935 heavy floods destroyed the major lowland crops on an average of only once in twelve to fifteen years; [16] in most years the flooding was light and favorable for good yields. For eight years before 1935 the records reveal that in only one year, 1930, did the river rise above the ten-foot mark at the gauging station above Utete, but since 1935 there have been only two years (1938 and 1949) in which the level did not exceed ten feet. In 1963 the Rufiji reached a new high-water record, and settlements on high ground near the river and in the delta were isolated for many weeks. Saville has suggested that the chief causes of the increasing frequency of floods are probably the accelerated clearing for cultivation (in response to the needs of the growing population) and the cutting and burning of the natural plant cover in the highland source areas of maximum precipitation, especially in the upper basins of the Kilombero and the Ruaha.

After heavy showers roads in the Rufiji Valley are impassable. Even during a "normal" rainy season, communications are disrupted from October to May for periods ranging from several days to three or four weeks and the interior valley is isolated from the rest of Tanzania. Because of inaccessability and scattered settlement, famine-relief measures have been ineffective. Many people are enabled to maintain a minimal diet by their ability to find wild edible plants, especially species of *Dioscorea*, buffalo beans, and immature coconuts. In 1963, however, families facing starvation in the flooded Rufiji Valley were dropped bags of American corn by air transports.[17]

THE INTERIOR PLAINS AND PLATEAUS (TYPE D)

In several large inland areas of Tanzania woodland and wooded grasslands have been drastically changed by agricultural and pastoral activities, and the unremitting pressure of these activities has permitted only small patches of regenerating bush and thicket or thin strips of original grasses. It is estimated that such areas of actively induced vegetation [18] (the "cultivation steppe" of British writers) support about 25 percent of the population of the country on a little less than 8 percent of the total area. The mean density is about 100 persons per square mile, and many of the settlements have a history of recurrent food shortages that have required relief measures.

THE NORTHEASTERN PLAIN (SUKUMALAND) (TYPE D-1)

The most extensive of these "cultivation steppes" is Sukumaland—the Mwanza, Kwimba, Maswa, and Shinyanga Districts, southeast of Lake Victoria, occupied chiefly by Sukuma tribesmen. Here in some 11,000 square miles of open, gently rolling country live one million people and about five million livestock units, the largest concentration of cattle, sheep, and goats in Tanzania. About 70 percent of the settled land is given to grazing and 20 percent to cultivation; the remainder is little used at present. The probable seasonal minimum rainfall ranges from about 20 inches in the

[16] A. H. Saville: A Study of Recent Alterations in the Flood Regimes of Three Important Rivers in Tanganyika, *East African Agric. Journ.*, Oct. 1945, pp. 69–74; reference on pp. 71–72.

[17] The Rufiji District Council sent President Kennedy a dugout canoe and a stuffed crocodile as an expression of their thanks.

[18] The term "actively induced vegetation," introduced by Gillman, is used in official publications and maps of Tanzania. See Clement Gillman: A Vegetation-Types Map of Tanganyika Territory, *Geogr. Rev.*, Vol. 39, 1949, pp. 7–37.

Maswa and Shinyanga Districts to about 30 inches in the Kwimba and Mwanza Districts. There are no permanent streams, and the Sukuma live in villages near springs and sources of shallow groundwater at the foot of the countless small granite hills that rise above the almost treeless plains.

The Sukuma formerly practiced a shifting cultivation, but this is no longer possible because the pressure of population on available water resources and arable soils is too great. The gradual abandonment of shifting cultivation for a more nearly permanent system of field cultivation has impaired soil fertility, but the gravest problem is the deterioration of grasses and soils brought about by overstocking.[19] The government's schemes to reduce the number of livestock and to introduce other management practices, such as the collection and use of manure for fertilizer, have received only slight positive response and acceptance by the Sukuma.

The staple cereals are grain sorghum, bulrush millet, and corn. Grain sorghum occupies the largest acreage, and as a measure of insurance against the erratic rainfall it is planted not only on the light soils of the steeper slopes but on the heavy clays of the valley bottomlands as well.[20] Rice

is a traditional minor cereal and is grown on terraced slopes by the impounding of surface runoff and seepage. Most cultivators grow sweet potatoes in small plots; some are dried and stored for use in the event of a food shortage, but this practice is apparently no longer common.[21] Peanuts are an important field crop and are usually interplanted with cereal grains. Manioc, though not popular, is widespread, partly because for many years administrative officers ordered that it be planted in each village as an antifamine measure.[22] Cotton was introduced into the Lake Region during the German administration and has become the major cash crop there. In ability to withstand drought in February and March and to recover from the ravages of insect pests, cotton has a better reputation than any of the grains in Sukumaland.

British administrative officers, like the Germans before them, noted that the migration of large numbers of Sukuma was commonplace.[23] This movement has continued to the present—in general, from congested villages in northern Sukumaland to the west and south. In the Geita District, in accordance with a development plan,

---

[19] Of some 2,500,000 cattle in the Sukuma districts in 1948, about 60 percent, or 1,500,000 died or were slaughtered as a result of the 1949 drought and food shortage. The sudden reduction in pressure on grazing resources permitted the recovery of grasses in many parts, but the most conspicuous result was the spread of new growth of shrubs and trees, which are usually held in check by the browsing of livestock. However, within four or five years the cattle population was again equal to that of 1948, and by 1960 the number had increased to 4,500,000.

[20] The Sukuma cultivator prefers to hold several small, rather widely scattered plots, each of which he considers suitable for certain crops. Dispersed holdings improve the odds that at least one plot will receive adequate soil moisture. For an excellent study of how two tribes in Kenya reduce agricultural risks by dispersal of their fields and other methods see Philip W. Porter: Environmental Potentials and Eco-

nomic Opportunities—A Background for Cultural Adaptation, *Amer. Anthropologist,* Vol. 67, 1965, pp. 409–420.

[21] In other places too, the sweet potato has declined in popularity. For example, in Chunya, a District with a small population but with frequent shortages of food, the sweet potato is grown as a snack to allay hunger but not as a major food crop. Few people today bother to boil and dry the potato for storage, even though almost every year there is need for a greater reserve of food.

[22] Communal fields of grain sorghum also were planted by compulsory village labor, and the grain was distributed to those in need when food was in short supply. But this scheme met with a great deal of popular resistance, and today there are few collective fields of sorghum.

[23] D. W. Malcolm (Sukumaland [London, New York, Toronto, 1953], p. 15) noted the abandonment of village sites in the 200 square miles of hills across southern Maswa, which were densely populated some 50 years ago.

30,000 Sukuma were resettled as individual farmers on consolidated holdings that provide both cropland and grazing. This is one of the few schemes in which the break from a communal-tribal agricultural system has been successfully carried out.[24] In other districts the movement has been from the hillsides to the valleys.

Far more Sukuma migrate of their own volition than by compulsion. "Frequent hunger" is almost always the reason given for leaving the home villages. Although the quality of the rainfall is the critical factor affecting crop production and consequent food supply in Sukumaland, there is no single preeminent cause for the recurring shortages of food. Movement out of the home area is a traumatic experience for the Sukuma, and for most of them, probably, the decision to migrate is the result of a combination of circumstances taking place over several years; these would include the grazing resources and supplies of surface water, and the spread of *Striga* in the cropped areas.[25] The cumulative effects on crop yields gradually "condition" the cultivator to accept the drastic step of migration as a solution to his difficulties.

The absence of a major famine in Sukumaland since 1953 is the result of several factors. The Sukumaland Development Scheme provided £800,000 for the improvement of water supplies, chiefly by the construction of surface-water catchments

works. Many small, new dams on seasonal streams now provide a year-round water supply. Scores of villagers formerly confined to worn-out soils near the granite outcrops have moved from the rocky ridges to the more fertile alluvial soils of the plains. And, most important, in contrast with the neighboring Central Region, the economy of Sukumaland has changed greatly during the past twenty years. Since 1945 cotton production in Sukuma has increased sixfold, and the average cash income per family is about ten times the 1949 level.

THE NORTH-CENTRAL PLATEAU (TYPE D-2)

Crop failures and food shortages are frequent on the plateaus of the Mbulu and Kondoa Districts and the consequences of overstocking are even more pronounced than in Sukumaland. The upland population of the two districts is about 250,000. Most settlements are between 5000 and 7000 feet in elevation, where the mean annual rainfall ranges from 26 to 34 inches; in a few of the highest settlements the range is from 40 to 60 inches. The 80 percent probability for annual rainfalls is less than 20 inches in northern Mbulu and central Kondoa, the most densely populated parts. Grazing is limited by tsetse infestation of the woodland that surrounds the settled land. In both Mbulu and Kondoa, lands free of tsetse are carrying too many head of livestock, and problems of soil erosion are exceptionally serious. Heavy grazing has hindered regeneration of the more palatable grasses, and species of lower nutritive value, such as wire grass (*Pennisetum schimperi*), have become dominant.[26] The acceleration of soil erosion in Kondoa was noted by the German administration more than half a century ago. Since that time increased erosion has created large areas of gullies and incipient badlands,

[24] Fuggles-Couchman, *op. cit.* [see footnote 9 above], p. 79. Because of widespread antipathy to the new rules for cultivation and land use, these objectives of the Sukumaland Development Scheme were finally dropped in 1955.

[25] *Striga hermonthica* and *S. asiatica*, witchweeds, are semiparasites that attack the roots of legumes and grasses, including grain sorghum. Grain sorghum is especially vulnerable to *Striga*, which spreads rapidly and unless controlled by uprooting or crop rotation will necessitate abandonment of the field. N. V. Rounce (The Agriculture of the Cultivation Steppe of the Lake, Western, and Central Provinces [Capetown, 1949], p. 23) mentions "wholesale movement of a village" as a result of *Striga* infestation.

[26] In the Mbulu watershed massive overstocking has reduced even the wire-grass cover.

with widespread loss of grazing and crop-land.

Corn is the leading staple and, especially on the Mbulu plateau, is much preferred to the other grains of the cereal complex—eleusine, wheat (in Mbulu only), and a bitter variety of grain sorghum (for beer). Food shortages are usually brought about by the failure of the corn harvest. Until World War II wheat was a minor crop in Mbulu, but in 1945, when the corn crop failed, expansion of wheat acreage was encouraged by the government as an antifamine measure.[27] But wheat production is frequently reduced by severe damage from rust.

THE CENTRAL STEPPE (TYPE D-3)

About 400,000 people, nearly all Gogo tribesmen, live in the Manyoni, Dodoma, and Mpwapwa Districts of central Tanzania. Gogoland has by far the most frequent famines in the country. It is said that good harvests in Gogoland are the exception rather than the rule, and that there is scarcity of food in some Gogo settlements every year. Although human fatalities from starvation have been relatively few in recent years, the general situation is still much as it was described in 1950: [28]

> The Central Province is notorious for its aridity and the uncertainty of its rainfall. It achieves a consequent additional notoriety from its widespread periodic famines. The margin between adequate and inadequate food supplies is so slender that, not only the African population, but also most responsible officers in this Province exist in a continual atmosphere of anxiety, wondering whether they will pull safely through another season. This atmosphere, side by side with the effects of a fluctuating existence, makes the orderly development of the resources of this Province, in order to

combat the recurrent famines, a difficult problem.

For the most part central Tanzania is a gently rolling steppe, ranging in elevation from about 3200 to 5000 feet above sea level, and broken here and there by isolated hills and small, grotesquely weathered masses of granite and gneiss. A common characteristic is internal drainage into pans and large depressions such as the Bahi Swamp.[29] Few streams flow for more than a few months each year. Except for Masailand and western Pare in the north, this is the driest part of Tanzania, and shortages of food are usually attributed to the rainfall characteristics. Mean annual rainfall in the central steppe is about 23 to 28 inches, all but two inches of which comes during five months of the year. Everywhere less than 20 inches can be expected at least once in five years, and in the Dodoma District the interval is three years.[30] Although prolonged drought is the more common disaster, flood is also a well-known destroyer of crops.

The usual practice of the Gogo is to burn a patch of cutover deciduous bush, till the plot by hoeing, and broadcast bulrush millet and grain sorghum. Formerly the well-drained reddish-brown soils were preferred for almost all cereals, but now the heavier grayish soils in areas of slight relief are much used. Fields are replanted to grains without rotation as long as possible—usually five to ten successive years. Grain sorghum is one of the first crops sown on soils of medium and heavy texture, and its

[27] "Agriculture in Tanganyika" (Department of Agriculture, Dar es Salaam, 1945), p. 11.
[28] Ann. Rept. of the Provincial Commissioners 1950, Dar es Salaam, 1951, p. 1.

[29] During a favorable year about 500 tons of fish are taken from the Bahi Swamp. The catch is dried and sold in local markets. For some years in the Central Region the government encouraged the peasants to raise fish (Tilapia) as a pond crop, but results were disappointing, and efforts to establish fish farming in Tanganyika were abandoned in 1956 (Ann. Rept. Dept. of Agriculture 1956, Dar es Salaam, 1957, p. 46).
[30] The average number of days of rain per year at Dodoma is fifty-five, including only seven days for the seven months from May through November.

yield is greatly reduced when heavy rains early in the season delay weeding and cause waterlogging.

Corn is not important anywhere in the central steppe. The Germans were concerned about the expansion of this crop at the expense of the millets, and under their administration plantings of corn in new areas were prohibited. Only a small acreage is given to pulses, chiefly cowpeas, peanuts, and Bambara nuts. Some wet rice is grown in the Bahi Swamp, but soil salinization has reduced production in recent years. Castor beans have achieved some popularity as a cash crop during the past decade, but production is significant only when rainfall is ample and seasonally well distributed. Intensive propaganda for the expansion of manioc and sweet-potato plantings has had little lasting effect. A fast-maturing variety of bulrush millet was introduced into the Central Region in 1953 as a famine-relief measure. It was popular but within several years lost its character from outcrossing with local varieties.[31]

In spite of the danger of trypanosomiasis in many places, the central steppe supports large numbers of cattle.[32] In 1952 about 40 percent of the Gogo were cattle owners, but population growth and the accelerated devastation of grazing resources have combined to lower the percentage of Gogo who own more than a few head of cattle. Nearly all families own goats or sheep. The family heads still consider themselves husbandmen rather than cultivators, and after the seed-bed has been prepared, most of the tasks of crop production are left to the women.

In central Tanzania, as in Sukumaland, efforts have been made by the government for several decades to induce owners to sell a great number of their animals each year. The goal has been an annual cull of 5 percent to 10 percent of adult cattle. But even

this modest objective has not been attained for more than two or three successive years.[33] In recent years when drought has occurred stock sales have risen, but marketing and transportation facilities are inadequate to cope with the large increase of sales that occurs during the worst droughts, as in 1953 and 1961–1962.

In the past, epizootics and drought were far more effective than propaganda or regulations in reducing the number of livestock. A German observer estimated that before the rinderpest epidemic of 1905 the average holding was from ten to thirty cattle, several times larger than it is today; but the human population then was much smaller. Veterinary services in Tanzania have prevented catastrophic losses from disease for many years. And it now appears that the many new wells and boreholes provided by the government during the late 1950's have greatly reduced stock mortality from thirst. Previously, as in 1953–1954, cattle losses from drought in central Tanzania were greater than 50 percent.

> In some places as much as 80 per cent of the herds perished. The mortality rate is an indication of the overstocking . . . In 1954 a great many moribund beasts were killed and used for food. Sometimes one bullock would provide less than 30 pounds of meat. However, it is told that in a previous famine, 1919, many people lay down and died beside their cattle rather than eat them, so that the attitude in this respect has become more rational. These large numbers of dying cattle did provide some meat for their owners, there was a large cash income from the sale of hides, and the cash was used to purchase [imported] grain. By the end of 1954 the greatly reduced herds found enough grazing for survival and were in better condition than at the same period in 1953. However, they provided no "untimely meat" and no

---

[31] *Ann. Rept. Dept. of Agriculture 1956*, Dar es Salaam, 1957, p. 16.

[32] There was no tsetse problem in the central steppe until the 1920's (H. S. Senior: Gogo Development [Dar es Salaam, 1953], p. 30).

[33] Sometimes, when persuasion failed, official action was taken to compel owners to sell part of their cattle. But compulsory destocking measures were met with evasion and could not be strictly enforced.

cash crop of hides. Now that cotton fabrics have largely replaced skins as wearing apparel, the people need the money from skins or they lack any sort of protective clothing.[34]

But during the severe drought of 1961–1962 the number of cattle in Gogoland *increased* slightly, to a total of 700,000 head. The effects of successive years of massive overstocking are the deterioration of grazing and soil resources and increasing difficulty in meeting food requirements. It appears that today there is no effective way by which the herds may be held even to the level of their natural rate of increase.

THE RIFT VALLEY (TYPE E)

The Masai District, about 23,000 square miles, lies almost entirely within the eastern branch of the Great Rift Valley. With a population of some 70,000, Masailand is one of the most sparsely settled parts of Tanzania, and its problems of food supply are unique. This part of the Rift Valley ranges in elevation from about 3200 feet in the south to about 7000 feet in the north, and in mean annual precipitation from 18 inches in the south to 32 inches in the north. In at least one year in five annual rainfall is 20 inches or less. Agriculture and stock raising in about one-third of Masailand is seriously handicapped by the lack of surface water, by tsetse-fly infestation, and by the presence of East Coast fever.

About 50,000 nomadic Masai tribesmen live in this part of the Rift Valley and tend some one million cattle, half a million sheep, and about 15,000 donkeys. Milk is the staple food. Prolonged drought, resulting in heavy loss of livestock, is almost the only cause of food scarcity among the Masai today.[35] During the past twenty years

famine relief has been required only three times—in 1946–1947, 1949, and 1961–1962. Droughts are frequent, but in the vastness of their land the Masai can move with their animals to places that escape the worst effects, especially Ngorongoro Crater and the Serengeti Plain, where most of the stock usually manage to survive. In this century no other disaster has approached the catastrophic rinderpest and smallpox epidemics in the early 1890's, which resulted in a livestock and human mortality estimated to be about 75 percent for both.

In a small area northwest of Lake Natron, the northern part of the Rift Valley in Tanzania, some 5000 Sonjo tribesmen live precariously by the cultivation of grain sorghum, sweet potatoes, and a little corn. They tend goats and are noted for the care they devote to beekeeping. All the acute shortages of food on record in the Sonjo county (1922, 1929–1930, 1946–1947, 1954–1955, 1961–1962) have resulted from crop loss due to drought.

The seasonally inundated bush and grassland flats at the base of the Rift Valley near the southeast end of Lake Manyara are inhabited by the Mbugwe—several thousand agriculturists who keep cattle and donkeys and catch fish in the lake. Their land has a look of desolation and poverty, and several attempts have been made to resettle them in places where water supplies are more reliable and soil drainage is better. All these efforts have failed. When persuasion proved ineffective, coercion was sometimes used, but as soon as official pressure was relaxed, the people returned en masse to their old homesteads.[36] Mbugwe

---

[34] "Cattle," Dodoma Disrict Book, p. 1.

[35] In 1959 some 30,000 cattle died in the northern part of the Masai District as the result of the accidental use of faulty serum by the Veterinary Department in an inoculation cam-

paign against bovine pleuropneumonia. It is reported that most of the herdsmen erroneously attributed this disaster to the influence of the District Commissioner, whose wife had been speared to death by some Masai a few years earlier.

[36] The reluctance of the Mbugwe to move has been attributed to several causes, including the presence of tsetse in the new areas and the difficulties of clearing the land for cultivation.

agriculture depends on a sufficiency of water descending from the adjacent Mbulu highlands to alluvial fans in the valley. Thus the population and the quality of land use are sensitive to the economic activities in the highlands that affect surface runoff and groundwater retention, especially grazing and browsing and the cutting and burning of vegetation for open-field cultivation. There is no doubt that the Mbugwe live close to the minimum requirements for subsistence, but according to historical records they have suffered fewer acute shortages of food than their more numerous neighbors on the "well-watered" uplands above the valley.[37] Unlike the highland tribes, the Mbugwe rely on plantings of grain sorghum and bulrush millet, which are more dependable than corn, the staple above the valley.

Famine relief has not been required in Tanzania since mid-1963. In general, this is a result of rainfall characteristics favorable for crops and grazing. But in some parts of the country extraordinary efforts by the government and the local people have begun to change rural economies from subsistence to commercial production, with income from cash crops sufficient to pay for imported food when staple grains fail. A margin of safety is provided by increased diversification, for commercial plants are usually *added* to the cropping complex and do not replace traditionals. This kind of economic transformation is not as easily

accomplished in most other areas of Tanzania as it was in Sukumaland, where both the cultural and the natural milieus are favorable for the large-scale cultivation of cotton. Where there are rigorous physical limitations to cultivation, as in Gogoland and other semiarid regions, the improvement of the livestock economy, rather than of farming, should hold priority in development schemes. However, in nearly all such schemes reduction of the cattle herds is the first step, and it is well known that local resistance to culling is more rigid and intense than it is to changes in farming practices.

All-weather main and secondary roads are requisite to the elimination of famine, for they make it possible for imported foodstuffs to reach distressed populations and for cash crops to be moved out. In fact, the construction and improvement of feeder roads have long been the commonest of the "self-help" famine-relief programs, which include the clearing of tsetse bushland (everywhere a grueling and most unpopular project) and the building of small dams and hafirs (usually favored in cattle areas). But good roads alone are not always an effective stimulus to greater production; some of Tanzania's most poverty-stricken areas are near the highways that connect the major market centers.

Clearly, acute shortages of food are complex in cause and effect, involving not only physical and abstract economic elements but group attitudes and values as well. Famine is a powerful motivating force, and governments faced today with crises of food supply are moved to actions that may drastically change the face of the land. Official projects to alter land-use systems, to introduce new foods plants and commercial crops, and to relocate peoples and their livestock in new types of settlements are often contrary to local tradition and without popular acceptance. But such changes are almost inevitable in Tanzania, as in other countries where scarcity is frequent and widespread.

C. Wallace Dierickx, who studied the Mbugwe closely, states (in a private communication to the writer) that there is great fear of stock raiding by Masai in the more vulnerable "new" areas.

[37] See H. A. F.'s [H. A. Fosbrooke] review of an article by Robert F. Gray, *Tanganyika Notes and Records*, No. 36, 1954, pp. 77–78. However, this is contradicted by official correspondence on file in the Shinyanga District, which show that the Mbugwe obtained food for famine relief so frequently from their more fortunate neighbors that the goodwill with which the assistance had been given broke down, and emergency supplies of food are no longer sent to them from that District.

IV. POPULATION-LAND RELATIONSHIPS: EUROPEAN INFLUENCES

European influence in Africa has varied greatly. Generally speaking, the degree of influence is related to the extent and permanence of European settlement and varies with the extent and nature of European administrative and economic involvement (Udo, 1966). For example, French influences in the independent *francophone* countries of West and Equatorial Africa are distinctly more evident than are British influences in independent *anglophone* countries (e.g. Church, 1969; Morgan and Pugh, 1969).

Throughout Africa, European imprints are inevitably more obvious in urban areas than in rural areas. The morphology of pre-European cities has been modified (Kay, 1967b; Lloyd *et al.*, 1967; Mitchel, 1961), and they have continued to expand together with more recently established towns (Mabogunje, 1968; McMaster, 1968; Steel, 1961). This growth and expansion may be attributed to pressure on resources in rural areas as well as to the economic and social opportunities that towns offer (or at least appear to offer). Both migration and urbanization must be considered important factors in the study of population-land relationships in Africa (Kuper, 1965; Prothero, 1968).

In rural areas with no permanent European settlement, economic contacts with Europe are particularly evident in the expansion of crops for sale and export. (See Part II.) More fundamental effects may be observed in areas where agricultural land was taken over "permanently," depriving Africans of some of the best and potentially most productive lands on the continent. Yet as a proportion of the total area of Africa south of the Sahara, the amount of alienated land was small, even when European settlement was at its maximum. This proportion has now been reduced in Kenya and in the Congo (Kinshasa), but in Southern Africa European control remains total, and its direct and indirect effects on African population-land relationships are considerable.

In southern Nigeria European influences were indirect in almost all respects. There was no permanent settlement, no alienation of land, and little plantation agriculture, despite the existence of a plantation economy in the neighboring Southern Cameroons established during the German colonial era and continued under British mandate and trusteeship (Udo, 1965; Bederman, 1966).

Christian missionaries provided the first strong European contacts with southern Nigeria. Among their achievements was the establishment of Nigeria's first educational system. Yet the most significant European contribution was the introduction of cocoa trees to the southwestern part of the country. Change is manifest not only in the large amount of land allocated to the crop, but also in the prosperity of Nigerian cocoa farmers (Galetti et al., 1956). In some areas, however, staples must be imported to offset a related decline in food production (Morgan, 1963). Urban expansion has stemmed in large part from indigenous foundations, particularly in the Yoruba area. Providing adequate amenities at a pace comparable to the rate of this expansion has been a problem, although the manifestations of this disparity are less severe than in other parts of Africa and elsewhere in the developing world (Mabogunje, 1962, 1965, 1968).

At the time the following paper was written, the oil resources of the Niger delta and adjacent areas were unexploited. They have now been developed to provide the major source of wealth in Nigeria, but their full influence and impact has yet to be realized and the situation has been much complicated by the disruptions of civil war.

15. The Influence of European Contacts on the Landscape of Southern Nigeria

W. B. MORGAN

In West Africa, as in many other parts of the world, man's activities have considerably modified the landscape. Even before the first contacts with Europe West African cultivators cut down vast areas of forest and replaced it by cropland and fallow. Pastoralists annually set fire to grassland and bush. European intervention brought economic changes which are reflected in new attitudes to land, cultivation and stock rearing, and these have produced further landscape modifications. In the French territories the settler with his plantation has introduced landscape elements which are at once obvious in their departure from West African traditions. In the British territories settlers are for the most part lacking, and yet European influences have produced marked changes through the medium of the peasant cultivator and the artisan. Southern Nigeria, with its policy of development through the African peoples themselves, affords several excellent examples.*

Southern Nigeria includes politically the Western and Eastern Regions and the

* *Principal dates of British occupation.* 1861: British occupation of Lagos. 1885: Protectorate declared over the "Niger Districts," *i.e.*, "the territories on the line of coast between the British Protectorate of Lagos and the right or western bank of the Rio del Rey." 1886: a Royal Charter granted to the National African Co., later the Royal Niger Co. 1893: Niger Coast Protectorate declared, *i.e.* "Niger districts," together with their hinterland. 1899: Charter of the Royal Niger Co. revoked. British Government assumed direct control of the Company's territories in 1900; Company's territories south of Idah included in the Niger Coast Protectorate (renamed Southern Nigeria Protectorate). 1906: Colony of Lagos and Protectorate of Southern Nigerian amalgamated under one administration. 1914: Colony and Protectorate of Nigeria (including Northern Nigeria) inaugurated.

Southern Cameroons; for convenience, reference will occasionally be made to neighbouring portions of Northern Nigeria with which it has or has had close economic or social contacts. Before the arrival of European traders in the fifteenth century the peoples of the territories now included in Southern Nigeria had produced a variety of social systems and agricultural practices which were, in part, responses to the different physical environments. The latter are defined broadly in terms of vegetation, soil and moisture distributions in so far as these are significant for man, *i.e.* the physical environments are "milieux" in the sense used by Richard-Molard.[1] Relief features produce only local differences except in the extreme east where the range of altitude is much greater. Since the physical factors vary in their significance for man from place to place the environmental boundaries differ in character according to local conditions. In Southern Nigeria two of these boundaries are defined mainly by vegetation distribution, and one by rainfall distribution, as will be shown below. Due to the modifications by man (with which this paper is concerned) physical environments are not static. The constant cutting and burning of trees, shrubs and grass, the modification of soils by cultivation and pastoralism, all produce changes in the appearance of the landscapes concerned—and even movement of the physical environment boundaries. Keay has pointed, for example, to the degradation of rainforest to savanna on a large scale.[2] Two of the following physical environments are based on Keay's "vegetation zones" which it is suggested may be more usefully recognized as broad physical regions of the type defined above. The vegetation has suffered too much modification and the terms of

From *The Geographical Journal*, 125, 1959, pp. 48–64. Reprinted by permission of the Royal Geographical Society.

Keay's definition are too broad for "natural" vegetation zones to be distinguished.

Guinean (Fig. I). The chief climatic characteristics are an annual rainfall in excess of fifty inches, less than three months' dry season, mean monthly humidities at dawn of ninety per cent, or more throughout the year, and normally less than two weeks of dry "harmattan" air from the north-east.[3] Soils are acid and heavily leached. They vary in consistency from the fine *ilepa* clays of the Yoruba uplands to the coarse sands of Benin and of the Awka and Awgu escarpments of Iboland. River alluvia, terrace and beach sands and gravel and estuarine muds appear in the lower reaches of the chief valleys and along the coast. Over the greater part of the area the climax vegetation is dense, lowland rainforest. On floodlands tall grasses take its place, whilst on the coastal fringe are freshwater and mangrove-swamp communities. The secondary vegetation cover consists mainly of woody plants which form a dense cover within five years of the abandonment of any clearing. The limit of this type of cover, which coincides with Keay's limit of "lowland rainforest," has been used to define the boundary of this environment. This limit is determined chiefly by length of rainy season and incidence of high humidities during the dry season. A distinction may be observed between the northern fringes of the region with a high proportion of deciduous trees in the climax forests and the more southerly portions where, with an annual rainfall of over seventy inches, evergreen species are dominant. Keay, however, claims that the vegetation differences between the northern and southern portions of his "lowland rainforest zone" are no greater than differences

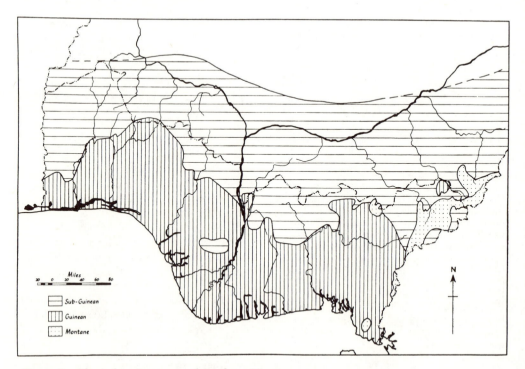

Figure 1.—Physical environments of Southern Nigeria.

between other parts of the zone and he prefers to regard it as one vegetation unit.[4] The Guinean physical environment extends from sea level to an upper limit of approximately three thousand feet. It includes plateaus of crystalline materials and granites in the west and extreme east. In the Ibadan and Ilesha districts in the west, and in the outer hills of the Obudu and Oban plateaus in the east, erosion surfaces occur at approximately one thousand feet above sea level. Erosion surfaces at approximately two thousand feet occur in north-western Yorubaland, Ekiti, and the Oban Hills. These surfaces are broken by granitic *inselberge* and other residual features. They are drained southwards by streams for the most part deeply incised in valleys with convex slopes and little or no flood-plain. Between the crystallines or basement complex areas there is a broad synclinal trough occupied in the west by the valley of the lower Niger, and in the east by Cretaceous and Tertiary sediments forming eastward-facing *cuestas* nowhere more than one thousand seven hundred feet above sea level. In the south the trough is occupied by the alluvia of the Niger and Cross river deltas forming a wilderness of creeks and levées fringed by sand bars and lagoons.

Sub-Guinean. Like the Guinean environment the sub-Guinean has two rainfall maxima in almost every year providing annual totals of between forty and sixty inches. The term sub-Guinean is used to suggest the close climatic relationship. It follows Richard-Molard's suggestion that in West Africa areas with two rainfall maxima should be classified as "Guinean" whilst those with a single maximum should be termed "Sudanic."[5] The northern boundary has in consequence been defined by the northern limit of stations with more than 75 per cent multi-peak years [6]—a 75 per cent occurrence being taken as an arbitrary figure for reasonable expectation by a cultivator of the occurrence of two or more rainfall peaks. The dry season lasts between three and four months, but during that season the effect of the harmattan is more pronounced than in the Guinean environment. For two to three months in the year mean monthly relative humidities at dawn are less than eighty per cent. Soils are acid and heavily leached. In this environment clays are mainly confined to valley-bottom lands and the greater part of the surface is occupied by sands or sandy loams. These often form only a thin mantle over concretionary ironstone, which is of common occurrence. Keay claims that the climax vegetation type is rainforest in the southern third of the area changing northwards into a transition woodland containing a mixture of fire-tolerant and fire-tender trees growing together in a closed canopy over shrubs and grasses.[7] Rainforest outliers extend far to the north, but always in exceptionally well-watered situations. Conversely the fire-tolerant species of the savanna woodlands extend to the southern limits of the environment wherever exceptionally well-drained soils occur. A notable occurrence of this type is in the isolated portion of savanna in the Sobo plains of Benin. Little can, however, be said of vegetation distributions without discussing the effects of cultivation and pastoralism, for a secondary vegetation of grasses and fire-resistant trees and shrubs is everywhere dominant. The sub-Guinean environment ranges in altitude from two hundred feet above sea level in the lowlands of the Niger valley to three thousand feet above sea level on the fringes of the Obudu plateau and the Bamenda highlands. In Southern Nigeria it consists essentially of the watersheds at between one thousand and two thousand five hundred feet above sea level between the Niger and Benue on the one hand, and the rivers flowing directly to the coast on the other. Except in northern Iboland, broad erosion surfaces with residual features are developed on the basement complex. In Iboland these are replaced by erosion surfaces developed on *cuestas* formed on sedimentary materials. With the exception of the Ogun and the headwaters of the Osse, the Anambra and the Aboine, drainage flows northwards to the Niger-Benue trough.

Montane. The mountain environments, *i.e.* the environments over three thousand five hundred feet above sea level, are climatically distinct by their lower temperatures. Precipitation on the Obudu and Bamenda plateaus and on Cameroon Mountain is for the most part high, generally over one hundred inches, but there are considerable variations according to exposure. On Cameroon Mountain mist lasts for long periods at altitudes of three thousand five hundred to six thousand feet and is of common occurrence on the more northerly plateaus. On the latter, however, the dry season is more marked and the harmattan more prolonged in effect. Exposure to strong winds producing high evaporation rates is a marked feature at altitudes of over five thousand feet. Soils vary in character from the clays of the more level plateau surfaces to the course sands and gravels of the steeper slopes; all are highly acid. On the Bamenda plateau, at over five thousand feet, a clay topsoil with a remarkably high humus content is developed over clays derived from basalts. Forest and grassland communities containing distinct species for the most part define the Montane environment, notably Mist or Evergreen Montane Forest and Dry Montane Forest. Keay's boundaries of his Montane vegetation zone have been adopted. Some of the species are found only on one plateaus, *e.g.* the mountain bamboo, *Arundinaria alphina,* and the conifer, *Podocarpus sp.,* which occur in Bamenda, but are unknown on Cameroon Mountain.[8] Woodland or scrub occurs up to approximately nine thousand five hundred feet above sea level depending on exposure, and grasslands below this height are for the most part secondary. The altitudinal range of the Montane environment extends from approximately three thousand five hundred feet above sea level to thirteen

thousand three hundred and fifty feet at the summit of Cameroon Mountain. There is a prominent erosion surface at between three thousand five hundred and four thousand feet. Residuals eroded in granites and lavas and the remnants of former volcanoes stand up above the general level cut for the most part in crystalline materials.

LANDSCAPE CHANGES BEFORE THE ARRIVAL OF EUROPEANS

By the sixteenth century settlement in the sub-Guinean environment and on the fringes of the Guinean appears to have produced communities of town dwellers depending on rotational bush fallow cultivation instead of on more primitive shifting methods. In the former system fallow land is constantly recleared and virgin forest is no longer sought.[9] In consequence, permanent settlement and the development of ordered government over a wide area became possible. In the west the powerful kingdom of Oyo was established on the uplands fringing the upper Ogun basin, whilst Ife and Ilesha were founded just within the rainforest environment. To the east, towns like Awka in the grasslands of northern Iboland appear to have established an early importance in trade and manufacture and probably in political influence.[10] It seems likely that the density of population in the sub-Guinean environment was greater than in the Guinean. In the former two crops a year could be produced on land easy to clear, thus reducing the area needed for cultivation. Here also could be grown the greatest variety of crops in Southern Nigeria, including all the known grains and root crops. To cultivators who were limited in their trading contacts this variety gave immense advantages in diet and in the supply of raw materials. Agriculture was developed in this environment at an early date for it seems probable that it contains the centre of origin of the West African species of yam.[11] The descriptions of Clapperton, Bowen and Burton in the nineteenth century suggest that before the advent of the cattle import from the north, amongst the Yoruba at least, cattle were formerly more common.[12] Dry season pasture on crop remains provided manure for the cultivated land and made possible a more stable agricultural system. The demand for crop land and pasture resulted in the removal of the original forests and their replacement by grasslands containing trees that were fire-resistant, or protected because of their usefulness. Grass established itself wherever dry conditions followed the main harvest so that woody plants had difficulty in taking root during the first stages of fallow. To the south the occurrence of savannas was limited by more humid or only short dry season conditions.

Before European influences were felt it seems probable that population densities in the Guinean environment were extremely low. Cultivators lived in scattered temporary clearings and depended mainly on root crops, particularly yams. Tree products, chiefly palm oil, kernels and wine, coconuts and various fruits were of great importance, so that many Guinean communities lived as much by gathering as by cultivation. With tools made of soft local iron the removal of the big trees of the rainforest was a difficult operation. The period when burning was possible was extremely limited. On the fallows woody plants quickly re-established themselves and needed considerable labour for removal. To the Yoruba the forest communities were the "epo," or "weeds" living in a remote part of the kingdom of Oyo.[13] Exceptions were the towns of Ife and Ilesha, probably seeking defensive shelter in the northern edge of the forest, and the city of Benin. The latter was established on the sandy soils of the Tertiary outcrop. These provide better drained conditions for cultivation and may have supported a less dense forest. In addition, location close to the creeks of the Niger delta gave access to easy trading routes and to abundant supplies of fish, important in a region which

produced very little meat owing to the lack of pasture and to problems of disease in cattle. In the south-east, the Guinean environment of Ibo- and Ibibio-land may also have been comparatively easy to clear since the soils consisted mainly of deep, well-drained sands. Probably dense settlement in Orlu and Owerri, Ikot Ekpene and Abak was established at an earlier date than in the heavily forested regions of the west. In the extreme east the densely forested hills of the Cross river basin still support only a few widely scattered villages where shifting agriculture is still practised. Of the early occupation of the Montane environments very little is known. In Bamenda, peoples appear to have immigrated from the Cross river valley in the late seventeenth or early eighteenth centuries and reduced most of the original forest to grassland. Later, Tikar immigrants came from the north and founded towns like Bali, Bafut and Kumbo on defensible hill tops and ridges. These were followed by Fulani pastoralists who introduced large herds of cattle on the increasing area of grassland.[14] The Obudu plateau and Cameroon Mountain are smaller in area and appear to have been avoided by the main currents of migration. The higher levels are occupied mainly by Fulani pastoralists seeking areas freer from cattle disease where pastures may easily be maintained.

EUROPEAN INFLUENCES ON THE RURAL LANDSCAPE

The first contacts with Europeans were in the Guinean environment at Benin; and later, on the beaches of the south-western lagoon coast and in the creeks of the Niger and Cross river deltas. The early Portugese traders introduced maize, cassava, groundnuts, sweet potatoes, tobacco and various fruits including several varieties of citrus. Of these, maize and tobacco spread rapidly—particularly the former, which had become, by the seventeenth century, one of the chief crops of the sub-

Guinean communities.[15] Maize became an important secondary crop in the Guinean environment, where it appears to be the only cereal which will produce abundantly under the highly humid conditions. Cassava did not spread so rapidly since yams were the preferred root crop until fallows were reduced by land shortage. None of these importations produced any great change in the Southern Nigerian landscape. However, they increased the variety of crops, made possible more widespread cultivation and improved crop rotations and combinations producing more food and supporting larger numbers of people. The trade established became mainly an export of slaves in exchange for manufactures, including iron and, at a later date, steel implements. The slave traffic resulted in concentrations of population at the coastal landing places, and clearance of the surrounding forest. Outlying villages and hamlets were raided and depopulation occurred in areas immediately inland from the slave markets, or near powerful states like Oyo in Yorubaland. The Egba of south-western Yorubaland, the Ibibio and the southern Ibo all suffered severely. The import of steel "matchets" made possible easier and more effective clearance of the forest [16] which became more attractive to settlement once it was no longer raided for slaves.

In the seventeenth and eighteenth centuries a trade in palm oil and kernels began. Eventually, after the action of the British naval squadrons and the establishment of the Protectorate of Lagos in 1861, the palm produce trade took the place of the slave trade and encouraged the occupation of the rainforest areas. From the evidence in Government intelligence and assessment reports it appears that the Ibo-speaking peoples were invading the south-eastern portions of the Guinean environment from the seventeenth century onwards.[17] They cut down the forests, replacing them by villages and hamlets surrounded by oil palm groves, farmlands and forest remnants. The oil palm forest of south-eastern

Nigeria is the product of this Ibo invasion and settlement. It provides a distinctive humanized landscape related to trading contacts with Europe.[18] Ibo immigration resulted in a contraction of the area occupied by the Ibibo-speaking peoples who were forced to retreat beyond the Aza River. There they developed an economy based, like that of the Ibo, on root crops and oil palms and able to support high densities of population.

The river valleys which had previously been avoided, partly because of the great danger of malaria, began to attract people in search of trading sites. The Etung clan of the Ekoi peoples moved down to the Cross river about 180 years ago in search of trade, building villages and establishing farms in areas formerly covered by forest. Many of them began to grow food crops, for sale to the population of the coastal ports and of the crowded areas to the south.[19] Inland, similar movements took place. In the Southern Cameroons people left the old slave-trade routes in the narrow valleys of the escarpments for the foothills zone where they planted oil palms and traded in palm produce.

Today south-eastern Nigeria is one of the most densely populated parts of West Africa with several Ibo and Ibibo districts containing over a thousand persons per square mile. Population is now concentrated along main roads, near railways and important river routes and along the coast where many small fishing villages, such as Bonny, Brass and Opobo have become ports. The extent of the modern road and railway network is illustrated in Figure 2. Remnants of the original forest survive only in a few scattered patches. The fallows of woody plants have been reduced in area and seldom does their vegetation obtain any great height before it is cut down again. In places fallow plants are now sown. For example, some Ibo plant "icheku" (*Acioa barterii*) whilst many Ibibo plant "nya" (*Macrolobium macrophyllum*).[20] In the Port Harcourt district mangrove swamps

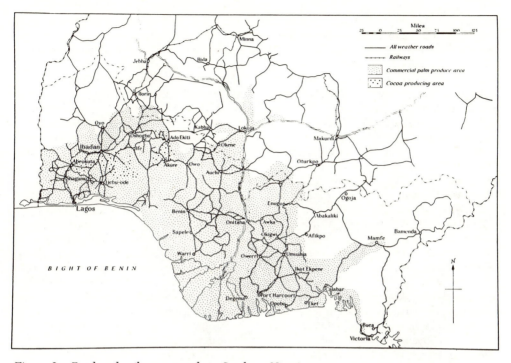

Figure 2.—Road and railway network in Southern Nigeria.

have been modified by cutting in order to supply pit props to the Enugu collieries.

In the south-west large-scale clearance of the rainforest did not begin until the nineteenth century when the Fulani armies invaded the Yoruba kingdom of Oyo, destroying a large number of settlements. Refugees fled southwards to the shelter of the Guinean environment where they made fresh clearances with imported "matchets" and defended themselves with European guns. On the northern edge of the rainforest was founded a new capital of Oyo to which the cultivators of the surrounding hamlets were forced to migrate by decree.[21] However, the capital of the Alafin of Oyo declined in importance and political power shifted to new cities founded on the sites of forest villages, such as Ibadan, established c. 1820. The invasion of the Guinean and southern portions of the sub-Guinean environments by refugees produced displacement of the original inhabitants, and the Egba peoples were forced southwards, founding the fortified town of Abeokuta c. 1830 on high rocks at the edge of the savanna. The warfare and the provision of new weapons and tools led to a southward shift of the Yoruba with a consequent change of landscape. Farmlands were cleared around the new towns excepting for the intervening strip of defensive home woodland or scrub, the igbo ile. The export of slaves in the first half of the century, of ivory, palm produce and timber in exchange for metal ware, cloth, "matchets," salt, spirits and guns led to the growth of ports like Badagry, Lagos, Ikorodu and Epe with their associated clearances. In their hinterland Ibadan, Abeokuta and Ijebu struggled to gain control of the trade routes. Between these three nuclei of settlement and cultivation lay the forest, forming a frontier or no-man's-land. It now forms a forest reserve.

To the east, in Ife and Ondo Provinces, away from the main trade routes between Oyo and the coast, great areas of original forest still remained. These were to be in large part removed by the development at the turn of the century of increasing timber exports and by the production of rubber and cocoa. All suitable timber within twenty miles radius of the ports was cut down. Further inland the rivers supplied the means for wood-cutters to penetrate still deeper into the rainforest, and they were soon followed by rubber tappers.

The demand for "Lagos rubber" began with an export of 56 lbs. in 1893 which rose to over five million lbs. in 1895.[22] The chief sources were the tree *Funtumia* (*Kicksia*) *elastica* and the vines *Landolphia* and *Clitandra*. The districts around Lagos were quickly worked out and tapping advanced rapidly inland; rubber camps were formed in the forest, many of which, particularly in Benin Province, became permanent settlements with associated croplands. Many people left traditional hilltop sites and abandoned the collection of palm produce for the more lucrative rubber industry. The effect was shown in the decline of palm produce exports as rubber exports increased. Despite ordinances intended to protect rubber trees and vines there were few left by 1900, even as far from the coast as northern Ondo Province, and the rubber export had decreased to 600,000 lbs. Rubber planting was introduced, but was never very successful in Nigeria, for to compete with the Malayan product plantations were needed. Large scale development required foreign capital, but investment in land by non-Nigerians was discouraged. Village plantations of *Funtumia* were made around Benin and a few companies acquired estates in 1904, planting *Ceara* and *Hevea*, chiefly in the Sapele area.

The rapid destruction of Nigeria's rubber resources strengthened the case for forest conservancy along "somewhat similar lines to that in India." [23] The first forest reserve was constituted at Ibadan in 1899 to preserve timber and improve rubber yields and a Forestry Department with Indian-trained officials was formed in 1901. Although this department did not achieve its original aim of reserving twenty-five per cent of the area of Nigeria for forest, it was able to acquire extensive tracts in the former inter-tribal and inter-state frontier woodlands. Thus the landscape is still dominated by dense stands of trees in areas which would otherwise have been available for agricultural expansion. To the work of this department Nigeria owes many village wood lots, urban plantations for fuel, and the planting of numerous exotics including teak, cassia and blue gum. Roadside tree plantings have greatly improved the appearance of many Nigerian highways and provide shade for pedestrians. In the Cameroons roads are often bordered by *Ficus* species introduced by the Germans. In some areas, for example in the Oban Hills of Calabar Province and in central Benin Province, the creation of forest reserves resulted in the reduction of the area available for shifting cultivation. Periodic migration into virgin brush was prevented and cultivators were forced to adopt rotational bush fallow methods in fixed locations. In effect, the landscape became almost static in appearance. Woodland and cultivated land became stable, standing out as clearly demarcated entities.

By the turn of the century numerous plants were introduced into Nigeria mainly through the agency of Government botanical stations. Seedlings were supplied to peasant farmers in the hope of developing production for export. For a short time coffee proved attractive, but prices were poor compared with cocoa, the planting of which spread rapidly in the Lagos hinterland. Areas adjacent to the railway, which was built as far north as Oshogbo by 1907, were highly valued for cocoa farms. Partly with Government encouragement kola trees were interplanted and gave a secondary resource. "Gbanja kola" (*Cola nitida*) seed was introduced from the Gold Coast, yielding larger crops of nuts which were generally preferred for flavour and storage qualities to the nuts of the indigenous variety "abata" (*C. acuminata*). Initially cocoa growing depended on the issue of seed, the provision of instruction by the Agricultural Department and the building of fermenting and drying houses. Its distribution coincided largely with the distribution of Agricultural Department effort.[24] The first commercially productive areas were around Ilaro and Ibadan. As the road system developed planting extended eastwards as far as Owo occupying the rainforest regions of central Yorubaland. Immigrants entered in huge numbers particularly from Oyo and Ilorin Provinces. Since penetration was from the north, the savanna-ward fringe of the rainforest was cleared at an early stage although conditions here are marginal for cocoa cultivation. The forests were replaced by a landscape of fallow shrubs, small wood lots, mixed cocoa and kola plantations and farmlands divided by densely forested valleys (Fig. 3). Dense settlement concentrated on the fertile *ilepa* clays of the hill tops. As old areas declined in productivity the cocoa landscape advanced eastwards and south-eastwards.

Outside the south-west cocoa was early introduced into Benin, Onitsha and Calabar Provinces. It did not become a popular crop, partly because oil palm production was already well established, partly because the Agricultural Department was not so concerned to develop cocoa planting there, and partly because of the lack of suitable soils. In the Southern Cameroons cocoa was grown on huge estates by the Germans, and in the same region the oil palm and above all the banana were also developed as plantation crops by European companies. The Tiko plains became in effect a forest of regularly spaced bananas, labour was imported from adjacent areas and estate villages were created. At the same time, portions of the adjacent upper Cross River

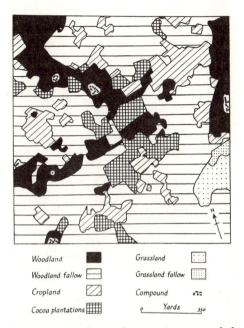

Woodland
Woodland fallow
Cropland
Cocoa plantations
Grassland
Grassland fallow
Compound
Yards
0   350

Figure 3.—Land use elements in a cocoa belt near Iwo.

basin were heavily depopulated and reverted to forest.

The sub-Guinean environment of southern Nigeria comprises the Oyo Province of Yorubaland, the Kukuruku region of northern Benin Province, northern Iboland and the north-western foothills of the Bamenda plateau. The total area is very much smaller than that of the Guinean environment and the changes which have occurred in the landscape due to European influences have been much less profound. Indeed the north-western foothills of Bamenda have neither roads nor railway and have remained almost entirely unaffected by recent economic development.

As described in an earlier paragraph, the kingdom of Oyo was invaded by Fulani armies at the beginning of the nineteenth century. Many of its towns and villages were destroyed and an area of over five hundred square miles between Shaki in the west and Ilorin in the east was severely depopulated. The capital, Old Oyo or Katunga, was abandoned and the site, together with the "finely cultivated valley" described by Clapperton in 1826, became overgrown with deciduous forest.[25] A landscape once similar in appearance, judging by Clapperton's description, to the open savanna lands in the south of the province at the present day, was thus completely changed. That change was due to internal and not European influences, but the continued existence of forest on land once highly valued for cultivation was due to a changed sense of land values caused by European commercial development. In the mid-nineteenth century the Guinean environment offered greater security not only because of the shelter afforded by its forest, but because of its proximity to ports trading in guns. In the late nineteenth century and at the present day its oil palm produce and cocoa offer greater returns per acre whilst its rapidly growing commercial centres offer more attractive social amenities. Northern Oyo is too far from main roads, the railway and markets to be resettled. Those parts of the region which are accessible to modern commerce have changed in appearance, although to a lesser degree than the Guinean areas immediately to the south. Firstly, large numbers of males have gone away either permanently or temporarily to seek work or land in the cocoa belt; in proportion to the size of the population the area cultivated has in effect been contracted. Secondly, the demand of the cocoa farmers for food has encouraged the commercial cultivation of yams, cassava, maize and guinea-corn so that farmers have tended to move towards the main routeways and markets. Thirdly, much of the region is now more important as a provider of pasture for the droves of Fulani cattle which are brought down to the markets of Ibadan and Lagos. Attempts were made to encourage increased cotton production for export, but the bulk of the cotton is still sold to the flourishing local textile industry which extends over the border

into Ilorin Province in the Northern Region.

In the Kukuruku or Afema region (northern Benin Province) in the nineteenth century subsistence cultivation of guinea-corn and yams was practised by a people who lived in hilltop villages. Many of the villages were ringed with walls and occupied rocky retreats which were refuges from the Fulani armies, whilst the more fertile lands at the lower levels were abandoned to forest.[26] The British Administration first entered the district in 1904. Under its influence the old settlement sites were abandoned and villages moved down to the plains. The hills have been abandoned to forest and scrub whilst the vegetation of the plains has been in large part removed and replaced by farmlands. Oil palms flourish on the riverain lands and their growth has been encouraged. Since 1935 cocoa and kola have been introduced, but have not been very successful owing to the occurrence of a marked dry season. Generally, the region is too distant from the major markets for export produce to obtain a large share in the benefits of modern commerce. The Kukuruku region does, however, grow foodstuffs, especially yams, for sale in areas to the south and west producing cocoa and oil palm products. The difficulties in developing a cash economy on the basis of agriculture have resulted in a tendency for males to emigrate in search of work elsewhere. Barring the re-location of settlements and farmlands there have been few major changes in the landscape under British rule.

In northern Iboland landscape changes have been more profound than elsewhere in the sub-Guinean environment, partly because of the increasing population pressure on local resources and partly because of the region's greater accessibility to main routes and markets. On the uplands between Awka, Enugu and Nsukka, Ibo farmers had early reduced the forests to open grassland with scattered low bushes. Within these grasslands they established "towns" each containing between ten thousand and sixty thousand people in dispersed compounds. Around the towns they developed a defensive screen of woodland. Modern transport conditions have encouraged a move of settlement to the roadsides whilst other new villages are being established outside former town boundaries.[27] With the increasing importance of oil palm produce in the economy the pace of planting has increased despite the fact that the region, with its marked dry season, is marginal for palm oil and kernel production. Below the easternmost escarpment at Enugu coal mining in the escarpment valleys has brought an abrupt change of landscape with its associated spoil heaps, mine buildings and miners' settlements. Close by are timber plantations, chiefly of teak, to supply pit props and fuel for the rapidly growing township of Enugu. Increasing population density in northern Iboland has created many problems. On the sandier soils the reduction of fallows and the fixing of paths and settlements due to overcrowding have led to both sheet and gully erosion. In addition great *embizes* or gullies as much as three hundred feet in depth occur at Agulu and on the eastern or Awgu escarpment. These features have been modified in part by small dams, wave-bedding and sowing with selected earth-holding plants which produce yet another landscape in Southern Nigeria.[28] In the extreme northeast in the areas accupied by the Izi Ibo, where trading contacts are poorly developed, the British occupation has resulted in the abandonment of old fortified sites, and settlement dispersal on to the farmlands.

In the Montane environment European influences on the rural landscape have been slight. The areas concerned have little original agricultural produce to offer for export, are remote from markets and poorly supplied with transport facilities. Since European settlement in Nigeria has not been encouraged there has been no development in these areas comparable to that in East Africa. Under German rule there was some reduction in the number of males in the Cameroons highlands in order to supply labour to the lowland plantations. At the same time the establishment of more peaceful conditions in south-eastern Nigeria and the Cameroons generally encouraged the immigration to these highlands of increasing numbers of Fulani pastoralists. Most of these came seasonally, but many have since become permanent settlers, and with this invasion of pastoralists the grassland area has undoubtedly increased at the expense of the remaining forests.

THE CHANGING URBAN LANDSCAPE

With the British occupation the earth walls surrounding the Yoruba towns were allowed to crumble and decay, whilst the wooden palisades of many of the Guinean villages were removed or allowed to rot. Earthworks and ditches became overgrown or were filled for road and building extensions. As already mentioned, hilltop sites were abandoned for sites near the farmlands where more open towns were laid out with broad streets in a rectangular pattern (Fig. 4). Burton's Abeokuta with its "narrow and irregular" streets was pierced by modern thoroughfares, whilst its tamped mud and thatching was replaced by brick, mixtures of mud and cement, concrete and corrugated iron. The area of scrubland around the town equivalent to the Yoruba *igbo ile* was gradually cleared and divided into farm holdings. In Yoruba towns generally, the traditional courtyard type of house gave way to a two storey mansion in the "Brazilian" style, copied by the descendants of former slaves from a Portuguese housetype in Brazil. In this type the courtyard is replaced by verandahs and balconies with ornamented rails. In Iboland a similar house-type has tended to replace the former compound unit. In the more important centres the offices, stores and houses of Government officials and of European and Syrian traders were established. African traders built large stores and shops. The condition of Nigerian towns, however, cre-

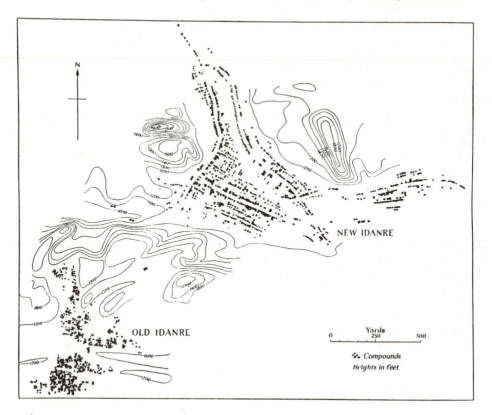

Figure 4.—Idanre villages in Ondo Province, from aerial photographs, 21 May, 1951.

ated problems for European settlement. Many of them were situated close to swamps or had pools of stagnant water in the numerous borrow-pits dug for the extraction of clay. The dense crowding of people within the town provided in itself a source of insect-borne disease. The chief medical official of Lagos wrote in 1900: ". . . the sites of European towns are, for the most part, far from being suitable for the erection of dwellings. Speaking generally, they are to be found on a low-lying sea coast, and either on or near swamps, lagoons, or river estuaries. The houses of Europeans are, as often as not, in close proximity to the native huts, or even actually amongst them. . . ."[26] Swamp drainage was begun in Lagos and Ibadan by 1900 and the reclaimed land was set aside for building purposes. In Lagos reclamation was extensive. Retaining walls were built along the foreshore, mangroves were cut and the MacGregor Canal dug to serve as a marsh drain. Beach sand and harbour dredgings, derived mainly from the extensive harbour works of 1907–17, were used to fill depressions so that the area of the island was increased and the harbour deepened.[30] Health measures became important in the planning or controlled expansion of Nigerian towns. On the peripheries of the built-up areas farmers were ordered to plant only short crops. In many of the towns European quarters were segregated. Regulations were made to create uninhabited zones of a quarter-mile in width between the Nigerian and European areas. In the recent past European quarters were frequently built to windward and planted with shade trees. Thus Government stations are frequently located on a nearby hill or rise on one side of a town or village. In these the houses and office blocks are widely dispersed and surrounded by lawns, gardens and tree-lined avenues. In some cases landscape gardening has been attempted. The provision of piped water supplies meant the construction of reservoirs and around some of these there is a careful spacing of lawns and trees in order to improve on the previous scene. Reservoirs like that of Ibadan or Ife provide small examples, although the reservoir at Okene in Kabba Province (just outside the limits of Southern Nigeria) with its terraces, its ordered planting of exotic trees and its two artificial islands is the most outstanding. Quarters for other Europeans—traders, soldiers, engineers and those in the professions—were established on similar lines to those built for Government officers. Separation of quarters was maintained as late as 1939 when Government recommendations for town planning recognized the need for a separate European residential area surrounded by an open space, but suggested that it should not be too far from the business area since otherwise few Europeans would be able to "avail themselves of the advantages of separation." [31] Today separation is tending to disappear as more and more Nigerians enter the higher ranks of administration and take managerial positions. The garden suburbs created by the British administration are becoming a part of the Nigerian urban landscape.

Within the Southern Nigerian towns immigration led to overcrowding and the rapid growth of unplanned sprawls outside the old walls. Streets were narrowed by the extension in some cases of the frontages of private property. In Epe, for example, the realization of the value of land resulted in the reduction of some street widths from twenty to six feet. [32] In Lagos the courtyards within the compounds were occupied by shacks built of bamboo and corrugated iron, thus producing densely populated slums. Between the compounds the streets of bare earth were heavily eroded during rainstorms. In some cases building foundations were undermined; in others, gutters were left above street level. Street widths had to be regulated and minimum building standards enforced. Tarred roads with concrete gutters were made and during the first decade of this century town planning was attempted.

Planned towns with broad streets at right angles to one another and with building plots of uniform size were laid out at the New Town of Ebute Meta forming a mainland extension of Lagos, and at Port Harcourt, Aba and Enugu. Modern waterworks and power stations were constructed whilst timber plantations were established to maintain domestic and public fuel supplies. Many of the larger markets were laid out anew and improved by the building of concrete shelters. Public buildings of brick, concrete and steel were erected. Where formerly a town had consisted of a number of crowded villages focusing on a central market and the area occupied by the ruling authority, now it had in addition distinct business, shopping and government districts with planned spacious suburbs. Traders from other parts of Nigeria have come to the towns in increasing numbers and occupy separate quarters. The Yoruba towns, for example, acquired districts occupied mainly by Hausa who had come from Northern Nigeria. Some degree of segregation thus occurs between different Nigerian communities within a town, and often leads to contrasts in types of housing, market and other amenities.

Since 1945 the pace of Nigeria development has increased. Investment has been made in new industries and Government loans or gifts have financed agricultural and resettlement schemes, and public services and institutions. Locally new types of landscape have resulted.

In the new agricultural schemes the large scale organization of peasant cultivation has been attempted, frequently combining the use of mechanized equipment. The Eruwa Mechanized Farming Scheme, initiated in 1951, includes a considerable acreage of contour-ploughed land under pineapples for the local canning industry. The contrast between the huge ordered fields under a single crop and the small patches with their mixed crops on the neighboring lands is startling. In the Eastern Region, plantation schemes for the cultivation of oil palms, cocoa, rubber, cashew and coffee, and of citrus fruits are being developed. In the Western Region a scheme of integrated rural development, including the use of hydro-electric power, is planned for the Upper Ogun River basin. The Upper Ogun Estate with its contour-ploughed strips and improved pastures has already been established. Improved pastures exist also on the Fashola Government Farm near Oyo, whilst on the Obudu plateau the Eastern Regional Production Development Board has a 20,000 acre ranch. Other schemes include swamp reclamation for rice-growing in the deltas of the Niger and Cross rivers, and market gardening at Enugu, using contour ridging and nightsoil compost.[33] Thus a variety of schemes has been initiated which, if successful, will greatly modify the Nigerian scene.

With regard to the development of industrial landscapes there are at present only a few manufacturing industries. These are concerned with canning food, bottling fruit juice, mineral waters and beer, preparing tobacco, milling flour, crushing groundnuts and oil palm fruit, and making margarine, soap and metal oil-containers. At Apapa, opposite Lagos, the Nigerian equivalent of an industrial trading estate has been laid out on reclaimed land; a broad, level area has been provided with roads and drainage ready for occupation by warehouses, factories and offices.

The examination of landscape changes in Nigeria has shown that European influences have produced the most marked effects in the towns, since these are the centres of commerce and political authority. In the rural areas the greatest changes have occurred in the Guinean environment where perennial crops, producing for external exchange, dominate the landscape. The introduction of modern methods of transport and modern trading facilities has done more to effect these changes than any other factor. In the lowlands of the Eastern Region the development of an oil-palm bush landscape began as early as the end of the eighteenth century. In the west the "cocoa belt" landscape was not developed until towards the end of the nineteenth century, but was assisted by earlier population movements due to the Fulani conquest of Oyo. In the sub-Guinean and Montane environments, generally unsuited to the cultivation of perennials like cocoa and the oil palm, landscape changes have been much less marked. In the former they are associated mainly with changes in settlement distribution and in the latter with an increase in pastoral activities. Development schemes involving resettlement of population and the introduction of modern agricultural techniques are producing, as yet on a small scale, new types of landscape. There is little industrial development at present, although the trading estate at Apapa gives some indication of a possible industrial and commercial urban landscape of the future.

NOTES

[1] Richard-Molard, J., "Afrique Occidentale Française," Paris, 1949, pp. 39 et seq.

[2] Keay, R. W. J., "Outline of Nigerian vegetation," 2nd edition, 1952, pp. 21–3.

[3] For an account of the harmattan see: J. Richard-Molard, op. cit., pp. 14–17.

[4] Keay, R. W. J., op. cit., pp. 14–15.

[5] Richard-Molard, J., *op. cit.*, pp. 18–26 and 39–50.

[6] Buchanan, K. M., and J. C. Pugh, "Land and people in Nigeria," 1955, p. 28.

[7] Keay, R. W. J., *op. cit.*, pp. 9, 21–3 and 23–6.

[8] *Ibid.*, p. 37.

[9] Morgan, W. B., "Some comments on shifting cultivation in Africa," Research notes, Department of Geography, University College, Ibadan.

[10] For comments on early Yoruba and Ibo history see: S. Johnson, "The history of the Yorubas," 1921; M. D. W. Jeffreys, "The Awka Report," 1931 (Government Intelligence Report).

[11] Leverhulme Trust, "The West African Commission, 1938–39," 1943, pp. 16–19.

[12] See: H. Clapperton, "Journal of a second expedition into the interior of Africa," 1829, especially pp. 56–7; T. J. Bowen, "Adventures and missionary labors in several countries in the interior of Africa from 1849 to 1856," 1857; R. F. Burton, "Abeokuta and the Cameroons Mountains," 2 vols., 1863, especially pp. 321–2.

[13] Johnson, S., *op. cit.*, pp. 12–14.

[14] Government Intelligence and Assessment Reports for Mamfe and Bamenda Divisions.

[15] On the introduction of crops to West Africa see: R. Portères, "Vieilles agricultures de l'Afrique intertropicale: l'agronomie tropicale," 1950, pp. 489–507; "The West African Commission," pp. 16–19; A. Adandé, "Le maïs et ses usages dans le bas-Dahomey," *Bulletin de l'IFAN*, 15 (1953), pp. 220–82. Maize was also introduced by Arabs from the north; see R. Portères, "L'introduction du maïs en Afrique," *J. Agric. trop. Bot.*, App. 2 (1955), pp. 349–86 and 477–510.

[16] See note on the effects of introducing the steel axe into the Amazon basin in: P. Gourou, "The tropical world," translated by E. D. Laborde, 1953, p. 26, n. 2.

[17] Government Intelligence and Assessment Reports for Aba Division.

[18] See "The West African Commission," pp. 24–5. The only case of direct European influence in the development of the oil-palm bush landscape appears to have been the German attempt in the Southern Cameroons in 1903 to enforce the planting of 25 palms for each standing hut and 50 for each new one. See H. R. Rudin, "Germans in the Cameroons, 1884–1914," 1938, pp. 258–61.

[19] Mackay, J. H., "A regional survey of the Ikom-Oban area," June 1944, unpublished typescript.

[20] "The Nigerian Handbook," 1953, p. 130.

[21] Johnson, S., *op. cit.*, pp. 90–3.

[22] See: Annual Reports for the Colony of Lagos, 1900–1903; Annual Reports for the Colony of Southern Nigeria, 1906–1907; W. N. M. Geary, "Nigeria under British rule," 1927, pp. 56–8; "The West African Commission," pp. 25–6.

[23] Holland, J. H., "The useful plants of Nigeria," Part I, 1908, *Bulletin of Miscellaneous Information, Additional Series* IX, Royal Botanic Gardens, Kew, p. 39. See also pp. 40–6.

[24] Annual Report of the Nigerian Agricultural Department for 1921, p. 4. See also comments on the effect of cocoa introduction, in H. Ward Price "Report of land tenure in the Yoruba provinces," 1932, especially in Part II. For the development of cocoa "regions" and forest clearance see: R. Galletti, K. D. S. Baldwin and I. O. Dina, "Nigerian cocoa farmers," 1956, pp. 1–7, 19–22 and 23–5.

[25] Clapperton, H., *op. cit.*, p. 35.

[26] Temple, O., "Notes on the tribes, provinces, emirates and states of the Northern Provinces of Nigeria," 1922, pp. 247–52.

[27] See Morgan, W. B., "The grassland towns of the Eastern Region of Nigeria." *Trans. Inst. Brit. Geogr.* 23 (1957), pp. 213–24.

[28] Grove, A. T., "Soil erosion and population problems in south-east Nigeria," *Geogr. J.*, 117 (1951), pp. 291–306; A. T. Grove, "Land use and soil conservation in parts of Onitsha and Owerri Provinces," Geological Survey of Nigeria, *Bulletin*, No. 21, 1951; R. A. Sykes, "A history of the anti-erosion work at Udi," *Farm and Forest, 1* (1940), pp. 3–6.

[29] Strachan, Dr. Henry, Paper on the health conditions of West Africa, 1900, p. 4—quoted in R. R. Kuczynski, "Demographic survey of the Colonial Empire," *West Africa*, 3, p. 17.

[30] Annual reports for the Colony of Lagos, 1900–1903; Annual reports for the Colony of Southern Nigeria, 1906–07; W. N. M. Geary, *op. cit.*, pp. 146–7 and 253–5.

[31] Government of Nigeria, "Selection of sites for towns and government residential areas," Lagos, 1939.

[32] Annual Report for the Colony of Lagos, 1902, p. 43.

[33] For an account of agricultural development schemes see: K. M. Buchanan and J. C. Pugh, *op. cit.*, pp. 159–70.

European interest in the highlands of Kenya was linked to the need to develop an economic base for a new country. The land was settled with little knowledge of local population-land relationships; in appropriating what seemed to be unoccupied territory, Europeans failed to recognize the extensive nature of indigenous agricultural systems, in which only a limited part of the total area is in production at any one time. Nor did they realize that inter-tribal warfare and the ravages of human and animal diseases had also played a part in producing the "empty" areas they chose to settle (Ominde, 1968).

The exclusive allocation of land to Europeans (designed to exclude Asians but subsequently extended to Africans) produced what is described as "a European tribal reserve." Africans were not allowed to own land, yet they supplied the labor force for European farms and occupied some alienated areas as unauthorized squatters. With technological advantages, European farmers were able to extend production to areas impossible for Africans to cultivate with traditional methods; with commercial advantages, Europeans were able to cope with environmental fluctuations and to balance returns from good seasons against bad seasons. Thus the highlands, which occupy only a small part of the total area of Kenya, contributed in inverse proportion to the total export production of the country (Fair, 1963).

With the independence of Kenya in the early 1960's the exclusive rights of Europeans ended, and African farmers began to settle the highlands in a series of schemes discussed in a subsequent paper (Carey Jones, 1960). The interlude of European occupation is an example of the structure and nature of alien population-land relationships in an area where climatic modifications have produced conditions attractive to settlement (Millman, 1968).

16. The "White Highlands" of Kenya

W. T. W. MORGAN

The term "the White Highlands" was derived from the official policy that certain agricultural lands in Kenya should be reserved for settlers of European origin. The termination of this policy after a period of nearly sixty years makes this an appropriate time to examine which were the areas included in the White Highlands and why.

To early explorers and administrators, the cool climate and absence of population

From *The Geographical Journal*, 129, 1963, pp. 140–155.
Reprinted by permission of the Royal Geographical Society.

over large areas of the highlands of what is now called Kenya suggested the possibility of European settlement. In 1901 much of this land lay within the boundaries of Uganda and Sir Harry Johnston was able to report (Cmd. 671) ". . . here we have a territory (now that the Uganda Railway is built) admirably suited for a white man's country, and I can say this, with no thought of injustice to any native race, for the country in question is either utterly uninhabited for miles and miles or at most its inhabitants are wandering hunters who have no settled home, or whose fixed habitation is the lands outside the healthy area." The first Land Regulations (of the East Africa Protectorate) were published as early as 1897 but little alienation took place until after the construction of the Uganda Railway, which reached Nairobi in 1899 and Lake Victoria in 1901, when settlement was greatly encouraged and the regulations were replaced by the Crown Lands Ordinance, 1902. Under this Ordinance, grants of Crown Lands could be made freehold or by leases of up to ninety-nine years. The Commissioner of Lands was not empowered to sell or lease any land in the actual occupation of the natives and further, if any grants were made which were subsequently found to contain African settlements, these settlements were deemed to be excluded from the lease so long as they were occupied. It was never contemplated that grants of land could be made to Africans, who had already selected the areas they chose to occupy. However, another immigrant community was interested in farming land in the highlands, the Asians, particularly as represented by the labourers brought from India to assist in the building of the railway. Under pressure from the Government of India, the contracts of these workers could be terminated in East Africa instead of in India, if the worker so desired. It is clear that by 1902 grants of Crown Land for agricultural purposes in the highlands were being restricted to Europeans or

Americans, so that, although applications were invited from Indians to lease agricultural land, the area lying between Kiu and Fort Ternan was specifically excluded. This policy was approved by Lord Elgin, the Secretary of State for the Colonies, in July 1906. Thus the Commissioner of Lands would only grant Crown Land for agricultural purposes within the highlands area, which was understood to extend from approximately Kiu to Fort Ternan railway stations, to Europeans. Furthermore, the lease could not be transferred without the approval of the Commissioner, who would presumably apply the same policy to the transfer as he had to the original grant. When the Crown Land Ordinance, 1915, replaced that of 1902 a further extension of this policy was written into section 36 as follows: "There shall by virtue of this Ordinance be implied in every lease granted under this part to a European a covenant that he shall not without the consent of the Governor in Council appoint or allow a non-European to be a manager or otherwise to occupy or be in control of the land leased."

Following the end of the 1914–18 war, the Ex-Soldier Settlement Scheme granted land only to Europeans under the Ordinance of 1915 and the Crown Lands (Discharged Soldiers Settlement) Ordinance of 1921. It was particularly these grants which extended beyond the limits of Kiu and Fort Ternan and to areas away from the railway, such as Uasin Gishu and Trans-Nzoia. By 1922, the Lands Department reported that the Crown Land remaining available for alienation was practically nil.

The restrictions on Indians' holding land in the Highlands were attacked in a despatch of the Government of India in 1920 and the status of Indians within Commonwealth countries was discussed at the Imperial Conference of 1921. This led to the publication of the "Devonshire White Paper" in 1923 in which the existing practice in both initial grants and transfers was reaffirmed. It is significant that this authoritative statement of the policy of restriction of land ownership to Europeans was in a paper entitled "Indians in Kenya." Again the question of grants of land to Africans was not considered: it was a decision on the ownership of land not occupied by Africans, whose land had been guaranteed to them by the creation of the various reserves. As a part of the general statement of policy it was declared that: "Primarily, Kenya is an African territory and His Majesty's Government think it necessary definitely to record their considered opinion that the interest of the African natives must be paramount, and that if, and when, their interests and the interests of the immigrant races should conflict, the former should prevail."

By this stage, the term "Highlands" had begun to take on a special meaning. The first explorers and administrators had used the term in the sense of the area climatically suited for Europeans to live in, for which the lower limit was generally agreed as 5000 feet above sea level. During the process of settlement the term came to mean those areas over 5000 feet which were not occupied by the African tribes. Through the land-grant policy operating this came to mean the land which only Europeans might own or manage. It was a curious fact, however, that the area within which the restriction operated had not been defined, other than as lying between two points on the railway and even then the eastern point was variously described as being either Kiu or Kibwezi. Areas which were clearly not included were defined by the proclamation of recognized African areas in 1926, which were placed under the Native Lands Trust Ordinance in 1930. A European boundary was suggested by the Commissioner of Lands in 1924 and others, by the Governor and by a Sub-Committee of the Executive Council in 1926. The Governor's definition enclosed an area three times as large as that suggested by the Sub-Committee and it was recorded that "these two boundaries have no points in common, except where they intersect."

In April 1932, the Secretary of State for the Colonies appointed a commission under the chairmanship of Sir Morris Carter to consider and report on certain land problems in Kenya. The Report of the Kenya Land Commission was submitted in July 1933 and subsequently published, together with three large volumes of evidence. It was not until this Report that the policy of the exclusion of African right-holders in the Highlands was authoritatively stated, and implemented, with compensation, by the Wyn Harris Commission in 1939. The sixth term of reference of the Commission was "to define the area, generally known as the Highlands, within which persons of European descent are to have a privileged position in accordance with the White Paper of 1923." The area so defined by the Commission was substantially that recommended by the Sub-Committee of the Executive Council in 1926. This was smaller that that expected by the European community and land was allocated for African use beyond the borders of the reserves gazetted in 1926. To allay the resultant fears of the European settlers the Commission recommended that the borders of the European Highlands should be safeguarded by Order in Council, so that the European community would have the same security in regard to the land reserved for them as the Africans. Thus, a "European tribal reserve" was to be created similar to the African Land Units. These boundaries were defined in the 7th Schedule to the Crown Land Ordinance under authority of the Kenya (Highlands) Order in Council 1939, which also established a Highlands Board with a majority elected by the European Elected Members of Legislative Council, to advise and make representations to the Governor on the disposal of land in the Highlands. Thus it was not until thirty-three years after the declaration of a "White Highlands" policy by the Secretary of State that the boundaries of the area concerned were delimited (see Figs. 1 and 2).

The Kenya Land Commission recognized that a tribal approach to the allocation of

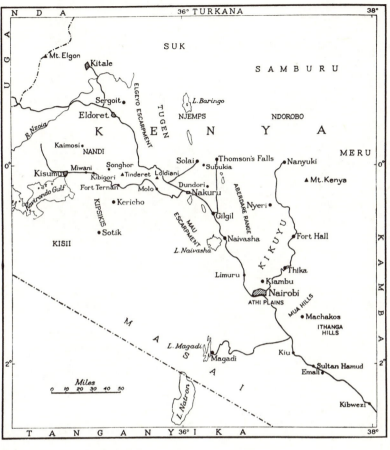

Figure 1.

land, as embodied in the Native Lands Ordinance which guaranteed the reserves, was the only one practicable at the time, although it was anticipated that this condition would change. The system was made less rigid by grouping the reserves into nine "Native Land Units," some of which contained more than one tribe, and Native Leasehold Areas were established without reservation to any particular tribe or tribes. The East Africa Royal Commission 1953–5 commented that "the approach on a tribal basis to questions of land tenure and land use is incompatible with the development of a modern economy, and this applies equally to a purely racial approach to the Highlands question. . . ."

The reservation of the Highlands for Europeans by administrative practice was ended by the Land Control Regulations made in 1961 under the authority of the Kenya (Land) Order in Council, 1960. The provision that a non-European might not manage or control land granted to a European in the Highlands was removed from the Crown Land Ordinance by the Crown Lands (Amendment) Ordinance, 1960, although approval still has to be sought for change of ownership. Approval, however, is given by specially constructed Divisional

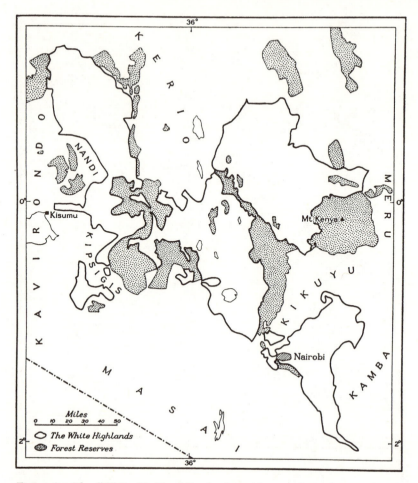

Figure 2.—The "White Highlands": the heavy line encloses the "Scheduled Areas" plus the area of Asian farming near Kisumu. Forest Reserves are stippled.

and Regional boards which may only refuse permission on limited economic grounds. It is specifically provided that if the transaction involves persons of different race and it is refused, appeal may be made to the Governor. A parallel development of land control has occurred in African areas. The Working Party on African Land Tenure, 1957–8, recommended the recognition, by registration, that rights amounting to full ownership under customary law amounted to freehold. It also recommended a system of control over land transactions by Divi-sional and Provincial Boards whose members were predominantly African. The Native Lands Registration Ordinance and the Land Control (Native Lands) Ordinance were enacted simultaneously on 28 July 1959, and from that date onwards it was legally possibly for a member of any race to purchase or lease land in the African areas to which title had been registered. This depends on an arrangement between a willing seller and a willing buyer, however, and this has not yet occurred. Following the Kenya (Land) Order in Council,

1961, the Land Control (Native Lands) Ordinance, 1959, was replaced by the Land Control (Special Areas) Regulations 1961, the provisions of which are almost identical with the Ordinance. The term "native lands" has now been replaced by "special areas," while the term "White Highlands" has always been avoided officially; but they may be described as the "Scheduled Areas," following the description in the Agriculture Ordinance, 1955. If Africans have so far proved unwilling to sell land to people of other races or tribes, this has not been true of Europeans. Individual purchases of European land by Africans now take place, but in addition there are two Government schemes to assist such African settlement, one for "assisted owners" and another on the "small holder" scale.

In determining which areas became part of the White Highlands two factors were paramount: the construction of the Uganda Railway and the extent of unused land. The Uganda Railway was constructed from Mombasa to Port Florence (now Kisumu) in order to connect the areas around Lake Victoria, especially Uganda, with a sea-port. The railway, however, had difficulty in paying its way and it was not helped by the virtual lack of traffic originating between Uganda and the sea (Hill, 1949). Since the railway passed through highlands judged to be suitable for European occupation, settlement was encouraged as a means of providing revenue for the railway and taxes to pay for administration. The railway was so essential to early settlers that only land within reach of it was regarded as being of any commercial use, and the boundaries of the Highlands were for many years described only by reference to two points on the railway, at first from Kiu to Fort Ternan, and later from Sultan Hamud to Kibigori. Kiu and Fort Ternan are the approximate edge of the highlands of over 5000 feet, an altitude commonly regarded as resulting in a climate healthy for Europeans. The alignment of the railway therefore helped to determine the areas first settled by Europeans. From Kiu the railway lay between the dry plains of the Masai to the south and the highlands with their higher rainfalls occupied by the Kamba and Kikuyu tribes to the north. Crossing the eastern Rift Valley at its highest point, a route had to be found between the Mau escarpment and the volcanic masses of Loldiani and Tinderet into the Nyanza or Kavirondo Rift Valley leading to the lake.

The railway provided the means for Europeans to enter the Highlands, but they soon spread into distant areas which were not served by the railway until ten or twenty years after settlement. This particularly applies to the Uasin Gishu and Laikipia plateaus. To explain the nature of this settlement, it is necessary to examine the distribution of the African population at the time. The most densely populated areas were where agricultural cultivating tribes were settled in areas of adequate rainfall and fertile soil. These included the high rainfall areas of Nyanza, bordering on Lake Victoria, and the most favourable highland areas such as the slopes of Mt. Kenya, the Aberdares, Elgeyo and the hills of Ukambani. The intervening areas were extensive plains (over 5000 feet) where a smaller and uncertain rainfall made extensive grazing the main support of life. This made these areas unattractive to the cultivating tribes and were made more so by the presence of the warlike pastoral people. The most important of these were the Masai (see Fig. 3). European settlement did not take place in the densely settled agricultural areas, but almost entirely on the sparsely inhabited plains. These plains could never have supported more than a sparse population under African methods of utilization, but at the time of the entry of the Europeans large sections were normally uninhabited due to the history of the Masai. The Uasin Gishu plateau takes its names from the Masai clan which formerly occupied it. This clan was defeated by other Masai and the Nandi in the middle of the nineteenth century and

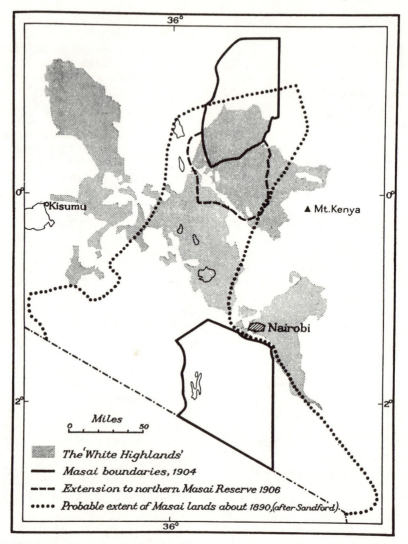

Figure 3.—Masai lands after the first Masai Treaty. The present Masai Land
Unit is approximately the 1890 area south of the Highlands.

the grazing lands had remained unused
ever since. Similar inter-tribal fighting had
also taken place in Laikipia, but the entire
tribe was weakened by cattle plague and
smallpox in 1890, to the extent that .the
Kikuyu and Kamba were able to slave-raid
the Masai *manyattas* and some Masai had
to be protected by government officers. In
these circumstances the Masai were willing
(or were persuaded) to move away from the
Naivasha area, where the railway crossed
the floor of the rift valley and to accept
two reserves guaranteed to them "so long
as the Masai as a race shall exist." This was
agreed in 1904 but, despite extensions to
the northern reserve in 1906, the division

of the tribal lands was unsatisfactory, particularly in weakening the authority of the Masai Laibon, Lenana; and in 1911 the northern Masai moved into a greatly enlarged southern reserve, encouraged by reports of the dying instructions of Lenana (Sandford, 1919). Large areas had thus been preserved for nomadic grazing by the warlike propensities of the Masai. Intertribal warfare in other areas had also resulted in unpopulated zones which lay as "no-man's-land" between tribes. The best authenticated of such zones is that lying between the Kisii and the Kipsigis, now occupied by the European farms of Sotik. Thus, with the establishment of the rule of law, there were found to be extensive areas formerly kept empty or nearly so by tribal warfare, which were now available for settlement. Although the majority of these lands had not been attractive to the agricultural Africans, Europeans could farm in these areas with the aid of such innovations as the ox-drawn plough and the bore-hole. The European could also afford to set off the profits of a good year against the failure of a harvest in a year of drought, which would force an African cultivator into starvation.

Thus, of the 12,000 square miles (excluding forest reserves) of European settled land, 7000 consist of old Masai grazing grounds, evacuated under agreements between 1904 and 1913. The remaining areas, including the Uasin Gishu plateau, were almost completely uninhabited. Despite this and the protection of the rights of African cultivation on alienated land under the Crown Land Ordinances of 1902 and 1915, disputes over land ownership between Europeans and Africans arose and continue. Many of these involve small parcels of land, partciularly bordering the Kikuyu Land Unit. They have received attention out of proportion to size and were investigated by the Carter Commission and settlements made. The sources of dispute may be classified under three headings. The first is the incomprehension of getting out-right ownership of land by tribes where ownership has a communal basis and where inheritance is governed by custom. As Senior Chief Koinange complained to the Carter Commission: ". . . we found that the Europeans who came on to our githikas, as we thought simply as ahoi, that is, people who come as temporary occupiers, had turned themselves into the owners and the real owners into the tenants." Thus no original objection might be made to European settlement, because they were regarded by Africans as tenants-at-will and, by the time the nature of the leasehold grants had become understood, the source of friction was present. The second source of dispute lay in the question: when was land vacant and thus available for settlement? The practice of shifting agriculture (or "bush fallowing") meant that unused land could be allocated to a European which an African would later claim had been kept in reserve for future cultivation. In a similar way pasture which had been used for many years and had become fouled and of poor quality would be left unoccupied for a period to permit its recovery. When the pastoralists returned they sometimes found Europeans in possession. The third general source of dispute arose because European-imposed law and order enabled some tribes to move on to land which they would not formerly have used for fear of the Masai or other enemies. Here they met Europeans who were moving on to the same land which had been previously unoccupied. This is clearly the basis of the Kamba complaints over the Mua and Ithanga Hills.

The Highlands, as defined by the Carter Commission, consisted of a number of blocks of land, separated by African land or Forest Reserves. The latter were included in the Highlands for convenience but were not available for settlement. The various parts of the Highlands are very different and originated as settled areas in different ways. To aid the discussion, fourteen regions have been recognized (Fig. 4)

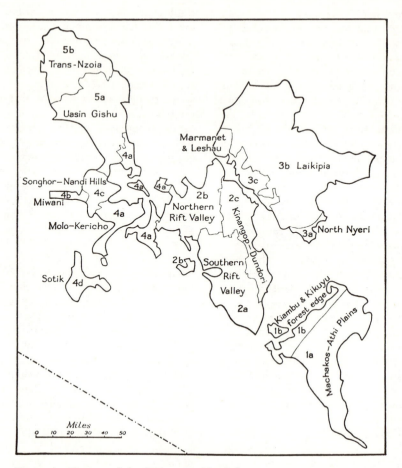

Figure 4.—Regions of the "White Highlands."

based on a compromise between natural environmental types and the history of settlement, with boundaries adjusted where possible to follow Agricultural Sub-Committee areas. The relation of the alienated area to relief and rainfall may be seen in Figure 5 and Figure 6. Flanked by the great extinct volcanoes of Mt. Kenya (17,058 feet) and Elgon (14,178 feet), the alienated area straddles the Great Rift Valley, which here is at its highest point, so that the floor reaches to 6000 feet at Naivasha. On either side lie the elongated Aberdare and Mau highlands rising to 13,000 and 10,000 feet.

The first Administration of "up country" Kenya was centred on Machakos until after the construction of the railway, when it was moved to Nairobi. The capital of the East Africa Protectorate, however, remained at Mombasa until 1905. This area was the scene of early settlement which now forms a triangle of land between Emali, Nairobi and Fort Hall. Between Emali and Nairobi the boundary is essentially the railway line from Mombasa, beyond which lie the extensive Masai grazing lands. To the east lie the Machakos hills, where greater relief brings increased rainfall as well as greater security from the raids of the Masai.

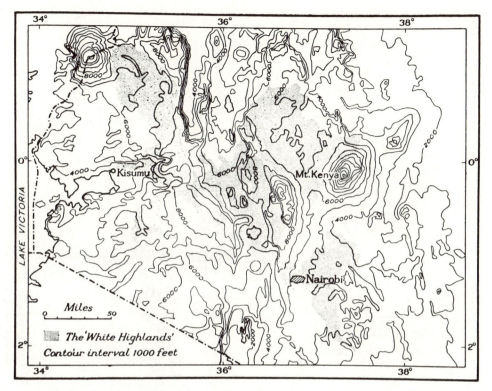

Figure 5.—Alienated farm land and relief.

This is the home of the Kamba tribe. Between Nairobi and Fort Hall the land is rising towards the lower slopes of the Aberdares, the densely populated Kikuyu Land Unit. The triangle thus lies between two populated hill-lands and between three tribes. It appears not to have been securely held by any tribe, but cattle of any of the tribes might be grazed here according to the state of inter-tribal conflict. European settlement separated these three tribes and undoubtedly assisted in maintaining peace and lessening cattle raiding, but there is no evidence of any deliberate policy involved. Most of this area consists of the dry ranching country of Machakos and the Athi plains (1a), from 4000 to 5500 feet, with rainfall from 30 to 20 inches a year or less. Land holdings are mostly of large estates either grazing beef cattle at ten acres to

the beast or growing sisal, this being the principal centre of sisal production in Kenya. The northern and western portion of this triangle, however, is of very different country (Fig. 4, 1b). Here the Kikuyu were clearing and cultivating their rich forest lands behind a belt of "boundary forest" which they had left between themselves and the Masai of the plains. The railway reached the edge of this forest at Nairobi in 1899 and then skirted its southern and western edge on the way to Kisumu. Here there was good land not being used for fear of the Masai and because of the result of a recent smallpox epidemic. Under ample rains of 30–50 inches, the volcanic slopes have weathered into a deep, rich, red soil, and altitudes ranging from 5500 to 7200 feet give a climate kind to man and to his crops. A Dr. Boedeker is generally

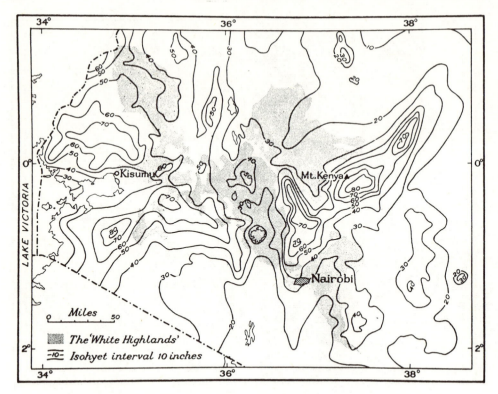

Figure 6.—Alienated farm land and annual rainfall.

regarded as having been the first "white settler," when he bought land from one Wangengi near the outpost of Fort Smith in 1897. Following the arrival of the Uganda Railway, more land was obtained by purchase and Crown grant along the edge of the forest towards Thika, and in the vicinity of the railway as it climbed towards the escarpment at Limuru. The former belt now contains some two-thirds of all the European-owned coffee in Kenya, while the higher belt around Limuru grows tea and provides Nairobi with milk. This is exceptionally good agricultural land, but it has led to the common misconception that all the Highlands are equally fertile.

From Limuru, the railway descends to the floor of the Rift Valley, which it crosses at its highest point, never below 6000 feet. Sheltered between escarpments and in the

lea of the Aberdares, this is an area of dry, short-grass, thorn-tree savanna or high-altitude, temperate-type grassland. This was another portion of the extensive Masai grazing lands, but it was attractive to European settlers because of the presence of the railway, cool climate and, where rainfall was adequate, the possibility of growing maize or wheat. By the treaty of 1904, the Masai agreed to evacuate this area and keep to two reserves, one to the south and the other in Laikipia. To the north, the floor of the Rift Valley is lower and drier and occupied by other tribes, the Njemps, Tugen and Suk. Farms were rapidly taken up in this area between 1904 and 1906, and it was here that Lord Delamere spent so much money to discover the principles of successful farming in this unknown land. In its utilization, the floor of the Rift Valley may be divided into a southern ranching area and a northern mixed farming area, distinguished by an annual total of rainfall of more or less than 30 inches. Except for riparian land around Lake Naivasha, the Southern Rift (2a) is given over to extensive ranching of beef cattle, or sheep on the higher areas, using natural short grass—thorn tree-grazing. In the area of the Northern Rift (2b), by contrast, annual rainfall totals of between 30 and 50 inches enabled settlers to grow maize and export it by rail through Nakuru, "the capital of the White Highland." Agriculture here has progressed far towards high-standard mixed farming, particularly in the Subukia valley, with a greater proportion of grass leys and more pedigree cattle than any other region. Crops include maize, wheat, barley, oats and sisal and some pyrethrum, while in addition to the dairy cattle there are large numbers of wool sheep, pigs and poultry. These two sections of the Rift Valley are bordered on the east by a high plateau lying between the volcanic mass of the high Aberdare (av. 13,000 feet) and escarpments dropping down to the floor of the Valley. This is the very flat Kinangop plateau at 7–8000 feet and the hill mass of Dundori rising to over 9000 feet (2c). In the lee of the Aberdares this area does not receive the heavy rains of the Kikuyu lands on the eastern slope, and totals between 30 and 40 inches and the cool climate induced by altitude gives rise to a natural temperate-type grassland. It is occupied by extensive fields of wheat, and is the major producer of barley and oats in Kenya as also of pyrethrum. Dairy cattle and sheep are important and it is the leading area for pigs.

The division of the Masai into two reserves was not satisfactory, even after the extension of the northern, Laikipia, reserve in 1906, and by the second Masai Treaty of 1911 the tribe agreed to move into a single, greatly enlarged, southern reserve. Thus were evacuated extensive plains lying on the flat lava flows originating from Mt. Kenya and the Aberdares and extending northwards on to a peneplain of basement rocks, mostly over 6000 feet (3b). The total rainfall is low, between 15 and 30 inches, but settlers rapidly took up large ranches for extensive grazing on the natural grassland, although the coveted Leroghi plateau on the northern boundary was awarded to the Samburu, who were being pushed southward by the fierce Turkana. Of necessity ranching here must be on an extensive scale, as was the Masai practice, and in this region are nine out of the eleven estates in the Highlands of over 50,000 acres. On its western boundary the Laikipia plateau rises towards a narrow belt of forest reserve which separates it from the settled areas of the Rift Valley. In this higher area of Marmanet and Leshau (3c) rainfall reaches over 30 inches and smaller mixed farms growing wheat and barley have been established. A similar, better-watered, forested boundary lies to the south in the saddle of land between Mt. Kenya and the Aberdares in the area of North Nyeri (3a). This lies at the northern end of Kikuyu land and, as in Kiambu, a belt of forested land was left unoccupied as a no-man's-land with the Masai. The first District Commissioner was appointed to Nyeri in 1902 and European settlers first arrived in 1904, although land grants were not made until 1906. The arrival of more peaceful conditions enabled more Kikuyu to move into the area between the Chania and the Amboni rivers, but in 1910 they were moved back south of the Chania by Government order and more European farms were established in the following years (Carter, Evidence: Vol. I, p. 520–1). As in Kiambu, this is fertile land, suitable, according to altitude, for growing coffee and wheat and for mixed farming.

Having crossed the floor of the Rift Valley, the railway ascended the western escarpment by the easiest route, lying between the smooth-crested Mau escarpment to the south (10,000 feet) and the volcanic mass of Loldiani (9874) feet to the north. Here were thick forests including bamboo, inhabited by none of the major tribes but only by small bands, or "hordes," of the hunting and honey-collecting Ndorobo. The cool climate and ample rainfall might be expected to have encouraged rapid settlement, but in fact the process was slow. In 1903 free grants of land were offered in this area but, although potential arable land in 640 acre blocks was taken up, ranches of 5000 acres at Molo were not. A trickle of settlers, many of South African origin, arrived in the next few years and another major allotment of land was made at Londiani in 1911. The farm lands remain in rather distinct blocks separated by forest reserves, but the Molo-Kericho (4a) has now become a well established community famous for sheep (Molo lamb), and for such cool-climate crops as pyrethrum, wheat, barley and oats. Kericho is a special area on the edge of the Mau forest where rainfall is not only heavy (over 70 inches) but is spread throughout most of the year. Attempts were made to settle ex-soldiers here following the First World War, but the scheme failed in 1924 and this district has now become the centre of the prosperous tea industry of Kenya (Fearn, 1961).

Beyond Kericho, on the lower flanks of the Mau extending from the lavas on to the basement peneplain, lies the isolated fragment of Sotik (4d). This is the only fully documented instance of settlement being deliberately encouraged to separate two warring tribes. The pastoral Nilo-Hamitic Kipsigis (or 'Lumbwa') to the east were in a state of semi-permanent hostilities with the cultivating Bantu Kisii to the west. Government officers inspected the area in 1906 and recommended that this block of land was suitable for farming by Europeans and should be settled by Europeans as a buffer zone. The land was pastoral land and known to belong to the Kipsigis, but it was hoped that the loss of this land would force the tribe to become more agricultural, and thus settled, on the ample land remaining to them. This policy has been strikingly successful and this form-

erly warlike pastoral tribe has now become prosperous and agricultural. The alienated land remains largely pastoral except for small, favoured areas which grow tea.

A tribe very similar to the Kipsigis is the Nandi, whose lands lay to the north of the railway line as it descends into the Kavirondo rift in the Songhor-Nandi Hills area (4c). They were formidable fighters and their raiding of neighbouring Europeans and Africans for cattle and the railway line for metal required a major military expedition in 1905. The Tinderet forest provided cover for fugitives from the law, so that the tribe was ordered back from this south-eastern boundary in 1906 and the land from the Nandi Hills down to Songhor was alienated (Huntingford, 1953). Former forest lands now grow tea. The boundaries of the Nandi reserve were defined and guaranteed in 1907. Unfortunately further alienations took place. At Kaimosi there was an empty neutral belt between the Nandi and the Bantu tribes to the west. The Nandi were told in 1908 that they might occupy this land, but did not do so and in 1913 farms were auctioned to Europeans and the remainder alloted under the Ex-Soldier Settlement Scheme in 1919. Further settlement under this scheme was made within the northern boundaries of the reserve at Kipkarren in an area being similarly little used. Both of these areas were admitted to consist of land belonging to the Nandi tribe, and since 1921 the revenue obtained from the leases has been given to the Nandi Local Native Council and its successor.

The southern boundary of the Nandi reserve lies along the crest of the Nandi escarpment overlooking the Kavirondo Rift Valley. At its foot lay another neutral zone, this time with the Nilotic Luo of the plains who called such an area mbawa. The railway was built along this stretch of Kisumu, thus delimiting a zone between the Luo to the south and the Nandi above the escarpment. This land lies just below 4000 feet and was regarded as outside the area of European privilege. Here farms were made available to Asians in 1903, and the Miwani area has now become the principal centre of sugar production in Kenya on large Asian-owned estates (4b). All of the alienated land, both European and Asian, on the floor of the Kavirondo rift may be said to represent the former land left vacant for inter-tribal fighting between the Luo and the Nandi or the Kipsigis and also between the various branches of the Luo.

East and north of the Nandi reserve lie the plains of Uasin Gishu and Trans-Nzoia, extending northwards to the foothills of Mt. Elgon and eastward to the high forest edge of the Rift Valley at the Elgeyo escarpment (5a and 5b). Here lived the Uasin Gishu section of the Masai until they were utterly defeated by Masai from the Rift Valley and the Nandi, sometime before the arrival of the British. Early travellers in this area all tell of the emptiness of these plains except for occasional raiding parties of Nandi, Masai or Karamajong. Although mostly drier than the Elgeyo forests to the east or the Nandi reserve, nearer the Lake, to the west, this plateau was covered with natural grazing and at an altitude in the south suitable for wheat (5a) and, in the north, for maize (5b). Until the construction of the through route to Uganda in 1925 and the branch to Kitale in 1926, however, it was remote from the railway, and when the Foreign Office offered it as a home for Jews in 1903, the offer was rejected. Nevertheless a few settlers began to enter the south of the area along the Elgeyo border, but the first wave of settlement came from South Africa, following the Boer War. In 1907 Kommandant James Van Rensburg visited Nairobi and obtained Government permission to lead a trek into this empty land, and in 1908 he returned with his party who settled in the Sergoit area. Another trek was led by Kommandant C. J. Cloete in 1911 and these laid the foundations of the distinctive Afrikaner community of Uasin Gishu centered on Eldoret. This settlement did not penetrate beyond the

Nzoia river, but when Government officers inspected that area in 1910 and again in 1912 they reported on its emptiness and its general suitability for settlement. The first farms were put up for auction in 1913, but a number had to be withdrawn for lack of bidders even at eightpence per acre. Substantial settlement did not follow until the Ex-Soldiers Settlement Scheme, 1919. In that year, however, it was discovered that some farms had been allocated on Suk Land, and the grants were withdrawn and the farmland included in the Suk reserve. The Trans-Nzoia is now a leading producer of maize with good grade and pedigree cattle, often on grass leys and with a small belt of coffee at the foot of Mt. Elgon.

We have described above the evolution of the White Highlands up to their change of status in 1961. The way is now open for Africans to purchase land and to farm in these areas, and this process is assisted by the Land Development and Settlement Board established on the 1 January 1961. The Board has funds amounting to £13,181,000, of which £3,410,000 is an outright grant by the British Government which may be used to subsidize the smallholder schemes. In addition the British Government have lent £4,071,000, the Colonial Development Corporation £1,500,000 the World Bank £3,000,000 and West Germany £1,200,000. These last three loans may not be used to purchase land but to develop it with the fundamental objectives of increasing production and increasing land settlement. This is being accomplished by Assisted Owner (or Tenant) Projects and Smallholder Schemes. The first scheme is intended for "yeoman" farmers who can produce a third of the necessary capital, and it is intended that the farm should provide a reasonable standard of living and a nett income of at least £250 a year after meeting annual loan charges at 6½ per cent. So far some 125 projects have been approved, involving about 100,000 acres in farms of 50–300 acres in area. The scheme is non-racial and includes two Europeans and one Asian. In the Smallholder Scheme the land is bought as a block from a European farmer, sub-divided and laid out with roads, schools, markets, etc., by the Board. The cost of each holding is subsidized by an average of £73 and smallholders are settled with the aid of loans normally repayable over twenty-five or thirty years. There are both high and low density schemes. A low density scheme is designed to produce a reasonable standard of living and a nett income of at least £100 after meeting loan charges, and a typical holding would be of 30 acres. High density schemes aim at a nett income of only £25–£40 per annum, which can be obtained on 7–20 acres. So far some 350,000 acres have been bought or are planned for Smallholder Schemes but, whereas approved owners may be found in any part of the former White Highlands, smallholder schemes are generally sited in areas contiguous to existing African land and are reserved for settlement by members of that tribe. Priority is being given to settlement from the densely populated Kikuyu, Maragoli and Bunyore areas, but the general intention is to provide one high and one low density scheme for each tribe in so far as this is possible and there is need.

Thus we see that the White Highlands are not only abolished as a legal or administrative concept but that the process of conversion to African ownership is well under way. It is most noticeable, however, that the only tribe which used any significant proportion of this land before the Europeans, the Masai, are taking no part in the present take-over. The effect of the European settlement will have been to settle these areas with cultivating peoples who formerly would not have entered the area for fear of the Masai or other pastoral tribes.

What then has been the result of nearly sixty years of European settlement? The most significant change has been the increase in the African population. At the Census held in 1948 the Districts entirely or almost entirely composed of alienated land (Thika, Nairobi, Nanyuki, Laikipia, Nakuru, Trans-Nzoia and Uasin Gishu) amounted to 13,193 sq. miles and contained a total population of 664,480 persons, of whom 582,708 were Africans, 24,087 Europeans and 57,685 other non-Africans. The provisional results of the Census of August 1962 give a total of 1,002,000 for this area. An analysis by race is not yet available. Fifty years earlier almost all of this land was either empty land reserved for inter-tribal battles, or grazed over by wandering Masai herds. The population of this area at that time cannot be known, but in the area now used by the Masai the density of population in 1948 was four per square mile. In the White Highlands the density was fifty. Although termed the White Highlands, it will be noted that they were occupied by over 200 Africans to every European.

The origin of white settlement lay in the need to establish an economy which would be able to pay for the necessary expenses involved in developing and governing the new country. The site of most of the economic activity of Kenya today, therefore, is in the Highlands. Here are the areas best served by railways and roads, flourishing towns (which, in addition to the capital of Nairobi, include Nakuru, Eldoret, Kitale, Thika, Kericho and Nyeri) and the centres of industry. In part this is due to the difficulty of buying land in African areas. Natural grassland and bush savanna has been replaced by fields of maize, wheat or sisal, and the near-useless disease-ridden Masai herds by pedigree or grade beef and dairy cattle (Table I). The total farm land of the Highlands amounts to 11,571 sq. miles, or just over 5 per cent of the land area of Kenya, yet it accounts for the majority of the exports, particularly in the four leading commodities, coffee, tea, sisal and pyrethrum (Table II).

If white settlement was necessary at the beginning of the century because of the lack of knowledge, capital and the desire

TABLE 1. LAND USE AND LIVESTOCK, WHITE HIGHLANDS, 1959

Land use

	1,000 acres
Sisal	177.9
Tea	36.1
Sugar	24.8
Coffee	67.8
Wattle and other plantation crops	87.4
Wheat	253.9
Maize	133.2
Barley	47.2
Oats	29.9
Other 'scheduled' crops	14.8
Pyrethrum	27.9
Other crops	78.4
Grass leys	216.5
Natural grazing	5390.8
Other land incl. forest	827.4
Total	7,414.0

Livestock

	1,000 head
Dairy cattle:	
Pedigree	14.7
Grade	390.3
Native	22.4
Beef cattle:	
Pedigree	1.5
Grade	238.0
Native	291.4
Sheep:	
Native	90.2
Wool breeds	411.7
Other	45.5
Pigs:	
Breeding sows	12.7
Breeding boars	1.0
Other	54.4
Poultry:	234.9

Source: Agricultural Census 1959.

for money on the part of Africans, to what extent is this true today? Fearn (1961) has shown that the major stimulating effect of the European settlement on Nyanza was by introducing Africans to the cash economy and growing for the market rather than by direct instruction. However, the dedicated work of many agricultural and veterinary officers has had an effect, and African farms may now be seen with crops of a quality suitable for export markets, and good quality cattle. With an orientation to the market well established and increasing skill at supplying it, however, the need for capital becomes more acute. The European settler was able to bring his own capital and raise more by private arrangements. The commercial banks are now beginning to lend on a larger scale to Africans as a result of registration of titles in the tribal areas, and it may be assumed that this will be extended to African farmers in the former White Highlands. The majority of the necessary capital, however, may be expected from international agencies and governmental sources similar to the loans to the Land Development and Settlement Board made by Great Britain, the World Bank and West Germany.

The episode of the settlement by Europeans in certain areas of the Highlands of Kenya has dominated the economic and political history of the Colony. This has left an inheritance which will form part of the problems and the opportunities facing an independent State.

ACKNOWLEDGEMENTS

The author has been permitted to study records in Provincial and District Offices and the Lands Department, Nairobi. He has received valuable advice and criticism from Government officers, including Mr. A. Horner, Mr. J. A. O'Loughlin, Mr. F. D. Homan and also Mr. S. H. Fazan. They are in no way responsible for expressions of opinion, however, which remain the responsibility of the author.

TABLE 2. PRINCIPAL EXPORTS 1960

	Coffee	Tea	Sisal	Pyrethrum
Percentage of total value of exports	29.2	12.5	13.0	8.6
Total production 1,000 tons	31.1	13.6	62.6	8.5
Non-African production 1,000 tons	25.2	13.5	59.6	6.7
Percentage non-African to total production	81.0	99.3	95.2	78.8

REFERENCES

Agricultural Census 1959 (Non-African) Summary of results. E. A. Statistical Department Kenya Unit, April 1960.

Cavendish-Bentinck, F. 1939. *Indians and the Kenya Highlands.* Nairobi.

East Africa Royal Commission 1953–55 *Report* Cmd 9475, 1955.

Fearn, H. 1961. *An African Economy.* Oxford University Press.

Hill, M. F. 1949. *Permanent Way.* Nairobi: E. A. Railways and Harbours.

Huntingford, G. W. B. 1953. *The Nandi of Kenya.* Routledge and Kegan Paul.

Huxley, Elspeth 1935 *White Man's Country.* Chatto and Windus.

—— 1957. *No Easy Way.* Nairobi: K.F.A. and Unga Ltd.

Indians in Kenya. Official Gazette of the Colony and Protectorate of Kenya, Vol. XXV, No. 899. Nairobi, 17 August 1923. (The "Devonshire White Paper").

Johnston, H. H. 1901. *Report by His Majesty's Special Commissioner in the Protectorate of Uganda.* Cmd. 671, July 1901.

Kenya Land Commission. 1933. *Report.* Nairobi: Government Printer (The "Carter Commission").

Land Department. 1922. *Land and Land Conditions in the Colony and Protectorate of Kenya.* Nairobi: Government Printer.

Land Settlement Commission. 1919. *Report.* Nairobi: Government Printer.

Lipscomb, J. F. 1955. *White Africans.* Faber and Faber.

Report on Mombasa Victoria Lake Railway Survey. Cmd. 7025. London: H.M.S.O. 1893.

Sandford, G. R. 1919. *An administrative and political history of the Masai.* Waterlow.

Statistical Abstract. 1961. Nairobi: Government Printer.

Troup, L. G. 1953. *Inquiry into the general economy of farming in the Highlands.* Nairobi: Government Printer.

In Kenya the allocation of land for exclusively European settlement has ended, but it continues in Rhodesia (formerly Southern Rhodesia). There the extent of land allocated is much greater, and its distribution is closely correlated with favorable environmental conditions. Since the end of the last century, territorial segregation has been extended, to the detriment of Africans and to the benefit of Europeans. As formerly in Kenya, Africans provide the labor force on European farms and are therefore an integral element in the European system of production (see also Roder, 1964; and Oliver, Mason, and Floyd, 1964).

17. *Land Apportionment in Southern Rhodesia*

BARRY N. FLOYD

We are in this country because we represent a higher civilization, because we are better men. It is our only excuse for having taken the land.
—N. H. Wilson, *Southern Rhodesia Native Affairs Department* (1925)
It is illogical to reserve land in a particular area for purchase exclusively by members of one race, to the exclusion of members of the other race.
—Southern Rhodesia Select Committee on the Resettlement of Natives (1960)

The disposition of land between Europeans and Africans in Southern Rhodesia has been a matter of unremitting controversy from the colony's earliest days—in fact, ever since the slender "Pioneer Column" of European adventurers first crossed the Limpopo River in 1890.

Since land holds so important a place in the system of values in both Western and African cultures, it is not surprising that its division between the races posed major problems in the past and remains a critical component of Rhodesian affairs today. A rigid territorial segregation forms the basis for the entire social and political system of the country and is undoubtedly "the root cause of a deep-seated sense of injustice among Africans." [1] Indeed, African preoccupation with the pattern of land allocation has become intensive and almost fanatical. There can be little doubt that the color bar on the land—crippling, discriminatory, and irrational in the eyes of the indigenous peoples of Southern Rhodesia—is one of the major political issues in the contemporary life of this "white settler" country.

The intention here is to examine briefly

[1] Colin Leys and Cranford Pratt, edits.: A New Deal in Central Africa (New York, 1960), p. 176.

the contemporary pattern of the division of the land and to trace its historical evolution through the so-called "land apportionment" legislation of the Southern Rhodesia government. An attempt is made to assess the viability of a racial division of territory at the present stage of the country's development and also to suggest the future course Rhodesia should pursue if a true partnership of its peoples is ever to be achieved.

In 1958 an African population of some 2,550,000 (Table 1) had 41,950,000 acres for agrarian settlement (Table II); the European population of 207,000 had almost 48,000,000 acres. This disproportionate division is heavily accentuated by the fact

TABLE 1. ESTIMATES OF AFRICAN AND EUROPEAN POPULATION IN SOUTHERN RHODESIA, 1890–1960

	Africans	*Europeans*	*Ratio*
1890	400,000		
1902	530,000		
1911	700,000		
1921	847,000		
1931	937,000		
1940	1,390,000	65,000	21:1
1945	1,640,000	81,000	20:1
1950	1,930,000	125,000	15:1
1951	1,970,000	138,000	13:1
1952	2,030,000	152,000	13:1
1953	2,090,000	157,000	13:1
1954	2,150,000	158,000	14:1
1955	2,220,000	165,000	13:1
1956	2,290,000	178,000	13:1
1957	2,480,000	193,000	13:1
1958	2,550,000	207,000	12:1
1959	2,630,000	215,000	12:1
1960	2,885,000	225,000	13:1

Source: Central African Statistical Office.

Reprinted from *The Geographical Review*, Vol. 52, 1962, pp. 566–582.

TABLE 2. LAND APPORTIONMENT IN SOUTHERN RHODESIA, 1958

	Square Miles	Acres	% of Country
European areas[a] (crown land and "alienated" land)	81,230	51,987,000	53.5
Native Reserves	32,844	21,020,000	21.5
Special Native Areas[b]	20,122	12,878,000	13.0
Native Purchase Areas[c]	12,580	8,052,000	8.0
Undetermined areas[d]	89	57,000	0.5
Forest areas	4,984	3,190,000	3.5
Total	151,849	97,184,000	100.0

Source: Various government agencies
[a] Include 4,000,000 acres of game reserves and national parks.
[b] Land added to the Native Reserves in 1950.
[c] Areas where Africans may acquire land individually, as distinct from tribal tenure in the Native Reserves.
[d] Land owned by Europeans that may be sold to Africans if the owners so desire.

that more than 70 per cent of the Europeans are town dwellers and only about 50,000 derive their livelihood directly from the land, whereas the reverse is a truer picture of African dependence on the soil. Furthermore, vast acreages in the African area are unfit for agricultural settlement because of broken terrain, poor soils, lack of water, and tsetse infestation. Table II indicates the marked imbalance in territorial "cake cutting'.'

The cartographic representation of land apportionment in 1958 (Fig. 1) reveals immediately the complex and seemingly bizarre alignment of boundaries between the areas reserved for African settlement and those set aside for European occupance. However, when this map is compared with a map depicting, for example, relief, soils, average annual precipitation, or mean annual surface temperatures (Figs. 2–5), a partial correlation becomes apparent between the disposition of African land within Southern Rhodesia and certain environmental conditions less attractive for human habitation.

In general, the European area—comprising both "alienated," or freehold, property and crown land held under lease or

unoccupied—includes the greater part of the salubrious high veld (4000 feet and above), which forms a distinct northeast-southwest backbone to the country (Fig. 2). Considerable parts of the elevated Eastern Highlands also fall within the European area: at higher elevations the tropical wet-dry savanna climate of Southern Rhodesia is markedly ameliorated, and a more favorable temperature regime is established, particularly for white settlement (Fig. 3). Most of the better-watered parts of the country also fall within the European area (Fig. 4), since higher annual rainfall assures a greater reliability, making agriculture and animal husbandry less hazardous than in the dry and unpredictable low veld (below 3000 feet).

Among the more satisfactory soils for agriculture in Southern Rhodesia are the dark red and brown clay soils, derived from dolerite and "greenstone," heavy to work yet more productive, and better suited to sustained cropping, than the ubiquitous light, fine- to coarse-grained sandy soils derived from granitic rocks and sandstones (sand veld and *gusu*). Much larger areas of heavy red earths occur on European farms than in the African reserves or other

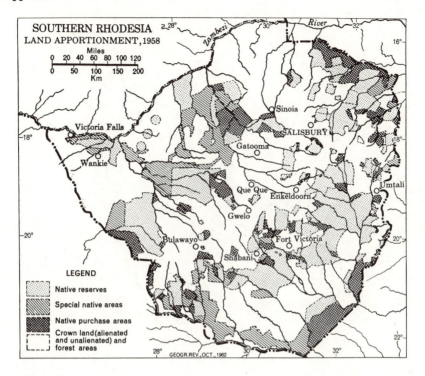

SOUTHERN RHODESIA
LAND APPORTIONMENT, 1958

Miles
0 20 40 60 80 100 120
0   50   100   150   200
Km

LEGEND

Native reserves

Special native areas

Native purchase areas

Crown land(alienated
and unalienated) and
forest areas

GEOGR.REV.,OCT.,1962

Figure 1.

native areas (Fig. 5). Indeed, many observers have commented on the fact that
when one is traveling by car in Southern
Rhodesia, it is frequently possible to tell
when one is leaving European land and
entering an African area by the abrupt
change from doleritic soils to granitic sands.
(In defense of this pattern, the European
settler argues that the indigenous farmer,
equipped only with a primitive short-
handled hoe, found the red-earth soils difficult to work and, despite their greater fertility, avoided using them.) The pedological
variation may be reinforced by a change in
topographic or physiographic features, from
the level plateau surfaces of the high veld
to the broken terrain of the middle and low
velds. But it is probably unwise to over-
emphasize these physical differences. In
the course of some fifteen thousand miles

of travel around the country on fieldwork,
the writer observed that variations in soils
and landforms may occur just as frequently
and noticeably *within* African or European
holdings as they do along the boundary
lines that separate the races territorially.

However, contrasts between the cultural,
man-made landscapes, as distinct from
changes in the natural setting, are admit-
tedly profound and more striking. Broad
fields of mechanically cultivated tobacco or
maize give way to pocket-handkerchief
patches of hand-tilled maize, millets, or
beans; and the lightly stocked grasslands of
a European ranch yield to the overstocked
and scrubby bushlands of a Native Reserve.
Brick-built, spacious, Western-style houses
contrast starkly with mud-block round huts.
The road itself may deteriorate from a
graded, black-topped surface to a rutted

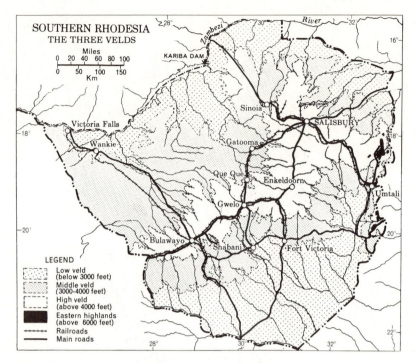

Figure 2.

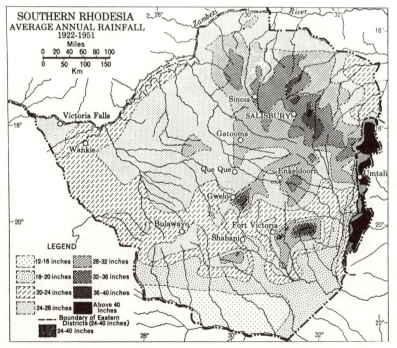

Figure 3.

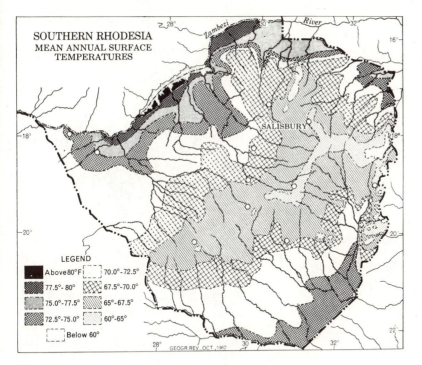

Figure 4.

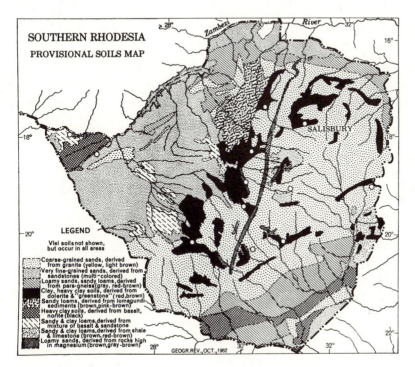

Figure 5.

dirt track; the change has been likened to that in certain states in the United States as one drives from one Congressional district to another.[2]

This, then, is the reality of land apportionment as written across the face of Southern Rhodesia today. It may prove salutary to trace now the historical development of this pattern of territorial segregation with the purpose of recognizing how former decision making, in accordance with racial and socioeconomic concepts fast becoming outmoded, has left an anachronistic heritage on the internal political map of the country. Clearly, this heritage will require radical modification if a stable future for both races in Southern Rhodesia is genuinely sought.

THE BEGINNINGS OF TERRITORIAL SEGREGATION

After the entry of the Pioneer Column into Southern Rhodesia, the provision of land for European settlers was one of the first matters to be taken up by the British South Africa Company, the administering authority—by royal charter—for the new state. A corollary was the provision of adequate land for the use of the native population, which was estimated to number some four hundred thousand in 1890 (Table I).

Matabele authority over most of Southern Rhodesia ceased as a result of the occupation, and land became the property of the British Crown. Private ownership of land was introduced, and large tracts were acquired by the B.S.A. Company for sale (or "alienation") to European immigrants. Farms of ten thousand acres were by no means uncommon, and this is still true today; some European ranches in the drier parts of the country exceeded one hundred thousand acres. Africans were also entitled to purchase and to own land, though in the early years few did. Private ownership was

a bewildering tenurial concept to the tribal Matabele and Mashona.

As a result of the expropriation of tribal lands, misunderstandings and resentment arose, which led to the appointment in 1894 of a Land Commission to deal with questions relating to the settlement of Africans on the land. The Commission recommended that two large territories be set aside for native occupation, the Shangani and Gwaai Reserves in Matabeleland, totaling about 2,486,000 acres (Fig. 6). For the Africans, who had had nearly 100,000,000 acres to exploit before the advent of the Europeans this was a drastic reduction of domain. The plan showed such poor judgment, and the lines of allocation were so ill considered, that the attempt to confine the native population within these two areas was never really practicable. But failure to make suitable provision for African lands may have been one of the prime causes of the Matabele Rebellion in 1896 and hence, indirectly, of the Mashona Rebellion of the same year.

These two wars forcibly called attention to the need for ensuring adequate reserves of land for the native population in view of the encroachment of European settlers and miners, who were already "picking out the eyes" of the better land and the more promising resources. The B.S.A. Company was given firm instructions "to assign to the natives inhabiting Southern Rhodesia, land sufficient for their occupation whether as tribes, or portions of tribes, and suitable for their agricultural and pastoral requirements, including in all cases a fair and equitable proportion of springs or permanent water." [3]

In this way the Native Reserves were established, solely for occupation by Africans under traditional tribal ways; only mineral rights were left open for European prospectors, a privilege that persists to the present day. By 1902 a general setting aside of land as Native Reserves had been accomplished; in that year the indigenous

[2] Thomas M. Franck: Race and Nationalism: The Struggle for Power in Rhodesia-Nyasaland (New York, 1960), p. 67.

[3] Report of the Native Affairs Committee of Enquiry, 1910–11 (Salisbury, 1911), pp. 10–11.

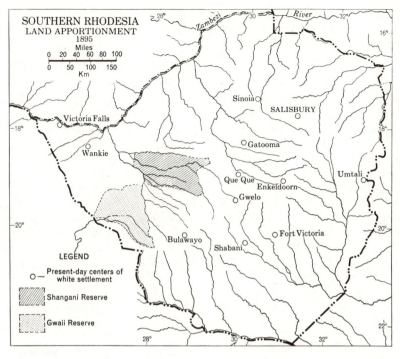

SOUTHERN RHODESIA
LAND APPORTIONMENT
1895
Miles
0 20 40 60 80 100
0   50   100   150
Km

Sinoia
SALISBURY

Victoria Falls

Wankie

Gatooma

Que Que
Enkeldoorn
Gwelo

Umtali

Bulawayo
Shabani

Fort Victoria

LEGEND

○— Present-day centers of white settlement

▨ Shangani Reserve

⬚ Gwaii Reserve

Figure 6.

population was estimated at some 530,000. However, the principle of complete segregation of land was not yet espoused, since an African could still "acquire, hold, encumber and dispose of land" on the same conditions as a nonnative.

It is worth noting how the areas and boundaries of the first reserves were arrived at, because, although modifications have certainly been made over the intervening years, the basic pattern of land allocation has persisted without radical change from the turn of the century down to the present time.

The European district officers who were made responsible for defining the reserves had little geographic knowledge of the country and no maps. They proceeded to their job without adequate directives or a uniform policy to which their crude surveying methods could conform. Small wonder that the resultant areal patterns of reserves varied greatly from district to district according to the degree of responsibility that individual officials showed in their task.

It is true that in Matabeleland the district officers were apparently advised to allow nine acres of arable land per native family.[4] However, handicapped by imperfect demographic knowledge of their districts, they were unable to follow the advice with any degree of certainty. (In any case, gross acreages for reserves in Matabeleland should have been arrived at by estimating numbers of cattle and the carrying capacity of the country, since livestock were of far greater importance than crops to peoples living in the drier, western parts of Southern Rhodesia.) In Mashonaland, to the east,

[4] Papers Relating to the Southern Rhodesia Native Reserves Commission 1915, [*British Command Papers*] *Cmd. 8674,* London, 1917, p. 7.

where data permitted, district officers appear to have allowed from fifteen to twenty acres of arable land per family. But in some parts of the country (for example, Mrewa District in the northeast) immense tracts were set aside for native occupance, and only small areas were assigned to crown land. Elsewhere, instead of demarcation of large blocks of little-known territory, the intricacies of tribal landownership were noted, and certain districts were peppered with dimunitive reserves interspersed between European farms—a policy that, if pursued over the entire country, might have had interesting consequences on race relationships in Southern Rhodesia.

Suffice it to say that the foundations for the present chaotic pattern of African- and European-owned lands were firmly laid at this time. The overall result of the formidable task was the creation of 108 reserves, ranging in size from less than five thousand acres up to hundreds of thousands of acres (Fig. 7).

DEVELOPMENT OF THE LAND-APPORTIONMENT PATTERN

It was not long, before discontent arose over the demarcation of the reserves on the part of the European population, especially the new settlers. In 1910 a special Native Affairs Committee of Enquiry was set up, but it made only minor changes in the disposition of African land. The Committee's estimate of land apportionment in 1911 was as follows: European areas, 19,032,320 acres (20.7 per cent of the total land area); Native Reserves, 21,390,080 acres (23.2 per cent); and unassigned, 51,628,800 acres (56.1 per cent).[5] The Afri-

[5] Report of the Native Affairs Committee [see footnote 3 above], p. 11.

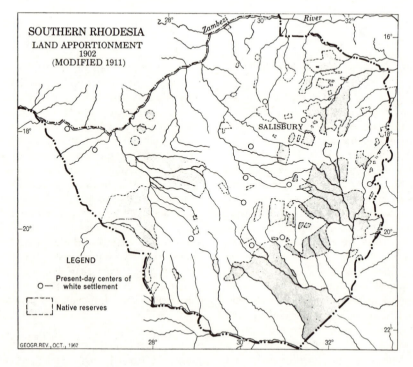

Figure 7.

can population in that year was about 700,000.

The report of the Committee failed to appease critics of the pattern of allocation, and it was necessary for another commission to be appointed in 1914 to make "final settlement of the matter." A thorough survey of Native Reserves by the new body revealed that some of the areas selected by the district officials could not even be located, owing to "defective topography"! It also engendered the observation that

> owing to the somewhat haphazard way in which reserves were originally marked out, land has been assigned to natives which is quite unsuitable for their purposes, though desirable from a European point of view, while land eminently fitted to carry a native population and actually inhabited by natives has been left open.[6]

For an independent, fact-finding commission this statement appears altogether too subjective. The criteria by which land was adjudged unfit for African agriculture yet favorable for European farming were not included in the Commission's report.

Elsewhere in the report the Commissioners expressed concern over the great numerical increase in native population and concluded that henceforth not every African could expect to till land or own cattle. This statement amounted to a rejection of tribal law and custom and was probably the first official sign of a developing realization that primitive traditions must sooner or later yield to the values of the new Rhodesian society. Although written in 1915, it has a singularly modern ring, because it expresses one of the cardinal principles behind the Native Land Husbandry Act of 1951, to which further reference will be made.

The detailed examination of land apportionment during the years of World War I led in 1920 to a regrouping of small reserves

[6] Papers Relating to the Southern Rhodesia Native Reserves Commission [see footnote 4 above], p. 9.

and to a clearer demarcation of European and African lands (Fig. 8). In that year there were about 847,000 Africans in Southern Rhodesia, more than double the number thought to have lived there at the time of the European occupation, scarcely thirty years before. Eighty-three Native Reserves were recognized and set apart "for the sole and exclusive use and occupation of the native inhabitants of Southern Rhodesia." Prospecting rights, however, were still in European hands, and of the 21,594,957 acres demarcated for African occupance, about 3,000,000 were acknowledged to be totally unsuitable for human habitation. Africans were still able to purchase and dispose of land throughout the country, though this right, for economic and social reasons, were exercised by very few.

In 1923 a significant step in the history of Southern Rhodesia occurred—the adoption of internal self-government. Barely two years later, because of a growing conviction that it was not in the best interests of either race to hold lands indiscriminately mingled, still another Land Commission was established.

The Morris Carter Commission of 1925, named after its chairman, claimed to find virtual unanimity among all classes of Rhodesians—farmers and town dwellers, missionaries, Native Department officials, and the Africans themselves (so far as they could grasp the subject)—for complete separation of races with respect to landholdings. The Commissioners came to the conclusion that tension was increasing as a result of contact between the races and that it could be diminished only by rigid territorial separation. Consequently, a policy of "possessory segregation" was officially endorsed, aimed at reducing points of contact between European and African landholders to a minimum. The right of Africans to own land anywhere in the colony was withdrawn. Instead, so-called Native Areas, some eighty-one in all, were set aside where only Africans would have the right to acquire and hold land as personal property, and where

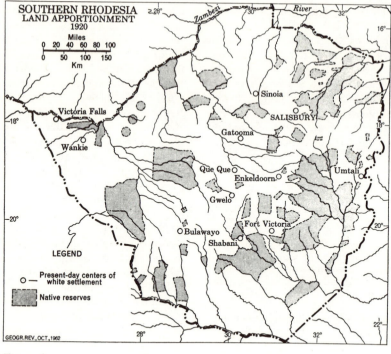

Figure 8.

they would be free from the intrigues of European land speculators. These lands, later known as Native Purchase Areas, were made to adjoin the Native Reserves wherever possible; in the reserves tribal tenure and land use continued as of old. The number of reserves was increased to ninety-eight but gross acreage was little changed.

Elsewhere in the country, only Europeans had the right to acquire new land. Africans residing in areas designated as European had no legal rights of occupancy and were required to move into Native Reserves. Since 1930 there has been a slow but steady stream of compulsory migrations from thinly settled crown land to overcrowded African lands. As late as 1955, some four thousand Africans were evicted from the European area. Their abandoned croplands were sometimes farmed after their removal but as often as not lay idle—a measure of the anachronisms and injustices that resulted

from racial segregation on the land. Table III sums up the changes that were recommended by the Morris Carter Commission and were incorporated into the first Land Apportionment Act, 1930. The African population in that year numbered some nine hundred thousand.

Although the policy of complete land segregation was supposedly agreed to by all, the problems of implementation so that both races would be satisfied with the division of the country were, of course, insuperable. The Commission found that "however unanimous members of both races may be in desiring separate areas, the evidence shows the widest diversity of opinion as to the amount of land which should be set apart for each race."[7] The Europeans were fearful of an overgenerous provision for the

[7] Report of the Land Commission 1925 (Salisbury, 1925), p. 7.

TABLE 3. LAND APPORTIONMENT IN SOUTHERN RHODESIA, 1930

	Square Miles	Acres	% of Country
European areas	76,796	49,149,440	51.0
Native Reserves	33,011	21,127,040	22.0
Native Areas[a]	11,663	7,464,320	7.8
Unassigned areas	27,802	17,793,280	18.5
Undetermined areas	107	64,480	0.1
Forest areas	923	590,720	0.6
Total	150,302	96,193,280	100.0

Source: Report of Native Production and Trade Commission 1944 (Salisbury, 1945), p. 11.
[a] The Native Areas were later renamed Native Purchase Areas.

natives; the Africans, suffering already from inadequate space for their traditional modes of living, strove for an increase in land.

Furthermore, the Commission was unable to start with a clean plate. The years of tedious demarcation and dispute leading up to the 1920 allocations precluded any radical readjustment; the existing pattern of land apportionment was too well rooted to be overthrown by a single piece of legislation. Nor was it by any means certain that the creation of large contiguous blocks for black and white settlement was really feasible. The environmental requirements of European and African farmers could hardly have been met to the mutual satisfaction of both. Given the physical conditions that prevail in Southern Rhodesia— the differences in elevation and landforms, water supply and soils, vegetation cover and distribution of mosquitoes and the tsetse fly—an equitable separation of land between the races was, of course, impossible to achieve. This is as true today as it was thirty years ago.

Thus in redrafting boundary lines between European and African areas the Morris Carter Commission had to content itself with making relatively minor changes. In keeping with the now established tradition, a reconsideration of the whole thorny issue was undertaken scarcely a decade after the Land Apportionment Act was passed. The act itself was repealed, and a reenactment introduced, in 1941.

The principle of territorial separation was again endorsed. The then Prime Minister, Sir Godfrey Huggins (later Lord Malvern), declared that the main purpose of land apportionment was

> to see that the European, by his energy, modern knowledge and science, may protect himself in the African environment and preserve all the characteristics of mind and body which he has acquired . . . and at the same time, under his influence, knowledge and care, he may raise the African to become morally and physically (i.e., in vigour) like a European.[8]

He further stated that geographical segregation and a certain amount of differential legislation would be necessary for some time to prevent degeneration of the European during the process of raising the African.

The main purpose of the new Land Apportionment Act was to tighten up conditions under which persons could occupy land in the Native Purchase Areas, but it also gave municipalities the authority to plan Native Urban Areas, in which it would

[8] Comparative Survey of Native Policy, [British Command Papers] Cmd. 8235, London, 1951, p. 79.

be lawful for Africans to occupy land in the periurban areas of European towns. In 1941 the African population numbered more than 1,400,000.

An amendment to the Land Apportionment Act was made in 1950, and at least twelve further amendments have been made since that date. With increasing pressure of population on the land in the reserves the government decided to reduce the extent of the Native Purchase Areas and thus provide more reserve land for tribal settlement by Africans. These new lands were called Special Native Areas, but in reality they were simply additions to the Native Reserves (Fig. 1). Sizable acreages were also acquired from European land and reclassified as Special Native Areas. The substance of these changes is summarized in Table IV.

Within the last ten years additions have been made to the areas available for African settlement under reserve conditions (Table II and Fig. 1). These extensions, however, have hardly kept up with the rapid increase in population, and it is in connection with the urgent problem of intensifying food production in the reserves that the entire matter of land apportionment has come to a head again in recent years.

In 1951, as was mentioned above, the Native Land Husbandry Act was passed, in a grim effort to come to grips with the rapidly deteriorating agricultural situation in the reserves. By that year some two million Rhodesian Africans had settlement rights to not quite one-third of the county. Implementation of the Land Husbandry Act has introduced dramatic changes in land use within the reserves, but its successful completion is jeopardized by the fact that the entire reform program must be executed within the restrictive framework of land apportionment, with all the maldistributions and anachronisms already described. The rising tide of African resentment against the present distribution of land in Southern Rhodesia threatens not only the agricultural reforms in the reserves but also the very security and political stability of the colony itself.

Since 1958, as Hanna [9] has observed, "there has been a slow, very incomplete, yet unmistakable thaw in the frozen rigidities of the segregationist policy based on the Land Apportionment Act." In 1961, after lengthy deliberations, the government even presented a plan for the gradual repeal of the Land Apportionment Act, but spirited

[9] A. J. Hanna: The Story of the Rhodesias and Nyasaland (London, 1960), p. 193.

TABLE 4. LAND APPORTIONMENT IN SOUTHERN RHODESIA, 1952

	Square Miles	Acres[a]	% of Country
European areas	74,075	47,407,792	49.0
Native Reserves	32,593	20,859,350	21.5
Special Native Areas[b]	6,461	4,135,427	4.0
Native Purchase Areas	8,835	5,654,325	6.0
Unassigned areas	26,728	17,105,918	18.0
Undetermined areas	98	62,563	0.5
Forest areas	1,543	987,745	1.0
Total	150,333	96,213,120	100.0

[a] "The African in Southern Rhodesia," No. 3, "Agriculture" (Salisbury, 1952), p.2.

[b] Additions to Native Reserves, acquired from old Native Areas and European areas.

debate in Parliament and widespread criticism from white settlers around the country seemed to assure that no positive move would be made for some time.

In defense of land apportionment, the conservative white argument continues to feature the necessity of spatial disengagement to preserve cultural values. When one walks the streets of Salisbury and other towns of Southern Rhodesia, one cannot help wondering to what extent this aim of disengagement of races has been achieved and questioning whether it is a defensible goal today, when the direction of world affairs is conspicuously a multiracial task. The historic facts that the country was finally occupied and subdued by force of arms and that the Europeans are the heirs to the land by right of conquest are also advanced as justification for land apportionment.[10] Probably the most frequent argument is that economic advancement for both whites and blacks in Southern Rhodesia is largely dependent on taxation of incomes and other contributions from the European community; hence more of the land should be in the productive hands of the whites. In this connection, it is sobering to reflect that only 1,100,000 acres were under the plow in the European area in 1957—barely 2 per cent of the total land allocated to the whites.

In the eyes of the African, there are few problems of agrarian and social development that could not be solved by acquisition of additional land. But what many Africans fail to appreciate is that the acquisition of more land alone would be, at best, only a temporary palliative for a situation which would recur in all its acuteness ten or twenty years after the new lands had relieved existing population pressures. It is mere wishful thinking to expect that

simply throwing open the country to African settlement and demolishing territorial segregation overnight would automatically solve all the ills of native rural society. The lesson from other countries and continents is painfully clear. It is yield per acre and output per farmer, not additional acreage, that will ultimately resolve the problem of successful African agriculture. Unless a radical change in occupational pursuits can be introduced into the African way of life, the vicious cycle of land and human degradation in the rural areas can never be broken.

This is not to say that racial segregation on the land is a viable political doctrine for the Southern Rhodesia of today. A policy of land reservation that safeguards racial interests and perpetuates gross differences in living standards would seem to be the antithesis of those governmental programs which profess to aim at elevating the indigenous masses to a more worthwhile, more productive, and more satisfying life. In the opinion of many, land apportionment has a stranglehold on Southern Rhodesia that is inhibiting its rational development and the formation of a genuine *esprit d'état* to be shared by all its inhabitants. The question has been posed: Under the rapidly changing political, social, and economic conditions in Africa and the world, when so many of the old colonial precepts concerning the "civilizing mission" and the "white man's burden" have been challenged and found wanting, is it not morally reprehensible to persist in the notion that territorial segregation will promote rather than destroy interracial harmony?

Clearly, it will be no simple task to eliminate the European idea of security based on land apportionment, which has been fostered over the years and generally accepted for a long time, and to replace it with the conception that a greater security rests with a genuine effort to work toward a real partnership of races, based on opportunities for advancement in all realms of human endeavor and in all geographical situations.

---

[10] Many Europeans in Southern Rhodesia are quick to point out that the system of land allocation adopted represented a fairer treatment of the African than was shown the Indian in North America.

But such a reevaluation of European strategy would now appear unavoidable.

A farsighted government might act now to repeal all discriminatory legislation at present in the statute books and replace it with new and enlightened land laws that would permit Rhodesians of all races to reside where they wish, acquire property according to their means and their ability to develop it, and generally to experience that freedom of movement and opportunity which is the legitimate aim of any democratic society. Particularly important, the "large tracts of land presently owned by resident or absentee Europeans, which are not being fully farmed or otherwise exploited, must be bought back by the government and redistributed to capable farmers regardless of race."[11]

Obviously, this transformation could not be accomplished overnight, nor would such

[11] Leys and Pratt, *op. cit.* [see footnote 1 above], p. 175.

haste be desirable. But it should be carried out with all expedition; procrastination to safeguard entrenched European interests might prove fatal. Protective legislation would still be necessary, of course, to prevent unscrupulous land dealings but this should not be governed by considerations of race or differing cultures.

A determined move to open up the country to all Rhodesians regardless of race would constitute an immense psychological step toward true partnership and would do more to ensure African support for the future of a multiracial Rhodesia than any other piece of constitutional reform. Cecil John Rhodes once promised to the peoples to Southern Rhodesia "equality of rights for every civilised man." Ideally, his namesake country should now aim to guarantee to all its citizens unconditional equality, and to provide those opportunities for cultural, economic, and social advancement without which the future of European occupance in Rhodesia is uncertain.

The allocation of large areas of good land to Europeans, coupled with the rapidly increasing African population, has led to congestion in the lands reserved for Africans, with accompanying pressures on limited resources. There is a striking contrast between efficient, large-scale production on European lands and poor organization and low productivity in African farming areas. The Africans urgently need more land, and the gross under-use of much of the European land adds further irony to the situation. Attempts to improve standards in African farming areas through the Native Land Husbandry Act of 1951 were prejudiced from the start, since they could operate only within the rigidly restricted framework of land apportionment (Floyd, 1962 a. and b.; Yudelman, 1964). The program has now been largely abandoned. Under such circumstances, African population-land relationships are maladjusted and face the prospects of further deterioration on the pattern of Matabeleland. When it was written a decade ago, this paper suggested that the contrast between the overpopulated and overstocked African lands of Rhodesia and the underdevelopment of much of the European area limited the reality of political and economic "partnership" between the two races. Subsequent political developments have destroyed the concept utterly.

18. *Overpopulation and Overstocking in the Native Areas of Matabeleland*

J. R. V. PRESCOTT

Scott has shown that land alienation in some African territories is causing considerable problems of population and stock congestion in the native areas (Scott, 1951; Fair, 1945; Doveton, 1937). These have been perennial problems which, all other solutions failing, have often been temporarily relieved by the extension of the native area into unallocated land. In Southern Rhodesia this palliative has been used three times, in 1930, 1950 and 1954. However, it is no longer available since all but 2 per cent of the land has been allocated, and the unallocated land is heavily infested with tsetse fly and has considerable problems of water supply. This situation makes the congestion in the native areas critical, and therefore it seems worth while to examine the nature and extent of the problem in Matabeleland in the light of land classification and agricultural methods, and to record the solutions which are being employed. Matabeleland was selected since it includes considerable areas where the annual rainfall is less than 20 inches and where problems are correspondingly more acute. The field-work was carried out during the winters of 1958 and 1959.

PHYSICAL REGIONS AND THE NATIVE AREAS

Southern Rhodesia is composed of two traditional provinces, Matabeleland and Mashonaland, which are named after the two main tribes found in the area. Matabeleland has an area of approximately 42,000 square miles and is situated in the southwest of Southern Rhodesia between the Zambezi and Limpopo rivers. Over most of the intervening area the Miocene peneplain is well represented, being significantly dissected by the post-Miocene cycle of erosion only near the Zambezi and Limpopo Rivers. The numerous rivers flow over gentle gradients from a watershed of 5000 feet, mostly to join the Zambezi and Limpopo Rivers at heights varying from 1500 feet to 2000 feet. Exceptions are the Nata and Tiriga Rivers which flow towards the Makarikari pan in Bechuanaland.

It has been recognized that "rainfall is the most important factor affecting both crop and animal production in the Central African Federation" (Engledow, 1950). Accordingly in the following brief description of physical regions in Matabeleland, effective rainfall and the length of the growing season have been used as two of the criteria for regional division. The figures for effective rainfall were calculated according to the formula devised by H. L. Penman (1948). Since it has also been recognized that livestock production forms a most important part of agriculture in Matabeleland (Staples and Murray, 1951; Welling-

From *The Geographical Journal*, 127, 1961, pp. 212–225.
Reprinted by permission of the Royal Geographical Society.

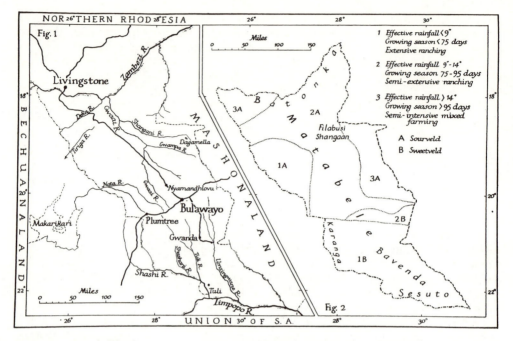

Figure 1.—Matabeleland.   Figure 2.—Physical regions of Matabeleland.

ton, 1953), the regional division takes account of the grazing quality of the veld (Fig. 2).

The classification according to effective rainfall and growing season gives three physical regions. Region 1 has either less than 9 inches effective rainfall per year or a crop production without irrigation. This region is best suited to extensive ranching based on veld grazing, since the conditions are too uncertain even for drought resisting fodder crops. Region 1 is located in the Limpopo valley and the area drained by the Makarikari pan. Region 2 has 9–14 inches effective rainfall and a growing season of 75–95 days. Within this region drought-resistant grain and fodder crops can be grown with some expectation of success. Accordingly the region is best suited to semi-extensive beef production, with arable production aimed mainly at providing cattle-feed reserves for winter and drought years.

Region 2 is continuous and has its greatest extent in the Zambezi valley. Region 3 has an annual effective rainfall of more than 14 inches and a growing season of more than 95 days. The area is still subject to moderate dry spells and is therefore only marginal for semi-intensive mixed farming which includes *Zea mays* and *Nicotiana tabacum*, in addition to *Sorghum sp.*, *Eleusine coracana* and fodder crops. The region is found mainly in the upper valley of the Shangani river and also in the extreme west, south of Livingstone.

The important distinction in the grazing quality of the land lies in the difference between "sourveld" and "sweetveld" (Rattray, 1957). The "sourveld" refers to those grasses which lose their food value after flowering, which means that cattle fed on "sourveld" will begin to lose weight from June to November. This type of grazing occupies the watershed and areas to the west. On the watershed the main species are *Hyparrhenia* and *Heteropogon,* both of which are tall and stand up well to heavy grazing pressure. Throughout the rest of the "sourveld" *Aristida* species are the most common. This is a shorter perennial with good resistance to heavy grazing. The "sweetveld" is predominantly composed of *Eragrostis sp.* and *Cenchrus sp.* Both these grasses retain their nutritional value after flowering, but they do not stand up well to heavy grazing pressure, which tends to be selective. The *Cenchrus sp.* is found on black, shallow soils, which are developed on basalt outcrops east of Tuli. Heavy grazing during the summer tends to compact the black soils with serious results for the next grass crop. These five physical regions must now be related to the native areas (Fig. 3).

The three types of native area indicate the successive attempts to solve the problems of population and stock congestion by the increase of area. The Native Reserves were delimited during the period 1894 to 1914, the Native Purchase Areas (N.P.A.) in 1930 and the Special Native Areas (S.N.A.) in 1950. A full description of the history of the native areas is to be found in Lord Hailey's *An African Survey —Revised* 1956 (Hailey, 1957). The Reserves are generally large and compact in the Zambesi valley and fairly distributed amongst the three physical regions, while in the Limpopo valley the Reserves are smaller and scattered, being located mainly in the extensive ranching zone of the "sweetveld." Fifteen of the N.P.A. have an area of less than 60,000 acres each, while the remaining two, Maitengwe and Mpimbila, are from 75,000–100,000 acres each. In all but one case the N.P.A. were made contiguous with existing Reserves (Gwatemba and Ghodhlawayo were attached to Belingwe Reserve in Mashonaland); however, only one was placed in the area of semi-intensive mixed farming while ten were situated in the extensive ranching zone. The S.N.A. were also created alongside existing

native areas. They are mainly large, and distributed in the extensive ranching zone of the Limpopo valley.

Half the native areas are situated in the two extensive ranching regions, those in the Limpopo valley representing 38 per cent of the total. Thirty-six per cent of the native lands are found in the region of semi-extensive beef production and the remaining 14 per cent in the region of semi-intensive mixed farming. Although the physical regions have been based on climate and grazing quality it is useful to relate the native areas to the best soils found in Matabeleland (Fig. 3). The most fertile soils in the Zambezi valley are clay loams developed along the contact zone between basalt and sandstones, while on the watershed and in the Limpopo valley they are red clays developed from band ironstone and dolerite. In both cases the main locations of the soils lie outside the native areas.

In order to complete the background picture of overpopulation and overstocking in Matabeleland, it is now necessary to supplement the information provided about the landscape with the relevant characteristics of the people and their farming methods.

When Matabeleland was first settled by Europeans there were about 500,000 Africans, most of whom belonged to the Matabele tribe. They were a warlike, stock-herding people, and had entered the area from the south through the Transvaal in 1823. They made little attempt to cultivate but acquired supplies of grain during raids on the weaker Mashona, who were cultivators in the moister northern areas of what is now Southern Rhodesia. The Matabele, who occupied most of the Zambezi valley and watershed, together with that part of the Limpopo valley which lies west of Gwanda, also raided the neighbouring tribes in Matabeleland for cattle and slaves. Three of these tribes were also stockherders and lived in the Limpopo valley south and east of the main Matabele area. Between Plumtree and the Shashi river there were small groups of Karanga whose parent tribe live in Bechuanaland. In the Limpopo valley lived the Bavenda and Sesuto tribes. The fourth small tribe in Matabeleland was the Batonka, a primitive group of fishermen and cultivators who occupied the riverine areas of the Zambezi valley. These vague tribal distributions have been crystallized within the native areas since 1894. Thus the Bavenda are found mainly in the Gwanda S.N.A. "H" and "F," the Karanga in the Raiditladi and Mphoengs Reserves and the Batonka in the Wankie native areas.

Since 1951 some members of the Shangaan and Filabusi groups of the Mashona people have been taken from congested areas in southern Mashonaland and settled in the underpopulated Shangani S.N.A. "A." The traditional antipathy between the Matabele and the other tribes is a factor which must be considered in any redistribution of population.

The pacification of the country meant that the stockholder had to begin growing their own grain, and gradually they became herders and cultivators. Each tribe developed its own agricultural method but they were all variations of the following theme. It is interesting to note the similarities of these methods with those of the Bemba described by Dr. Audrey Richards in the *Journal* three years ago (Richards, 1958).

The chief allocates arable land to the headman, who in turn allocates it to the kraal chief, who in turn allocates it to the individual families. The men clear the trees leaving only fruit trees and trees with ritualistic significance. Thus *Uapaca kirkiana* (*Muhobohobo*), and *Parinari curatellifolia* (*Muhacha*) were left for food and *Gardenia thunbergia* for ritual. The ground is broken by hoeing and then just before the first rains the felled trees are burnt. After the first rains the seeds are sown and covered by a shallow hoeing which also burries the ash. A small portion of the area is planted separately to *Arachis Hypogaea* (*Nzungu*) and *Voandzeia subterranea* (*Nyimo*). The greater portion is sown with a mixture of *Sorghum sp.*, (*Mapfunde*) *Eleusine Coracana* (*Rupoka*), *Pennisteum spicatum* (*Munga*), *Curcurbita pepo* (*Mapudzi*) and *Vigna eatjang* (*Nyemba*). Some *Zea mays* is planted but always in individual holes. In the first season one weeding is carried out by a communal work party (*Nimbe*).

A man will start with 2 acres and each year gradually extend his farm until at the end of the fourth year he will have 4 acres under crops. He will then allow the first cleared area to revert to bush. Although there is no definite fallow period it is believed that land in this area takes an average of thirty years to regenerate. Peters and Trapnell working in Northern Rhodesia suggest thirty-five years and twenty years respectively (Peters, 1950; Trapnell, 1953). This means that a man with one wife will need at least 34 acres of arable land if he is to farm without shortening the fallow period. Most men have two or three wives and so their arable needs are greater. There is thus shifting cultivation in all areas except the moist valley bottoms (vleis) which are cropped continually under *Zea mays*.

There is no integration between livestock and arable farming. The women are the main cultivators and the young men and women herd the cattle. Since settlements are usually located near water the cattle tend to remain near the kraals although, except in regions where there are known carnivores, they are not penned. After drinking in the morning the cattle are driven into the veld to graze. They are seldom driven far and accordingly graze the same area until it is completely bare. Gradually these denuded areas extend outwards and soil erosion may develop, following one of two patterns. If the ground is broken either for cultivation or by hoof pressure then deflation may occur during the winter. This type of erosion has been particularly serious on the shallow basalt soils in Gwanda S.N.A. "H." If the grounds is not broken it may form a skin through baking, which means that during the first rains run-off is considerable and flash-flooding occurs, creating some spectacular gullies on river bank sand causing silting in reservoirs.

These farming methods would, by themselves, have produced important landscape changes, but the changes have been more rapid and far-reaching as a result of the high rate of population growth (Fig. 4). The graphs reveal that, despite the increases in native land there has been a continuous fall in the area available for each individual to the present level of 16 acres per person. Prior to European occupation the landscape was characterized by a low density of kraals near which there were a few small gardens. The kraals were separated by wide stretches of virgin woodland which provided common grazing and firewood. As the two following examples show, the present pattern reveals a close density

of kraals around which are large fields, the intervening areas are usually composed of fallow land, and there are extensive tracts near stock-watering points which have been denuded of all vegetation.

Figure 5 represents a typical section of a native area in the extensive ranching zone, being part of Gwanda S.N.A. "D," which has a great number of granitic residuals in the form of inselbergs. Fields extend to the base of these outcrops and most of the land is under cultivation or is resting from recent cultivation. With so little area for grazing it is not surprising that considerable sections of the river banks have been denuded of vegetation, allowing the partial development of gullies. Recent estimations indicate that this S.N.A. contains twice as many cattle and people than it should. Figure 6

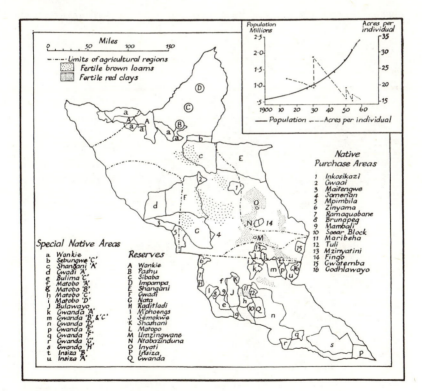

Figure 3.—Native areas in Matabeleland.

Figure 4. (inset).—Population growth.

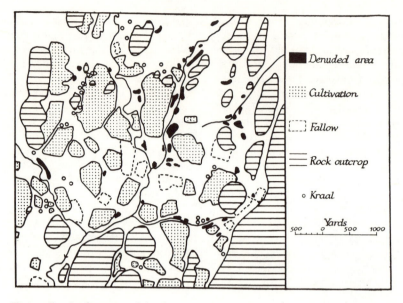

Figure 5.—Settlement and land use pattern of part of the northern section of Gwanda S.N.A. "D."

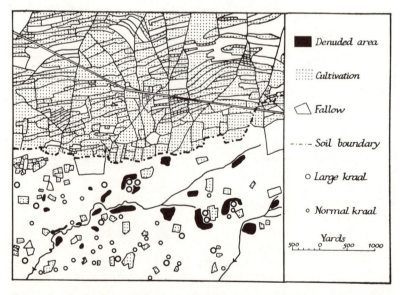

Figure 6.—Settlement and land use pattern of a section of the north bank of the Nata River in the Nata River Reserve.

shows a section of the north bank of the river Nata which drains into the Makarikari pan. The land use pattern here presented is unusual for an extensive ranching region in Africa. In the north there is a fragmented block of arable land, which almost exactly coincides with the contact soils between the sandstones on the ridge and the basalts in the valley. Each plot is the land cultivated by one wife. The larger plots are farmed by a number of wives married to one man, since, when a man marries a second wife, he clears a farm for her and tries to make it contiguous with the plot of his first wife. The clayey valley soils are used mainly for settlement and grazing. Some of the kraals in the Nata Reserve are unusually large, containing as many as twenty huts compared with the normal number of four or five. Although exact figures are not available I am advised that there is a preponderance of women in this Reserve, which means that each man tends to have more wives than men in other areas. The significance of the restricted grazing area and the large kraals is seen in the zones where the vegetation cover has been completely removed and where some soil erosion is taking place. The shortage of grazing land in the Reserves described has led the people to practise a form of transhumance (*lagisa*). In the southern sector of Nyamandhlovu S.N.A. the Nata river floods during the period January to April before draining south-westwards to Bechuanaland. After the floods have subsided the majority of the cattle from northern Nyamandhlovu and western Nata Reserve are brought into the valley, for winter grazing, by a number of selected families. The cattle graze there until immediately before the onset of the first rains, when they are driven back to the home kraals so that the herders can prepare their farms. A similar system is also practised by the people in Gwanda S.N.A. "D," "E" and "F," who move their cattle into the recently flooded portions of the Shashani and Tuli valleys during winter.

This brief analysis of the physical and cultural landscape makes it possible to attempt a geographical interpretation of the problem of congestion in the native areas.

The figures on which the following analysis is based were collected by the Department of Native Agriculture of Matabeleland. The census of stock and families was made by officers attached to the native areas. The population and stock capacity, which represent the optimum number of people and cattle which the area can support under ideal conditions of distribution and agricultural practice, were assessed by a team of agricultural officers. These officers carried out extensive tours and also made use of air photograph analysis. From these figures it has been possible to calculate the degree of over- or understocking and over- or underpopulation for each unit and these values are shown in the Appendix. Since there is considerable interaction between the facts of overpopulation and overstocking it seems most valuable to consider them together. Accordingly the values for each unit were plotted on a single graph and by inspection six groups were distinguished (Fig. 7). The main characteristics of each group are shown in Table I, and their distribution is shown in Figure 8.

Before analysing these figures it must be observed that it has been necessary to neglect two factors, for reasons of length, which make the situation more critical. First, it has not been possible to consider the distribution of population in each native area. In some native areas which appear to be only lightly overpopulated, there is a maldistribution of population, which is causing more serious resource deterioration than might be expected. An example of this is provided by Shangani Reserve which shows an over-all excess of three persons per thousand acres. This low figure masks the concentration of people at Dagamella in the Shangani valley. Dagamella is the name of a former lake bed composed of fertile alluvium. These fertile soils have attracted large numbers of people, and the soils are becoming impoverished as a result

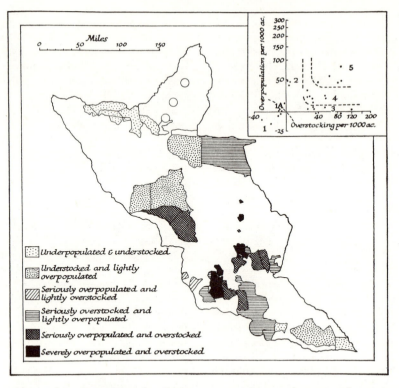

Figure 7 (inset).—Relationship between overstocking and overpopulation in the Native Reserves and Special Native Areas, Matabeleland; Figure 8.—Overstocking and overpopulation in the Native Reserves and Special Native Areas, Matabeleland. (No data available for unshaded areas)

TABLE 1.

| | 1,000 acres | | Average Stock capacity per 1,000 acres | | | Families of 5 Members | |
| | | Available | | | Excess | | Excess |
Group	Area	area		Stock	stock	Population	population
1	1,059	837	37.3	19,773	−12,637	2,531	−1,513
1A	3,195	2,828	42.8	108,388	−12,261	10,803	2,948
2	124	120	93.9	12,082	194	2,068	1,114
3	3,122	2,629	51.0	210,549	62,513	13,312	7,699
4	1,251	1,175	74.4	96,697	35,998	11,162	4,554
5	520	391	73.2	62,524	37,731	7,199	5,184
Total	9,271	7,980	—	510,013	111,538	47,075	19,986

of overcropping and overgrazing. Second, it has not been possible to consider stock other than cattle due to lack of statistics. During the fieldwork, numerous small herds of sheep, goats and donkeys were seen and they must all contribute to a reduction in the stock-carrying capacity of the veld.

Understocked and underpopulated areas. This group includes Gwanda S.N.A. "E" and "F," Wankie S.N.A. and the Wankie Native Reserve, which form about 11 per cent of the area of the Reserves and Special Native Areas, and accommodate 5 per cent of the population and 4 percent of the stock. The areas are situated in the extreme north-west and south-east of Matabeleland (Figs. 8 and 3) and have two common characteristics. In each area there is a measure of tsetse fly infestation which is greatest in Gwanda S.N.A. "E," whither it is carried by game migrating from Portuguese East Africa. Further, water supplies are difficult to obtain in Wankie, because the water-table in the Karroo sandstones is at considerable depth, and in Gwanda because of the low rainfall. These areas are unattractive by virtue of their low carrying capacity. Immigration into them would seem to depend upon the prior provision of stock and population watering points, which could only be achieved at considerable expense.

Understocked and lightly overpopulated areas. This group includes Shangani S.N.A. "A," Gwanda S.N.A. "H," Nyamandhlovu S.N.A. and the Gwaai Reserve. Together they form about 34 per cent of the native areas and accommodate about 23 per cent of the population and 21 per cent of the stock. Although all the areas have a low stock capacity, their inclusion in a single group is due to a variety of factors. The Shangani S.N.A. "A" has only recently been developed and it is into this area that members of the Filabusi and Shangaan groups have been moved. There has not yet been time for the stock density to increase to the stock capacity of the land; it is interesting, however, that overpopulation precedes over-

stocking in this new area. The Gwaai Reserve has been included in this group, due to the fact that in recent years there have been considerable numbers of cattle deaths resulting from the noxious weed *Dichapetalum cymosum* (*Nkauzaan*) which has appeared in the Reserve. So far as can be determined the cattle deaths have not caused any emigration of population from the Reserve. Gwanda S.N.A. "H" and Nyamandhlovu S.N.A. are closely akin to those native areas described in the first group. The slight overpopulation in these areas can be attributed to accessibility in the case of Gwanda and the provision of water supplies in Nyamandhlovu. In 1959 nineteen pans in Nyamandhlovu were deepened to 15 feet in an effort to supply permanent water to allow settlement.

Areas seriously overpopulated and lightly overstocked. This group is composed of three small Reserves, Mphoengs, Raiditladi and Mzingwane, which together make up less than 2 per cent of the native areas. All three have a high stock capacity and are clearly attractive areas for settlement. It is difficult to account for the higher level of overpopulation than overstocking in Mphoengs and Raiditladi, but the answer may be partially found in their location on the Southern Rhodesian boundary with Bechuanaland and the fact that the people of these Reserves are Karanga, a group which is also found in Bechuanaland. The excessive population of Mzingwane is due to its periurban situation 5 miles from Bulawayo, which provides the principal attraction for African labour in Matabeleland.

Areas seriously overstocked and lightly overpopulated. This group contains Bulima S.N.A. "C," Bulawayo S.N.A. "A," Matobo S.N.A. "A," Insiza S.N.A. "A," Gwanda S.N.A. "D" and "G" and the Shangani Reserve. With the exception of the Shangani Reserve and Bulawayo S.N.A. "A" these areas have a low stock capacity and are situated in the extensive ranching region of the Limpopo valley (Fig. 8). The low stock capacity is reflected in the low population densities of the units, but seems to have offered less hindrance to the development of high stock densities and consequent overstocking. Although the Shangani Reserve is in the physical region suited to semi-intensive mixed farming, the geological structure imposes considerable limits on land use. The westward flowing rivers, such as the Shangani and Gwampa, have cut valleys in the Kalahari sandstone series and in certain areas have reached the underlying basalt. Settlement is concentrated in the valley bottoms where cultivation is possible throughout the year. *Zea mays* is grown during the summer and vegetables during the winter. The cattle are also herded on the better grazing of the valley floors. This neglect of the sandstone ridges (*Gusu*), due to the absence of water except at considerable depth, and concentration of settlement and farming along the valley floors, has led to a deterioration of the resource value of the valleys. An attempt is being made to organize native agriculture along the following lines. Settlement and arable land will be established on the contact zone between the sandstone series and basalt on the valley sides. During the summer the cattle will be grazed on the *gusu* ridges which will support one beast to 60 acres. With the end of the rains the cattle will be brought down to graze near the settlements for about two months, and then taken to the valley bottoms. After the harvest the cattle will be brought to the cleared fields to graze as long as possible before being returned to the valley floors until the end of the dry season. The high density of population in Bulawayo S.N.A. is a partial consequence of its nearness to Bulawayo.

Areas seriously overstocked and overpopulated. This group contains Matobo S.N.A. "C," Insiza S.N.A. "B," Gwanda S.N.A. "A" and "B" and the Insiza, Gwanda and Nata Reserves. These areas comprise 14 per cent of the total native areas and accommodate 24 per cent of the population and about 20 per cent of the stock. The Insiza and Gwanda Reserves have a high

stock capacity together with high population and stock densities. The remaining areas have low stock capacities but about the same degree of overstocking and overpopulation. Much conservation work is being undertaken in Nata Reserve and during 1959 six dams were built with a total capacity of 150 million gallons. In addition, fifteen pans were deepened to provide permanent water for settlement.

Areas severely overstocked and overpopulated. About 6 per cent of the native areas fall into this group, the particular units being Matobo S.N.A. "D," and Matopo, Shashani, Semokwe, Ntabazinduna and Inyati Reserves. Together they accommodate 15 per cent of the population and 12 per cent of the stock. The first four units are located in the Matopos range of hills, which consists of a series of spectacular granite outcrops presenting a bare rounded profile. These outcrops in the case of the Matopo Reserve reduce land available for use to 27 per cent of the total area. Despite this fact, stock capacity is moderate to high, and since the Reserves have been long established they have attracted people over a considerable period.

Ntabazinduna and Inyati have high stock capacities by virtue of their location on the watershed; however, this is not the only factor accounting for their severe overpopulation. Ntabazinduna is situated only 12 miles from Bulawayo and the Inyati Reserve is placed in the centre of an important gold mining area which offers attractive employment possibilities.

It is not possible to be precise about the position in the Native Purchase Areas. They were designed to be areas where Africans could acquire freehold land rights to a farm varying in size from 50–350 acres. At the end of 1958 the land purchased in the N.P.A. throughout Southern Rhodesia amounted to 1,180,000 acres, with an average farm size of 200 acres. Unfortunately the designated areas were not always unoccupied land and thus the scheme has not been applicable in some areas due to the numbers of original settlers, not all of whom wished, or were able, to purchase land. In Matabeleland the scheme is working in six areas, Gwatemba, Godhlawayo, Zinyama, Samenan, Inkosikazi and Tuli. Accurate information is not available for the remaining ten, but examination indicates that they have the characteristics of areas that are both overstocked and overpopulated.

This review indicates that the development of population and stock congestion is a more complex process than might be imagined. Prior to European settlement it seems likely that nowhere in Matabeleland was there an optimum level of stock or population, although there was no doubt a greater density of settlement on the watershed than in the low veld of the Limpopo and Zambezi valleys. With the creation of native areas stock and population congestion has developed to some extent on all but the poorest land. Eventually, the final stage in all cases will be serious or severe overstocking and overpopulation, and thirteen areas have already reached this condition. There seems to be two ways in which this ultimate condition may develop. On the land with the highest stock capacity overpopulation is at first in excess of overstocking, while on the land with moderate stock capacity overstocking is at first in excess of overpopulation. It has also been noticed that location near manufacturing or mining centres, such as Bulawayo or Inyati, is a significant factor in accounting for congestion.

Having considered the nature and extent of the problem of congestion it is now necessary to examine the attempts which are being made to reduce its severity and incidence.

SOLUTIONS TO THE PROBLEM OF CONGESTION

Some of the local attempts to minimize the problem, such as the provision of increased water supplies, and the change of farming methods in the *gusu* area of the Shangani Reserve, have already been described. The following account indicates the large-scale solutions which are applicable to all Matabeleland, and will show in which areas these solutions are at present being applied.

In an effort to grapple with the serious situation in the native areas, the Southern Rhodesian government passed the Native Husbandry Act in 1952. This act aims at control of land utilization and allocation, and is intended to promote the efficient use of land in the following ways. First, the Act encourages good husbandry and the protection of all natural resources such as soil and water. Second, stock level is to be limited to the carrying capacity of the veld. Third, the Act prevents fragmentation of holdings and encourages amalgamation of individual units into larger organizations. Fourth, the Act makes provision for the establishment of town and business sites.

The first stage in the application of the Act is the collection of the data being analysed in this paper. It is on this data that plans are based and their implementation is producing important landscape changes. Arable land is being consolidated into large blocks and contour ploughing is everywhere apparent. Kraals are arranged in regular lines and community centres are provided. In areas where this has been done there is a marked absence of denuded sections of river bank. In Matabeleland the final planning stage has so far only been achieved in parts of the Matopo Reserve, where the situation was chronic. The accompanying map of part of this Reserve indicates the features of a planned landscape (Fig. 9). The other native areas are being planned along similar lines and priority is being given to those areas where the situation is most serious.

It would appear, however, that the plan alone cannot succeed, for the population and stock estimates on which the plan is being based in Matabeleland show that there are 100,000 people and 111,000 cattle for which no provision can be made. The stock surplus can be dealt with by compulsory destocking over a number of years, but the surplus population make it essential to find supplementary solutions.

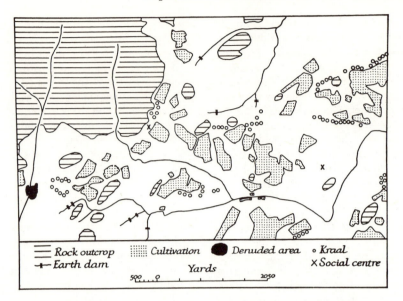

Figure 9.—Settlement and land use pattern of part of the Matopo Native Reserve, where the Native Husbandry Act (1952) has been implemented.

A preliminary survey has indicated that there are at least 4500 acres of the Shashi and Tuli river valleys, in Matobo S.N.A. "B" and Gwanda S.N.A. "D," which could be irrigated. Estimating the need of each family as 4 acres of irrigated land, this development would accommodate about 5600 persons. The families resettled in this area will be encouraged to stall-feed one beast for sale to the Cold Storage Commission. The main problem would be to maintain soil fertility under constant cropping. Green manuring is not entirely satisfactory and it may be necessary to subsidize the purchase of bagged fertilizers.

Since the best use of land is extensive ranching it has been suggested that co-operative farms should be established. Herds would be amalgamated and supervised by the most efficient farmers, profits being distributed on the basis of cattle contribution. Investigation into the possibility of such organizations are being undertaken in Gwanda S.N.A. "D," "G" and "F."

It has further been suggested that the use of squatter labour on European farms, coupled with the restriction of immigration by alien Africans, would assist in reducing congestion in the native areas. In 1959 the government introduced legislation prohibiting further immigration of alien Africans into Bulawayo and Salisbury urban districts in order to combat the effects of slight industrial recession which was causing unemployment. This only affected urban native locations and contributed nothing to the solution of congestion in the rural native areas. It is likely that any large-scale restrictions on labour movement by Southern Rhodesia would produce similar action by neighbouring states, involving the return of Southern Rhodesia's African immigrants. It is to be doubted whether European farms and expanded industrial undertakings could absorb more than a small fraction of the surplus population.

Large-scale irrigation and cooperative farming would seem to offer the greatest contribution to the solution of overcrowding in the native areas, and both will require considerable organization and capital investment.

This paper has described the incidence of overpopulation and overstocking in the native areas of Matabeleland. It shows that, even if all the native areas held their maximum population and stock densities, there would still be a surplus of nearly 100,000 persons and 111,000 stock. The deleterious effects of this situation on the physical resources of the area are noted. The value of the veld is being reduced through overgrazing, which is upsetting the normal balance of vegetation at the expense of the more nutritious grasses. Around waterholes in the drier part of the country, land is being denuded of vegetation, and erosion is occurring, although spectacular gullies are few because of the low gradients. Some waterholes are becoming dry for the first time in living memory, yet there is no evidence of increasing desiccation from the available rainfall records. Finally, the solutions which are being applied to the problem are described.

The implications of the situation do not relate only to the physical landscape. The significance of congestion in respect of the social life of the Africans and the economic life of the country can be readily imagined, and is worth study. However, it is possible that the greatest significance of the situation may lie in its influence on the political concept of "Partnership," which forms the basis of the Central African Federation. Lord Hailey has written that the alienation of land in African territories is "the most powerful influence in determining the character of the relations between the indigenous population and a colonial administration" (Hailey, 1957). The congested native areas are in direct contrast with the underdeveloped European farm lands, and this contrast seems to reduce the possibility that "Partnership" will become an effective reality.

APPENDIX 1.

S.N.A.	Per 1,000 acres					
	Population Capacity	Population Density	Excess Population	Stock Capacity	Stock Density	Excess Stock
Shangani "A"	4.6	4.7	.1	55.6	48.0	−7.6
Bulima "C"	7.5	8.5	1.0	50.1	103.4	53.3
Bulawayo "A"	19.5	20.2	.7	78.9	110.9	32.0
Matobo "A"	3.0	3.5	.5	40.0	163.8	123.8
Matobo "C"	4.0	6.1	2.1	53.5	84.5	31.0
Matobo "D"	7.4	16.5	9.1	66.5	146.7	80.2
Insiza "A"	12.6	12.3	−.3	62.5	149.7	87.2
Insiza "B"	10.1	13.7	3.6	69.2	93.6	24.4
Gwanda "A"	9.3	12.8	3.5	93.4	147.0	53.6
Gwanda "B"	9.4	15.4	6.0	93.5	117.8	24.3
Gwanda "D"	1.7	3.5	1.8	33.4	64.9	31.5
Gwanda "E"	1.7	1.6	−.1	33.3	27.6	−5.7
Gwanda "F"	2.0	1.3	−.7	33.5	30.7	−2.8
Gwanda "G"	2.0	1.6	−.4	33.4	67.7	34.3
Gwanda "H"	1.6	1.7	.1	33.3	28.8	−4.5
Nyamandhlovu	2.7	2.9	.2	40.0	32.5	−7.5
Wankie	4.1	2.2	−1.9	42.5	15.3	−27.0

Note: The population figures are expressed in families with an average size of 5 members.

APPENDIX 2.

S.N.A.	Per 1,000 acres					
	Population Capacity	Population Density	Excess Population	Stock Capacity	Stock Density	Excess Stock
Matopo	12.0	53.9	41.9	72.1	242.5	170.4
Shashani	7.7	19.2	11.5	81.4	142.8	61.4
Semokwe	3.0	12.9	9.9	58.0	154.1	96.1
Insiza	11.5	15.8	4.3	94.3	143.8	49.5
Gwani	2.6	4.6	2.0	42.5	41.8	−.7
Gwanda	1.8	5.0	3.2	51.7	82.0	30.3
Shangani	4.7	5.3	.6	58.8	83.5	24.7
Ntabazinduna	10.7	27.2	16.5	64.3	155.6	91.3
Nate	4.4	8.4	4.0	66.7	93.2	16.5
Inyati	17.0	26.0	9.0	97.2	137.9	40.7
Mphoengs	7.3	17.0	9.7	102.4	103.7	1.3
Raiditaldi	7.3	15.1	7.8	85.3	87.6	2.3
Mzingwane	24.4	33.8	9.4	94.0	97.0	3.0
Wankie	7.4	4.6	−2.8	40.0	25.4	−14.6

Note: The figures for population are expressed in families, with an average size of 5 members.

REFERENCES

Doveton, D. M. 1937. The human geography of Swaziland. *Trans. Inst. Brit. Geogr.* 8, especially pp. 47–54.

Engledow, Sir Frank. 1958. *Agricultural policy in the Federation of Rhodesia and Nyasaland.* Report to the Federal Minister of Agriculture by the Federal Standing Committee on Agriculture Production, in collaboration with Prof. Sir F. Engledow, c.m.g., f.r.s., C. Fed. 77, p. 24.

Fair, T. J. D. 1945. The Drakensberg native locations. *S. Afr. geogr. J.* 27, 65–72.

Hailey, Lord. 1957. *An African Survey—Revised* 1956. Oxford University Press.

Penman, H. L. 1948. Natural evaporation from open water, bare soil and grass. *Proc. Roy Soc.* A 193, 120.

Peters, D. U. 1950. Land usage in Serenje District. *Rhodes-Livingst. J.* 19, 14.

Rattray, J. M. 1957. Grass and grass associations of Southern Rhodesia. *Rhod. agric. J.* 54, 197–234.

Richards, I. A. 1958. A changing pattern of agriculture in East Africa: the Bemba of Northern Rhodesia. *Geogr. J.* 124, 306–7.

Scott, P. 1951. Land policy and the native population of Swaziland. *Geogr. J.* 117, 435–7.

Staples, R. R. and C. A. Murray. 1951. Farming systems in Southern Rhodesia. *Rhod. agric. J.* 48, 413–27.

Steel, R. W. 1955. Land and population in British Tropical Africa. *Geography 40*, 1–17.

Trapnell, C. G. 1953. *The soils, vegetation and agriculture of north-eastern Rhodesia.* Report of the Ecological Survey, para. 143. Lusaka: Government Printer.

Wellington, J. H. 1953. A tentative land classification of Southern Africa. *S. Afr. geogr. J.* 35, 16–25.

The division of land in Rhodesia is not as sharply defined as it is in the Republic of South Africa. The distinction between Non-White and White populations permeates all aspects of life in the latter country and influences the entire range of population-land relationships, both in the countryside and in the towns (Brookfield, 1957). Restrictions governing place of residence and movement of population militate most severely against the Africans, although there is a growing tendency for the concentration of all racial groups into prescribed areas (Fair, 1969).

For some time the limited resources of the African reserves have displayed evidence of population pressure. In the past these pressures were relieved in part by the outflow of African labor to European mining and industrial enterprises and farming areas. Movement of population is now strictly controlled, although economic advantages, which are heavily weighted in favor of the White population, can only continue with dependence upon Non-White labor. At the same time, African reserves are being developed politically as "Bantustans," to give the people a degree of independence. Efforts are also being made to give them some measure of economic viability. The long-term prospects for these and other policies are impossible to determine, but it is the intention of the government that ultimate control in all matters shall remain with the White population (see also Brookfield, 1957; Fair, 1969; Nel, 1962; Sabbagh, 1968).

19. *Population Patterns and Policies in South Africa, 1951-1960*

T. J. D. FAIR AND N. MANFRED SHAFFER

The population geography of the Republic (until May 31, 1961, the Union) of South Africa is complex. There are at least four main ethnic groups: Whites, both English- and Afrikaans-speaking, of European descent; Natives or Africans (termed Bantu by the Bureau of Census and defined as members of any aboriginal race or tribe of Africa); Coloreds of mixed White and non-White blood; and the Asians or Asiatics, mainly Indians.

In recent years, various writers [1] have

[1] Among the more important are: K. M. Buchanan and N. Hurwitz, "The Asiatic Immigrant Community in the Union of South Africa," *Geogr. Rev.*, Vol. 39, 1949, pp. 440–449; K. M. Buchanan and N. Hurwitz, "The 'Coloured' Community in the Union of South Africa," *Geogr. Rev.*, Vol. 40, 1950, pp. 397–414; L. T. Badenhorst, "The Future Growth of the Population of South Africa," *Population Studies*, 1951, pp. 4–36; J. H. Moolman, *Explanation of the Population Distribution Map*

From *Economic Geography*, 40, 1964, pp. 261–274. Reprinted by permission.

analyzed the population geography of these groups, their cultural patterns, the changing proportions of each in the total structure, the changing patterns of distribution, and the significance of these trends in relation to the South African government's current policy of "apartheid" or separate development."

These studies are based upon censuses taken up to the year 1951 or earlier. In September 1960, the first census in nearly ten years was taken, and the preliminary results of the distribution of population were made available in 1961.[2] The object of this paper is to examine some of the more significant changes in the proportions between the groups, particularly between White and non-white, and in the pattern of their distribution over the past 10 years. This has been a critical period and certain aspects of the Government's apartheid policy, embarked upon in 1948, should now be measurable. Moreover, the effects on the redistribution of population of the expansion of mining, agriculture, and industry, which the country enjoyed after the Second World War, may also be gauged.

Government concern as to the significance of these changes is reflected in the recent appointment of a number of commissions of inquiry and the publication of their reports; [3] the establishment of new depart-

ments of State; [4] and the further enactment of legislation and the stricter implementation of existing legislation governing the movement of persons of different races from place to place, and their residence in particular areas.[5] Much of the Government's interest in population growth and its redistribution is motivated by the growing disparity in numbers between Whites and non-Whites (Table I). In 1921 there were 3,900,000 more non-Whites than Whites (3.6 to 1); in 1951 the difference was 7,400,000; and in 1960 it had risen to 9,700,000 (4.2 to 1).

The present pattern of population distribution in South Africa is illustrated in gen-

---

of the Union of South Africa, Natural Resources Development Council, Pretoria, 1951; J. H. Wellington, Southern Africa, Cambridge, 1955, Vol. 2, pp. 201–270; F. F. Winklé and M. F. v.d. Merwe, "Economic Expansion of the Union as reflected by the Shift of the White Population 1936–1951," Finance and Trade Review, Vol. 2, 1956, pp. 1–8; H. C. Brookfield, "Some Geographical Implications of the Apartheid and Partnership Policies in Southern Africa," Trans. and Papers No. 23, Inst. British Geogrs., 1957, pp. 225–247; Monica Cole, South Africa, London, 1961, pp. 653–675.

[2] Bureau of Census and Statistics, First Results of the Population Census, 6 September, 1960, Geographical Distribution of the Population, Special Report No. 234, Pretoria, 1961.

[3] Commission for the Socio-economic Development of the Bantu Areas within the Union of

South Africa (Tomlinson Commission), Summary of Report, U. G. 61/1955, Pretoria; Witwatersrand and Vereeniging Native Areas Zoning Committee 1955–1956, Report unpublished (an investigation into sites for new African townships for the growing African population of this important mining and industrial region); Commission on Smallholdings in the Peri-urban Areas of the Union of South Africa, Report U.G. 37/1957, Pretoria; Commission of Inquiry into European Occupancy of the Rural Areas, Report 1959–1960, Pretoria.

[4] The Department of Native Affairs was divided into two separate departments in 1958 as Bantu Administration and Development, and Bantu Education; a division for Coloured Affairs within the Department of the Interior was established in 1951, and raised to a fully independent department in 1958; and a department of Asiatic Affairs was established in 1960.

[5] Natives (Urban Areas) Consolidation Act, No. 25 of 1945, as amended. Apart from defining and describing the powers and the duties of urban local authorities in respect of the African population within their areas, this Act, inter alia, allows also for the control and limitation of the influx of Africans into urban areas, and for the removal of Africans if they are surplus to the labor requirements of such areas. The Natives Resettlement Act, 1954. To provide for the removal of Africans from areas of Sophiatown, Martindale, Newclare, and Pageview in Johannesburg and to resettle them in Meadowlands and Diepkloof, new African townships to the southwest of the city. The Group Areas Act, 1957. To consolidate the group (i.e., racial groups) areas legislation embodied in Acts dating from 1950.

TABLE 1. POPULATION: SOUTH AFRICA

	Total	Whites	Coloreds	Asiatics	Bantu
1951	12,671,452	2,641,689	1,103,016	366,664	8,560,083
1960*..............	15,841,128	3,067,638	1,488,267	477,414	10,807,809
Percentage increase					
1951—60	25	16	35	30	26
Percentage Urban					
1951	42	76	62	77	27
1960*	44	80	63	80	30

Source: *First Results of the Census,* 6 September, 1960, "Geographical Distribution of the Population," Special Report, No. 234.
*Preliminary results.

eral terms in Figures 1 and 2.[6] It possesses

[6] The census unit upon which Figures 1 to 6 have been based is the magisterial district, an administrative unit, of which there are 277 in South Africa. The urban and rural populations are not differentiated in this study, but the sizes of magisterial districts in the neighborhood of the larger urban or metropolitan centers are sufficiently small for such centers to be clearly

three outstanding characteristics: (1) the higher density of population in the wetter eastern half of the country and in the south and southwest Cape, the marked drop in density of both Whites and non-Whites

recognized. The High Commission Territories of Basutoland, Swaziland, and Bechuanaland are excluded from the analysis.

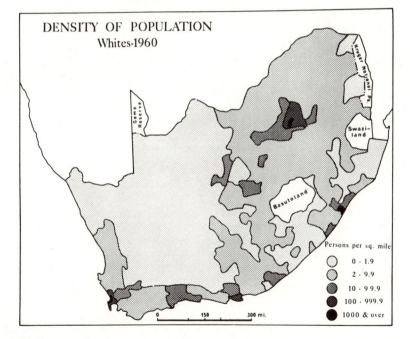

DENSITY OF POPULATION
Whites-1960

Persons per sq. mile
○ 0 - 1.9
◉ 2 - 9.9
◉ 10 - 99.9
● 100 - 999.9
● 1000 & over

Figure 1.

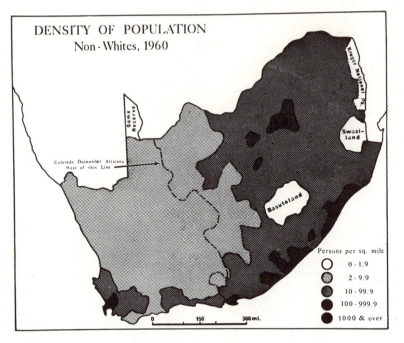

Figure 2.

roughly coinciding with the 400 to 600 mm. isohyets; (2) the high urban concentration of population particularly in the eight major metropolitan areas (Table II),[7] which con-tain 29 per cent of the total population, and 56 per cent of the White and 66 per cent of the Asiatic population; and (3) concen-rand—Vereeniging region, Cape Town, Port Elizabeth, Durban, East London, Pietermartiz-burg, Bloemfontein, Kimberley.

[7] Southern Transvaal or Pretoria—Witwaters-

TABLE 2. POPULATION: EIGHT MAJOR METROPOLITAN AREAS

A. Number in each racial group				
	Total	Whites	Coloreds	Asiatics	Bantu
1951	3,652,539	1,444,201	416,110	232,805	1,559,423
1960*	4,694,530	1,723,777	568,938	315,737	2,086,078

B. Each group as a percentage of its South African total				
	Total	Whites	Coloreds	Asiatics	Bantu
1951	28.9	54.6	37.7	63.5	18.2
1960*	29.4	56.1	38.2	66.0	19.3

Source: *First Results of the Population Census,* 6 September, 1960, "Geographical Distribution of the Population," Special Report, No. 234.
  *Preliminary results.

trations of non-White groups in specific areas—Bantu in the Reserves, Coloreds in the western portion of the Cape Province, and Indians in the coastal belt of Natal.

This pattern is derived from well-established historical and natural foundations: the arrival of Europeans at the Cape of Good Hope in 1652; the entry of Bantu tribes from the northeast in the seventeenth and eighteenth centuries; the advance of the Voortrekkers into the interior after 1838; the importation of Indian laborers and others to the sugar cane plantations of Natal from 1860 to 1914; the birth of the Colored population in the southwest Cape after the arrival of Europeans; the discovery and subsequent mining of diamonds, gold, and base metals in the interior after 1860; the growth of ports and railways to serve the hinterland so created; and the potentialities for intensive agriculture in the wetter eastern half of the country and along its southern coast.

Inherent in these patterns and in the growth trends and shifts that have occurred over the past 40 years are a number of population problems that today have assumed important proportions. They are the rapid growth of Whites and non-Whites in the major urban centers, the depopulation of much of the farming area by Whites and their replacement by non-Whites, and the growing overpopulation of many of the Bantu Reserves. All are closely linked and are live political, social, and economic issues, to which government interest in the past 10 years has been strongly directed.

URBAN GROWTH

Figure 3 indicates the remarkably few areas in which an increase of any consequence in the White population has been registered during the period 1951–1960. Modest increases are recorded in the smaller metropolitan centers of East London, Bloemfon-

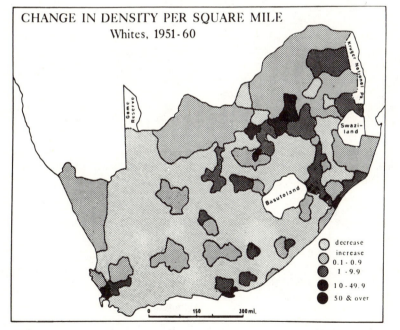

Figure 3.

tein, and Kimberley, as well as in small urban centers (population not exceeding 25,000) along the highway and railway line from Johannesburg to Durban. Advances made in the low veld of the Eastern Transvaal after the eradication of malaria in the mid-1940s and the opening up of the area to the irrigation of citrus and subtropical fruits have persisted, as has the growth of White population in the sugar belt of Natal north of Durban where the growing of timber (*Eucalyptus saligna*) has also become important since World War II. Increases have also occurred within the Vaal Hartz irrigation area north of Kimberley as a result of the enlargement of that scheme.

By far the largest increases, however, have taken place in the four major metropolitan areas of the Southern Transvaal, and in Cape Town, Durban, and Port Elizabeth, in which are employed nearly 80 per cent of all workers in manufacturing activities in South Africa. There have also been big increases in the recently developed goldfields of the Orange Free State, Western Transvaal (Klerksdorp), and Far West Rand. In these three mining areas, the White and non-White populations have nearly trebled between 1951 and 1960, from 136,000 to 385,000. In fact, over the period 1936–1960, out of a total increase of 1,060,000 Whites in South Africa, more than 90 per cent was accounted for in the comparatively small industrial, mining, and agricultural heartland in and around the Southern Transvaal and the Orange Free State Goldfields and in the areas centering on Cape Town, Port Elizabeth, and Durban.[8]

The steady urbanization of the White population in South Africa is evident from the fact that 53.4 per cent of their total was living in towns in 1921, 76 per cent in 1951, and 80 per cent in 1960. In the period 1936–1951, industrialization, stimulated by the expansion of gold production

and by World War II, surged ahead, and the net national income nearly quadrupled to a little over $3 billion. During this period, large numbers of Whites left the land and the smaller towns and moved into the large commercial and industrial centers. However, in the decade 1951–1960, while the economy has continued upward (net national income was nearly $6 billion in 1960–1961), it has been estimated that as much as 94 per cent of the growth of the White population in the Southern Transvaal, containing 32 per cent of South Africa's Whites, was due to natural increase. Only the remaining 6 per cent could be attributed to a net gain through migration.[9] It would seem either that the major period of movement of Whites off the land is past or that the addition of these migrants from the rural areas now makes little impact upon the growth rate of the urban population as a whole. Only immigration from overseas can now supplement on a large scale the growth from natural increase of Whites in the urban areas. However, since the rapid falling off in immigration after 1948, the average net immigration of people of European descent since 1951 has been only 3800 per annum; though, by a system of assisted immigration now instituted, it is hoped that this number will be considerably raised.[10]

All non-White groups in South Africa continue to display an increasing urbanization during the period 1951–1960. Asiatics living in towns increased from 77 per cent to 80 per cent of their total number, Coloreds from 62 per cent to 63 per cent, and Bantus (the least urbanized) from 27 per cent to 30 per cent. The greatest period of city-ward movement on the part of Bantus,

[8] L. P. Green and T. J. D. Fair, *Development in Africa,* Johannesburg, 1962, p. 79.

[9] Dr. L. T. Badenhorst, University of the Witwatersrand, personal communication.
[10] It has been estimated by the 1820 Memorial Settlers Association that some 40,000–50,000 immigrants per year are necessary if South Africa's White population is to reach 10 million by the turn of the century. *The Star,* Johannesburg, 4th June, 1962.

however, took place between 1936 and 1946 when an uncontrolled "flood" created housing problems in and around major cities during and after World War II, producing the unsightly shanty towns so widely publicized. Since the advent of "influx control" initiated by the present government in 1948, the urban flow of Bantus has been strictly controlled through municipal Bantu Affairs departments, and the housing problem has been all but overcome.

It is virtually impossible, however, to determine the net gain of the Bantu urban population from migration to towns compared with growth from natural increase.[11]

[11] One estimate, not considered thoroughly reliable, made for the municipal area of Johannesburg indicates that in the period 1957–1961, of a total growth of 73,000 Africans, natural increase (*assuming* 2 per cent per annum) accounted for 45,000, leaving the increase from net migration as 28,000 (or 1.31 per cent per annum).

In the past 10 years the resettlement and rehousing of Bantus on a vast scale in and around the major cities has involved the taking in of large numbers of squatters and others from peri-urban areas and their placing in the new greatly expanded Bantu townships;[12] and it is not easy to distinguish these people from those from more distant rural areas.

There can be little doubt that influx control measures have considerably slowed down the flow of rural Bantus to the towns. What is significant, however, is that, irrespective of such control on immigration, the

[12] For example in the southwestern African townships of Johannesburg, now covering 26 sq. miles, the number of houses for Africans in 1946 totalled 10,000. In 1960 there were 55,000 houses and 25,000 beds in hostels for single men, to be increased to 74,000 houses and 30,000 beds by 1965. This pattern has been repeated in all the major metropolitan centers.

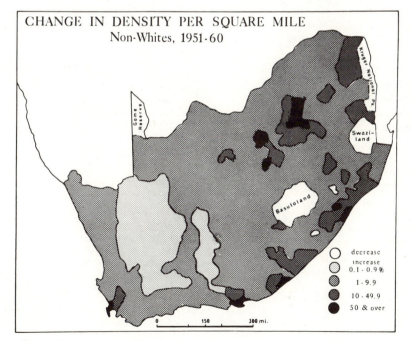

CHANGE IN DENSITY PER SQUARE MILE
Non-Whites, 1951-60

○ decrease
◔ increase
  0.1 - 0.9 %
◒ 1 - 9.9
◕ 10 - 49.9
● 50 & over

0   150   300 mi.

Figure 4.

growth by natural increase of urban Bantus is itself assuming large proportions. For example, in Johannesburg, excess of births over deaths among the Bantu population has increased from 7.18 per 1000 in 1951 to 19.3 per 1000 in 1960. Likewise, the ratio of males to females, which was as high as 23 to 1 in 1910, has been reduced from 2.8 to 1 in 1936 to a virtual parity of 1.1 to 1 in 1960. These changes are reflected in the increasing youthfulness of the Johannesburg Bantu population; for those under 18 years of age in 1951 represented 27.6 per cent of the total compared with 55 per cent in 1960.[13]

Thus, whereas in the Johannesburg metropolitan area non-Whites (including Asiatics and Coloreds who in 1960 formed only 12 per cent of non-Whites) outnumbered Whites by only 4000 in 1936, the difference in 1960 was 317,000 (706,851 non-Whites and 389,690 Whites).

However, natural increase alone may be insufficient to meet the White and non-White labor requirements of expanding industry in the towns. In Durban, for instance, a recent analysis[14] indicates that, if manufacturing industry continues to grow at a rate which has marked it in the past, supplies of Bantu labor, including that available from a limited adjacent zone from within which labor is permitted to be drawn, may very soon be exhausted.

In Durban, both the urbanization and the growth of the Indian population are as significant as for the Bantu. Though forming only 3 per cent of the total South African population, in Durban (where live 49 per cent of South Africa's Indians) the Indian population represents 35 per cent of the total. It exceeded that of the Whites for the first time in 1951; and, in 1960, Indians numbered 231,000 compared with 194,000 Whites. This rapid increase has

produced not only a serious housing shortage for Indians in Durban, but also a comparatively high rate of unemployment.[15]

Similarly, in Cape Town, where Coloreds exceed Whites for the first time in the Census of 1951 (by 25,000), the difference between these two groups has now grown to 87,000. Since the urban growth of both Indians and Coloreds is primarily due to natural increase, government measures have not been directed toward curbing their cityward flow but rather to segregating them within the towns and cities from the areas occupied by Whites under the Group Areas Act of 1950.[16]

DISLOCATION WITHIN METROPOLITAN AREAS

It is very difficult to demonstrate, with any degree of precision, changes in the distribution of population which are directly attributable to the Group Areas Act or the policy of *apartheid*. Bantus resident in White urban areas are governed by the Natives (Urban Areas) Consolidation Act, No. 25 of 1945, as amended; this was enacted, *inter alia*,

> for improved conditions of residence for Natives in or near urban areas, and the better administration of Native Affairs in such areas; for the registration and better control of contracts of service with Natives in certain areas, and the regulation of the ingress of Natives into and their residence in such areas.

In all of the major metropolitan areas, local government authorities are delegated the responsibility of enforcing the provisions

[13] Data from Johannesburg Municipal Native Affairs Department.
[14] John R. Burrows, *The Population and Labour Resources of Natal*, Pietermaritzburg, 1959, pp. 170.

[15] "Indian Employment in Natal," in *Natal Regional Survey*, Vol. 11, Cape Town, 1961. In 1951, in Natal, the ratio of unemployed males to total males aged 15–64 was 1:118 for Whites, 1:13 for Coloreds, and 1:14 for Indians, p. 131.
[16] See L. Kuper, H. Watts and R. Davies, *Durban: A Study in Racial Ecology*, London, 1959; and P. Scott, "Cape Town: A Multiracial City," *Geogr. Journ.*, Vol. 121, 1955, pp. 149–157.

of the Act. As a result, the non-White populations of the major centers are being resettled in areas specially designated for their residence. The largest of these is the South-Western Bantu Township, an area of approximately 26 square miles, from 6 to 15 miles southwest of the Johannesburg city center. In 1960, the Township had a population of 376,577.[17] In 1951, there were but 142,439 persons resident in the area. Between 1951 and 1960, the Bantu population of the Johannesburg municipality declined from 244,729 to 162,332, a decline of 33.67 per cent as compared with an overall metropolitan area increase in the Bantu population of 33.87 per cent.

In Pretoria, the Bantu population of Riverside declined from 10,548 in 1951 to 61 in 1961, while Vlakfontein grew from open veld to a new Bantu township of 47,576. Although the Bantu population of Durban municipality increased between 1951 and 1960, it was at a slower rate than the metropolitan area average. New Bantu townships such as Kwa Mashu, Umlazi Glebe, and Umlazi Township absorbed 27,128 new residents. The Bantu population of Cape Town municipality actually declined between 1951 and 1960, as it did also in Goodwood, Bellville, and Parow—all White areas. A new Bantu township at Nyanga on the Cape Flats now houses 21,711 Bantus.

What is needed is some measure of the amount of dislocation or displacement which

[17] Including Diepkloof and Meadowlands. There were 34 whites and 127 Coloreds also resident in the area.

transpired between 1951 and 1960. Most "segregation" indices, concentration indices, and forms of the Lorenz curve fail to observe the location of the phenomena within the region. It is apparent that any measure must make some assumptions about the "expected" population at the later period.

If the rate of change in each of the subregions is equal to that for the region as a whole, then a subregion's "computed" population for 1960 can be obtained from

$$C_{i_2} = \frac{\sum_{i=1}^{n} x_{i_2} - \sum_{i=1}^{n} x_{i_1}}{\sum_{i=1}^{n} x_{i_1}} x_{i_1} \quad i = 1,\ldots,n$$

where x_{i_1} is the 1951 population in the ith subregion and x_{i_2} is the 1960 population in the ith subregion. C_{i_2} is the "computed" population of the ith subregion in 1960. There are n subregions in each metropolitan area and m population (racial or ethnic) groups.

By calculating the difference between each subregion's actual 1960 population and the "computed" population, summing the differences (disregarding signs), and dividing the sum by 2, it is possible to obtain the net absolute dislocation (Δ) for each population group.

$$\Delta = \frac{\sum_{i=1}^{n} x_{i_2} - C_{i_2}}{2}$$

The values for each group in the five major metropolitan areas are detailed in Table III. Absolute dislocation was greatest

TABLE 3. NET ABSOLUTE DISLOCATION OF POPULATION (Δ) IN MAJOR METROPOLITAN AREAS OF SOUTH AFRICA, 1951−1960

	White	Colored	Asiatic	Bantu	Total
Pretoria	21,238	1,249	208	48,551	68,415
Johannesburg	10,638	8,250	1,465	190,444	222,068
Durban	7,358	241	3,825	28,191	32,672
Cape Town	24,352	28,725	331	22,423	56,928
Bloemfontein	3,100	339	0	2,364	6,121

in Johannesburg where over 222,000 persons were involved. As is to be expected, absolute dislocation was least in Bloemfontein, the least populous of the five centers. Bantu dislocation was greatest in Johannesburg, White and Colored dislocation was greatest in Cape Town, and the Asiatic dislocation was greatest in Durban.

Perhaps more meaningful is a relative measure or index of dislocation (δ) which weights the net absolute dislocation by the total 1960 population. From Table IV it can be observed that relative dislocation

$$\delta = \frac{\Delta}{\sum_{i=1}^{n} x_{i_2}}$$

for Bantus is highest in Cape Town, where Bantu housing schemes are more recent than those of Johannesburg. Asiatic dislocation is highest in Johannesburg, reflecting, in part, the movement from the central city to Lenz and Lenasia. Colored and White dislocation in Pretoria is considerably greater, relatively, than in the other centers. White dislocation in the latter metropolitan area reflects, in part, the increased suburbanization of Whites, many of whom are professional people.

It appears that the Government decision to segregate racial groups is bearing fruit, if the amount of dislocation which has taken place within the five metropolitan areas during the past nine years can be employed as a useful criterion of movement. With the exception of designated proclaimed

townships, the Bantu population in 1960 in each subregion was less than the "computed" population for 1960.

RURAL POPULATION TRENDS

These trends toward a growing concentration in a few areas of all South Africa's racial groups have prompted the government to review, in the past ten years, the wider field of rural-urban relationships affecting both Whites and non-Whites. The report of a recent commission of inquiry [18] indicated that, since the mid-1930s when the present period of economic expansion and urbanization commenced, there has been a steady decline of White people in rural areas from 643,000 in 1936 to 552,000 in 1958. Moreover, in the period 1936–1960, the proportion of Whites living in rural areas as well as in small country towns of less than 2500 persons fell from 41.9 per cent to 23.0 per cent of the total White population. Between 1945 and 1959, no fewer than 5419 farms were vacated by their White occupants.[19] Most of these farms were located in the drier areas of the pastoral west, and in the maize and wheat areas of, respectively, the Orange Free State, and

[18] *European Occupancy of the Rural Areas, op. cit.,* 1959–1960.
[19] Among the wide variety of physical, social, and economic reasons advanced were an excessive subdivision of farms which yielded uneconomic units, as well as the buying up of large numbers of farms, and so the creation of large farm units, by wealthy farmers.

TABLE 4. INDEX OF DISLOCATION OF POPULATION (δ) IN MAJOR METROPOLITAN AREAS OF SOUTH AFRICA, 1951–1960

	White	Colored	Asiatic	Bantu	Total
Pretoria	.216	.346	.053	.480	.326
Johannesburg	.055	.289	.108	.612	.405
Durban	.076	.020	.033	.276	.100
Cape Town	.175	.157	.073	.690	.159
Bloemfontein	.101	.109	.000	.067	.087

the southwestern and southern parts of the Cape Province.

This downward trend is well exemplified in Figures 3 and 4; but in South Africa, unlike similar trends elsewhere, this decline has been matched by a rapid increase of non-Whites; namely, of Bantus in the eastern half and of Coloreds in the western half of the country (Figs. 5 and 6). Excluding the Bantu Reserves, the ratio of Whites to non-Whites in the rural areas has consequently declined from 1 to 3 in 1921 to 1 to 6 in 1951.

Figures 5 and 6, illustrating the percentage of Whites in the total population in 1951 and in 1960, clearly show that the "shrinkage" (or dilution) of White South Africa, referred to by Brookfield,[20] has persisted. Over most of the eastern half of South Africa, Whites now number less than 20 per cent of the total population outside of the

major metropolitan areas. Not only have White farmers moved off the land but also large farming areas are being maintained by an increasing number of Bantu and Colored farm workers and their families for absentee White landowners.

The findings of the Commission on rural depopulation among Whites and the measures proposed to counteract it have given encouragement to those in and out of government who for long have complained, rightly or wrongly, that the concentration of activity in a few localities is an undesirable char cteristic of South Africa's economic expansion. Moreover, combined with the government's determination to reduce the flow of Bantus to the cities and to "White" farms, an ambitious program of rural development in both White and non-White areas has recently been set in motion.

Arising, in part, directly from the Commission's recommendation that it is of the utmost importance to the people of South

[20] Brookfield, *op. cit.*, p. 232.

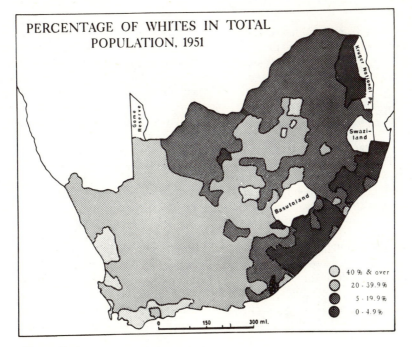

PERCENTAGE OF WHITES IN TOTAL POPULATION, 1951

40 % & over
20 - 39.9 %
5 - 19.9 %
0 - 4.9 %

Figure 5.

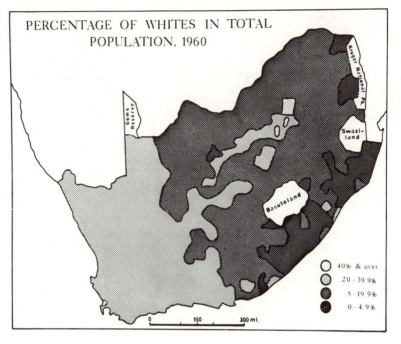

PERCENTAGE OF WHITES IN TOTAL
POPULATION, 1960

40% & over
20 - 39.9%
5 - 19.9%
0 - 4.9%

0   150   300 mi.

Figure 6.

Africa "to strengthen the White occupancy of the *platteland* (rural areas)," the government has announced its intention to develop two new large irrigation schemes in the Pongola, and in the Orange and adjacent Fish and Sundays river valleys. Ultimately, 150,000 and 750,000 acres respectively will be brought under irrigation, the latter involving a 30-year project of gigantic proportions. Together, the two schemes will attract nearly 60,000 Whites including their families and an ancillary population of an, as yet, uncalculated number. In addition, some 75,000 Bantus will be settled on that part of the Pongola scheme to be developed within the adjacent Bantu Reserves, while a smaller number of Coloreds will be settled in the lower part of the Orange valley.[21]

Moreover, since the publication of the report of the Commission for the Socio-economic Development of the Bantu Reserves,[22] the government has shown increasing zeal in developing these areas. This is not only to assist their agricultural rehabilitation and industrialization in order to contain more effectively the present heavy and dominantly agricultural population, but is also in pursuit of the policy of separate development and the restriction of the flow of Africans to "White" areas. These Reserves at present cover 13 per cent of the area of South Africa, and in 1951 contained 43 per cent of its Bantu population of 8.5 million people. The average density in the Reserves is 63 persons to the square mile, compared with 27 per square mile for South Africa as a whole.

Measures now being implemented to achieve the stated objectives are the de-

[21] Republic of South Africa, Secretary for Water Affairs, *Report on the Proposed Orange River Development Project*, W.P.X.–'62, 1962–1963.

[22] Tomlinson Commission, *op. cit.*

velopment of a number of agricultural, irrigation, and forestry schemes, the encouragement of Bantu-directed industry and commerce and of European-directed industries requiring large numbers of semi-skilled labor; the latter industries are on the borders of, but not within, the Bantu Reserves.[23] Associated with all these measures is the establishment of new towns in the Reserves; these are planned to absorb much of the population now living on overcrowded and run-down farming land and will give them employment in new industries and tertiary activities. The Tomlinson Commission estimated that, in order to achieve the objectives set, half of the population of 3.6 million living in the Re-

serves in 1951 would have to be taken off the land and given alternative occupations, in and around the Reserves, at the rate of 50,000 new jobs a year; this estimate did not include those already employed on a migratory labor basis in the mines, industries, and farms run by Whites.

The policy of "separate development" as it affects the Bantu Reserves in South Africa now envisages the establishment of politically-independent "homelands," or *Bantustans*, created out of consolidated Bantu Reserves, for each of the five main linguistic groups.[24] A greater measure of economic viability is envisaged through the measures indicated above and through close economic linkages to the "White" dominated areas

[23] By government decree, private European capital and entrepreneurship are excluded from the Reserves, but a government-sponsored Bantu Investment Corporation will assist the financing of African industrial enterprises.

[24] A draft constitution for a measure of political independence for the Transkei has already been accepted by the Transkeian Territorial Authority. *Fortnightly Digest of South African Affairs*, Vol. 9, May 14, 1962.

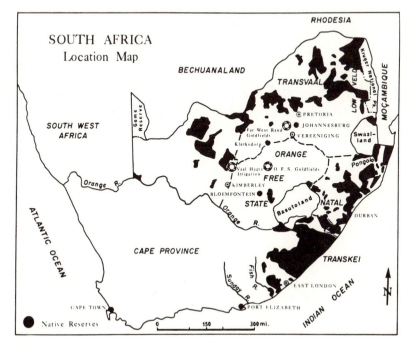

Figure 7.

of South Africa. The government is confident that these plans will, by the mid-1970s, generate a steady movement of Bantus from the White areas to the "homelands" and so *reverse* the trends that have for so long persisted.

As a program of rural improvement, there are few who do not commend these efforts; for up to now no planned and comprehensive attack upon these backward areas has been made on the scale now envisaged. However, as a means to attain even the partial *physical* separation of Black and White in South Africa, on the scale and in the time required, the policy must be seriously questioned. Plans entail a formidable buildup of primary and secondary industry in the rural areas in competition with the powerful centripetal attraction to secondary industry of the existing metropolitan centers, with the drive and enterprise of White entrepreneurs excluded from the Reserves themselves, and in the face not only of high costs involved in the provision of a basic infrastructure but also of the limited natural endowment of many of these areas.[25] Moreover, the scale of the operation can be appreciated by the fact that 55 per cent (about 6 million) of the Bantu, 1.5 million

Coloreds, and .5 million Indians are already economically committed with the 3 million Whites in mining, agriculture, commerce, and industry in the so-called "White" areas.

The late Sir Patrick Abercrombie wrote of that eternal dilemma of the planner, "when to follow trends and when to fight against them."[26] The population trends of the past ten years in South Africa have shown that there is an increasing measure of urbanization on the part of both White and non-White, and an increasing participation by both in the primary, secondary, and tertiary activities of the Republic. These trends enter into every aspect of the social, economic, and political fabric of South Africa. Government legislative machinery is now, however, geared more highly than ever before to attempt to achieve an increasing measure of physical separation of the races which is the goal of the policy of separate development. It is a formidable task.

ACKNOWLEDGMENTS

The writers make grateful acknowledgment to Daniel R. Irwin of the Cartographic Laboratory, Mississippi Valley Investigations, Southern Illinois University, for the preparation of the maps accompanying this paper.

[25] T. J. D. Fair and L. P. Green, "Development of the Bantu 'Homelands'," *Optima*, Vol. 12, 1962, pp. 7–19; D. Hobart Houghton, "Economic Dangers of Separate Bantu Development," *Optima*, Vol. 9, 1959, pp. 188–198.

[26] Sir Patrick Abercrombie, "From Brighton to Liverpool," *Town and Country Planning*, Vol. 24, 1956, p. 571.

V. POPULATION-LAND RELATIONSHIPS:
READJUSTMENT

The papers in Part II illustrate spontaneous accommodation to changing circumstances in population-land relationships. Because changes have occurred over long periods of time, the processes have developed gradually. But for a variety of reasons there may be the need for readjustment to take place in a short time and under careful direction (Wilde, 1967).

Political changes may make available to Africans land once held exclusively by Europeans. Such was the outcome of the Algerian war, which in 1962 culminated in the independence of Algeria and the large-scale departure of French *colons*, whose holdings were expropriated and nationalized (Clarke, 1969). In the process of readjustment, the Algerians have applied socialist principles to land allocation and management. State farms account for about two-fifths of the agricultural exports, though they employ only about one per cent of the agricultural workers. Thus, readjustment has done little to alleviate the economic conditions of most of the people. In no part of Africa south of the Sahara has there been a similar mass exodus, although the scale of readjustment in Kenya has been significant since the departure of most of the European population. Elsewhere change is taking place on a small scale but points the way to possible future developments that could involve large numbers of people and large areas of land.

In Kenya, the European hold in the highlands began to weaken following the Mau Mau rebellion in the 1950's and eventually was relinquished in the 1960's without political disruption. "Decolonization" and subsequent resettlement of the land by Africans were stages in the readjustment process following independence. Radical readjustments in population-land relationships had already taken place during the later stages of the rebellion, when large numbers of the Kikuyu people were resettled according to plans that envisaged revolutionary changes in African farming systems (McGlashan, 1958, 1960). Resettlement is now being achieved through a number of different schemes, the promotion of which involves consideration of the needs of the people and their relationships to the national economy, and recognition of political factors, particularly inter-tribal rivalries. As yet it is too early to evaluate the success of resettlement in Kenya, either in alleviating problematic population-land relationships or in contributing to the total economy of the country (Morgan, 1963).

20. *The Decolonization of the White Highlands of Kenya*

N. S. CAREY JONES

Professor Morgan's paper of June 1963 (*Geogr. J. 129*, 2 (1963) 140–55) told of how the "White Highlands" of Kenya came into being. The decolonization of the area has begun and it may be worth looking at some of the geographical considerations that have governed the process, particularly since the introduction of the million-acre settlement scheme made it necessary to plan it (see Fig. 1).

The early story of the land settlement schemes is a history of rapidly changing thought as events moved rapidly towards independence, and as political influence in Kenya shifted from the Europeans to the Africans. The opening of the "White Highlands" to Africans took place in 1960 with the amendment of the laws that had excluded African landownership from the area. During the preceding six years great changes had been taking place in the African reserves. Under the Swynnerton Plan, the Government was conducting a major revolution in African landownership

and farming. The Plan was a brilliant synthesis by Mr. R. J. M. Swynnerton of the various projects for African agricultural development that had been formulated, brought together for an intensive drive and given a coherent philosophy. Its bases were twofold. The first was the change of land-ownership from customary tenure to individual freehold. This involved the enclosure and registration of existing rights and, where there was excessive fragmentation in over-populated areas, the sorting out of scattered fragments and their re-assembly in areas around the homestead in roughly the same proportions of kind of land as was held before. The purpose of this was simply to give, through individual ownership, the greatest incentive to farmers to make the jump from subsistence agriculture to modern planned farming for money and to bring together in viable farming units the scattered fragments that often went unused and could not be farmed economically. The second base was the provision on these con-

From *The Geographical Journal, 131*, 1965, pp. 186–201.
Reprinted by permission of the Royal Geographical Society.

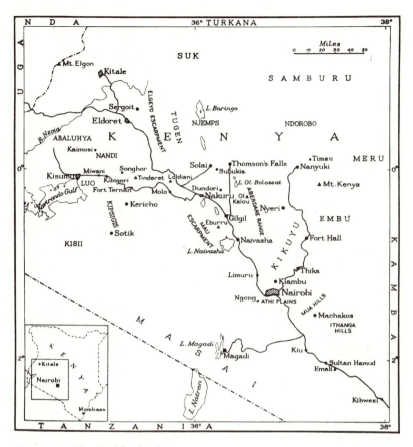

Figure 1.—The Highlands of Kenya.

solidated or enclosed farms of farm plans or lay-outs, with rotational schemes, the introduction of exotic, high-yielding live-stock and of high-priced cash crops. This was possible because of the pioneer work of Mr. L. H. Brown and others on African small farming systems. The whole was to be geared into the complex and highly organized agricultural marketing system of Kenya, designed to bring to the farmer a steady and high return for his produce, and with the provision of agricultural long-term credit to farmers who could now pledge their land against borrowings and through permanent title could plan ahead for their farms. Steady, organized marketing is one

of the keys to agricultural development, since it enables farmers to plan ahead with one of their major uncertainties removed. They have plenty of others, in weather and disease. It is also necessary in order to eliminate the small middleman, who cannot organize large-scale marketing, who is uncertain of the prices that he can obtain and must, in the prices he pays, protect himself against the uncertainties of his own selling. In addition, the transition from subsistence to cash farming is a big psychological jump for the farmer to make. He must be able to make this with some assurance, and he needs a big incentive in the highest possible prices, if he is to do so.

The Swynnerton Plan revolution was designed to take place over about fifty years, and met with a lukewarm reception among Africans, who regarded any Government activity with suspicion. It failed equally to be popular with Europeans, who resented the idea of taxes, which they regarded as "their" money, being used for African purposes. However, as a result of the Emergency, most of the Kikuyu politicians were detained and the opposition to the Government removed. It was possible to proceed with land consolidation and registration of title in the Kikuyu areas, with the cooperation of the people. As a result the Plan made rapid progress in those areas and in some others where there was little land pressure. Agricultural production began to rise rapidly, by about 15 per cent per annum, as the Plan progressed in one of the most populous areas in the country. The Kikuyu tribe had already suffered from land pressure, with the result that some had very small holdings and still have (an attempt was made generally to site very small uneconomic holdings around the new villages which had arisen out of the Emergency). This is not the occasion to go into the ramifications of the Swynnerton Plan, but it is necessary to be clear that land pressure and the existence of a near-landless and landless class already existed in the Kikuyu areas, and that the Plan, by introducing a new rigidity into land titles, heightened this division of landed and landless, which was enhanced by the political consciousness of the Kikuyu, the tribe closest to the capital, who had been able to observe from the Europeans what could be obtained by political pressure.

The other great area of population pressure lay around Lake Victoria; the Luo on the plains beside the Lake and the Abaluhya to the north. The Abaluhya, with population densities in some areas of 1400–1600 per square mile, failed over six years to respond to the persuasions, cajoleries and pressures of the Government to accept the idea of land consolidation. As poor farming practices, soil erosion and increasing numbers impoverished them more, they huddled for protection under their traditional system and were suspicious of the efforts of a government that they blamed for their position. But their political consciousness was negative, unlike the positive and active consciousness of the Kikuyu. The problem of the Luo was to get them to accept large irrigation schemes, and attempts to do so have so far failed. It is necessary to understand something of this background in order to understand the course that settlement took. There were three main overpopulated areas, all bordering on the "White Highlands." Their inhabitants looked over the border and saw the more developed agricultural system of the Europeans, whose capital had brought into production land which had previously been in Masai occupation and little used. Most tribes had claims on parts of the Highlands, either against the Masai or against other tribes, particularly in those no-man's-lands described by Prof. Morgan. This led very soon to the claim to tribal "spheres of influence" in the Highlands, which often overlapped, but at that time were thought of as excluding other tribes from settlement rather than necessarily taking the land from Europeans. Many tribes, indeed, were protesting their long-term future from encroachment by the overpopulated tribes. Not to take account of these claims could well have led to tribal warfare.

Even before the first constitutional talks on independence, before the opening of the Highlands to all races, and before the last officially-sponsored European settlers had completed their agricultural training and chosen their farms, the first settlement schemes were being considered. It was realized that without Government action, the opening of the Highlands would achieve nothing. Europeans would not sell their farms to Africans. Africans could not afford to buy them. The first scheme devised was a "yeoman" scheme. It was intended to buy small European farms or parts of farms, over a wide area. The idea was to introduce into the Highlands Africans who would farm, if not on the same scale as Europeans, at least on something approximating to it. Their small numbers and their dispersal would make them acceptable to Europeans and the latter would help and advise them. The pattern of agriculture would be unchanged. (A similar scheme, a few years earlier, for bringing in European "yeoman" farmers, to bolster up the European position, had been quickly dropped after economic investigation of the social services that would be needed for them.) The preparation of this project was scarcely completed when it was realized that, with independence in the air, however distant, a scheme of this kind would not meet African aspirations or needs. Meanwhile the first independence conference, followed soon after by the Congo débâcle, had had a sharp and drastic effect on the Kenya economy. The outflow of funds increased. The much greater inflow of capital stopped. Large foreign potential investors stated their intention of marking time for two years to see what would happen. Unemployment rose in the towns as the investment already in the pipeline was completed. European farmers, with an uncertain future, ceased developing their farms and got what they could from the land quickly. This reduced employment on the land, as did the pressure of the growing trade unions for higher wages. The lesser political leaders talked of taking over the European lands at independence. To add to the over-population already existing in the Kikuyu, Abaluhya and Luo Reserves were the new unemployed from the towns and farms who moved back to the Reserves —many of those from the farms had been born, grown up and worked on the same European farm. These pressures mounted in the next few years and sharpened the tribal "spheres of influence" attitude, as the Kikuyu and Abaluhya had formed the bulk of European farm labour and, it was feared, would claim the land that they had worked on.

As a result of all this, the settlement schemes went through some rapid metamorphoses. By early 1961 "peasant" schemes had been added to the "yeoman" scheme. These provided for small holdings and the idea at the time was that they should be on the edges of the Reserves and merged with them in their administrative and social arrangements. By mid-1961 a "high density" scheme had been added. This was to provide for a lower standard for the more over-crowded tribes, since the peasant schemes required settlers to have capital and good farming experience which the growing numbers of unemployed and landless lacked. By mid-1962 the "high density" scheme was merged into the "million-acre" scheme. Up till then, the location of settlement had depended on European farmers offering land for sale and on the price being such that a viable small-holder scheme could be mounted. If not, then no scheme emerged unless the farmers were prepared to reduce their price. As schemes were in units of 5000 acres this required joint action by sellers. With the million-acre scheme, which would make a significant impact on the agriculture of the Highlands, it was necessary to drop this haphazard method of location and to plan the five-year programme ahead. This had to be done so that European farmers knew where they stood, and so that the organization would not dissipate its energies over too wide a field, which would be expensive and mitigate against the speed which was essential if the object of the schemes was to be achieved; that is, to take the steam out of the land pressure, so that an orderly transition from European to African ownership could take place over the years without breaking the economy (see Figs. 2, 3 and 4).

The first thing was to prepare a land classification map. The "White Highlands" are very variable. The total Highlands contain some of the richest agricultural lands of Africa, but mainly associated with the well-drained slopes of the Aberdare Mountains, Mount Kenya and other hill areas. Of

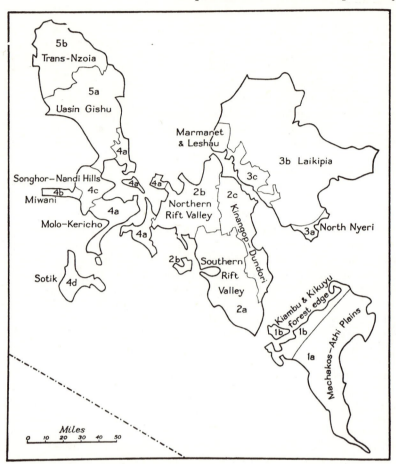

Figure 2.—Regions of the "White Highlands."

these good lands about one-fifth only was in European hands, and of the "White Highlands" only about one-fifth was represented by these good lands. On the land classification map the soils were divided into good, medium and poor, or alternatively into land suitable for high density settlement, low density settlement and dairy—or beef —ranching areas. For example, the whole of Area 1a. (Machakos-Athi Plains), Area 2a. (Southern Rift Valley), Area 3b. (Laikipia) and a large part of Area 4d. (Sotik) fell into the third category and were generally unsuitable for settlement. Areas 5a. and 5b.

(Trans-Nzoia and Uasin-Gishu) fell into the middle category, i.e. they could be resettled but were preferably farmed on a large scale. Area 2c. (Kinangop-Dundori) fell into all three, from the rich lands on the edge of the Aberdares down to the high, level plains which were used by Europeans for wheat and livestock (but on which many European farmers had failed) to the badly-drained area around Lake Ol Bolossat. The map was a great over-simplification, since the classification can change rapidly within a mile or so, but it gave a general indication of where the successful settlement schemes

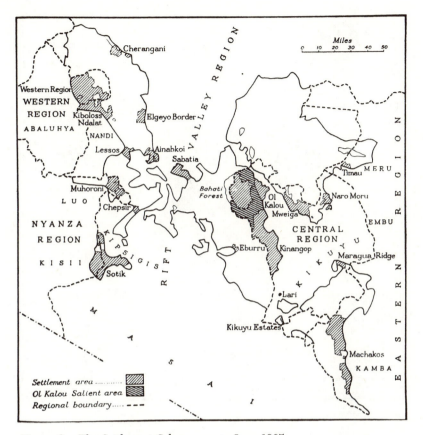

Figure 3.—The Settlement Schemes up to June 1965.

could be mounted. It served as the starting point for planning the "million-acre" scheme. The term "million-acre" is itself a generalization, since the original scheme started at one million acres plus 180,000 acres of yeoman and peasant schemes, and plus the 200,000 acres bought in 1961–2 under the earlier schemes. It was then reduced in negotiation by certain areas carried forward from 1961–2, by the need to provide for "compassionate cases" (the purchase of isolated farms owned by elderly and infirm Europeans which were no longer properly farmed, attracted illegal squatters and presented a security risk to their neighbours), and for an "assisted owner" scheme introduced in place of the "yeoman" scheme but

which did not fall within the terms of the finances available. A million-acre boundary line was broadly drawn (to include the yeoman and peasant schemes as well, since the scale of operations now demanded close planning and the economical use of equipment, machinery and staff, while the land classification map gave guidance for all schemes). The schemes were intended to exclude: (a) ranching lands, since these were unsuitable for settlement and unlikely to produce more than they were doing if settled; and, (b) plantations (coffee, tea, sisal, etc.) since these were already fully developed and their break-up would only reduce the value of production; their purchase price would be very high; and they

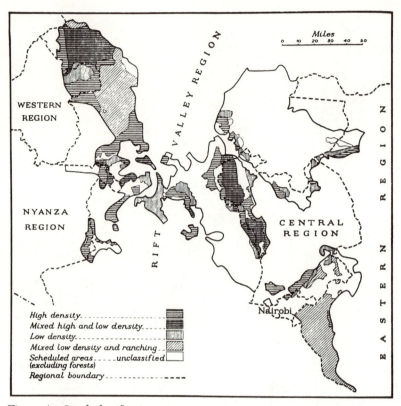

Figure 4.—Land classification map.

would not give any additional occupation of the land beyond the existing labour force. The boundary line excluded these areas, except where there were countervailing political reasons, and where they fell within areas generally suitable, when it was assumed that they would not actually be bought. This assumption was not always correct, since it proved impossible to leave a few isolated European farms in bad security areas.

Having established the areas suitable for settlement it was then necessary to see how they fitted the political needs. The foremost of these was to provide within their own "spheres of influence" for the most densely populated tribes and to see how far it was

possible with safety to stretch their spheres of influence. It had also to be born in mind that some share of the European lands must go to each of the major tribal groups, even if they had little or no need of more land, since the original desire to keep other Africans out of their sphere of influence later developed into a desire to share in the spoils. This was foreseen by Sir Michael Blundell when he laid down in 1961 that each major tribal group must have a scheme.

It was easy to cut out Area 3b. (Laikipia) and the lower parts of 3c. (Marmanet and Leshau) and 3a. (North Nyeri), and area 2a. (Southern Rift Valley) which were unsuitable; 2b. (Northern Rift Valley) and 4a. (Molo section) were excluded because so many tribal spheres of influence met or crossed uncertainly there.

The first problem came with the Kamba whose only outlet was in the unsuitable area 1a. (Machakos-Athi Plains). Here the tension was low, relations between the Europeans and Kamba generally satisfactory, and some farmers had no desire, and in fact refused, to sell. On the other hand, the Kamba country is generally poor, and in spite of a massive and successful programme for the rehabilitation of the land under Mr. Hughes Rice, some over-population existed. It was hoped at one time to be able to achieve mixed Kamba-Kikuyu settlement in the north, but this proved to be impossible as tribal feelings hardened. The Kamba eventually had themselves placed in the new Eastern Region, as did even the Embu and Meru who had been closely associated with the Kikuyu in the Mau Mau, but preferred not to be in the same Region as them. Some large-scale cooperative dairy-ranching farms were therefore planned for the Kamba, and gave them a large acreage of land even if few settlers.

Area 1b. (Kiambu and Kikuyu Forest Edge) was omitted as comprising highly developed plantations from which there could be no gain in settlement.

An attempt was then made to see how far westwards the Kikuyu could be settled, and the Area 2c. (Kinangop-Dundori), although very mixed in character, was allocated to them within the schemes up to the edge of the Rift Valley Scarp. This area included a Masai ceremonial circumcision ground, claimed by the Masai to be 7000 acres, which they used every seven years and which they had continued to use after Europeans took over their land. It was impossible to provide for this in the middle of Kikuyu settlement, and to maintain unoccupied any area of land among a land-hungry people. A small scheme was planned on the Eburru mountain in the middle of 2a. (Southern Rift Valley) for mixed Masai-Kikuyu who had established agriculture on the Masai side of the border of the Masai

and Kikuyu tribes at Ngong near Nairobi, as it was thought that they might be accepted there. In the event it was found that the mountain's water supplies, obtained from volcanic steam jets, was insufficient to allow further development or the settlement of more than the existing Kikuyu labour force.

Area 4d. (Sotik) was included as a rather later part of the programme. Some of the area around the edges is good and there are tea plantations (excluded) in the northern strip and potential tea development, but the bulk of the area is poor, ill drained and not really suitable. It was, however, impossible to expect European farming to continue in this area, which had always suffered from its isolation and poor communications, and had depended largely on milk production. This had found an outlet in Area 4a. to the north (Kericho), where the big tea estates had supplied milk as part of their rations to their large labour force. This market had, however, shrunk as the trade unions had insisted on the labour being paid in cash, with the result that the workers drank Coca-Cola instead of milk. The Kenya Cooperative Creameries gave notice that they would be forced to close what had become an uneconomic dairy in the area and the continuation of farming had become very difficult for the Europeans there. It is interesting to note what happened in this no-man's-land between the Kisii and the Kipsigis tribes. A boundary between the two was mapped sharing the area, and settlement commenced on either side of the boundary. There was no friction between the two groups of settlers, but at first some minor raids were made by men from the Reserves on either side on the settlements of the other tribe. These soon died down and the schemes are going well.

The remainder of Area 4a. (excluding the tea estates) was included in the million-acre boundary, but this area was not included in annual programmes and was cut out because of the reduction in size of the million-acre project. The tribes around were not pressed for land and there was no great racial tension.

Area 4b. (Miwani) was a highly controversial one, claimed alike by the Luo to the west, the Nandi to the north and the Kipsigis to the south. The Luo were greatly overpopulated and had suffered in recent years from the record high flooding of Lake Victoria, which was popularly attributed to the construction of the Owen Fall Dam at Jinja, although the dam is supposed to maintain normal river flow pending agreement with Egypt and the Sudan for compensation to Tanganyika, Kenya and Uganda for any raising of the Lake levels, and pending the time necessary to use the compensation for making other arrangements for the inhabitants of the areas which would be permanently flooded. The Luo also suffered because of their unwillingness to cooperate in any irrigation and drainage schemes in the plains around the Lake. The Nandi and the Kipsigis were not pressed for land, but viewed any intrusion of the Luo within their "spheres of influence" (which overlapped anyway) with hostility and threatened aggressive action. The Government, therefore, had a particularly knotty problem: to meet the real needs of the Luo without endangering the security position of the area. In the end the area set aside for Luo settlement (the only outlet for the Luo in the Highlands) was pushed as far as possible and included nearly all of Area 4b. There was the further factor that opening the area to the hard-pressed Luo endangered the security of the Asian settlers there and maintaining their right was likely to arouse strong racial feelings which might take the form of political pressure on them or on other Asians elsewhere. The area had serious disadvantages of a technical kind. The land was really unsuitable for settlement except under sugar, when the productivity was great. The value of production under sugar was about seven times that of any alternative form of husbandry, and this affected the number of settlers that could be put on the land, since any increase in population-carrying capacity is related to

an increase in production and to increased capital being put into such land as will take it. Sugar development required more capital than was available under the high-density schemes, while the peasant schemes, where development capital was provided by the World Bank and the C.D.C. and was plentiful, required the settler to bring some capital of his own. It was therefore difficult to provide an outlet in the area for the unemployed and landless. In addition, there were doubts whether the World Bank and the C.D.C., with sugar commitments elsewhere in the world and with a world sugar surplus, would accept sugar as the basic crop of a settlement scheme, even though it would do no more than replace some of Kenya's sugar imports.

The three isolated parts of Area 4a. to the north were included for settlement by the Elgeyo and other tribes. Area 4c. (Songhor-Nandi Hills) was also included together with a small part of Area 5a. (Uasin-Gishu) adjoining, but these suffered from the cuts in the million-acre scheme and were never included in the annual programmes.

There remained the problem of providing for overcrowded Abaluhya tribes, and a roughly rectangular area of about 200,000 acres was set aside on the western border of Areas 5a. and 5b. (Uasin-Gishu and Trans-Nzoia) but mainly in Trans-Nzoia, for them.

As independence approached nearer tribal feelings hardened. Counter-pressures were exerted to the movement into the Highlands of the Luo and, in the struggles over the Regional boundaries, the Abaluhya sought a greater area in the Trans-Nzoia, including Kitale, the capital. The main fear, however, was of the expansion of the Kikuyu. This, particularly, seems to have governed the approach of the other tribes to the Regional Boundaries Commission, which was sitting, and no tribe was prepared to be associated with the Kikuyu in a Region. The battle over the new constitution was taking place and it was clear that considerable Regional powers would be insisted on and granted. (In the event the constitution was much more ambiguous on this than was apparent and many of the Regional powers were given in one part and taken away in another.)

The Regional Boundaries Commission grouped the tribes according to the wishes indicated to it, and dealt with the disputed areas largely by following the million-acre boundary line; e.g. in the Sotik (4d.) area, in the Miwani area and in the bloc set aside for the Abaluhya by including it in the Western Region. The one exception was the Kinangop—Dundori area, where they pushed the boundary farther to the west in the northern part and up to the Bahati forest. This brought into the new Kikuyu area and new Central Region a greater area of good land suitable for settlement. The Government, with only a given acreage of settlement available to it, reluctant to extend the Kikuyu share (already 40 per cent of the whole) at the expense of other tribes, and anxious to provide for as many landless and unemployed Kikuyu as possible, moved its settlement line west to coincide with the new Regional boundary, but left out of settlement an area of highly unsuitable land running from Thomson's Falls to Ol Kalou and beyond including the Ol Bolossat swamps, which became known as the "Ol Kalou Salient."

With the publication of the Regional Boundaries Commission Report new pressures were set up. The Report was generally well received, with two exceptions. The Abaluhya tribes found themselves in the Western Region with no administrative centre and sought to include Kitale and a further large portion of Trans-Nzoia; while the Kikuyu found towns such as Thomson's Falls and Nanyuki, on the border of the new Central Region, included in the Rift Valley Region. This latter also entailed the construction of new district administrative centres. Agreement was nearly reached to give the Abaluhya their demand but failure by the other tribes to accept the inclusion of Thomson's Falls or Nanyuki in the Central Region prevented agreement on this for the time being.

The settlement scheme boundaries had left two large mixed-farming areas untouched: on the one hand, the Northern Rift Valley (2b.) and Molo (part of 4a.), and on the other, the greater part of Trans-Nzoia (5b.) and Uasin-Gishu (5a.). The former were excluded because of their controversial nature and the latter because they were fundamentally better suited to large-scale farming. Their exclusion had the advantage of keeping in being the areas that provided the milk, butter, wheat and maize which fed the towns and supported the small processing industries of the country, especially during the time when so much land was undergoing an agricultural transition and it was clear that small-holder settlement, even if more productive, would result in a different pattern of production. It was obviously impossible to hold these areas, any more than the ranching areas, as a miniature "White Highlands." So, parallel to the settlement schemes, encouragement was given to Africans, through the Land Bank, to purchase complete European farms or parts of them and to become large-scale farmers. This had become increasingly possible with the growing wealth of a great number of Africans. At the same time the "compassionate case" farms were being resold to Africans at reduced prices. The areas excluded from the schemes were thus becoming areas of larger-scale farming by persons of all races and, indeed, of all tribes, since considerations of tribe did not affect purchases of this kind, other than the fear an individual might have of a spear in his back if he bought land in the "sphere of influence" of another tribe and too near to that tribe's Reserve. It was hoped that by these various means a re-shuffling of the European farming population would take place; that those who were unable to accept the idea of independence and an African government would be able to sell out, and that those who looked to a future in the country would stay. In fact many farmers who were bought out in settlement areas purchased farms in nonsettlement areas. This, it was thought, would enable the country to rid itself painlessly of unacceptable and unaccepting persons who spent a lot of time in giving it a bad name.

The publication of the Regional Boundaries Commission Report enabled the European farmer to see better where he stood. The whole of the old "White Highlands" included in the Western and Nyanza Regions were scheduled for purchase and the farmers in those areas naturally pressed, but unsuccessfully, for earlier settlement. Similar pressure came from the farmers in the Sotik area, whichever side of the Regional boundary line they were, on account of their worsened economic position. The farmers in 4c. (Songbor-Nandi Hills) pressed for re-inclusion in the schemes because their means of communication with the railway line ran through the Nyanza Region and they seem to have imagined this as presenting an insuperable obstacle to farming. They were also subjected to increasing stock thefts, etc. In the Machakos—Athi Plains area there was sporadic trouble on individual farms, but generally tension was low. The political difficulties were centering themselves on the Central Region, particularly in the Kinangop—Dundori area, which had become the new district of Nyandarua.

Here there was a completely new and large addition to the Kikuyu homeland. It was, in fact, unfamiliar country to the Kikuyu, high country, where maize took ten months to ripen, cold, much of it poorly drained and with only medium soils. Nevertheless it appeared to many as a promised land. It had also been the scene of much Mau Mau activity and many European farmers there had not only lived through a harrowing time but taken an active part in suppressing the Mau Mau. It attracted the unemployed and landless from the Kikuyu Reserve in some numbers, particularly when political leaders there, besought for land, knew of no other way of dealing with the people than to say: "Go to Nyandarua." But chiefly it attracted the newly unemployed Kikuyu from the farms of the Rift Valley Region, who were actively encouraged by the tribes of that Region to move out. Even the Embu and Meru to the east encouraged Kikuyu to move to the Central Region and there seems to have been a general pressure to contain the Kikuyu there, although it received no official or overt political support. This tendency to try to localize the problems of the Kikuyu was like not only sealing up the lid of the kettle and the spout as well, but putting more steam in while doing so. As a result of it people moved into the area in increasing numbers, squatting where they could and increasing the security problems of the area.

At an early stage the Government had recognized the dangers in the Kikuyu situation and had arranged with the Kikuyu leaders to complete the settlement of their areas in three years instead of five, in return for which the Kikuyu leaders had undertaken to try to stem the flow into the Central Region. They had, however, reckoned without the pressure from the other tribes and the rise of a host of minor leaders promising free land to all at independence. There was a basic misconception in the public mind: that land could be had for all who needed it; but a quick study of the area to the west and north of the Aberdares within the Central Region had shown that the 25,000 families already employed there could only be increased to 33,000 by settlement on sound, economic holdings. Anything else meant a return to subsistence agriculture and the destruction of the economy of the area. Free land would have meant the breakdown of land values and the inability of farmers to borrow to develop their land. This surge into Nyandarua not only endangered the area itself but the rest of the country as well. The Government had every reason to fear that at independence there would be an even greater surge, squatting and the effective seizure of European farms, since farmers would be unable to operate, the driving out of Europeans and a reversion to subsistence agriculture doing incalculable harm to the country as a whole. If the Kikuyu seized land in this way other tribes were likely to copy them and this would lead to inter-tribal warfare in disputed "spheres of influence." Even if it did not spread, it would require a semi-military effort to re-establish the position, an effort which no African government could have contemplated. This, indeed, had been the underlying philosophy of settlement, to save the economy by an orderly transition of land ownership over large areas from Europeans to Africans combined with further development of the land in sound economic holdings. As independence approached this was largely being achieved, under immense difficulties and at great speed, and the deteriorating situation in Nyandarua endangered the whole. Kikuyu settlement, anyway, had been bedevilled for a long time by doubts as to whether it was wise to take up the new holdings being offered, or to await the promised free distribution of land at independence. The Prime Minister moved quickly. He ordered a "crash" programme of settlement and nearly the whole resources of the organization were diverted to settling 4000 families and the whole of south Nyandarua in the six weeks before independence. He himself toured the area and told the people firmly that they would only get land through the Government schemes and could not take it. He told the minor politicians not to attack the Government's settlement policies but to support them.

This left north Nyandarua for 1964/5, but omitted the Ol Kalou Salient, an area largely unsuitable for settlement, suitable only for the ranching of acclimatized cattle and for the occasional wheat crop. Here a new danger appeared. Farming became increasingly difficult. Labour became unresponsive. Many farmers, with memories of the part they played in the Mau Mau and expecting reprisals, became apprehensive. In addition to all this, a considerable number of farmers in the Salient were Afrikan-ers of South African origin. As feelings and emotions became more and more stirred up against South Africa these had added cause for apprehension. Farms began to be abandoned; not legally, so as to render them liable to take-over by the Government, but effectively as they were left in the care of neighbours who took grazing leases over them. For these reasons the Government sought further funds to purchase and settle the area. It would have been impracticable to divert funds from other areas, since this would simply have created new problems in those, such as not being able to complete Abaluhya and Luo settlement, which would have caused those tribes to make farming impossible for the remaining Europeans whose land they had been led to expect. It had become clear that European farming could not continue in the District. The problem was what to do with the lands in the Salient. They could not be broken up into small holdings; the sheer cost of fencing alone was beyond the capital available to a smallholder under the scheme. A simple system of wheat and dairy farming on a large scale was devised and fourteen "cooperatives" were planned to operate them. It had always been held, soundly, that the pattern of settlement development should be more on the lines of the Israeli *Moshavim* than of the *Kibbutzim*, i.e. individual holding, with a Cooperative to undertake marketing, processing and mechanized farming of those operations that put too much strain on the available labour at certain seasons, since the management decisions to be taken in large-scale mixed farming were complex and difficult. Even many European farmers had not appreciated this, in spite of the efforts of Mr. A. Storrar, to whom much of the development of European farming had been due over the years with the Government's farm planning advisory service and soil conservation service. Management was a scarce factor of production and likely to be scarcer, while there was a wealth of knowledge on small farming systems which could be adapted to the Highlands and were within the competence of the small farmer. Where, however, it was necessary to take over unsuitable lands it was necessary to devise a simple agricultural pattern that could be worked cooperatively with success on a large scale. The first of such enterprises had been started in the Machakos-Athi Plains Area with straightforward cooperatives.

As settlement had got under way with increasing impetus it had, however, raised problems of its own. In the early days the Land Development and Settlement Board had laid down that any labour on a farm bought for settlement which had been in employment for over four years should have priority for a holding on the subsequent scheme or on some other scheme. This was possible when the selection of settlers was centrally controlled, as it could be arranged for a man to take a holding in a scheme in his own tribal area, if there was one. In certain cases alien labour which had lived in an area for a long time was accepted by the local people. Under the new constitution the selection of settlers was given to the Presidents of the Region, although they were required to consult the Minister, and the machinery of selection became regionalized. Plots were notified to the Region as they became ready and the Region selected candidates to take them. With the pressure for these opportunities that was generally exerted, those evicted from other Regions had little chance. All over the Rift Valley Region settlement schemes for tribes from their Reserves involved considerable displacement of alien labour; mainly Kikuyu in the south and Abaluhya in the north. These persons either squatted on the new settlers' holdings, making the economy of the holding unworkable, or migrated in search of empty or badly run European farms to squat on. Thus, while the position of some persons was greatly improved, that of others became much worse. In practice more problems were being solved than

were being created, but this was by no means obvious, especially as the schemes could not provide land for all, and the creation of the Regions had severely restricted the overcrowded tribes. The problem of displacement loomed large and affected political thinking. It became larger as a result of the methods of selecting settlers under the "crash" programme referred to earlier. Here the President of the Region delegated his powers to a series of local political committees and the schemes instead of absorbing, as intended, all the existing labour force on the farms, plus a large number of recent immigrants to the area, absorbed only about 25 per cent of the labour force, while others from the Reserve, and even one from Mombasa, were selected. The President of the Region took the view that all Kikuyu, wherever they were and wherever they came from, should have a fair chance of getting one of the new holdings. But this served to create a large displacement problem, which the Government can still solve in the north Nyandarua schemes provided that selection is not left to the Region.

The displacement problem caused a change in approach, aided by other powerful influences. Mrs. Huxley and others argued that it was bad in principle to break up large farms, that everywhere in the world the movement was to larger farming units, and that small holdings were uneconomic. These arguments ignored the advances made in Kenya in economic small-scale agriculture, ignored the wastefulness of mechanized agriculture (its efficiency is efficiency per man in countries where labour is scarce, and not efficiency per acre), ignored the broken nature of much of the land in Kenya which is simply not worth cultivating at all by machinery, and ignored the moves in many advanced countries for settlement by intensive small-scale agriculture. It was based, too, on an exaggerated idea of the degree of development in European farming in Kenya. On the whole, European farming had made its biggest strides since the last war, but it was still in mid-development, with capital being ploughed back year by year. Some mixed farms were fully developed, some barely developed at all, but most could offer plenty of room for further production. (It may well have been true, as many Europeans argued, that if the capital for the settlement schemes were made available to them they could also achieve greater production and absorb more labour. But this was not the problem.) A similar view was taken by those politicians whose contacts with Russia and Eastern Europe had been close, and where the same philosophy reigned. They ignored the manifold problems all too evident in Communist agriculture, particularly those of management.

What seems to have determined opinion at a time when the settlement schemes were too young to demonstrate any achievements, as they are now beginning to do, was the displacement problem. Simply stated: you set up a collective which includes all the persons at that time on the farms included in it and you immediately have all the advantages of large-scale agriculture and solve your displacement problem. If this ignores both the management problem and the fact that the number of persons who can be engaged on the land is related to the capital put into it, that is another matter, and these two problems can be tackled in other ways. It does, innocently, recognize that of the mixed farming lands suitable for small-holding development the bulk has been taken. So the pattern for the future has become the "collective"; a sort of compulsory cooperative. It will remove settlement from all those things in the Constitution that hedge it round. Farms will be bought only at a price at which a collective can operate the land successfully. Labour of any tribe on the land will stay there. This has great advantages for the overcrowded tribes who will no longer be restricted to their own Regions. The collectives will have their own new problems, but they will be economic ones rather than

political. It is easy to pour scorn on the collective from both the administrative and economic points of view, if not the social. But Kenya has new problems to solve and must decide which are most important and which means come nearest to solving them. The pressure for land has grown and not diminished as time has gone on, especially as the new Government has shown its intention of not letting anyone seize land. This tends to show itself in hostility to the idea of Asians buying land and of Europeans who have been bought out for settlement buying land elsewhere. Not far away is the hostility to the idea of Europeans owning land at all. Indeed, since January 1964, very few Europeans have bought land. It has become a matter of argument as to how long those remaining still have. Expert opinion suggests that to try to take over European farms in less than 8–10 years would do irreparable damage to the economy. By that time the steady development of the old Reserves, together with a planned transfer in the European areas, would enable the economy to carry the strain without causing suffering to many, which an earlier transfer could do.

There is an alternative. In the Masai lands below the Mau Escarpment lie 1,400,000 acres of good agricultural land untouched. The Masai use it rarely for grazing as it is too high and cold for them. Nor will they allow it to be developed, even for their own benefit, and rejected a recent scheme for a ranch on 200,000 acres of it. Thoughts had been turning to the idea of renting this land from the Masai, thus bringing it under development and providing the Masai with money to improve the lower, warmer lands that they prefer. The Prime Minister has declined to countenance any infringement of Masai rights, and it is clear that it will be some time before the Masai are themselves prepared to contemplate anything of this kind.

Professor Morgan refers on page 151 to the Kipkarren and Kaimosi farms. These, together with "Murray's Farm" at Meru, became classified as the "Nandi Salient," lands which it was recognized had been wrongly alienated. The case of "Murray's Farm" (actually parts of three farms lying between two rivers named similarly in the early days) was by no means so clear, and the Carter Commission decided that the area had not been wrongly alienated. But dispute continued. The Nandi Salient farmers paid their rents to the local authority but, as independence approached, it was clear that they would never be able to sell their leases to other Europeans or tribes, and that the Nandi regarded them as belonging to them. Here the early pressure came from the Europeans to be bought out and it was expected that they would be able to renew their leases with the Nandi and continue farming. There appeared to be little tension between them and the Nandi. There was no possibility of recovering the cost of purchase and the Kenya Government took the view that it should not use its development funds on nugatory expenditure to correct a mistake made by Britain. In the end the farms were purchased from savings on the administrative costs of settlement schemes.

What is interesting, however, is the change in African attitudes over the short period of negotiation. As settlement (outside the Kikuyu areas where the hope of free land proved an obstacle for some time) gained in popularity and became fashionable, the Nandi decided that they wanted the land to settle for themselves. European farming could not continue there. Similar pressures began to grow in connection with "Murray's Farm." Here race relations were excellent. The Meru had ample first-class land, much of it far from fully developed. A settlement scheme was being prepared for them nevertheless on the northern lower slopes of Mount Kenya near Timau. In 1962 they were prepared to exchange their claim on "Murray's Farm" for free land of an equivalent value in the settlement

scheme. By 1963 growing political pressure made them demand not only "Murray's Farm" but the settlement scheme as well (on much poorer land than their own) and yet more land.

What happened was that the increased tribal exclusiveness together with the Regional Constitution had led to tribal jealousy. Why are we getting so little and other tribes more? This was coupled with another and unexpected factor. The original hope was that the settlement schemes would effectively take the steam out of the land pressure; that they would provide a sufficient relief to unemployment to ease new pressures; that when the Africans found out what the European lands were really like the demand for them would fall away. Then agriculture could go on normally and no doubt in time Europeans might give up farming, but this would be up to them. Meanwhile the progress in agriculture in the Reserves under the Swynnerton Plan would make European farming of less significance. What did much, but not by any means all, to change this was the schemes themselves. They are carefully planned. Individual holdings are based on economic farm budgets, are laid out with proper soil conservation measures, roads of access to holdings, villages and trading centres, and through their cooperatives are linked to the highly-developed European marketing system. They are achieving what they set out to do economically. They are too good to miss. Added to which the unemployment problem has grown to a size not originally expected. The ownership of land is the basic social insurance of the country. More and more people want the opportunity, not only for security, but for wealth, offered by the schemes. (A good farmer can greatly improve on the minimum, conservative farm budgets.) It is likely, therefore, that the pressure for settlement, in whatever form, will grow rather than diminish.

APPENDIX

Note on costs of settlement   This note is provided to bring up to date the figures provided by Prof. Morgan.

The total cost is £24,986,000, of which £9,816,000 is non-repayable grant; the balance is borrowed. The sources of funds are:

Britain	Grant	£9,316,000
	Loan	£10,462,000
Germany		1,200,000
World Bank		1,640,000
C.D.C.		830,000
Land Bank and Agricultural Finance Corporation, Kenya		1,418,000
Farming operations		120,000
		£24,986,000

This is spent thus:

Land Purchase	£12,032,000
Development Loans to Settlers and Co-operatives	7,539,000
Subsistence to Settlers before crops come in	509,000
Pre-settlement development of land	1,231,000
Administrative costs	1,815,000
Advisory Services etc. by other agencies	1,860,000
	£24,986,000

The cost of the scheme per settler is:

High Density	Recoverable from settlers	£368
	Met by grant	246
		£614
Low Density*	Recoverable from settlers	£648
	Met by grant	322
		£970

---

* The 'peasant' and 'yeoman' schemes have been merged in the Low Density Scheme.

Resettlement may result from factors other than political change. For example, the Belgian *paysannat* schemes in the Congo were aimed at improving agricultural production through organizing land use (Miracle, 1967). In the valleys of the Nile, the Zambezi (Rhodesia) and the Volta (Ghana), thousands of people were displaced as reservoirs for power and irrigation submerged vast areas (Hilton, 1967; Warren and Rubin, 1968). The success of large-scale agricultural schemes based on mechanized production has been limited; their faults and failures may be linked to difficulties encountered in utilizing new methods of production (Davies, 1964b; White, 1958). Nevertheless, both colonial and independent African governments have planned and executed a variety of settlement schemes (Chambers, 1969).

In the Chipangali scheme in Zambia, the need for resettlement was related to land allocations made about the turn of the century. Here (as elsewhere in tropical Africa) tsetse fly infestation was a problem (Turner and Baker, 1968). Initially, planning was inadequate and reflected insufficient understanding of the local environment, its inhabitants and their problems. The present scheme attempts to correct previous errors and is important as a model for development in other parts of Zambia (Kay, 1967a). The history of resettlement schemes in Africa indicates that even when population-land relationships are unsatisfactory, there can be no firm assurance that balance can be satisfactorily redressed.

21. *Resettlement and Land Use Planning in Zambia: The Chipangali Scheme*

GEORGE KAY

After the Second World War the Colonial Office committed itself to "an endeavour to raise rapidly the standards of living of African populations"[1] and it accordingly instigated a vigorous policy of economic and social development in the colonies. The basis of progress in underdeveloped countries must, in the long run, be through improved education in all its many aspects, but a variety of problems and possibilities have invited immediate attention. One such problem, found in widely separated parts of tropical Africa, is the overcrowding and mismanagement of land by primitive cultivators and pastoralists. In several areas maladjustment of population to land has

From the *Scottish Geographical Magazine, 81*, 1965, pp. 163–177. Reprinted by permission.

required both movements of population and programmes of agricultural improvement in order to conserve natural resources and increase productivity. This has been the case in the Eastern Province of Zambia where serious overcrowding of the Native Reserves in the North Charterland Concession led to large-scale resettlement schemes between 1940 and 1946. These, however, did not provide adequate relief to all parts of the Reserves and resettlement programmes are still considered necessary.

This paper first outlines the origin and character of the problems of overcrowding and the role of resettlement schemes in the campaign to alleviate the situation. And, secondly, it describes in some detail the Chipangali Resettlement Scheme and the Regional Plan [2] for Chipangali which reveals current technological, economic and social measures designed to bring about the optimum use of the natural resources of marginal lands in Zambia.

THE NORTH CHARTERLAND CONCESSION
AND NATIVE RESERVES

In 1895 the North Charterland Concession, based on treaties made between the paramount chief of the Ngoni and a German adventurer and trader, was recognised by the British South Africa Company and the High Commissioner for Central Africa. The concession occupied 10,000 square miles in the south-east corner of Zambia (Figure 1), and all land and mineral rights within it were held by the North Charterland Exploration Company and all administrative powers were held by the British South Africa Company. The tribes of this area, notably the Ngoni (who held sway over the others), the Chewa, Nsenga, Ambo and Kunda, thus became little more than tenants of one European company and subjects of another. The defeat of the Ngoni during their rebellion of 1897–8 confirmed these relationships and also gave the Europeans rights of conquest which

the tribesmen understood more readily than those of treaties and agreements. By the end of 1899 effective administration had been established throughout the concession and the stage was set for economic development.

No economic occurrences of minerals were discovered, but a European agricultural industry soon developed. It was at first based on cattle ranching and depended on the market for cattle in Southern Rhodesia. Cotton and rubber also held promise and plantations of both were established. By 1912, however, the cattle industry had declined and both cotton and rubber had proved unsatisfactory. Tobacco, on the other hand, grew well and, encouraged by the United Tobacco Company and later assisted by Imperial Preference, tobacco planting developed rapidly. It reached a peak in 1927 when leaf to the value of £225,000 was exported. Since 1927 European farming has enjoyed mixed fortunes, but has never regained the prosperity of that year, and it finally collapsed in 1955. There is now only a handful of European farmers in the Eastern Province, but, with few exceptions, all estates alienated during past decades have remained in European hands (Figure 1).

Land alienation was permitted by the North-Eastern Rhodesia Order in Council of 1900 and Africans could be removed from their land provided that they were compensated. The Order (Clause 40) also required the British South Africa Company to "assign to the Natives inhabiting Northern Rhodesia land sufficient for their occupation, whether as tribes or as portions of tribes, and suitable for their agricultural and pastoral requirements including in all cases a fair and equitable proportion of springs or permanent water." [3] This legal machinery for clearing land of its African population and for the creation of reserves was never formally applied in full in the Eastern Province until 1928, but nevertheless a policy of racial separation of farming areas was pursued from an early date

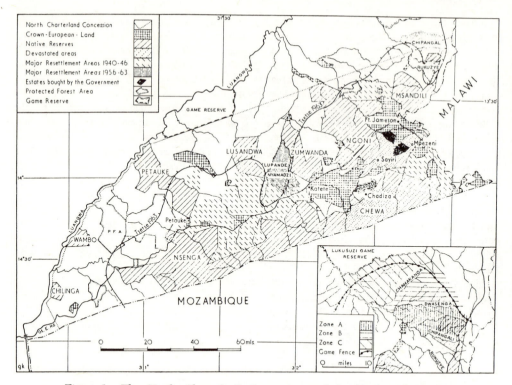

Figure 1.—The North Charterland Concession and (inset) the Chipangali Resettlement Area. Based on the 1:500,000 map of Zambia published by the Survey Department, Lusaka (1962), supplemented by manuscript maps consulted at Petauke and Fort Jameson and by reference to publications cited in the list of references.

The Msandile, Ngoni, Zumwanda, and Chewa Reserves are referred to in the text as the Fort Jameson Reserves; the Lusandwa, Petauke, Wambo, Chilinga, and Nsenga Reserves are referred to as the Petauke Reserves. Some small areas of Crown (European) Land, mostly belonging to mission stations, have been omitted. The key to the main map also applies to the inset.

where such separation facilitated development.

The first European farms were laid out around Fort Jameson, which, for strategic reasons, had been sited in the heart of Ngoniland. This Ngoni core area was heavily populated and by 1903 difficulties of alienating such land led to the appointment of the East Luangwa Land Commission to investigate the situation. The Commission defined an area south-west of Fort Jameson for the sole use of natives and

into which Africans from European estates could be moved; and in 1906 Mpezeni Reserve was demarcated south-east of Fort Jameson for the personal use of the paramount chief and his entourage. Thereafter the matter rested until 1913 when it was reviewed because of the developing tobacco industry. F. V. Worthington[4] then considered that "in view of Clause 40 of the Order in Council (see above) it is necessary first to determine the requirements of the natives and to satisfy them; the balance of the land then becomes available for Land Settlement." This simple argument prevailed and accordingly a survey of the entire Eastern Province was made and 19 reserves were provisionally defined. However, only in Fort Jameson District were serious attempts made to concentrate the African population into these provisional reserves.

None of these early reserves was legally constituted, though within the North Charterland Concession they were acknowledged and accepted by both Europeans and Africans. In order to clarify and crystallize the pattern of land holding within the concession the Colonial Office appointed a Native Reserves Commission shortly after it assumed administrative responsibility for the country in 1924. The Commission recommended the establishment of nine Native Reserves which, in Fort Jameson District at least, represented the first provisional reserves with various additions and extensions.[5] In spite of the North Charterland Exploration Company's protests and the lengthy litigation that followed, the nine reserves were excised from the concession and set apart in perpetuity for the sole and exclusive use and occupation of the natives by the Northern Rhodesia Crown Lands and Native Reserves Order in Council of 1928. The government then pursued a vigorous policy of moving all Africans within the concession into the Native Reserves and this task was virtually completed by 1930. Thus a pattern of land occupation which had been emerging during the previous thirty years was given legal recognition and precise territorial definition, and the North Charterland Concession was divided into three broad classes of land:

1. Land alienated to Europeans   ca.   640 square miles.
2. Native Reserves   ca. 3,466 square miles.
3. Unoccupied and unalienated land   ca. 5,894 square miles.

If the Native Reserves Commission of 1924 had been able to satisfy the terms of Clause 40 of the North-Eastern Rhodesia

Order in Council problems of overcrowding in the Reserves should not have arisen. The Commission, however, "did not have the advantage of expert agricultural advice . . . (and it) underestimated the amount of land necessary for native requirements."[6] It also hoped that the carrying capacity of the Reserves would be greatly increased by an extensive programme of water development and by widespread agricultural education, but neither of these measures could be implemented sufficiently to alter the situation materially. Consequently the Reserves were overcrowded as soon as they were formed; in fact, large parts of them had already been overcrowded for many years. The carrying capacity of the Eastern Province plateau under the African agricultural systems which then prevailed has since been calculated to be 22 persons per square mile.[7] The general extent and degree of overpopulation in the Reserves at the time they were recommended and in 1942 are indicated in Table 1. W. Allen [8] has demonstrated that where land carrying capacity is exceeded "without a compensating change in the system of land usage a cycle of degenerative changes is set in motion which must result in deterioration or destruction of the land." By 1930 the complex process of land degradation could be readily observed in many parts of the Reserves.

The disastrous effects of overpopulation and overstocking in the Reserves attracted the attention of officials from 1929 onwards, and government concern grew throughout the thirties as the severity of the situation increased. At first responsibility for land degradation was placed on the Africans and their "wasteful methods of cultivation," and it was argued that the solution to the apparent shortage of land lay in its better use. Gradually it was realised that agricultural improvement alone could not remedy the

TABLE 1. POPULATION DENSITY IN THE NATIVE RESERVES OF
THE EASTERN PROVINCE IN 1924 and 1942.[9]

Reserve	Area (Square miles)	1924		1942	
		Number	Density	Number	Density
Msandili	264	15,151	57	22,539	85
Ngoni	784	42,961	55	63,561	81
Chewa	756	37,045	49	53,350	70
Zumwanda	177	5,707	32	9,800	55
Fort Jameson Reserves	1,981	100,864	51	149,250	75
Nsenga	960	38,450	40	43,218	45
Lusandwa	172	5,000	29	6,213	36
Petauke	293	5,500	19	6,666	23
Wambo	44	1,050	24	2,308	53
Chilinga	16	500	31	1,263	79
Petauke Reserves	1,485	50,500	34	59,668	40

Note: The figures, particularly those for 1924, are best regarded as estimates. The
first census of the African population of Zambia was taken in 1963, and it revealed a
population 35 per cent in excess of the current official estimates. This would suggest
that the figures in the above table are likely to be understatements of the true
situations in 1924 and 1942.

situation, and that agricultural change was virtually impossible whilst excessive population pressure persisted. Large-scale resettlement, accompanied by the widespread compulsory adoption of basic soil and water conservation measures, and an intensive campaign of agricultural education, appeared to be the most promising means of arresting the destruction of natural resources and giving the villagers a chance to improve their lot. The government therefore accepted the recommendation made by K. G. Bradley and R. H. Fraser [10] in 1938 that the North Charterland Concession should be purchased *en bloc* for the resettlement of the excess population of the Reserves, and negotiations with the North Charterland Exploration Company began in 1940. The company agreed to sell the unalienated land of the concession and the price of £154,000 was fixed by a Court of Arbitration in September 1941. Some alienated lands were purchased at the same time. Thus the opportunity to redistribute the African population was created and once the decision to do so was made the tremendous task was undertaken with commendable alacrity.

Thorough ecological and demographic surveys were made of the Reserves and of the habitable parts of the purchased land.[11] These revealed that there were 98,000 Chewa and Ngoni in excess of the carrying capacity of the Fort Jameson Reserves and that the Petauke Reserves were overpopulated by 35,000 Nsenga and 8,000 Ambo. Unfortunately, the carrying capacity of the purchased land suitable for settlement under traditional systems of land usage was only 78,000. Alternative systems of land use were dependent upon agricultural education which was not immediately available and which, it was thought, could lead to only a slow rate of agricultural improvement. It was therefore decided to resettle the "new areas" according to their carrying capacity under prevailing systems of land use, and they were allocated as follows:

Ngoni and Chewa land for 35,000 people;
Nsenga   land for 35,000 people;
Ambo   land for 8,000 people.

This plan provided full relief to the Reserves in Petauke District, but removed only 36 per cent of the excess population of the Fort Jameson Reserves. By the end of 1946 about 45,000 people had been moved in their village groups from the Reserves to the major resettlement areas (Figure 1) where the siting of villages and the allocation of land was carefully planned and controlled. But not all the land purchased was suitable for major resettlement schemes. The escarpments and hills between the plateau and the Luangwa valley, other areas of difficult topography, areas heavily infested with tsetse fly, and small, irregular-shaped pockets of land, were thrown open to uncontrolled settlement. Throughout the purchased land, however, all villagers were required to accept simple measures of agricultural control and to observe local authority rules and orders designed to conserve natural resources.

Within the Reserves rehabilitation schemes and agricultural extension work helped nature to heal her wounds, but in the most devastated parts of the Ngoni and Chewa Reserves (Figure 1), where excessive overcrowding continued, their effects were negligible. In these areas processes of land degradation were too far advanced to be checked easily. Agricultural improvement was difficult, if not impossible, until congestion had been reduced still further to manageable proportions. A survey of the Ngoni Devastated Area in 1954-55 [12] confirmed that *both* resettlement and agricultural change were necessary to remedy the situation which would only deteriorate with delay. Opportunites for large-scale resettlement were no longer available and the potentialities

of marginal lands had to be examined. Eventually three large areas and several small pockets of land were selected and plans for their development were prepared. Chipangali is one of these areas and is intended to provide relief to the southern parts of the Ngoni Reserve and to facilitate rehabilitation schemes there. Rukuzye, adjacent to Chipangali, is another and provides new land for Chewa people from Msandili Reserve. The third is the Lupande-Nyamadzi region which was planned to take excess population from the Chewa Reserve (Figure 1). The resettlement schemes in these three areas are very similar and have experienced similar problems, and the following account of the Chipangali Resettlement Scheme is, in general terms, representative.

THE CHIPANGALI RESETTLEMENT SCHEME, 1956 TO 1962

Until recently the Chipangali resettlement area was an inhospitable place and remained virtually uninhabited in spite of its proximity to overcrowded parts of Msandili Reserve. It is a well-wooded, undulating plateau region, broken by numerous isolated rocky hills or *kopjes*. The soils, known as sandveld or plateau soils, are generally derived from ancient crystalline rocks, mostly granites, and they are sandy and of low fertility. Relatively rich, red loams derived from metamorphic rocks are found locally and they have a greater agricultural value; unfortunately they are of very limited extent. Other regions of similar soils in the Eastern Province, however, are heavily utilised, and these mediocre soil conditions alone have not made the area unattractive. Inadequate water supplies and tsetse fly have proved more substantial obstacles to settlement. The Chipangali region is part of the upper Rukuzye basin and is crossed by many streams and *dambos* (i.e. shallow, linear depressions which are waterlogged or flooded for part of the year). Unfortunately, prior to any programme of water development, most of these dried up each year by July or August and from then until late November, when the rains break, surface water was almost non-existent. Tsetse fly infestation was very heavy and, partly because of the nearby Lukusuzi Game Reserve, fresh incursions were frequent. These conditions made Chipangali particularly unattractive to cattle-keeping peoples. That difficult country such as this should be considered for resettlement demonstrates the scale of land shortage in the Eastern Province and the urgency of problems of overcrowding in parts of the Reserves.

The Chipangali area was surveyed in December 1955 by the Senior Entomologist of the Department of Tsetse Control who reported that it might be divided into three zones (Figure 1: insert). Zone A, between the Chipangali and Dwasenga streams, was almost fly-free and was suitable for both human settlement and cattle-keeping. Zone B, between the Dwasenga and the Chamakanga streams, was only lightly infested with tsetse fly and was suitable for human occupance and for inoculated cattle during the ploughing season. Zone C, between the Chamakanga and the Lukusuzi Game Reserve, harboured resident tsetse fly and required intensive control measures; it was not suitable for settlement. The Department of Water Affairs investigated the water resources of the area and found that deep wells almost invariably struck water and that the construction of dams and weirs would greatly reduce runoff and much improve the dry-season supply of surface water.

These surveys indicated a greater potential for resettlement than had been envisaged and the Department of Agriculture prepared a plan for the development of the area between 1956 and 1965. It was intended that during this period 36 villages and about 600 farmers comprising a total population of over 7,000 would be moved from the Ngoni Reserve to Chipangali. The villagers were to be settled in Zone B where

their disturbance of the tsetse's habitat would oust the fly and make cattle-keeping possible there within a very short time. Tsetse control measures in Zone C would prevent later incursions of fly from the north and west and, in time, prepare this area also for settlement. The villages would provide an effective barrier between the tsetse infested areas to the north and Zone A where farmers were to be settled and where oxen, on which they depend so much, could be safely introduced immediately. The allocation of Zone A for the use of individuals who wished, through participation in the Peasant Farming Scheme, to abandon traditional village life and take up commercial farming reflected a major change in economic and social policy since the earlier resettlement schemes were implemented. In the postwar period the government has actively sought to develop commercial African farming and to devise ways in which a family may obtain a reasonable living from the land. The Peasant Farming Scheme, started in 1948, has had an important and successful role in the Eastern Province,[13] and it is not surprising that almost half of the land available for settlement at Chipangali should have been set aside for farmers in spite of the relatively low density of population permitted by such settlement.

Early in 1957 work began to prepare Chipangali for its new occupants. Main and secondary roads were constructed, wells were sunk, dams and weirs were built, farm sites were demarcated and a nine-acre plot on each was stumped and made ready for cultivation. A community centre was established and equipped with a school, a dispensary, a welfare hall, a courthouse, two general shops, a grinding mill and a producers' co-operative marketing organisation. The Department of Agriculture and the Department of Game and Tsetse Control built permanent centres in the area and appointed staff to work and reside there. Visits to Chipangali were arranged for headmen and others from the Ngoni Reserve, the resettlement scheme was well publicised within the Reserve, and generous offers of transport and assistance to establish themselves in their new homes were made to those who were willing to move.

It was expected that response to the scheme would be slow at first, but that the transfer of people would gather momentum within two or three years. By July 1958 five villages and eighteen farming families had been settled in Chipangali but, contrary to expectations, resettlement then failed to accelerate and at the end of 1962 only twelve villages and fifty-nine farmers (a total population of about 2,000) had moved into the area. By then £43,000 allocated to the scheme by the Commissioner for Rural Development and considerable sums from other government departments had been spent there, and a further £10,000 was on loan to the Peasant Farmers. Much of this money had financed the infrastructure necessary for development, but installations lay unused, or under-used, because the expected numbers of settlers had not been forthcoming.

This failure can be attributed to a complex of factors, most of which, unfortunately, are intangible and difficult to remedy. The conservatism of the Ngoni is undoubtedly significant and so is their attachment to their home land is spite of its extraordinarily difficult conditions. Chipangali has long been known to them as an area unsuitable for man and beast, and news and rumours of death amongst the cattle of the first settlers strengthened these opinions. Official propaganda on developments and prospects at Chipangali did not overcome the reluctance of most Ngoni to venture into these new lands and, of course, compulsory transfers of people have not been possible. The considerable distance (about 60 miles) between Chipangali and the southern part of the Ngoni Reserve, and the fact that the resettlement area does not form part of the Ngoni tribal area, but lies in a formerly disputed frontier zone, have also contributed to the slow and disappointing rate of resettlement. Movement to

Chipangali would sever contacts with one's relatives and society, and established tribal authorities feared that they might lose their following if the scheme were successful. They have therefore been reluctant to persuade their people to move whilst ostensibly supporting the government's plans. To try to reduce such fears Chipangali has been gazetted as part of Chief Sayiri's Area, and this may encourage his people in particular to transfer their residence. And, finally, the tantalising prospects of resettlement on European estates adjacent to the Ngoni Reserve (Figure 1) may have increased reluctance to move sixty miles into a strange land.

Partly because the large numbers of settlers expected were not forthcoming, the Chipangali Resettlement Area has suffered severely from fresh incursions of tsetse fly. There may be a general upsurge in the fly population along the whole fly-front in the Eastern Province; certainly other areas have also experienced much trouble in recent years. It is, however, quite probable that close village settlement throughout Zone B would have provided an effective barrier to any tsetse invasion, whereas the few and scattered settlements and the increased movements of people and cattle may well have facilitated, if not caused, the encroachments. Whatever the causes, by 1962 Zone B had become heavily infested and even Zone A harboured resident fly. Cattle losses were severe, and it was only by prophylactic treatment that the cattle population could be maintained. Under these circumstances it was impossible to continue with the original scheme and Chipangali had to be replanned.

The success of the Chipangali resettlement scheme depends very much on the campaign against the tsetse fly. The use of prophylactic drugs, such as Prothidium, is expensive, and there is a very real danger that with their long continued use resistant strains of trypanosome will develop. If this were to happen a most valuable weapon for use on crucial occasions on the fly-front would be lost. It is therefore more practical at present to eliminate trypanosomiasis by the eradication of the carrier than by control of the actual disease organism in cattle. And it is easier to oust the fly by disturbing its eco-system than by direct means. To this end a dual policy has been adopted which consists of a major offensive to establish a forward line, and a strategic withdrawal of development to consolidate the position in the south-east and prepare for effective expansion of settlement later. The tsetse fly depends entirely on blood, and the offensive operation is directed against its food supply. The upper Rukuzye basin is being enclosed by a seven-feet high game fence (Figure 1: inset) which should prevent all large game moving from the north and west into the Chipangali and Rukuzye resettlement areas. South of this fence all game are being systematically exterminated. These measures should greatly reduce the food supply of the tsetse and, in fact, they could be so effective as to reduce the fly population to negligible proportions. Meanwhile development north of the Dwasenga stream has been halted, and Zone A is being cleared of tsetse fly and closely settled to prevent further incursions.

The anti-tsetse measures consist largely of selective clearing and pruning to remove or modify dense vegetation which provides the fly with the essential conditions of humidity, shade and shelter during the dry season. Without these conditions the fly is in danger of an untimely end through dessication. Such conditions are most common in woodlands along dambo fringes and in riverine zones, and the removal of all small trees and shrubs and the pruning of large trees to a height of eight feet in these areas can open the woodlands sufficiently to make them unsuitable for the fly. Spraying the vegetation with residual insecticides during the dry season reinforces the effects of bush clearing.

Plans for resettlement and development clearly must be reconciled with plans for tsetse control, and in 1962 it was decided to restrict work to Zone A. A revised scheme was therefore prepared, and the *Regional Plan for the South-East Chipangali Area,* which envisages an expenditure of about £38,000, was approved in 1963. There had already been considerable development in this area and it contained all the 59 occupied farms and three of the twelve villages in the whole Chipangali area. Under the original plan most of this area was reserved for farmers, but both villagers and farmers are now being encouraged to move in, though it is intended to keep the villages and farms separate as far as is possible. Most vacant land has been allocated for village settlement which is most efficient in ousting the tsetse. The main block of farms occupies the centre of the region, and villages are to be arranged around them. Some farms have been cleared, and one occupied, in the extreme south-east corner, but settlement in this part will be determined by the relative numbers of villages and farmers wishing to move to Chipangali, and an alternative plan for the development of village gardens there has been prepared. The pattern and density of settlement proposed (Figure 2) will admit a population of more than 2,000 persons, and if this is achieved there should be little difficulty in keeping this area free of tsetse fly. The frontier of settlement then can be pushed forward into Zone B where nine villages now remain as outposts.

The pattern of land use proposed for Chipangali is a model of conservation planning, and seeks to make optimum use of the natural resources whilst ensuring that they are preserved for posterity. It is adapted, as far as possible, to present social and economic practices but makes generous allowance for future developments. The network of watershed roads and details of the water conservation and supply measures (most of which already exist) are shown in Figure 2, and the character of the community centre has already been described; further discussion will therefore be restricted to productive uses of the land.

Four main categories of land, each with a distinctive use, can be recognized:

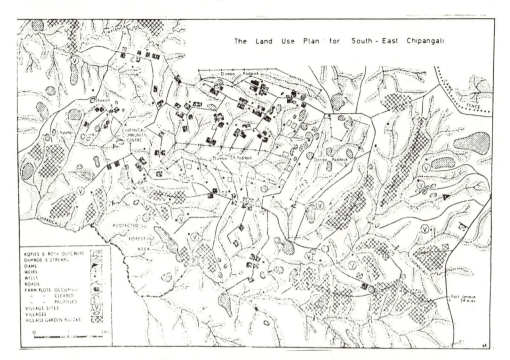

The Land Use Plan for South - East Chipangali

Figure 2.—The land use plan for South-East Chipangali. Based cn the manuscript plan made available by the Department of Agriculture, Fort Jameson.

1. Kopje and rock outcrops—amenity value only;
2. Plateau, with relatively poor soils—wet season grazing; pole and fuel supply area;
3. Plateau, with relatively good soils—arable land;
4. Dambo and dambo fringe—dry season grazing.

The areas of the plateau surface where poorer soils predominate are for communal grazing and for the collection of poles and fuel. Cutting of trees on steep slopes and along stream and dambo margins (except for tsetse control purposes), however, is prohibited by local authority rules in order to restrict soil erosion. The villages are sited in these grazing areas which, as far as is possible, are clearly separated from the garden blocks in order to minimise herding problems. The garden blocks and the farms are in areas where relatively good soils predominate. And the dambo and dambo fringes provide dry-season grazing. It is, however, a common practice to graze dambos indiscriminately for the greater part of the year, and three large dambo areas are being fenced to demonstrate the value of controlled grazing. The means of control and allocation of grazing within these dambo paddocks has not been laid down, and it is hoped that the residents at Chipangali will form their own organisations to manage such affairs. Any such organisations would, of course, receive the benefit of professional advice. An area of about 2,000 acres enclosed by the Chipangali and Chamatunda streams and a line of kopjes is also being set aside from general usage and is scheduled as a Protected Forest Area. When the need arises this area will supply the timber requirements of the region and will be replanted as necessary in order to maintain a regular supply.

Incoming villagers are encouraged to improve their agriculture, and the allocation and lay-out of the village gardens are designed to facilitate change (Figure 3). Each household is allocated a strip of land extending from a watershed road to the edge of a dambo. Each strip is approximately ten acres, and is separated from its neighbours by a footpath or cart track on an uncultivated section five yards wide. Soil erosion is checked by contour banks at a vertical interval of about thirty inches and by cultivation on ridges parallel to them. These measures are compulsory under local authority rules, and each cultivator is responsible for their construction on his land. Each block of gardens is also protected by windbreaks. To assist incoming cultivators the Department of Agriculture clears two acres in each strip adjacent to the road, and supplies fertilisers (sulphate of ammonia) for the first year's crops. Thereafter progress on each holding depends upon the initiative and energy of the household concerned. The holdings can be cultivated by hoe or by plough, and they are large enough to allow either subsistence production by traditional methods or the develop-

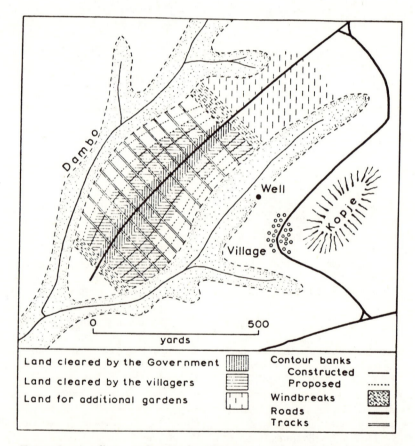

Figure 3.—A village garden block. This plan was prepared by the author from information and illustrations supplied by the Department of Agriculture, Fort Jameson; it does not represent any actual situation.

ment of a commercial small-holding. The Department of Agriculture's extension staff encourage the latter, and they teach improved planting techniques, principles of mixed husbandry, the use and value of fertilisers and how to integrate cash crops, such as Burley tobacco, into a rotation which will meet not only subsistence requirements but provide a surplus (mostly of groundnuts and tobacco) for sale. It is hoped that eventually a commercial livestock industry will also develop.

Progressive individuals, who are willing to leave their village community and wish to become full-time commercial farmers, are encouraged to take a Peasant Farm. On each farm nine acres of good arable land are cleared prior to the farmer's occupation, and on taking the farm he is supplied with all basic farm equipment, with oxen unless he already possesses his own, and with seed and fertilisers for the first year's sowing. If he proves to be a promising farmer a further six acres of arable land are cleared for him the following year; all arable land on the farms must, of course, be protected by graded contour banks. The costs of all the initial clearing and of the goods supplied are debited to the farmer, and most Peasant Farmers at Chipangali began their careers with debts of about £200 repayable over a ten year period. Each Peasant Farmer signs an agreement whereby he is required to reside on and to cultivate his farm and to follow principles of land conservation and good husbandry as laid down by the local staff of the Agricultural Department; persistent failure to respect these terms can lead to eviction. The Agricultural Department's extension staff provide general supervision and advice, and various bonuses and subsidies have been paid to encourage good farming.

The holdings are distributed (Figure 2) so as to permit each to develop from the original nine or fifteen-acre plot into a self-contained farm of 100 to 150 acres. Development again depends upon the individual, and in 1963 several farmers already had

more than thirty acres under the plough, and would soon be able to afford to enclose their farm units and to manage the larger areas efficiently. Three farmers were discussing with the local Agricultural Officer how they should lay out their farms. A typical farm plan is shown in Figure 4. Whilst present practices prevail, each farm will consist of a large arable block on the best soils within the holding, dry and wet season grazing paddocks where the natural grazing will be improved by selective clearing and controlled stocking, a fruit and vegetable plot which may be irrigated, a homestead paddock for general purposes, and a wood and fuel lot on any rough land that falls within the farm boundary. It is hoped that ley-farming will be practicable on the arable land, and the sown grasses will be grazed between two movable fences used to subdivide the block. The capital costs of implementing such a farm plan, notably the costs of fencing and road building, receive a 50 per cent subsidy which averages about £200 per farm; this is a considerable incentive for an able man to prove himself worthy of such a farm by developing his original plots. But farming at Chipangali is not easy, and relatively few farmers managed to make satisfactory incomes from groundnuts and Turkish tobacco which were the main cash crops until recently. Now Burley tobacco has largely replaced Turkish, and has proved a more satisfactory and profitable crop, and the prospects of a commercial livestock industry also hold promise for the future. There is, indeed, reason to believe that a thriving agricultural community, both on the farms and in the villages, can emerge at Chipangali where a few years ago the tsetse fly held sway. The future depends largely upon the people.

Chipangali has benefited from experience gained in rural land use planning and the development of farming in other parts of Zambia during the past fifteen years. The area, however, still faces major agricultural problems which are found throughout the

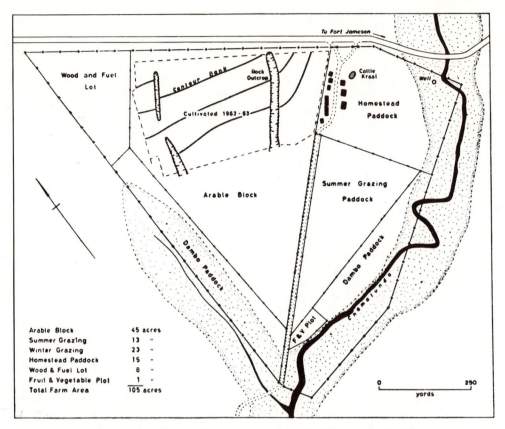

Figure 4.—A typical farm plan. Based on an actual farm plan (Chipangali Farm No. 25) made available by the Department of Agriculture, Fort Jameson.

territory and which deserve early attention. In particular there is an urgent need for teaching farm management, and labour management in particular. Agricultural extension work at present is almost limited to technical aspects of conservation and production; this is insufficient for most farmers who lack the experience and business acumen to become efficient without further vocational training. Present levels of productivity could provide a reasonable living for a farmer and his family and provide some wage employment for others, if the farms were managed efficiently. And the emergence of a prosperous farming community could be accelerated by teaching

farm management, rather than relying entirely upon the farmers learning slowly from their own, often bitter, experience. There is also need for a legally recognised and socially acceptable system of land tenure which is compatible with capitalised commercial farming; at present all land is held under customary laws of land tenure. This topic has received much attention in Zambia and it seems likely that some rational system will emerge in the near future. The allocation of land at Chipangali, both on the farms and in the villages, will facilitate the application of any such system because each family's rights are already quite well defined.

The success of the Regional Plan for the south-east, and the future of the larger Chipangali resettlement area, depend very much upon the willingness of Ngoni to move into the region and on the continued supply of funds for development there. The position is likely to be complicated as unoccupied Crown (European) Land is made available for resettlement and development. During 1963 a block of vacant European farms near Chadiza was purchased by individual agreements with their owners, and this area (Nzadzu) is now being developed as an alternative resettlement scheme for people from the southern parts of the Chewa Reserve (Figure 1). Nzadzu has, in fact, assumed priority over the Lupande-Nyamadzi resettlement area which has encountered difficulties similar to those at Chipangali.

It is quite probable that all unused Crown Land will be acquired by the government, and plans for its optimum use have been discussed already. It is understandable that the Ngoni and others are reluctant to move to distant areas such as Chipangali while there is hope that they may obtain better lands nearer their present homes. It is also reasonable that, when opportunity arises, the government should give priority to development of the less difficult and more promising lands. But Crown Land is limited; there are approximately 400,000 acres of farmland alienated to Europeans in the Eastern Province. According to the current estimates of the total land required for resettlement, this area, though of very great benefit, could not accommodate all of the excess population of the still overcrowded Ngoni and Chewa Reserves. There will remain a need for Chipangali and similar areas. To ensure that good use is made of the very considerable sums already invested in that area, there must be no withdrawal, nor even a temporary delay, of development of Chipangali before it is firmly established as a settled area with a contented and prosperous population.

NOTES

[1] Secretary of State for the Colonies, *Despatch No. 29, 1947.*

[2] In Zambia the title *Regional Plan* is given to the detailed schemes of land use prepared for various areas by the Department of Agriculture.

[3] Worthington, F. V. *Report on Proposed Native Reserves.* Mss. in the Library of the Zambia Archives, 1913.

[4] *Ibid.*

[5] Lane-Poole, E. H. *The Human Geography of the East Luangwa Province.* Mss. in the Library of the Rhodes-Livingstone Institute, 1932.

[6] Eccles, L. W. G. (Chairman). *Report of the Land Commission on the North Charterland Concession.* Mss. in the Library of the Zambia Archives, 1942.

[7] Allan, W. African Land Usage. *Rhodes-Livingstone Journal,* 1945, III, pp. 13–20.

[8] Allan, W. *Studies in African Land Usage in Northern Rhodesia.* Rhodes-Livingstone Paper 15. Oxford University Press for Rhodes-Livingstone Institute, 1949.

[9] Eccles, L. W. G. *Op. cit.,* 1942.

[10] Bradley, K. G. and Fraser, R. H. *A Report on the Native Reserves of Fort Jameson District.* Mss (SEC/AG/65) in the Zambia Archives, 1938.

[11] Allan, W. *Op. cit.,* 1949.

[12] Priestley, M. J. S. W. and Greening, P. *Ngoni Land Utilization Survey 1954–55.* Government Printer, Lusaka, 1956.

[13] Coster, R. N. *Peasant Farming in the Petauke and Katete Areas of the Eastern Province of Northern Rhodesia.* Agricultural Bulletin No. 15. Government Printer, Lusaka, 1958.

OTHER IMPORTANT REFERENCES

Fraser, R. H. Land Settlement in the Eastern Province of Northern Rhodesia. *Rhodes-Livingstone Journal,* 1945, III, pp. 45–49.

Green, R. N. and Verboom, W. C. *Regional Plan for the South-East Chipangali Area.* (Roneoed) Department of Agriculture, Fort Jameson, 1963.

Kay, G. *Changing Patterns of Settlement and Land Use in the Eastern Province of Northern Rhodesia.* Occasional Papers in Geography No. 2. Department of Geography, University of Hull, 1965.

VI. POPULATION-LAND RELATIONSHIPS: EVALUATION

Attempts to arrive at some measure of the relationships between people and land, to provide a quantitative index of adjustment or of maladjustment, are fraught with great difficulties. The simplest and most frequently used measure is population density, or the number of people per unit of area of land. It is a crude measure and is useful only in the most general terms. Low population density does not necessarily indicate satisfactory population-land relationships, nor vice versa. Crude density need not be discarded as worthless; at the same time it must be treated with great caution.

It is possible to refine the figures by determining whether occupied land is cultivable or cultivated; still, these indicators may be far from accurate. Land has many complex qualities, both actual and potential, and the use made of them will depend on the equally complex political, social, technical, and economic qualities of its inhabitants. A further complication is that few groups in the world are confined solely to their land. People in Africa south of the Sahara have become increasingly involved in an ever-widening network of economic relationships (Hodder, 1965). It can almost be said that subsistence production in the strict sense no longer exists; most people are engaged to some degree in processes of exchange (Bohannan and Dalton, 1962.)

To measure all of the variables in these situations is virtually impossible, even with the aid of sophisticated measures such as those derived from work in the Congo (Beguin, 1964; Henshall, 1967). Even if formulas were available, it would be difficult to compare the expectations of different groups regarding resources, for example. The examples of evaluating population-land relationships included here are not complex, but they do illustrate realistic attempts to solve particular problems.

This paper and the one following are concerned with the carrying capacity of land under indigenous agricultural systems. Both papers indicate levels which, if exceeded, will result in deterioration of the environment as expressed in falling levels of production. The virtue of the method devised by Hunter for Ghana is that it depends on available census data and might therefore be applied under comparable conditions in other parts of Africa. The results may be regarded not so much as ends in themselves, but rather as means of identifying areas where more specific and detailed work can be undertaken.

22. Ascertaining Population Carrying Capacity under Traditional Systems of Agriculture in Developing Countries

NOTE ON A METHOD EMPLOYED IN GHANA

JOHN M. HUNTER

One of the most interesting problems in the human geography of developing countries is how to estimate the carrying capacity of land under traditional agricultural systems. For any given natural vegetation zone occupied by a given ethnic group, or several ethnic groups with farming practices in common, what is the critical population density at which emigration is likely to commence? At what stage, and by what criteria, other than field observations of soil exhaustion and human malnutrition, may we judge a rural area to be overpopulated? At what stage, and to what extent, will pressure on the land act as a determinant of population growth?

The method outlined below is not offered as a substitute for field investigation, but it does seem to give certain broad indications which are of value when taken into consideration with other evidence. The data used here are drawn from Ghana. Possibly other tropical areas, where suitable data are available, could be examined in a similar way. Essentially the method compares population density with migration tendencies. This can be effected spatially by maps (Fig. 1) and graphically by scatter diagram (Fig. 2).

At the time of its last census, in 1960, Ghana was divided into 69 local council areas; these covered the whole extent of the country's 92,100 square miles, and are used here as conveniently sized units for purposes of calculation and mapping. Migration tendencies, as such, could not be recorded in the census returns, but "place of birth" data were collected and classified as follows: born in (1) this locality, i.e., locality of enumeration, (2) another locality in the same administrative region, (3) another administrative region, and (4) abroad (i) in an African country or (ii) elsewhere. Such birthplace data, however, are of lim-

From *The Professional Geographer*, *18*, 1966, pp. 151–154.
Reprinted by permission.

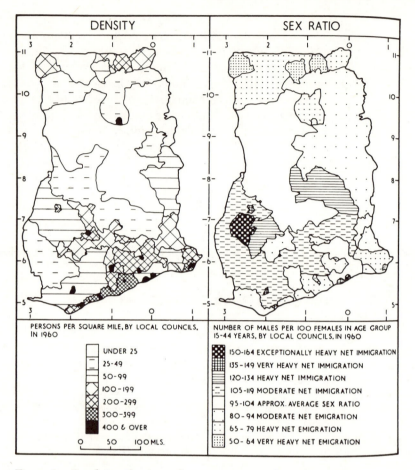

Figure 1.—Population density and sex ratio compared in Ghana, 1960.

ited geographical value because of the large size of the administrative regions; for example the Northern Region covers 37,723 square miles and the Western Region 13,051. On the other hand, sex ratio which can be calculated for each local council, gives a much finer indication of migration tendencies, especially when applied to the most active and mobile section of the population. The age-group of 15 to 44 years has been selected for the calculation of sex ratio because it contains the largest proportion of economically active persons, particularly those most likely to move in response to economic incentives. Normally males mi-

grate, perhaps temporarily and seasonally at first, and later, permanently, and only after some time do the womenfolk follow, if at all. Hence, an area with a high rate of economic growth, into which population is migrating, will have a large number of males in relation to females, whereas a declining area, or an area with such a low rate of economic growth that population is moving out in the search for employment, will have fewer males than females.

According to the 1960 census the average sex ratio in Ghana in the 15–44 age group was 98, ranging from 160 males per 100 females in the new port of Tema to 59

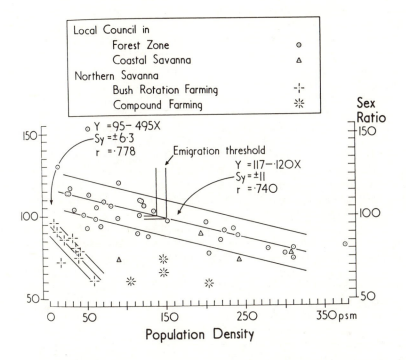

Figure 2.—Scatter diagram with regressions of sex ratio over population density, by local councils within major vegetational regions of Ghana, 1960.

males per 100 females in Frafra in the northern savanna. Clearly these are areas of exceptionally heavy net immigration and emigration, respectively. The key to Fig. 1 (part ii) suggests an eight-point scale of migration tendencies which has been used elsewhere in an analysis of population growth in Ghana.[1] Briefly, net emigration, or net immigration, results from the push and pull interaction of two sets of forces: positive inducements to migrate into economically attractive areas, such as the towns and cocoa farms of the southern forest zone on the one hand, and on the other, austerity and hardship, often due to overpopulation, in source areas of emigration.

When sex ratio and population density are compared statistically for the 69 local councils, no apparent correlation obtains.

Much more meaningful is a comparison within major vegetational zones. Apart from a relatively narrow coastal strip of savanna, Ghana may be divided very roughly along line of latitude 8°30′ N. into a northern savanna zone and a southern forest zone. If one excludes from the total number of local councils all urbanized councils (*i.e.*, those with 50 per cent or more of the total population enumerated in localities of 5,000 population or over), and non-urbanized councils where the sex ratio has been raised by an influx of male migrants for gold and diamond mining, one is left with "rural" councils which may be subdivided according to natural vegetation into (1) southern forest zone, (2) coastal savanna and (3) northern savanna. The latter may be divided further into (a) "bush rotation farming" councils and (b) "compound, *i.e.*, fixed farming" councils (Fig. 2).[2] Attention is here focused on the two regressions of Fig. 2: that for the northern bush rotation savanna and that for the southern forest zone.

In northern savanna areas of bush rotation farming, the coefficient of correlation between sex ratio and population density is r=0.778; whilst in the forest it is r= 0.740. Sex ratios are much higher in the forest than the savanna (Fig. 2, Y=117, cf. Y=95). In addition, the absorptive capacity of the forest, measured in terms of the regression coefficient, is much greater than that of the savanna (Fig. 2, 0.120, cf. 0.495).

The northern savanna areas start off with lower sex ratios and regress more sharply than the forest, with an increase in population density. In the circumstances, it is difficult to say what the carrying capacity of the northern savanna is, under present agricultural practices of bush rotation. If the sex ratio evidence is acceptable as an indication of migration trends, then the absorptive capacity is nil, since initial sex ratios are below 100, and diminish rapidly with mounting population pressure. This conclusion accords with field observations, and with the fact that net emigration has obtained for many decades in these areas

which have served as a labor reservoir for the southern forests. One must conclude that only a radical break-through in agricultural technique will remedy the situation.

In the forest, however, a firmer idea of the carrying capacity of the land can be obtained. The 34 forest councils, plotted in Figure 2, form a clear negative linear regression with a coefficient of correlation of r=0.740. If it is assumed that a sex ratio of 98 (the Ghana average) or 100 indicates the threshold between net emigration and net immigration, then, in the forest, under present agricultural systems, a population density of 140–152 per square mile would seem to be critical. Below this density there is net immigration, above it, net emigration. Here again it should be noted that changes in agricultural technique could affect the balance.

NOTES

[1] Hunter, J. M., "Regional patterns of population growth in Ghana," in J. B. Whittow and P. D. Wood (*eds.*), *Essays in Geography for Austin Miller,* University of Reading, Reading, 1965, pp. 272–90.

[2] The high population densities of the compound system form a special case now under investigation by the writer.

The significant part of this paper is its method for calculating the carrying capacity of land. The elements in Allan's formula are quite basic and reasonably easy to quantify, and the formula itself is simple to understand and to apply; nonetheless, the data required for it are not readily available for many areas of Africa (Allan, 1965). Further, the formula is most satisfactorily applied in a closed system of subsistence agriculture. Its value is much reduced when applied to systems that involve elements such as the production of cash crops or systems in which part of the population derives returns from employment other than agriculture.

23. *How Much Land Does A Man Require?*

W. ALLAN

Those who know their Tolstoy will recognize the origin of the title. Those who do not might profit by reading the story of Pakhom and the Devil.

In the study of African agriculture the question of how much land a man requires is one of paramount importance. It must be obvious that any area of land will support in perpetuity only a limited number of people. An absolute limit is imposed by soil and climatic factors in so far as these are beyond human control, and a practical limit is set by the way in which the land is used.

If this practical limit of population is exceeded, without a compensating change in the system of land usage, then a cycle of degenerative changes is set in motion which must result in deterioration or destruction of the land and ultimately in hunger and reduction of the population. The term "erosion," in its widest sense, is sometimes used for this cycle of destruction, but the word as it is generally understood has too limited a connotation to describe a process which results in radical changes in the whole character of the land; loss of mineral plant foods, oxidation and disappearance of organic matter, breakdown of soil structure, degeneration of vegetation; and the setting up of a new train of land and water relationships. The whole complex process of destruction is best referred to as *land degradation*.

For every area of land to which a given system of land usage is applied, there is a population limit which cannot be exceeded without setting in motion the process of land degradation. The limit may be termed the *critical population* or *carrying capacity* for that system of land usage. Any estimate of land carrying capacity is, of course, meaningless unless the area to which the calculation applies and the system of land

usage upon which it is based, are clearly defined.

This conception of land carrying capacity, and the possibility of its numerical expression, allows of a much more precise approach to the problems of African agriculture and land requirements. In the past both precision of approach and adequate knowledge have often been noticeably lacking. Consequently there has arisen a tendency to regard all African systems as wasteful and destructive, to be ignored, discarded and replaced by wholly alien and often impracticable methods of "improved agriculture"; a tendency which Gillman dismisses in the trenchant sentence, "the scope and nature of land and population problems change from place to place and can therefore not be solved by generalized methods elevated into bogus panaceas." [1] Estimates of land requirements have in the past been even more vague than the "panaceas" for improvement. In Northern Rhodesia and elsewhere Native reserves have been demarcated on a very insufficient knowledge of traditional land requirements, and in many cases the inadequacy of the land allowances has demonstrated itself within a remarkably short space of time.

The calculation of approximate carrying capacities for traditional African systems presents no insuperable difficulty, but it does require a close study and clear knowledge both of the land and the systems employed on it. Trapnell's admirable work, compiled and collected in the Reports of the Ecological Survey,[2] gives a clear picture of the traditional systems of Northern Rhodesia in relation to their environments and to the changing conditions of the present day. These systems are remarkable for their number and variety and, in some instances, for their complexity and admirable adaptation to environmental requirements.

From *Rhodes-Livingstone Papers*, No. 15, 1949, pp. 1–23. Reprinted by permission of the Institute for Social Research, University of Zambia.

They may, however, for present purposes, be treated as falling into two main groups: *Chitemene Systems* and *Soil Selection Systems.*

The chitemene systems are practised by certain forest tribes who rely for fertility on the ash of the trees which they lop or fell to make their gardens. Brushwood is generally hauled from an area much greater than that cultivated in order to obtain the necessary supply of ash. There is much variation within the chitemene group, from the primitive "small circle" method described in one of the following reports to complex and advanced systems practised by certain of the northern tribes. In all of these systems little or no selection is practised other than the choice of woodland convenient for felling and, in the case of the pure systems, the calculation of carrying capacity is relatively simple. The data required are: the area of available woodland, excluding stony and waterlogged tracts, the acreage of woodland used annually per unit of population and the period of time necessary for woodland regeneration.

In the soil selection methods of agriculture definite use is made of trees and grasses and of soil texture and colour as indicators of fertility. Indicators of both good and bad soils are recognized. The crops for which a particular vegetation-soil type is suitable, the period for which it can be worked and the phase in the succession at which it can be returned to for further cultivation, are known with a considerable degree of precision. Calculation of land carrying capacities for such systems is a more difficult matter.

The first requirement is, obviously, a rapid method of recognizing and mapping the vegetation-soil types. It is also necessary to know the traditional agricultural usage for each type; the duration of cultivation and subsequent rest; and to have an accurate numerical estimate of the acreage under cultivation at any one time for each unit of population. Another factor which must be known is the proportion of land in each vegetation-soil type which can be used for cultivation of the staple crops under the traditional system of land usage.

VEGETATION: SOIL UNITS

The ecological method of vegetation-soil classification developed by Trapnell and described in the Reports of the Ecological Survey [2] provides an excellent method of rapid mapping, where the original characteristics of the land have not been destroyed or obscured by prolonged over-population and over-cultivation. The units employed in this classification are distinguished by means both of vegetation and soil characteristics, and in some cases, contour and topography. They form part of a general classification of the soils of the Territory, which has been worked out over the last twelve years, and they are in general accordance with the classification used by Milne in compiling the East African Soil Map.

In estimating the carrying capacity of an area the first step is to determine and clearly define suitable vegetation-soil units for the area. As an example, the units which have been used in surveying large areas on the Copperbelt and in Ndola District are summarized:

Red earths

(a) Woodlands of *Brachystegia Hockii* and *B. longifolia* with many evergreens in the understorey; on deep brownish red to lighter clay-loams and loams.

(b) Woodlands of *B. floribunda, Isoberlinia tomentosa* and *I. paniculata;* on bright red to orange-red clay-loams.

Chipya Forest Types. High forest, commonly including *B. Hockii, I. tomentosa, Erythrophloeum africanum* and *Entandophragma,* with a luxuriant understorey of evergreens; on

(a) grey humic soils, varying marginally to more brownish or orange-toned sandy loams and loams; or

(b) soils of the Red Earth class (strong chocolate-red or brownish-red loams).

Copperbelt Loams and Sandy Loams. Woodlands of *I. paniculata, B. floribunda, B. longifolia* and *B. flagristipulata,* with much *B. floribunda* locally; on

(a) light-colored sandy soils, usually buff-coloured;

(b) loams of variable orange colouring; or

(c) yellow clay soils.

Pallid Sandy Soils. I. paniculata, B. longifolia, I. tomentosa, Uapaca kirkiana, etc., with poor understorey; on pure white to pale grey or pale buff sandy soils.

Stronger Sandy Soils. B. longifolia and *B. Hockii* with less *I. paniculata* and many evergreens in the understorey (including small *Marquesia*); on light buff to more orange-toned sandy soils.

Museshe Type. Much *Marquesia macroura* (museshe) with *B. Hockii, B. longifolia,* etc., and many evergreens in the understorey; on pale buff to more pinkish and orange-toned sandy loams and loams.

Musaka Type. Brachystegia utilis (musaka) pure or with some *B. longifolia, I. tomentosa, I. paniculata,* etc., and occasional evergreens; on light coloured, generally buff, sandy loams, usually shallow or with gravel near surface.

Musuku Museshe Type. Uapaca kirkiana (musuku), *U. nitida,* etc., forming scrub-woodland with spaced *M. macroura, B. Hockii,* etc., on shallow gravelly soils.

Sheet-Ironstone (Laterite) Types. Brachystegia flagristipulata with *I. paniculata, U. kirkiana,* etc., and sometimes a little *B. floribunda;* on soils of any colour, with many blocks, sheets or pellets of ironstone on the surface or immediately below it.

Dambo grassland and hill types are also distinguished. In field recording, the units are sometimes further sub-divided into variants regarded as typical of the type, poorer than the general run of the type (indicated by a negative sign) or better than the general run of the type (indicated by a positive sign), and the information obtained by recording the type number and sign is supplemented by general notes intended to aid in the construction of the final map.

MAPPING OF VEGETATION-SOIL TYPES

The first step in making a survey of an area, was to collect all existing maps and topographic information from which to compile a base map. In some areas, where prospecting surveys had been carried out by mining companies, very accurate base maps were available; in others, existing topographic information was so scanty and inaccurate as to be practically valueless. The base map was used in planning the system of traverses to be employed in the reconnaissance survey. Most recording work had to be done on foot with carriers, over trackless and uninhabited country, and it was therefore necessary to plan the work in relation to known or possible water supplies and points accessible to motor transport, reducing as far as possible the amount of food and water which the carriers must transport for their own use.

The traverse system usually consisted simply of a base line from which parallel traverse lines were laid off. Distance between the parallel traverse lines varied from half a mile to two (and occasionally three) miles, according to the degree of accuracy required, the time available, the nature of the country and the distribution of water supplies. In all the later work in the Western Province a grid system was used, with east to west traverse lines not more than one mile apart and north-south traverse line two miles apart (Fig. 1).

All measurements were made by means of liquid prismatic compasses and cyclometer wheels (checked as frequently as possible) and additional strikers were usually attached to cyclometer wheels to allow of finer measurements. The base-line was demarcated and the starting points of traverses beaconed by an Agricultural Officer. Trained African staff were employed to demarcate the traverse lines, by means of a simple blaze through woodland, felled bushes in scrub-bush area, and lines of poles crossing grassland. Numbered beacons were erected at the beginning and end of each traverse and at intervals of two miles along the traverse lines, to give fixed points of reference. In the case of the grid system these served as a check on the accuracy of the work. Each beacon consisted of a small tree trunk, the bark removed at the top, supported by a tripod or forked branches, with a metal plate bearing the number attached to the central post.

Actual recording along the base and traverse lines was done by European staff,[*] the line records being supplemented by lateral observations wherever possible and offset traverses when necessary. Some types can readily be distinguished at considerable distances; for example, the projecting crowns of the giant *Entandophragma* indicate Chipya forest types, while the characteristic colour of the spring flush of *B. floribunda* and other *Brachystegia*, and differences in the leaf shade and habit at other times of year, are distinguished at distances of a mile or more.

After some practice, recording becomes almost automatic and the work is wearisome in the extreme and very trying both for European and African staff. The occasional encounter with elephant, buffalo and lion adds a mild relief, but this is offset by an accumulation of less interesting annoyances; the apparently endless monotony of empty, lifeless, waterless woodland; thorn, bamboo thicket and ten-foot grass; swamp and reed beds; biting insects, snakes, veld sores and the intolerable itch caused by seed ticks and buffalo beans. Aerial photography is an extremely valuable auxiliary to ground survey, especially in areas of varied vegetation, but it adds greatly to the cost. The total cost of ground mapping using the 1×2

mile grid, was about 12s. per square mile. Before the War vertical aerial photography cost 20s. per square mile, exclusive of the cost of supplementary ground work and preparation of maps, but the method has the decisive advantages of speed, greater accuracy of detail and saving on staff.

The field data obtained from the traverses and supplementary observations were plotted on a scale of 1:50,000 and final maps, with the types shown in colour, were usually compiled on a scale of 1:125,000. The areas of each type were then computed from the maps by planimeter measurements.

The type of map obtained by this method, and the main traverses on which it was based, are illustrated by Fig. 1, a reproduction in black and white of a portion of the area surveyed in Ndola District as a preliminary to the movement of people from the congested areas on the margin of the Copperbelt.

ACREAGE CULTIVATED IN RELATION TO POPULATION

The estimation of this factor is also a matter of tedious field sampling, but the unravelling of family relationships which it entails adds a good deal of human interest and requires at least a foundation of sociological knowledge. The data have usually been collected in the course of tours and traverses, by picking individuals at random, ascertaining the relationships of the family to which the individual belongs, and measuring all the land in cultivation by the family group at the time of sampling. African gardens are almost invariable very irregular in shape, and areas were measured by making a detailed traverse with compass and chain round the perimeter of each section of the garden, plotting the traverse on squared paper and estimating the area from the diagram by a count of squares or by planimeter measurement. The process of individual sampling was repeated (and sometimes supplemented by complete surveys of village lands) to give a sufficient number of samples for a satisfactory esti-

[*] African staff can readily be trained to make simple line traverse but they proved to be slow, lacking in self-confidence and in ability to interpret their observations or to make sufficiently full and accurate notes.

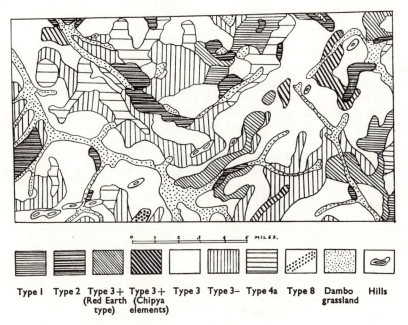

Figure 1a.—Vegetation-soil types.

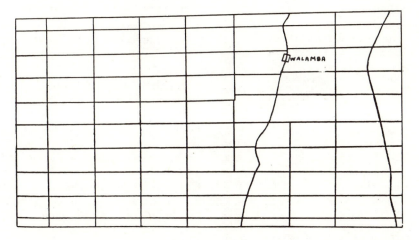

Figure 1b.—Main traverse lines on which the map was based. In this section the railway line was used as a base line and the motor road to the east of it as a north-south traverse line.

mate, or at least as many samples as the available time would allow.

From this method of sampling there has arisen the conception of the *garden family*. This is a measure of the number of people obtaining their food supply from a family land holding, and it is estimated by allowing one unit for each person, irrespective of age, obtaining the whole of his or her food supply from the holding, and an appropriate fraction for each person obtaining part of his or her supply. The following example for the family of a Tonga headman (in 1944) will serve to illustrate the

Nineteen people were wholly dependent for their food and nine were partly dependent, on this set of gardens during 1944. The "garden family" estimate is 21.83 units and the total acreage of staple crops (maize and kaffir corn) grown in the 1943–4 season was 27.37 acres. For this sample the estimate of area of staple crops per head of population is, therefore, 1.25 acres.

Figures obtained in this way for the Lamba of Mushiri's area are summarized in the Table below. They include:

A. Random samples of which details are

Vegetation soil-type	Area Measured (acres)		Cultivable percentage	
	Total	Cultivable	Range %	Mean%
Th	11,090	3,500		31.8
Th/Tr	109,450	34,580	27–32	31.6
Tr.	33,430	8,598	20–34	25.7
Bl/Tr/Th	63,070	13,875	19–23	22.0
Bl/Tr	76,855	13,670	13–22	17.8
Bl	62,570	4,520	5–11	7.2
	356,375	78,743	5–34	22.1

method of estimation. The relationship of each user of the gardens to the headman, as head of the family group, is shown.

Fed from Headman's Garden

Son, daughter-in-law and their 4 dependent children obtained ¼ of their requirements for six months	0.75
Son, his wife and one child obtained ½ of their requirements for the year	1.50
	2.25

Fed from Wives Gardens

One man (Headman)	1.00
His 3 wives	3.00
9 young or adolescent children of headman and his wives	9.00
Family obtained ¼ of their requirements for six months	0.75
Family fed for six months	1.50
Daughter (Husband away at work) and child fed for six months	1.00
Aged sister and her husband fed during year	2.00
Niece (deserted by insane husband)	1.00
Son-in-law (deserted by wife) fed for four months	0.33
	19.58

given in the first of the following reports.

B. Survey of a complete village group.

C. Independent estimates based on later sampling by D. U. Peters for a group settled outside the Reserve.

For the Lamba of Mushiri, the acreage of main garden in cultivation at any one time appears to be very nearly one acre per head of population, men, women and children.

Very similar figures were obtained from a survey made among the Ngoni and Chewa, who practise a comparable method of soil selection but whose traditional system of agriculture and staple crops differ from those of the Lamba. Samples consisting of 40 families taken at random and one complete village group gave a total population of 259 cultivating 280.9 acres of main crops, or approximately 1.08 acres per head of population.

As will be seen from the following reports, the Swaka, practising a *semi-chite-*

mene system on very poor, weak soils, commonly have more land in cultivation at one time and may average 1.5 acres of main gardens per head of population. The Western Lala, on the other hand, still with a predominantly *chitemene* tradition but in a state of change, average only about 0.7 acres of main crops per head of population.

Analyses of the data from Lamba, Ngoni and Chewa sources show no trace of correlation between garden acreages and soil fertility, though such a correlation might well be expected. Among the Swaka, however, the acreage cultivated on the poor, sandy soils which cover most of their area is considerably greater than corresponding acreages on the much more fertile but restricted belt of *B. Burtii* red loams. It is somewhat surprising that no closer correlation between soil fertility and the acreage cultivated per head of population has so far been found. Perhaps the area cultivated is determined by the physical capacity of the family, for all the peoples mentioned here are subsistence cultivators whose only implements are the axe and the hoe.

General adoption of the plough can, of course, by increasing the physical resources of the family, lead to much larger cultivated acreages and bring about an entirely new relation between population and the land. Of the Northern Rhodesian tribes, it is only among the Plateau Tonga of Mazabuka District and in a few neighbouring areas, that this situation has as yet arisen and even here, where the plough is in almost universal use, the increase in the acreage cultivated per head has been found to be unexpectedly small.

Aerial photography, provided it is sufficiently recent, can be of the utmost value in reducing the labour of field sampling in estimating cultivation acreages and in allowing wider and more adequate sampling. On vertical photographs the boundaries between land holdings are usually clearly distinguishable and the areas can be measured directly from the photographs, but the ground work necessary to ascertain the population relationship summarized in the "garden family" cannot, of course, be avoided.

THE CULTIVABLE PERCENTAGE OF LAND

Not all land is cultivable for crops. There is, again, an absolute and a practical limit to the proportion of any land surface upon which crops can be grown. According to H. H. Bennett[3] only about 11 per cent of the earth's land area is cultivable now or in the immediate future. O. E. Baker[4] also of the United States Department of Agriculture, has calculated that, of the 52 million square miles of land in the world outside the polar caps, only 10 million square miles is *ultimately* arable. This is an estimate of the absolute limit for the world; about 19 per cent of the total available land surface.

But a considerably lower limit is set by practical considerations. In a system of economic farming the practical limit is determined by the relationship between the cost of maintaining the land in cultivation and the amount and value of the product.

Bennett[4] has estimated that, of the 2,900,000 square miles in the continental United States, certainly not more than 953,125 square miles can be farmed even under the utmost pressure. In the 1935 census,[5] 415 million acres of land in the United States was classified as crop land. Of this area, 76 million acres was found to be unsuitable for cultivation under the price range for agricultural produce prevailing during the 1922–35 period, either because known methods of erosion control were too expensive or because of inherent soil poverty. In other words, it would appear that the absolute cultivable limit for the continental United States is not more than 33 per cent the total land surface and that the practical limit for the 1922–35 price range may have been little more than 18 per cent.

This *cultivable percentage* of land varies enormously from one part of the earth's surface to another. Norway, for example, is said to be only 4 per cent cultivable, while of the land surface of the Philippine Islands 55 per cent is believed to be cultivable, though only 12.5 per cent is in use.

The cultivable percentage of land in Northern Rhodesia, and probably over much of East Africa, is very low. Many people find it difficult to realize this or to accept such estimates as it has been possible to make, and I have introduced the foregoing notes to show that we are not unique in this respect and that even for an advanced society, with much scientific knowledge at its disposal and the skill and material resources to translate knowledge into practice, the cultivable percentage of land still remains low. Where, because economic and material resources and skill are lacking, marginal land cannot be brought into cultivation by manuring, application of artificials, grass leys, liming, drainage, irrigation or any of the means open to an advanced community, the cultivable percentage of land must obviously be lower still.

In the case of a predominantly subsistence agriculture, such as still prevails over much of Africa and virtually the whole of Northern Rhodesia, the *practical* limit to the cultivable percentage of land is set by physical and psychological factors; the material resources of the people and the amount of energy which they are able and willing to expend. For any large area the calculation of cultivable percentage is a matter of great difficulty. It has been pointed out [4] that, "astronomers announce to the last decimal place the mass and density of other planets; but the apparently unique soil supply by which we live on this one has so recently become an object of concern and measurement that men do well to guess within a million square miles of its usable extent."

Even when we are dealing with thousands, instead of millions, of square miles, estimation must, at best, include a good deal of guesswork. In the past this guesswork has been rather crude. It has often been assumed for practical purposes, as for example in demarcating some of the Northern

Rhodesian Native reserves, that one third of the land is uncultivable, irrespective of the system of usage or the resources of the people. Estimation of the proportion of any large area which is very obviously uncultivable, hill masses, large swamps, seasonally waterlogged areas and the like, is not very difficult. A careful survey of 1,840 square miles of land in the Eastern Province of Northern Rhodesia showed that 36 per cent of this area did in fact fall within the very obviously uncultivable category. But that is not to say that the remaining 64 per cent is cultivable, for it does include dambos and streams (other than extensive swamp areas), local hill slopes too steep for cultivation (other than the larger hill masses), outcrops, gravels, waterlogged areas, very shallow soils, areas of extreme poverty and soils infertile for many reasons.

How then is the cultivable percentage to be estimated?

An opportunity to make some investigation of the subject occurred in 1939, when aerial photography was applied to a large part (some 3,000 square miles) of the Native reserves on the railway line of Northern Rhodesia.* Over a good deal of this area congestion of population, a market for surplus food crops and the large-scale adoption of the plough had led to the cultivation of virtually every acre suitable for the production of maize; or at least this was a reasonable assumption. Consequently the acreage cultivable for maize showed up on the photographs as land under cultivation or resting under grass or scrub-fallow.

Large areas to which this assumption could be applied were selected and classified into the vegetation-soil types of the region. Measurements of cultivable and uncultivable areas within the samples were

---

* These were vertical photographs on an average scale of about 6 inches to 1 mile. Determinations of scale were made from survey data where available, or by means of direct measurements between points distinguishable on the photographs.

then made from the photographs and, from these measurements, the percentage of cultivable land was estimated. Figures obtained in this way are summarized in the Table below, the vegetation-soil types being indicated by the following notation:

Th: *Acacia Woodii* thorn soils of the Upper Valley Class.
Tr: Transitional soils of the Upper Valley Class.
BI: *Brachystegia-Isoberlinia* woodland on soils of the Southern Plateau Class.

corn which has a wider soil tolerance than maize. It seems likely, however, that at the time the photographs were taken neither manure nor kaffir corn were so widely used as to affect the figures very seriously.

The data obtained in this way, modified to accord with field observations and staple crops, have been used in estimating the cultivable percentages of other vegetation-soil types under different systems. For example, the Chipya soils of the Ndola District have been regarded as approximately equivalent to Upper Valley soils which are roughly one third cultivable for maize. These

	No. of 'garden families' in sample	Total population in sample	Area of main gardens (acres)	Area of main gardens per unit of population
A.	23	127	120.4	0.95
B.	8	40	44.0	1.10
C.	18	87	93.6	1.07
	49	254	258.0	1.01

The mean cultivable percentage for each type and combination of types is shown, together with the range for individual sample areas which were never less than 8,000 acres in extent.

The total area measured was almost 557 square miles and of this area about 22 per cent appears to be cultivable for maize. Of the Thorn type, containing the richest soils of the Upper Valley Class and among the most fertile in the Territory, about one third is cultivable. The variable but generally lighter and poorer soils of the Transitional type are cultivable for about a quarter of their extent, while the poorest soils of the Plateau Class are only about 5 per cent cultivable for maize.

These figures may err on the high side for an unmodified traditional agriculture with maize as the staple, for the increasing use of cattle manure has enabled the Tonga to extend their cultivation on to soils formerly regarded as uncultivable, and measurements of cultivable land include land under kaffir

Chipya soils are cultivated to kaffir corn under the Lamba system, but the wider soil tolerance of the staple crop is offset by the occurrence of uncultivable ironstone phases within this type. For purposes of calculation the Chipya soils have therefore been taken as approximately one third cultivable. The modifications, it must be confessed, are arbitrary and little better than guesswork. They are likely to remain so until further data can be collected by the application of aerial photography to selected areas.

It must be emphasized that the cultivable percentage of land, as the factor has been used in calculating carrying capacity, is strictly relative to the staple crop, the system of agriculture and the resources of the people. A forest type containing a predominance of species too hard to be cut, without excessive expenditure of energy and time, by means of the small, soft axes which are the only available implements, may be uncultivable however fertile the soil. To take an example from our own past: the great oak and ash forests of Britain were uncultivable for the Neolithic and Bronze Age peoples, although they contained some of the best soils, because they could not be felled with stone or even bronze axes. These forests were not seriously attacked until Roman occupation or finally cleared until Saxon times. Similarly, land which might be brought into cultivation by the use of stock manure remains uncultivable for a people who have no livestock and no means of obtaining any. Wet land is uncultivable if drainage is beyond the resources and social organization of the people. In this connection the Sishanjo gardens of Barotseland may be mentioned. Formerly the Lozi combined to drain large areas of saturated soil for these gardens but the practice entailed compulsory labour and was brought to an end under British Administration. Consequently some large areas once cultivated are no longer cultivable under the present system.

AGRICULTURAL USAGE

The next essential step is to ascertain the manner in which each of the vegetation-soil types is used under the traditional system of agriculture. Trapnell's work [2] has provided much information for the traditional systems of Northern Rhodesia, and further studies have been made on a number of the systems in connection with estimates of land carrying capacity and the resettlement of populations.

Most land can be classified for purposes of Native utilization into five simple categories originated by Trapnell. These are:

1. Useless land.
2. Partial cultivation land.
3. Shifting cultivation land.
4. Re-cultivation land.
5. Semi-permanent or permanent land.

Useless Land. Types which because of shallowness of soil, seasonal waterlogging or other factors allow of no cultivation whatsoever. The Sheet-Ironstone types of the Copperbelt classification, for example, are avoided by the Lamba even under extreme pressure and are regarded as falling within this category.

Partial Cultivation Land. Land largely unsuited to cultivation but allowing of use, generally for short periods only, in restricted sites. Such types are cultivated usually for two years (rarely three and exceptionally four years) and cultivation is followed by a full period of woodland regeneration. The 4a types of the Copperbelt region, *as used by the Lamba,* are examples of this class. They are commonly cultivated for two years and rested for a period which may be as long as twenty-five years.

Shifting Cultivation Land. Land used for a short term of cultivation followed by a long period of rest for woodland regeneration; differing from the last in that the percentage of cultivable soil is higher; the period of cultivation is also generally somewhat longer. Cultivation is usually for three to four (rarely five) years, with a regeneration period of twenty to twenty-five years. The type 3 soils of the Copperbelt classification fall largely within this category.

Re-cultivation Land. Land cultivated for longer periods, followed by a short rest under "scrub fallow" and a further cultivation, after which a longer rest period is usually given. The cultivation period on these soils, of which the Copperbelt Red Earths are examples, is usually five to eight years, followed by a scrub fallow of similar duration, a further period of cultivation and a longer period of rest; for example, six years cultivation, six years rest, six years cultivation and twelve or more years regeneration; the cycle being repeated indefinitely.

Semi-Permanent and Permanent Land. Land used for long term cultivation with brief "scrub" or grass fallows. The period of cultivation is commonly six to nine years, and ten to twelve years or even more in the best examples. A rest period equivalent to the period of cultivation is usually allowed, but in some cases cultivation for eight to ten years is followed by a scrub fallow of three to five years before further cultivation, or shorter cultivation periods of four to five years are alternated with fallows of two to four years duration. In estimating the land requirements of Lamba agriculture it has been assumed, on the little direct evidence available, that the Chipya types fall within this category and that they are permanently cultivable on a system of six to twelve years cultivation alternating with similar rest periods. This is rather a marginal case, for the Lamba are reluctant to clear Chipya forests on account of the labour involved, although they recognize the fertility of the soil, and some deny that they are cultivated at all. Nevertheless, the Chipya forest types are normally used by the neighbouring Lima and by the Lamba under pressure of population, and there is evidence that the Lamba cultivated them in the past when population density must have been very low. Another qualification may also be noted. Late fires are particularly fierce and destructive in the tall grass of cleared Chipyas (the name derives from the verb kupya—to burn) and it may be that the assumption of semi-permanent cultivation is only valid, especially in the case of the grey-soil Chipyas, if early-burning is practised, or under conditions of partial fire-protection such as occur naturally in areas of relatively dense settlement.

For simplicity of calculation the method of land usage has been reduced to a simple factor (called the *cultivation factor*). This is merely an expression of the number of "garden areas" required for each type to allow of the complete cycle of cultivation and regeneration normally practised on that type under the system to which the calculation applies. Thus, if a particular type is cultivated for two years and then allowed to regenerate for twenty-four years, it is obvious that thirteen garden areas are required; one in cultivation and twelve in various stages of regeneration. Similarly,

some three garden areas will normally be required for a re-cultivation type; and not more than two need be allowed for a semi-permanent type.

ESTIMATING OF LAND CARRYING CAPACITY

Given a sufficient knowledge of the factors which have now been briefly discussed, the calculation of land carrying capacity is a matter of simple arithmetic. For any single soil type, the area of land required per head of population is 100 CL/P acres, when C = the cultivation factor, L = the mean acreage in cultivation at any one time per head of population, and P = the cultivable percentage of the type. To revert to the simple example given above; if the cultivation factor is thirteen, if the cultivable percentage is five and if about one acre is normally maintained in cultivation per head of population, then 260 acres are required for each individual, and the permanent carrying capacity of the type, for this system of usage, is only about 2.5 persons per square mile. At the other extreme, the semi-permanent types with a cultivable proportion of about one third, have a permanent carrying capacity of well over one hundred persons per square mile.

As a complete example of the estimation of land carrying capacity we will take an area, approximately 379 square miles in extent, south of Ndola and the Copperbelt, which was surveyed in 1944. The following Table summarizes the data obtained from the survey and the factors, calculated for Lamba traditional agriculture, used in the estimate.

Column 1 lists the vegetation-soil types found within this area. These are the types defined with the addition of a further type of seasonally waterlogged uncultivable land.

Column 2 gives the total area in acres of each of these types, as measured on the map constructed from the survey traverses.

Columns 3A and 3B show the cultivation and rest periods for each of these types, based on traditional Lamba practice. The

Soil Type	Total Area (acres)	Years of Cultivation (A) and Rest (B)		P %	C	Area required per head (acres)	Total Carrying Capacity (persons)
		A	B				
1	4,380	Re-cultivation		33–34	3	9	487
2–	1,160	Re-cultivation		25	3	12	97
2	12,983	6–12	6–12	33–34	2	6	2,164
2–	1,650	Re-cultivation		25	3	12	137
3+	15,435	Re-cultivation		25–30	4	15	1,029
		5	20				
3	125,898	3	21	25	8	32	3,934
3–	43,615	2–3	22–28	15–25	11	55	793
4a	22,447	2	22–28	8–12	13	130	173
4a–	11,380	2	22–28	5	13	260	44
6	1,260	–	–	–	0	–	–
8	190	–	–	–	0	–	–
9	2,010	–	–	–	0	–	–
	242,408						8,858

rest periods are derived from Native information, supplemented by tree ring counts.

Column 4 gives the cultivable percentages allocated to each type for the Lamba system of kaffir corn cultivation. The surveys of which this example is part, were made in country formerly occupied by the Lamba from which the people had been removed some fourteen years before. Woodland previously cleared for cultivation could generally be distinguished by the habit of the regrowth, and observations on the extent of previously felled and unfelled woodland were made during the traverses. These observations were used to modify the "yardstick" data obtained from the aerial photographs.

Column 5 shows estimates of the total number of "garden areas" required for each type, derived from Columns 3A and 3B.

Column 6 gives the total acreage of land required per head of population for each type (100 CL/P, assuming that L=1).

Column 7 gives estimates of the carrying capacity for the total area for each type, obtained simply by dividing the figures in Column 2 by the corresponding figures in Column 6.

According to this estimate, the general mean cultivable percentage for the whole area of 378.76 square miles is about 22, and the carrying capacity for the Lamba system of kaffir corn cultivation is 8,860 persons; or, in other words, the critical population density, for this particular area and system, is in the region of 23 or 24 persons per square mile.

In the Eastern Province of Northern Rhodesia, where this method of calculation has been applied to large areas as a basis for resettlement of population, very similar estimates of critical density were obtained, although soils, systems and crops differ from those of the Lamba. The following examples, taken from the earlier Eastern Province surveys, are for areas in the Fort Jameson District and for the Ngoni-Chewa methods of maize cultivation.

The general estimate of critical population density for the total area of 955.6 square miles, on the basis of the Ngoni-Chewa system of maize cultivation, is 25 persons per square mile.[*]

* For a total area of 2,010 square miles in Fort Jameson and eastern Petauke the estimate

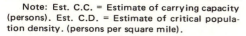

Area Surveyed (acres)	Estimated C.C.	Estimated C.D.
97,550	4,600	30.4
143,660	5,565	25.0
40,900	1,350	21.1
46,800	2,480	33.3
19,600	1,135	37.0
110,300	3,970	23.0
79,100	1,860	15.0
19,500	500	16.4
54,200	2,440	28.8
611,610	23,900	25.0

Note: Est. C.C. = Estimate of carrying capacity (persons). Est. C.D. = Estimate of critical population density. (persons per square mile).

It must again be emphasized that these estimates are strictly relative to specific areas and to the systems employed on them. For much of Northern Rhodesia the critical density is undoubtedly well below this figure of 25 persons per square mile. The Swaka and Western Lala, described in the report which follows, give examples of areas and systems of lower carrying capacity. On the other hand, considerable areas of Upper Valley Soils cultivated under the Senga kaffir corn system of the Eastern Province, probably have carrying capacities of well over 100 persons per square mile. Another point worth noting is the effect of climate. The single rains (November-April) and long dry season (April-November) of Northern Rhodesia, impose a limit of one main crop each year. Under more favourable climatic conditions, and where there are extensive areas of fertile soils, land carrying capacities. are, no doubt, very considerably higher. For example, it has been estimated [6] that on good soils in the elephant grass belt of Uganda, the existing system of agriculture is able to support up to about 350 people per square mile. It appears, however, though it is not clearly stated, that this means 350

of mean critical density, based on Ngoni, Chewa and Eastern Senga practice, was 22 persons per square mile.

people per square mile of *cultivable land,* which may be a very different matter from the general carrying capacity. Humphrey, in his refreshingly realistic essay on the Kikuyu lands [7] allows, for the area with which he is dealing, a cultivable percentage of 50. This, he admits, is "probably a generous estimate," and he concludes that the problem posed by population densities little short of 550 per square mile can be solved only by drastic reduction of the agricultural population, in addition to radical changes in agricultural practice.

The conception of population carrying capacity does, of course, assume a more or less ideal distribution of population in relation to soils; or at least a mobility of population which will allow of the natural readjustment of local excesses before pressure on the land becomes too acute. Such conditions do not always obtain. Lack of natural water supplies sometimes prevents the exploitation of an area to the full extent of its carrying capacity and gives rise to local over-population and under-population. Equally or perhaps more important, as causes of maldistribution of population in relation to soils, are the barriers to free movement set by political divisions and by tribal and kinship ties. It is often the case that the area of one chief is supporting a population greatly in excess of the carrying capacity, while in the neighbouring chieftaincy population density is far below the critical point. Such conditions have sometimes arisen naturally; more frequently they are the result of the creation of Native reserves. Even where the area demarcated as a reserve is much more than adequate for present requirements, population has invariably failed to adjust itself to the new set of conditions. Preservation of the old boundaries of tribes, chieftaincies and social units, and the absence of any attempt at planned readjustment, has commonly given rise to extreme maldistribution of population.* The adjustment of such

* For example, in the Western Province prior

anomalies should be a cardinal principle
of land policy. Lord Lugard drew attention
to the subject twenty years ago in the following passage from the *Dual Mandate:*

> The larger question of the augmenta-
> tion of the area held by a tribe, or by
> an advanced community, whose in-
> creasing population has caused acute
> land hunger, while perhaps a neigh-
> bouring tribe has so decreased in num-
> ber that its lands are in excess of its
> needs, is one for the Government to
> deal with.
>
> If the facts are established a trans-
> fer of land must be made, but in my
> own opinion, in no case—whether the
> country is conquered territory or not—
> should a rental be demanded from the
> community which receives the addi-
> tional land. In days not distant it
> would have seized the land and would
> probably have eliminated its owners as
> well. The peaceful adjustment of such
> economic claims, when proved to be
> well founded, is the function of the
> suzerain Government.[8]

However, the purpose of this paper is to
give a brief indication of the method which
has been used in the estimation of land
carrying capacities in Northern Rhodesia,
not to discuss the implications which arise
from such studies. The immediate point is
that, in the practical applications of the
method, such considerations as water supply
and political and social factors must be
taken into account. In the resettlement
work, based on this conception of land
carrying capacity, wells and dams have been
provided where necessary to allow of the
full exploitation of each area, and systems
of land allocation have been devised and
applied to establish, and as far as possible
to maintain, an approximate population-land
balance. These methods of resettlement are
briefly described in the second paper of this
series and further notes and references will

be found in the Annual Reports of the
Department of Agriculture, Northern Rhodesia, from 1941 onwards.

So far, the method has been applied
mainly to the purpose for which it was
devised; the amelioration of congested conditions by transfer of populations to vacant
Crown Lands, or, in the case of the Eastern
Province, to land formerly owned by a
private company. But it provides also a
means of classifying and assessing the
urgency of land problems. Given the necessary vital statistics, which are too often
lacking, it is possible to estimate, for an
area in which population is as yet below the
land carrying capacity, when pressure on
the land may be expected to begin. There
are large areas of Northern Rhodesia where
it seems highly probable that critical population densities for the traditional systems
of land usage will not be reached for fifty
years or more; there are also areas in which
population is already five or six times the
carrying capacity. When populations are
below, or even approximately equal to, the
land carrying capacities, there is ample time
for the evolutionary development of agricultural methods, and attention may be
focused on the next, rather than on the
present, generation of landholders. On the
other hand, where the critical point has
already been greatly exceeded, immediate
and possibly drastic action is called for.
Sound planning, and the most profitable use
of resources which must always be limited,
require that the method of approach to land
problems should be in accordance with the
needs of each particular situation.

The two main weaknesses in the methods
which have been described in this paper
lie in the difficulty of arriving at satisfactory
figures for the percentage of cultivable land,
and in the great amount of labour involved
in survey and garden sampling. Both can,
to a large extent, be overcome by the use
of aerial photography, but during the war
this has been out of the question, and urgent
practical work has of necessity taken prece-
dence over improvement in technique.

---

to resettlement one half of the population occupied less than one twelfth of the available land.

Gillman[1] has pointed out that in Tanganyika
Territory two-thirds of the people are living on
one-tenth of the land and nearly two-thirds of
the whole territory is uninhabited.

THE EFFECTS OF OVER-POPULATION

It has often been suggested to me that relatively low estimates of land carrying capacities are at variance with existing population densities. Some areas are now carrying, and have for considerable periods supported, dense populations. Densities of the order of 300 people per square mile are not unknown in Northern Rhodesia and in other parts of Africa even higher concentrations have been reached.

This criticism overlooks the time factor and also the fact that population densities by themselves mean little, and acquire their full significance only when considered in relation to soils, climate and land usage. I have become accustomed to thinking in terms of a *Population-Land Factor* (denoted by the symbol Ml), which is simply the total population of an area divided by the estimate of carrying capacity. Thus, if Ml is 0.5, the critical density will not be reached until the population has doubled itself. If Ml is 6, this means that the area is carrying six times the number of people it can support in perpetuity under the system of land usage to which the estimate of carrying capacity applies. Population-land factors of the order of 6 or 7 are, in fact, the highest that have so far been noted in Northern Rhodesia, but the conditions of intense congestion which this figure denotes are of very local occurrence and have been in existence only for relatively short periods. For most of the overcrowded areas the population-land factor rarely exceeds 3. In parts of Fort Jameson District this factor of 3 corresponds to actual population densities of about 130 per square mile, while in parts of Mkushi the same value of the factor corresponds to densities of only 18 or 20 people to the square mile.

I have already pointed out that in other parts of Africa climatic and soil conditions may allow of much higher critical densities than is commonly the case in Northern Rhodesia. Leakey [9] says of the Kikuyu lands:

The lands of a certain section of the Kikuyu tribe are to-day populated to a density of 500 to the square mile; but in a few parts the figure is much lower. Where the density is over 250 to the square mile there is a continual complaint that there is no room to expand, no room to grow more than just the bare necessities of life and to graze stock.

It is quite possible that the critical density for the Kikuyu land and system may be something of the order of 200 people per square mile and more, though one does not usually hear complaints nor is there any general realization of land shortage until the critical density has been considerably exceeded for some time. A population density of 550 or 600 per square mile in the Kikuyu lands may quite possibly be much the same thing, in terms of pressure on the land, as a density of a mere 200 per squire mile for such an area and system as the Serenje highlands and the Lala method of *chitemene* which is practised there.* Both communities may be using up their land capital at about the same rate. There will, of course, be differences in other respects; one problem may admit of much easier solution than the other.

The carrying capacity of an area is an estimate of the number of people that area will support in perpetuity, under a given system of land usage, without deterioration of land resources. The area can, of course, carry a very much greater population for a number of years, but that population will be using up its land capital at a greater or lesser rate according to the degree of congestion.

---

* Examples of acute pressure on land at relatively low population densities (for a system complicated by the cattle complex) will be found in Schapera's *Native Land Tenure in the Bechuanaland Protectorate* (Lovedale Press, 1943). E.g. "The Malete (39.3 persons per square mile) and Tlôkwa (29.9 per square mile) have been forced within recent years to seek relief by buying additional land from neighbouring European farmers, and the Tali Reserve (25.7 per square mile) is notoriously overcrowded and overstocked."

Suppose that the population of an area is increased to three times the carrying capacity for a given soil selection system and that this system continues as the basis of land usage. The newcomers will tend to take up land which is regenerated, or in an advanced state of regeneration, and for some years there will be no appreciable effect whatever. After the first cycle or so of cultivation, regeneration periods must obviously be reduced and this process continues until a stage of temporary equilibrium is reached. At this stage the poorer soils will be worked more or less on a 2–3 years' cultivation period and a 6–9 years' scrub fallow. Rather better soils will probably be worked up to 5 or 7 years with more or less equal periods of rest, while the recultivation and semi-permanent soils will come into almost continuous cultivation with very brief periods of weed or grass fallow. Under such conditions erosion symptoms will appear and yields will decline slowly, though the decline will, of course, be partially masked by seasonal fluctuations. When the decline in yields begins to be seriously felt efforts will be made to increase the crop acreage by taking into cultivation land which would not normally be used; hills and steep slopes, dambos and water courses, and soils of very low productivity and little power of recovery. Next, the weaker soils will be abandoned: such data as we have suggests that this stage is reached when grain yields fall below 200 lb. per acre in the normal season. The former cultivators of the abandoned land may then offer work in exchange for the food surplus still enjoyed by the holders of the stronger soils, or they may be entitled to a share of the surplus by virtue of kinship obligations. In this way a period of increasing pressure and accelerated erosion on the stronger and more fertile soils is brought about. These stages will commonly be accompanied by migration of able-bodied men to the centres of employment and the stage finally be reached when the area is dependent to a large extent on food purchased from outside sources.

In 1941 a study was made of a highly congested area in Fort Jameson District; the area of Mpezeni, Paramount Chief of the Ngoni. The chieftaincy was found to be 54,000 acres in extent and, after detailed survey, the carrying capacity for traditional Ngoni agriculture was estimated to be about 1,300 to 1,400 persons. A total of 7,700 people, between five and six times the carrying capacity, were supposedly living within the chieftaincy. In short, an area which, because of the high proportion of mountain country, had a critical density of only about 16 persons per square mile did in fact appear to be carrying over 90 to the square mile.

The main reasons for the continued survival of this population were found to be as follows:

(a) The time during which these conditions had existed (about 15 years) was not sufficient to show the full effects of this degree of land pressure.

(b) Great areas of hill country and dambos, which would not normally be cultivated, had been taken into cultivation. The almost incredible mountain cultivation on the Nyamfinzi range was, until recently, a startling spectacle. Use of dambo grassland for *fipoka* gardens had seriously reduced grazing and was a sore point with the cattle-loving Ngoni.

(c) Under extreme pressure the population had burst its bounds and an irresistible tide had inundated adjoining private land and unoccupied European farms. In addition, a missionary organization had permitted cultivation, on payment, on land owned by the mission. By these means the effective acreage had, in fact, been increased by almost 50 per cent.

(d) A very heavy burden had been thrown on the limited soils of high fertility and resistance to erosion, the only soils left in the original area still carrying moderately good crops.

These soils, then in continuous cultivation, were feeding more than twice as many people as they would normally do.

(e) The Paramount Chief was importing from Nyasaland each year a considerable quantity of food for the use of his people.

The people in the original area were short of food but by no means at starvation level. This was ascertained by taking seven sample villages at random within the congested area and weighing their entire food stocks during the first fortnight of February. From these samples the following data were obtained.

GRAIN STOCKS OF NGONI VILLAGES
(FEBRUARY 1941)

Total population			Total grain stocks
Men	Women	Children	lb.
292	389	531	24,719

Making no allowance for a special reserve of seed against a possible need for replanting, or for loss in preparing flour and for other reasons, the grain stock represents not more than 20 days usage, and supplies would probably be exhausted by early March. There was much variation between villages; one exceptional village had enough grain for 46 days while in another the grain stocks represented only 4 days supply. It will be remembered, however, that in an African social system, kinship obligations tend to even out the distribution of food supplies.

In striking contrast to these samples, a village which had recently made an illicit move to unoccupied private land was found to have, at the end of February, grain stocks representing 81 days supply. The effects of falling yields first make themselves felt in the bad years and it should be noted that the sampling was done in a year following a good climatic season. It will also be noted that villages which would in all probability have reached the starvation level had already transferred themselves.

There is, then, a time lag between the beginning of over-crowded conditions and the point at which obvious symptoms of land degeneration and soil erosion appear. The length of this time lag clearly depends on a number of factors acting together; the type of land and the system used on it, the degree of congestion, the original population density and the rate of population increase, if any. A further variable time lag elapses before conditions of general food shortage are reached. Under some conditions the process of land degradation may result in food shortage within a very few years, while in other cases this result may not appear for twenty years or more.

Within ten years of the creation of reserves in the Mkushi District obvious land degradation and recurrent food shortages in some areas had reached such a stage as to attract the attention of District Officers, missionaries and other interested persons, and to create an insistent demand for additional land. The population densities in these areas were 18 to 25 persons per square mile. Other areas of the Territory, notably the reserves of the Northern and Eastern Provinces, provide similar examples for different systems and land categories. In the second Report of the Ecological Survey (North Eastern Rhodesia, paras. 316–20) Trapnell records a wide range of observations on areas where land degeneration and soil erosion had become marked, in relation to land categories, population densities and the time factor. These observations provide independent evidence of the relatively low carrying capacity of much of our land under the traditional systems, and they accord well with the estimates obtained by the methods outlined in this paper.

REFERENCES

[1] C. Gillman, Population Problems of Tanganyika Territory, *East African Agric. Journ.* October 1945.

[2] C. G. Trapnell and J. N. Clothier, *Soils, Vegetation and Agricultural Systems of North*

Western Rhodesia. Lusaka: Government Printer, 1937.

C. G. Trapnell, *Soils, Vegetation and Agriculture of North Eastern Rhodesia.* Lusaka: Government Printer, 1943.

³ H. H. Bennet, "Agriculture," *Jour. Min. Agric.* November 1943.

⁴ United States Dept. of Agric. Misc. Publication No. 321.

⁵ *United States Year Book of Agriculture,* 1938.

⁶ *Report on Nineteen Surveys Done in Small Agricultural Areas,* Entebbe: Government Printer, 1938.

⁷ N. Humphrey, *The Kikuyu Lands,* Nairobi: Government Printer, 1945.

⁸ Lord Lugard, *The Dual Mandate in British Tropical Africa,* Blackwood & Sons, 1926.

⁹ L. S. B. Leakey, *Kenya: Contrasts and Problems,* Methuen & Co., 1936.

Gould's paper is not concerned with carrying capacity but with the application of a method in which simple quantitative measures are used to assess the likelihood that producers will succeed under certain environmental conditions. Here the method is demonstrated with data from Ghana, and suggests that future research in population-land relationships may be based on more theoretical concepts than in the past (Henshall, 1967).

24. *Man Against His Environment: A Game Theoretic Framework*

PETER R. GOULD

Without cataloging the many and various definitions of human geography by professional geographers over the past few decades, it is safe to say that most have included the words *Man* and *Environment.* Traditionally, geographers have had a deep intellectual curiosity and concern for the face of the earth and the way it provides, in a larger sense, a home for mankind. Much of what we see upon the surface of the earth is the work of Man, and is the result of a variety of decisions that men have made as individuals or groups. Unfortunately, we have all too often lacked, or failed to consider, conceptual frameworks of theory in which to examine Man's relationship to his environment, the manner in which he weighs the alternatives presented, and the rationality of his choices once they have been made. Underlining a belief that such theoretical structures are desirable, and that they sometimes enable us to see old and oft-examined things with new eyes, this paper attempts to draw the attention of geographers to the Theory of Games as a conceptual framework and tool of research in human geography.¹ Upon its initial and

¹ References to Game Theory in geographic literature are almost nonexistent. What few references there are usually appear as peripheral points to a larger discussion on linear-programming solutions, for example: William L. Garri-

From *Annals of the Association of American Geographers,* Vol. 53, 1963, pp. 290–297. Reprinted by permission.

formal appearance in 1944,[2] a reviewer stated: "Posterity may regard this . . . as one of the major scientific achievements of the first half of the twentieth century," and although the social sciences have been relatively slow in considering the Theory of Games, compared to the widespread application of all forms of decision theory throughout engineering, business, and statistics, its increasing use in our sister disciplines of economics, anthropology, and sociology indicates a sure trend, fulfilling the extravagant praise heaped upon it at an earlier date.

The Theory of Games, despite its immediate connotation of amusements of a frivolous kind, is an imposing structure dealing, in essence, with the question of making rational decisions in the face of uncertain conditions by choosing certain strategies to outwit an opponent, or, at the very least, to maintain a position superior to others. Of course, we do not have to think in terms of two opponents sitting over a chessboard; we may, as geographers, think in terms of competition for locations whose value depends upon the locational choices of

others;[3] or, perhaps more usefully, in terms of man choosing certain strategies to overcome or outwit his environment. A good example of the latter is a Jamaican fishing village,[4] where the captains of the fishing canoes can set all their fishing pots close to the shore, all of them out to sea, or set a proportion in each area. Those canoes setting pots close to the shore have few pot losses, but the quality of the fish is poor so that the market price is low, particularly when the deep-water pots have a good day and drive the price of poor fish down still further. On the other hand, those who set their pots out to sea catch much better fish, but every now and then a current runs in an unpredictable fashion, battering the pots and sinking the floats, so that pot losses are higher. Thus, the village has three choices, to set all the pots in, all the pots out, or some in and some out, while the environment has two strategies, current or no-current. Game Theory has successfully predicted the best choice of strategies and the proportion each should be used, a proportion very close to that arrived at by the villagers over a long period of trial and error.

Man continually finds himself in situations where a number of different choices or strategies may be available to wrest a living from his environment. Indeed, without soaring to those stratospheric heights of philosophical, or even metaphysical, discussion, to which all discourse in the social and physical sciences ultimately leads, let it be said that to be Man rather than Animal is,

---

son, "Spatial Structure of the Economy II," *Annals,* Association of American Geographers, Vol. 49, No. 4 (December, 1959), pp. 480–81. It should be noted, parenthetically, that much of the mathematics used in Game Theory is the same as that used in linear programming, and one of the hopeful things about the new ways of looking at old problems is that a common mathematics underlies many of the same theoretical structures. In terms of efficiency, a key made from a little modern algebra may often open many doors.

[2] The basic work, now revised, is John von Neumann and Oskar Morgenstern, *Theory of Games and Economic Behavior* (Princeton: Princeton University Press, 1953). Excellent introductions are J. D. Williams, *The Compleat Stratygyst* (New York: McGraw-Hill Book Co., 1954); Anatol Rapoport, *Flights, Games and Decisions* (Ann Arbor: University of Michigan Press, 1961); while a complete critique and survey is R. Duncan Luce and Howard Raiffa, *Games and Decisions* (New York: John Wiley and Sons, Inc., 1958).

[3] W. L. Garrison, *Annals,* Association of American Geographers, Vol. 49, pp. 480–81, reviewing Tjalling C. Koopmans and Martin Beckmann, "Assignment Problems and the Location of Economic Activities," *Econometrica,* Vol. 25 (January, 1957), pp. 53–76.

[4] William Davenport, "Jamaican Fishing: A Game Theory Analysis," *Yale University Publications in Anthropology,* No. 59 (1960); an excellent case study drawn from detailed anthropological field work which provided the basis for assigning actual monetary values to the various choices presented to the village as a whole.

in part, to be able to recognize a variety of alternatives, and in a *rational* manner, reasoning from those little rocks of knowledge that stick up above the vast sea of uncertainty, choose strategies to win the basic struggle for survival. The perception that alternatives exist, and the recognition that their specific value, or utility, for a given time and place may depend upon an unpredictable environment, about which Man has only highly probabilistic notions based upon past experience, is clearly central to any discussion of man-environment relationships within a game theoretic framework. Thus, growing concomitantly with, and, indeed, embedded in, the Theory of Games, is a theory of utility intuitively raised, axiomatically treated, and experimentally tested in the real world.[5]

The Barren Middle Zone of Ghana (Fig. 1), a belt which, for environmental and historical reasons, has a very low population density, has one of the severest agricultural climates in West Africa,[6] with heavy precipitation followed by the extreme aridity of the Harmatten, which sweeps south from the Sahara. A further problem is that the high degree of variability of the precipitation makes it difficult for the farmers to plan effectively.[7]

Let us assume that the farmers of Jantilla, a small village in Western Ghana, may use

[5] The barbarous treatment of utility theory by those who fail, or refuse, to see the difference between a man declaring a preference because of the supposedly existing greater utility, rather than assigning a higher utility to a man's pref-

erence after it has been declared, did much damage at one time in the field of economics. The latter must always be kept in mind to avoid confusion; see Luce and Raiffa, *op. cit.*, p. 22.

[6] Walter Manshard, "Land Use Patterns and Agricultural Migration in Central Ghana," *Tijdschrift voor Economische en Sociale Geografie* (September, 1961), p. 225.

[7] H. O. Walker, *Weather and Climate of Ghana*, Ghana Meterological Department, Departmental Note No. 5 (Accra, 1957), p. 37, map (mimeographed).

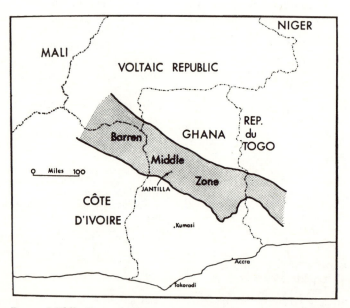

Figure 1.—The Barren Middle Zone of Ghana of low population density and extreme variability of rainfall.

the land to grow the following crops, each with different degrees of resistance to dry conditions, as their main staple food: yams, cassava, maize, millet, and hill rice.[8] In Game Theory terms the cultivation of these crops represents five strategies. In the same terms, and to simplify this initial example, let us make the somewhat unrealistic assumption that the environment has only two strategies; dry years and wet years. These strategies may be put into matrix form (Fig. 2), called the payoff matrix, and represent a two-person-five-strategy-zero-sum game, in which the values in the boxes represent the average yields of the crops under varying conditions, perhaps in calorific or other nutritional terms. For example, if the farmers of Jantilla choose to grow only yams, they will obtain a yield of eighty-two under wet year conditions, but the yield will drop to eleven if the environment does its worst. It should be noted that the values in the boxes have been chosen simply to provide an example of Game Theory, but this, in turn, emphasizes the close relationship of these methods to direct field work, for only in this way can we obtain these critical subcensus data. In a very real sense,

our tools are outrunning our efforts to gather the necessary materials. We might also note, parenthetically, that extreme accuracy of data, while always desirable, is not essential in order to use Game Theory as a tool, since it can be shown that payoff matrices subjected to a fairly high degree of random shock by injecting random error terms still give useful approximations and insights upon solution.[9]

A payoff matrix in which one opponent has only two strategies can always be reduced to a two-by-two game which is the solution for the complete game, in this case a five-by-two. We may, if time is no object, and we like dull, tedious work, take every pair of rows in turn and solve them for the maximum payoff to the farmers; but, fortunately, we also have a graphical solution which will point to the critical pair at once (Fig. 3). If we draw two scales from zero to one hundred, plot the values of each of the farmer's strategies on alternate axes, and connect the points, then the lowest point on the uppermost boundary will indicate which crops the farmers should grow to maximize their chances of filling

[8] Manshard, "Land Use Patterns . . .," pp. 226–29. See also Thomas T. Poleman, *The Food Economies of Urban Middle Africa* (Stanford: Food Research Institute, 1961).

[9] In linear-programming terms this would follow from the notion that the boundary conditions would have to change quite drastically, in most cases, in order for there to be a change in the mini-max point which would alter, in turn, the choice of strategies (see Fig. 3).

		Environment	
		Moisture Choices	
		Wet Years	Dry Years
Farmers of Jantilla Crop Choice	Yams	82	11
	Maize	61	49
	Cassava	12	38
	Millet	43	32
	Hill rice	30	71

Figure 2.—Payoff matrix for two-person-five-strategy-zero-sum game; crop choices against moisture choices.

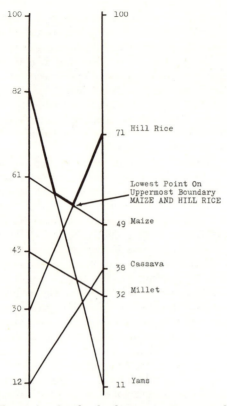

Figure 3.—Graphical solution to assign critical pair of strategies in two-person-five-strategy-zero-sum game.

and by calculating the difference between each pair of values and assigning it, regardless of sign, to the alternate strategy, we can find the proportion each strategy should be used. Thus, maize should be grown 77.4 per cent of the time and hill rice 22.6 per cent of the time, and if this is done the farmers can assure themselves the maximum return or payoff over the long run of fifty-four.

These proportions immediately raise the question as to how the solution should be interpreted. Should the farmers plant maize 77.4 per cent of the years and hill rice for the remaining 22.6 per cent, mixing the years in a random fashion;[11] or, should they plant these proportions each year? As Game Theory provides a conceptual framework for problems where choices are made repeatedly, rather than those involving choices of the unique, once-in-history variety, the cold-blooded answer is that *over the long haul* it makes no difference. However, when men have experienced famine and have looked into the glazed eyes of their swollen-bellied children, the long run view becomes somewhat meaningless. Thus, we may conclude that the farmers will hold strongly to the short-term view and will plant the proportions *each year* since the truly catastrophic case of hill rice and wet year could not then occur.

It is interesting to note, simply as an

their bellies.[10] Now we can take this pair of strategies, maize and hill rice (Fig. 4),

[10] This is simply the graphical solution to the basic linear-programming problem. The values, and the resulting slopes, have been deliberately exaggerated for the purposes of illustration.

[11] For a discussion on the necessity of a random mix of strategies see R. B. Braithwaite, *Scientific Explanation: A Study of the Function of Theory, Probability and Law in Science* (Cambridge: The University Press, 1955), pp. 236–39.

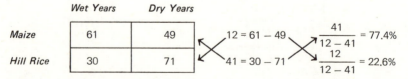

Figure 4.—Solution of two-by-two payoff matrix to achieve most efficient choice of crop proportions.

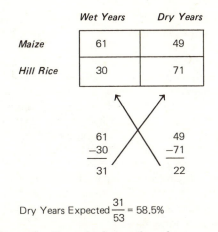

	Wet Years	Dry Years
Maize	61	49
Hill Rice	30	71

$$\begin{array}{cc} 61 & 49 \\ -30 & -71 \\ \hline 31 & 22 \end{array}$$

Dry Years Expected $\dfrac{31}{53}$ = 58.5%

Figure 5.—Vertical solution of two-by-two pay-off matrix to yield proportion of dry years expected.

aside, that solving this two-by-two matrix vertically tells us that over the long run we may expect dry years 58.5 per cent of the time (Fig. 5), if we assume the environment to be a totally vindictive opposing player trying to minimize the farmers' returns.

The solution of this little game raises some interesting questions for the geographer. Does the land-use pattern approach the ideal? And if not, why not? If the land-use pattern does not approach the ideal, does this imply a conscious departure on the part of the people, or does their less-than-ideal use of the land reflect only the best estimate they can make with the knowledge available to them, rather than any degree of irrationality? Do the farmers display rational behavior in our Western sense of the term despite all the warnings of the anthropologists about the illusory concept of economic man in Africa? If one were in an advisory position, would this help to make decisions regarding the improvement of agricultural practices? If the solution exceeds the basic calorific requirements of the people, is it worth gambling and decreasing the proportion of one or both crops to achieve a better variety of foods— if this is desired by the people? How far

can they gamble and decrease these proportions if inexpensive, but efficient, storage facilities are available, either to hold the surpluses of one year to allay the belt-tightening "hungry season" of the next, or to sell in the markets of the south when prices are high? Thus, the usefulness of the tool is not so much the solving of the basic problem, but the host of questions it raises for further research.

A further example from Ghana will make this clear (Fig. 6). For centuries the people living south of the great Niger arc have raised cattle and have driven them along the old cattle trails to the markets of Ghana.[12] The driving of cattle is a chancy

[12] Peter R. Gould, *The Development of the Transportation Pattern in Ghana* (Evanston: Northwestern University Studies in Geography, No. 5, 1961), p. 137.

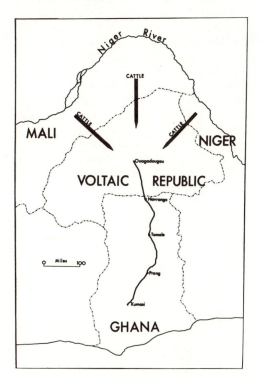

Figure 6.—Areas of cattle production and main route to traditional cattle markets.

business because, while Man can overcome cattle diseases such as rinderpest with modern veterinary medicines, he cannot yet predict the very dry years in this area of high rainfall variability through which the cattle have to be driven to market. Let us assume that the northern cattle traders of the Voltaic Republic, Mali, and Niger have the choice of selling their cattle in five markets: Ouagadougou, Navrongo, Tamale, Prang, and Kumasi. Each market thus represents a strategy and the traders may choose any one, or a mixture, of these in which to sell their animals. Let us further assume that Nature, or the environment, also has five strategies ranging from years with intensely dry conditions to unusually wet years. Thus, the strategies available to the cattle traders and the environment form a two-person-five-by-five-zero-sum game and may be represented by a five-by-five matrix which indicates, for example, the average price of an animal in various markets under different conditions (Fig. 7). The matrix indicates that a trader may gamble upon the season being a very wet one, in which case he would drive all his animals to Kumasi; but, if he guessed wrong, and the season was a less than average one, cattle would die or lose a great deal of weight on the way and he would get much less in Kumasi than if he had sold them in another market such as

Ouagadougou.[13] This, of course, is a deliberate simplification, for we are not taking into account the possibility of varying demands, the question of alternative local supplies at some of the markets, nor the probability of Ghanaian consumers substituting one source of protein for another, for example, fresh fish from the coast or dried Niger perch.[14] It might be possible to gather data to fill payoff matrices for other suppliers, but the situation would become much more difficult since we would be in the realm of non-zero-sum games that are, both conceptually and computationally, much more complex.[15]

[13] It has been suggested by Professor William Garrison that this problem might be readily handled in a practical sense by a standard linear-programming approach; a suggestion that would confirm Luce's and Raiffa's evocative comment on the Theory of Games that ". . . one can often discover a natural linear programming problem lurking in the background," *op. cit.*, p. 18.

[14] Peter Garlick, "The French Trade de Nouveau," Economic Bulletin of the Department of Economics, University of Ghana (mimeographed), p. 19.

[15] Zero-sum games are so called because upon choosing a particular strategy one competitor's gain (+) becomes the opponent's loss (—), the gain and loss summing to zero. Non-zero-sum games are those cases where an alteration in strategic choice *may* raise or lower the payoff for both players. Two-person-non-zero-sum

		Environment — Available Moisture Choices				
		Very Wet	Above Average	Average	Below Average	Intense Drought
Cattle Traders Markets	Ouagadougou	15	20	30	40	50
	Navrongo	20	15	15	20	5
	Tamale	40	30	20	15	10
	Prang	60	50	40	20	15
	Kumasi	80	70	40	25	10

Figure 7.—Payoff matrix in two-person-five-by-five-zero-sum game; market choices against available moisture choices.

Given the above strategies, what are the best markets the cattle traders can choose, and what are the best proportions?—"best" in the sense that over the long run the traders selling certain proportions of their cattle in these markets will get the maximum payoff. The solution of a five-by-five matrix in a zero-sum game is not as easy as the case where one opponent has two, or even three, choices. We do have, however, ways of choosing the strategies and *estimating* the proportions that should be used, the estimation being based upon a relatively simple iteration which converges upon the solution and which may be carried to any degree of required accuracy (Fig. 8). In the above example, the iteration has been carried out sixty times, and by counting the number of asterisks in each row of a market, which mark the maximum figure in each column of the estimating process, we can calculate that the traders should sell thirty-two sixtieths, or 53.4 per cent, of their cattle in Ouagadougou and then drive the remainder right through Navrongo, Tamale, and Prang to the Kumasi market (Fig. 9).

Let us pose the question, now, of what might happen if a really strong transportation link were forged between Tamale and Navrongo, such as the remaking and tarring of a road, so that upon arrival at the Voltaic-Ghanaian border cattle would no longer have to make their way on the hoof, but could be driven in trucks to the southern markets arriving in much better condition even in the very driest of seasons (Fig. 10). The payoff matrix would obviously change, and we might expect very much higher prices to prevail in Tamale, Prang, and Kumasi for the fat, sleek animals, rather than the bags-of-bones that often stumbled into these markets in former years. Again, the payoff matrix can be solved using the iterative method 160 times on this occasion (Fig. 11), to produce completely different choices and proportions from the previous example. Now it is no longer worthwhile for the traders to sell cattle in the Ouagadougou or Navrongo markets, but sell instead 62.5 per cent in Tamale, 25 per cent in Prang, and 12.5 per cent in Kumasi. Thus, an improved road link, a visible sign

games can be handled using the notion of imaginary side payments. *N*-person-non-zero-sum games may best be described as computationally miserable.

Environment
Available Moisture Choices

Cattle Traders *Markets*						*1*	*2*	*3*	*4*	.....	*59*	*60*	*Total*
Ouagadougou	15	20	30	40	50	15	65	115*	165*	.....	2,060	2,110*	32
Navrongo	20	15	15	20	5	20	25	30	40	.....	870	875	0
Tamale	40	30	20	15	10	40	50	60	70	.....	2,045	2,055	0
Prang	60	50	40	20	15	60	75	90	105	.....	1,875	1,890	0
Kumasi	80	70	40	25	10	80*	90*	100	110	.....	2,065	2,075	28
	15*	20	30	40	50								
	95	90	70	65	60*								
	175	160	110	90	70*								
	.	.	.	.	.								
	.	.	.	.	.								
	.	.	.	.	.								
	2,190	2,250	1,880	1,845	1,830								
			etc.										

Ouagadougou 32 $\frac{32}{60} = 53.4\%$

Kumasi 28 $\frac{28}{60} = 46.6\%$

Figure 8.—Solution by iteration of payoff matrix.

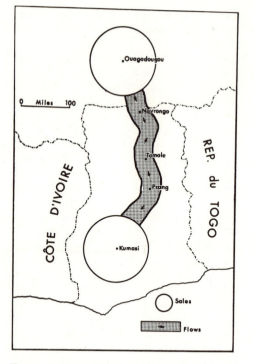

Figure 9.—Proportional sales and flows of cattle prior to road improvements and trucking.

the route, and it has become desirable to sell portions of the herds in the Tamale and Prang markets, the increases at these markets coming from former sales at Ouagadougou and Kumasi. Again, solving the payoff matrix points up some interesting questions for the geographer. First, it raises the whole question of estimating the effects of improving a transportation link—what will the flows be before and after? Can we obtain payoff values from one part of West Africa and use them to estimate changes of flows in other parts? Secondly, the question, again: how close does the behavior of the cattle traders approach that required to obtain the maximum payoff over the long run? Thirdly, what would be the effect of increasing the speed of communication so that cattle traders who started early in the season could inform others on the trail to the north about the conditions they find? And, finally, we should note the way an improved transportation link in effect extends the influence of one or more markets over others as the effect of distance is broken down allowing the demands of one center to impinge upon another.

By taking two examples from the traditional economy of Ghana, this paper has tried to point out the possible utility of the Theory of Games as a tool of research and as a conceptual framework in human and economic geography. That such frameworks are needed is evident, for without

on the landscape of a technological improvement, changes Man's perception and evaluation of the same choices available to him before, and as a result changes the patterns of flows and sales (Fig. 12). Now the flow has increased over the northern portion of

Environment
Available Moisture Choices

		Very Wet	Above Average	Average	Below Average	Intense Drought
Cattle Traders Markets	Ouagadougou	15	20	30	40	50
	Navrongo	20	15	15	20	5
	Tamale	80	80	70	70	80
	Prang	100	100	90	80	70
	Kumasi	130	130	120	90	60

Figure 10.—New payoff matrix indicating price changes in markets as a result of new road link between Tamale and Navrongo.

Environment
Available Moisture Choices

							1	2	3	4	.....	160	Total
Cattle Traders	Markets	Ouagadougou	15	20	30	40	50	50	100	150	190	.....	.	0
		Navrongo	20	15	15	20	5	5	10	15	35	.....	.	0
		Tamale	80	80	70	70	80	80*	160*	240*	310*	.....	.	100
		Prang	100	100	90	80	70	70	140	210	290	.....	.	40
		Kumasi	130	130	120	90	60	60	120	180	270	.....	.	20
			130	130	120	90	60*							
			210	210	190	160	140*							

Tamale $\dfrac{100}{160} = 62.5\%$

Prang $\dfrac{40}{160} = 25.0\%$

etc.

Kumasi $\dfrac{20}{160} = 12.5\%$

Figure 11.—Solution by iteration of new payoff matrix.

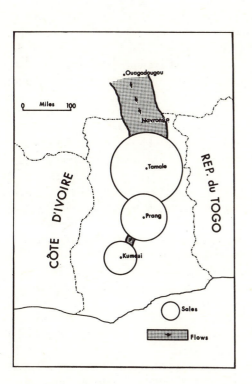

Figure 12.—Proportional sales and flows of cattle after road improvements and trucking.

these broad conceptual constructions in which to place our facts and observations it becomes an almost impossible task to raise and tackle, in a meaningful and lasting fashion, questions of Man's equilibrium with his environment, his perceptions and judgments about it, and the rules by which he reacts at different points in time and space? The work of Man is all around us upon the face of our earth, and is the result of men perceiving a variety of alternatives, subsequently limiting the range of choices according to their idea of what is useful and good, and *deciding* upon certain strategies to gain those ends. Thus, the whole body of decision theory, of which the Theory of Games is but one part, has an increasingly important role to play. Perhaps, in the same way that information theory has illuminated old problems of central-place structure, linear-programming solutions have helped our understanding of shifting flows and boundaries, and the theory of queues is throwing light upon problems ranging from those of the Ice Age to those of livestock production, the Theory of Games may also have a role to play.

VII. TOWARD A MODEL OF POPULATION-LAND RELATIONSHIPS

The papers in this volume illustrate the diversity of relationships between people and land in contemporary Africa. They show at work processes which produce conditions of relative rather than absolute adjustment and maladjustment. They show some of the ways in which indigenous agricultural systems have responded to internal stimuli, as in the growth of population, or to external stimuli, as in the growth in demand for export cash crops. They discuss the establishment and continuing influence of large non-indigenous agricultural systems, particularly in southern Africa.

Among the factors that influence the development of relationships, limitations imposed by the physical environment are fundamentally important. Recent work has pointed out that our understanding of the African environment is very restricted (Moss, 1969). To help overcome this deficiency, Moss has proposed an ecological point of view: ". . . resource assessment must be concerned with the measurement and evaluation of a complex of relationships between heterogenous features—soils, climates, plants and animals—and not with the collection of data concerning features within areas." This approach emphasizes the need for a conceptual differentiation between the *data* on physical environment, which may be a haphazard collection only partially relevant to agriculture, and *information*, all of which is related and relevant. Attention, he states, should be focused upon "functional relationships."

There is a comparable need for a conceptual framework that outlines the function and influence of human factors in population-land relationships. Recent discussions have suggested how such a framework might be structured. Ester Boserup (1965), a Danish economist, has set up a hypothesis which recognizes population as an independent variable conditioning changes in land, which are expressed in the agricultural system practiced. In essence, the hypothesis outlines increasing frequency and intensity in the use of land as a response to the increasing needs of a growing population. Five categories in the use of land are designated.

1. Forest fallow cultivation (with long fallow periods)
2. Bush fallow cultivation (with medium fallow periods)
3. Short fallow cultivation (with short fallow periods)
4. Annual cropping (land may be in seasonal fallow)
5. Multiple cropping (with two or more successive crops each year)

Basically, the first three categories differ from one another in the length of time land is cultivated and is in fallow, the cultivation period increasing progressively in length and the fallow period becoming correspondingly shorter. Mrs. Boserup postulates that in recent decades land use has been more intensive virtually everywhere in the under-developed regions. The development has been toward annual cropping, with or without irrigation.

She dismisses the idea that agricultural systems are adaptations to natural conditions, favoring the idea that they result from variations in population density instead. Such a direct dismissal is naïve. Also, throughout her argument she accords scant attention to the physical environment, even though it plays an important role in some of the developments she discusses, such as irrigated agriculture.

The view of population as the determinant variable in agricultural change is supported by current evidence from the developing world as well as by historical evidence from the developing world. Gleave and White (1968), after an independent investigation of relationships between population density and agricultural systems in West Africa, put forward ideas comparable to those of Mrs. Boserup. Although more aware of the influence of the physical environment, they appear to equate pressure with increasing population density: ". . . the stimulus for advance from one phase to the next in the development of population-land relationships comes from population pressure." Permanent use of the cultivable land (with manures and fertilizers replacing fallow) is identified as the key to agricultural advance and may be equated with Mrs. Boserup's categories 4 and 5 (annual cropping and multiple cropping). Gleave and White maintain that this phase has not been reached in West Africa. Such developments *are* limited; this collection of papers, however, includes examples of permanent cultivation. Whether development can continue in the face of present rates of population growth in rural areas is a major question. Ester Boserup's hypothesis requires *slow* (my emphasis) and sustained population growth; in the context of high and increasing growth rates in tropical Africa (Hance 1968, 1970; Steel 1970), this seems improbable.

The approaches to population-land relationships discussed in this volume lack a framework in which variables can be identified and examined. The Boserup hypothesis is based on economic considerations, and gives insufficient attention not only to the physical environment but also to social organization. Gleave and White consider a wide range of evidence but relate it to a conceptual framework which emerges implicitly rather than explicitly. A comprehensive model of population-land relationships for Africa south of the Sahara is beyond the scope of this book, but it is possible to set out some of the *characteristics* and *components* of a model, identifying its *phases* and the *processes* through which the phases are developed and linked with one another. These may be expressed diagrammatically.

CHARACTERISTICS AND COMPONENTS FOR A MODEL
OF AFRICAN POPULATION/LAND RELATIONSHIPS

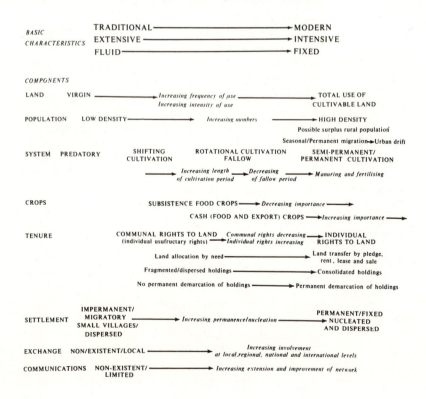

The framework envisages development along a continuum, from traditional to modern, from extensive to intensive, from fluid to fixed circumstances. These *characteristics* are not absolute; nowhere is it meant to imply that population-land relationships are other than dynamic and changing.

The *components* indicated are some of the most important in African population-land relationships. Population is clearly an important variable in the evolution of agricultural systems, but it is not possible to distinguish a cause-and-effect relationship as distinctly as Mrs. Boserup does. Yet as agricultural systems improve, part of the rural population may migrate to the towns, thereby linking rural population-land relationships with those of urban areas.

Phases in development cannot be clearly distinguished from one another in practice. There is a continuum in the fullest sense from pre-agricultural predatory use of the land to semi-permanent or permanent cultivation. Not only do intervening phases merge; it is also possible for more than one to be represented, as in the concentric zoning of land use around rural settlements. Under this system, the inner zones are most intensively used and are manured to maintain fertility. Progressing outward, the intensity of use decreases and fertility is maintained by increasing lengths of fallow (Morgan, 1968; Prothero, 1957a).

Crop changes occur, not only in the crops themselves but in the purposes for which they are grown. When emphasis is placed on producing cash crops, both for food and export, the importance of subsistence crops usually declines. These developments are closely linked with the extension of exchange systems at local, regional, national, and international levels. Both production and trade are influenced by extension and improvement in the communications network.

Also to be emphasized is land tenure, which provides organization in allocating land. Where there is ample land to meet all requirements, traditional communal organizations function successfully. Individuals do not hold rights to specific areas nor are there permanent demarcations of holdings. But as demands for land increase, communal holdings eventually are replaced by individually held areas with specified values. Land may be transferred by pledge, rent, lease, or sale, and the permanent demarcation of holdings becomes necessary. Within one agricultural community, both the traditional and more modern forms of land organization may operate, depending on the kinds of land available. For example, the limited areas suitable for irrigated agriculture acquire scarcity value and may be allocated in terms of individual rights; general farmland, however, is not in short supply, and continues to be allocated through the system of communal holding (Prothero, 1957b).

The diversity of settlement forms and patterns and limited knowledge of them make it difficult to outline valid generalizations; thus little attention has been given to the functions of these variables in population-land relationships. It is reasonable, however, to suggest that under conditions requiring more intensive use of land, a dispersed settlement pattern brings population into closer contact with the land than does a pattern of settlement nucleation.

Understanding relationships between population and land in Africa presents a major intellectual challenge, even to skilled observers. More attention needs to be given to the linkages between the *characteristics, components, phases,* and *processes* from which a model of population-land relationships may be built. Data must be gathered from a variety of disciplines and then coordinated and systematized. Above all else integrated analysis and evaluation are required. It is to be hoped that this book points toward methods for the achievement of these goals.

BIBLIOGRAPHY

Agboola, S. A. (1961). The Middle Belt of Nigeria—the basis of its unity. *Nigerian Geographical Journal 4*, 41–46.

Agboola, S. A. (1968). Some factors of population distribution in the Middle Belt of Nigeria: the examples of northern Ilorin and Kabba, in Caldwell and Okonjo (1968).

Allan, W. (1949). *Studies in African land usage in Northern Rhodesia.* Rhodes-Livingstone Papers No. 15, Oxford University Press, London.

Allan, W. (1965). *The African husbandman.* Oliver and Boyd, Edinburgh.

Anyare, L. (1963). *Ghana agriculture: its economic development from early times to the middle of the twentieth century.* Oxford University Press, London.

Baldwin, K. D. S. (1957). *The Niger Agricultural Project,* Blackwell, Oxford.

Barbour, K. M. (1959). Irrigation in the Sudan: its growth, distribution and potential expansion. *Transactions Institute of British Geographers 26*, 243–263.

Barbour, K. M. (1961). *The Republic of the Sudan.* University of London Press, London.

Barbour, K. M., and R. M. Prothero, eds. (1961). *Essays on African population.* Routledge and Kegan Paul, London.

Bederman, S. (1966). Plantation agriculture in Victoria Division, West Cameroon. *Geography 51*, 349–360.

Beguin, H. (1964). *Modèles géographiques pour l'espace rural Africain.* Brussels.

Biebuyck, D., ed. (1963). *African agrarian systems.* International African Institute, Oxford University Press, London.

Blij, H. de (1964). *A geography of Subsaharan Africa.* Rand McNally, Chicago.

Boateng, E. A. (1955). Settlement in the southeast Gold Coast. *Transactions, Institute of British Geographers 21*, 157–169.

Boateng, E. A. (1966). *A geography of Ghana.* Cambridge University Press, London.

Bohannan, P. (1963). "Land," "tenure" and land-tenure, in D. Biebuyck (1963).

Bohannan, P. and L. (1953). *The Tiv of Central Nigeria,* Ethnographic Survey of Africa, International African Institute, London.

Bohannan, P., and G. Dalton, eds. (1962). *Markets in Africa.* Northwestern University Press, Evanston, Ill.

Boserup, E. (1965.) *The conditions of agricultural growth.* Faber, London.

Brass, W., *et al.* (1968). *The demography of tropical Africa.* Princeton University Press, New Jersey.

Brokensha, D., ed. (1965). *Ecology and economic development in tropical Africa.* Research Series No. 9. Institute of International Studies, University of California, Berkeley.

Brooke, C. (1967). Types of food shortages in Tanzania. *Geographical Review 57*, 333–357.

Brookfield, H. C. (1957). Some geographical implications of the *apartheid* and partnership policies in southern Africa. *Transactions Institute of British Geographers 23*, 225–248.

Brookfield, H. C. (1962). Local study and comparative method. *Annals Association of American Geographers 52*, 242–254.

Buchanan, K. M. (1954). Recent developments

in Nigerian peasant farming. *Journal Tropical Geography 2*, 17–34.

Caldwell, J. C., and C. Okonjo (1968). *The population of tropical Africa*. Longmans, London.

Chambers, R. (1969). *Settlement Schemes in Tropical Africa*. Routledge and Kegan Paul, London.

Church, R. J. H. (1961). Problems and development of the dry zone in West Africa. *Geographical Journal 127*, 187–204.

Church, R. J. H. (1969). *West Africa: a study of the environment and of man's use of it*. Longmans, London.

Clark, C., and M. R. Haswell (1964). *The economics of subsistence agriculture*. Macmillan, London.

Clarke, J. I. (1969). North-west Africa since mid-century, in Prothero (1969).

Colbourne, M. (1963). *Planning for health*. New Africa Library, Oxford University Press, London.

Coppock, J. T. (1964). Agricultural geography in Nigeria. *Nigerian Geographical Journal 7*, 67–90.

Coppock, J. T. (1966). Agricultural developments in Nigeria. *Journal of Tropical Geography 23*, 1–18.

Courtney, P. P. (1965). *Plantation agriculture*. Bell, London.

Dalton, G. (1964). The development of subsistence and peasant economies in Africa. *International Soc. Sci. Journ. 26*, 378–389.

Davies, H. J. R. (1964a). The West African in the economic geography of the Sudan. *Geography 49*, 222–235.

Davies, H. J. R. (1964b). An agricultural revolution in the African tropics: the development of mechanised agriculture on the clay plains of the Republic of the Sudan. *Tijdschrift voor economische en sociale geografie 55*, 101–108.

Davies, H. J. R. (1964c). A study of tribal readjustment in the Nile Valley: the experience of the Ingessana. *Geographical Journal 130*, 380–389.

Davies, H. J. R. (1966). Nomadism in the Sudan. *Tijdschrift voor economische en sociale geografie 57*, 193–202.

Deshler, W. (1960). Livestock trypanosomiasis and human settlement in northeastern Uganda. *Geographical Review 50*, 541–554.

Deshler, W. (1963). Cattle in Africa. *Geographical Review 53*, 52–58.

Dickson, K. B. (1968). Background to the problem of economic development in north-

ern Ghana. *Annals Association of American Geographers 58*, 686–696.

Dickson, K. B. (1969). *A historical geography of Ghana*. Cambridge University Press, London.

Dresch, J. (1952). Paysans montagnards du Dahomey et du Cameroun. *Bulletin de l'Association de Géographes Français 222–3*, 2–9.

Dumont, R. (1966). *False start in Africa*. Deutsch, London.

Engmann, B. (1965). Population movements in Ghana: a study of internal migration and its implications for the planner. *Bulletin Ghana Geographical Association 10*, 41–65.

Fair, T. J. D. (1963). A regional approach to economic development in Kenya. *South African Geographical Journal 45*, 55–77.

Fair, T. J. D. (1969). Southern Africa: bonds and barriers in a multi-racial region, in Prothero (1969).

Fair, T. J. D., and N. M. Shaffer (1964). Population patterns and policies in South Africa 1957–60. *Economic Geography 40*, 261–274.

Floyd, B. N. (1962a). *Changing patterns of African land use in Southern Rhodesia*. Rhodes-Livingstone Institute, Lusaka.

Floyd, B. N. (1962b). Land apportionment in Southern Rhodesia. *Geographical Review 52*, 566–582.

Floyd, B. N. (1965). Soil erosion and deterioration in Eastern Nigeria. *Nigerian Geographical Journal 8*, 33–44.

Floyd, B. N. (1969). *Eastern Nigeria: a geographical review*. Macmillan, London.

Forde, C. D. (1953). The cultural map of West Africa: successive adaptations to tropical forests and grasslands. *Transactions New York Academy of Sciences 3*, 206–219.

Froelich, J. C. (1952). Densité de la population et méthodes de culture chez les Kabrés du Nord-Togo. *Comptes rendus du Congrès International de Géographie*, Lisbon IV, 168–180.

Frood, A. McK. (1967). The Aswan High Dam and the Egyptian economy, in R. W. Steel and R. Lawton, eds., *Liverpool essays in geography: a jubilee collection*, Longmans, London.

Galetti, R., *et al.* (1956). *Nigerian cocoa farmers*. Oxford University Press, London.

Gann, L. H., and P. Duignan (1962). *White settlers in tropical Africa*. Penguin Books, Harmondsworth.

Gillman, C. (1936). A population map of Tanganyika Territory. *Geographical Review 26*, 353–375.

Gleave, M. B. (1963). Hill settlements and their abandonment in western Yorubaland. *Africa 33*, 343–351.

Gleave, M. B. (1965). The changing frontiers of settlement in the uplands of Northern Nigeria. *Nigerian Geographical Journal 8*, 127–141.

Gleave, M. B. (1966). Hill settlements and their abandonment in tropical Africa. *Transactions Institute of British Geographers 40*, 39–49.

Gleave, M. B., and M. F. Thomas (1968). The Bagango valley: an example of land utilization and agricultural practice in the Bamenda Highlands. *Bulletin Institut Fondamental d'Afrique Noire, Série B, 30*, 655–681.

Gleave, M. B., and H. P. White (1968). Population density and agricultural systems in West Africa, in Thomas and Whittington (1968).

Goldschmidt, W., *et al.* (1965). Variation and adaptability of culture: a symposium. *American Anthropologist 67*, 400–408.

Gould, P. R. (1963). Man against his environment: a game theoretic framework. *Annals Association of American Geographers 53*, 290–297.

Gourou, P. (1953.) *La densité de la population au Ruanda-Urundi.* Institut Royal Colonial, Brussels.

Gray, R. F. (1963). *The Sonjo of Tanganyika: an anthropological study of an irrigation-based society.* International African Institute, Oxford University Press, London.

Gray, R., *et al.* (1962). Third conference on African history and archaeology. *Journal of African History 3*, 177.

Green, L. J., and T. J. D. Fair (1962). *Development in Africa.* Witwatersrand University Press, Johannesburg.

Grove, A. T. (1951a). *Land use and soil conservation in parts of Onitsha and Owerri Provinces.* Bulletin 21, Geological Survey of Nigeria, Kaduna.

Grove, A. T. (1951b). Soil erosion and population problems in south-east Nigeria. *Geographical Journal 117*, 291–306.

Grove, A. T. (1956). Soil erosion in Nigeria, in R. W. Steel and G. A. Fisher, eds., *Geographical essays on British tropical lands*, Philip, London.

Grove, A. T. (1957). *Land and population in Katsina Province.* Ministry of Agriculture, Kaduna, Nigeria.

Grove, A. T. (1961). Population densities and agriculture in Northern Nigeria, in K. M. Barbour and R. M. Prothero (1961).

Hailey, Lord (1956). *An African survey* (revised edition). Oxford University Press, London.

Hance, W. A. (1964). *The geography of modern Africa.* Columbia University Press, New York.

Hance, W. A. (1967). The Gezira Scheme: a study in agricultural development, in *African economic development* (revised edition). Council on Foreign Relations, Pall Mall, London.

Hance, W. A. (1968). The race between population and resources: a challenge to the prevailing view that Africa need not worry about population pressure. *Africa Report 13*, 6–12.

Hance, W. A. (1970). *Population migration and urbanization in Africa.* Columbia University Press, New York.

Hance, W. A., *et al.* (1961). Source areas of export production in tropical Africa. *Geographical Review 51*, 487–499.

Haswell, M. R. (1953). *Economics of agriculture in a savannah village.* H.M.S.O., London.

Haswell, M. R. (1963). *The changing pattern of economic activity in a Gambia village,* H.M.S.O., London.

Henshall, J. D. (1967). Models of agricultural activity, in R. J. Chorley and P. Haggett, *Models in geography*, Methuen, London, 425–460.

Herskovits, M. J., and M. Harwitz (1964). *Economic transition in Africa.* Northwestern University Press, Evanston, Ill.

Hill, P. (1963). *Migrant cocoa farmers of southern Ghana.* Cambridge University Press, London.

Hilton, T. E. (1959). Land planning and resettlement in northern Ghana. *Geography 44*, 227–240.

Hilton, T. E. (1961). Frafra resettlement and the population problem in Zuarungu. *Bulletin Institut Français d'Afrique Noire, Série B, 22*, 464–442.

Hilton, T. E. (1967). The Volta resettlement project. *Journal Tropical Geography 24*, 12–21.

Hodder, B. W. (1965). Some comments on the origin of traditional markets in Africa south of the Sahara. *Transactions Institute British Geographers 36*, 97–105.

Hodder, B. W. (1968). *Economic development in the tropics.* Methuen, London.

Hodder, B. W. (1969). West Africa: growth and change in trade, in Prothero (1969).

Hodder, B. W., and D. R. Harris, eds. (1967). *Africa in transition.* Methuen, London.

Hopkins, B. (1965). *Forest and savanna.* Heinemann, London.

Hunter, J. M. (1961). Akotuakrom: a case study of a devastated cocoa village in Ghana. *Transactions Institute of British Geographers 29,* 161–186.

Hunter, J. M. (1965). Regional patterns of population growth in Ghana, in J. B. Whittow and P. D. Wood, eds. *Essays in Geography for Austin Miller,* University of Reading, 272–290.

Hunter, J. M. (1966a). River blindness in Nangodi, Northern Ghana: an hypothesis of cyclical advance and retreat. *Geographical Review 56,* 398–416.

Hunter, J. M. (1966b). Ascertaining population carrying capacity under traditional systems of agriculture in developing countries. *Professional Geographer 18,* 151–154.

Hunter, J. M. (1967a). Population pressure in part of the West African savanna: a study of Nangodi, north east Ghana. *Annals Association of American Geographers 57,* 101–114.

Hunter, J. M. (1967b). The social roots of dispersed settlement in Northern Ghana. *Annals Association of American Geographers 57,* 263–290.

Hunter, J. M. (1967c). Seasonal hunger in part of the West African savanna: a survey of body weights in Nangodi, north east Ghana. *Transactions Institute of British Geographers 41,* 167–185.

Isnard, H. (1963). Agriculture et développement en Afrique occidentale. *Cahiers d'Outre-Mer 16,* 253–262.

Johnston, B. F. (1958). *The staple food economies of western Africa.* Stanford University Press, Stanford, California.

Jones, N. S. C. (1965). The decolonization of the White Highlands of Kenya. *Geographical Journal 131,* 186–201.

Jones, W. O. (1959). *Manioc in Africa.* Stanford University Press, Stanford, California.

Kay, G. (1964). Aspects of Ushi settlement history: Fort Rosebery District, Northern Rhodesia, in Steel and Prothero (1964).

Kay, G. (1965). Resettlement and land use planning in Zambia: the Chipangali scheme. *Scottish Geographical Magazine 81,* 163–177.

Kay, G. (1967a). *Social aspects of village regrouping in Zambia.* Department of Geography, University of Hull, Miscellaneous Series No. 7.

Kay, G. (1967b). *A social geography of Zambia.* University of London Press, London.

Kenworthy, J. M. (1964). Rainfall and water resources of East Africa, in Steel and Prothero (1964).

Kimble, G. H. T. (1960). *Tropical Africa.* 2 vols. The Twentieth Century Fund, New York.

King, J. G. M. (1939). Mixed farming in Northern Nigeria. *Empire Journal of Experimental Agriculture 7,* 271–284.

Kuper, H., ed. (1965). *Urbanization and migration in West Africa.* University of California Press, Berkeley and Los Angeles.

Langlands, B. W. (1966). *Bibliography on the distribution of disease in East Africa.* Makerere University College Library, Kampala, Uganda.

Lebon, J. H. G. (1960). On the human geography of the Nile Basin. *Geography 45,* 16–26.

Lebon, J. H. G., and V. C. Robertson (1961). The Jebel Marra, Darfur, and its region. *Geographical Journal 127,* 30–49.

Ledger, D. C. (1961). Recent hydrological change in the Rima basin, Northern Nigeria. *Geographical Journal 127,* 477–487.

Ledger, D. C. (1963). The Niger Dams project of Nigeria. *Tijdschrift voor economische en sociale geografie 54,* 242–247.

Lehrer, P. L. (1964). African agriculture in Kenya: a study of a changing system of subsistence farming. *Nigerian Geographical Journal 7,* 24–33.

Lloyd, P. C., *et al.* (1967). *The city of Ibadan.* Cambridge University Press, London.

McDonnell, G. (1964). The dynamics of geographic change: the case of Kano. *Annals Association of American Geographers 54,* 355–371.

McGlashan, N. D. (1958). Resettlement in the Meru district of Kenya. *Geography 43,* 209–210.

McGlashan, N. D. (1960). Consolidating land holdings in Kenya. *Geography 45,* 105–106.

McLoughlin, P. F. M. (1962). Economic development and the heritage of slavery in the Sudan Republic. *Africa 32,* 355–391.

McMaster, D. N. (1960). Change of regional balance in the Bukoba district of Tanganyika. *Geographical Review 50,* 73–88.

McMaster, D. N. (1962a). *A subsistence crop geography of Uganda.* International Geographical Union, World Land Use Survey, Occasional Paper No. 2, Geographical Publications, Bude, England.

McMaster, D, N. (1962b). The distribution of

traditional types of food storage containers in Uganda. *Uganda Journal 26*, 154–160.

McMaster, D. N. (1968). The colonial district town in Uganda, in R. P. Beckinsale and J. M. Houston, eds., *Urbanization and its problems*, Blackwell, Oxford.

McMaster, D. N. (1969). East Africa: influences and trends in land use, in Prothero (1969).

Mabogunje, A. L. (1962). *Yoruba towns*. Ibadan University Press, Ibadan, Nigeria.

Mabogunje, A. L. (1965). Urbanization in Nigeria: a constraint on economic development. *Economic Development and Cultural Change 13*, 436–438.

Mabogunje, A. L. (1968). *Urbanization in Nigeria*. University of London Press, London.

Mabogunje, A. L., and M. B. Gleave (1964). Changing agricultural landscape in southern Nigeria: the example of Egba Division 1850–1950. *Nigerian Geographical Journal 7*, 1–15.

Mercier, P. (1949). Densités de population dans le moyen—Dahomey. *Comptes Rendus du Congres International de Géographie, Lisbonne IV*, 181–191.

Middleton, J. F. M., and D. J. Greenland (1954). Land and population in West Nile District, Uganda. *Geographical Journal 120*, 446–457.

Miege, J. (1954). Les cultures vivrières en Afrique occidentale. *Cahiers d'Outre-Mer 7*, 25–50.

Millman, R. (1968). Kenya's "Tierra Templada." *Scottish Geographical Magazine 84*, 185–195.

Miner, H. (1967). *The city in modern Africa*. Praeger, New York.

Miracle, M. P. (1961). Seasonal hunger: a vague concept and an unexplored problem. *Bulletin Institut Français d'Afrique Noire*, Série B, 23, 273–283.

Miracle, M. P. (1967). *Agriculture in the Congo: tradition and change in African rural economies*. University of Wisconsin Press, Madison.

Mitchel, N. C. (1961). Yoruba towns, in Barbour and Prothero (1961), 279–302.

Morgan, W. B. (1955). Farming practice, settlement pattern and population density in south-eastern Nigeria. *Geographical Journal 121*, 320–333.

Morgan, W. B. (1959a). The distribution of food crop storage methods in Nigeria. *Journal of Tropical Geography 13*, 58–64.

Morgan, W. B. (1959b). The influence of European contacts on the landscape of Southern Nigeria. *Geographical Journal 125*, 48–65.

Morgan, W. B. (1963). Food imports of West Africa. *Economic Geography 39*, 351–362.

Morgan, W. B. (1968). The zoning of land use around rural settlements in tropical Africa, in Thomas and Whittington (1968), 301–320.

Morgan, W. B., and J. C. Pugh (1969). *West Africa*. Methuen, London.

Morgan, W. T. W. (1963). The "White Highlands" of Kenya. *Geographical Journal 129*, 140–155.

Mortimore, M. J. (1967). Land and population pressure in the Kano close-settled zone, Northern Nigeria. *Advancement of Science 23*, 677–686.

Mortimore, M. J. (1968). Population distribution, settlement and soils in Kano Province, in Caldwell and Okonjo (1968).

Mortimore, M. J., and J. Wilson (1965). *Land and people in the Kano close-settled zone*. Ahmadu Bello University, Department of Geography Occasional Paper No. 1, Zaria, Nigeria.

Moss, R. P. (1968). Land use, vegetation and soil factors in south-west Nigeria: a new approach. *Pacific Viewpoint 9*, 107–127.

Moss, R. P. (1969). The appraisal of land resources in tropical Africa: a critique of some concepts. *Pacific Viewpoint 10*, 18–27.

Moss, R. P., and W. B. Morgan (1970). Soils, plants and farmers in West Africa, in J. P. Garlick, ed., *Human ecology in the tropics*, Pergamon Press, Oxford.

Murdock, G. P. (1960). Staple subsistence crops of Africa. *Geographical Review 50*, 523–540.

Nel, A. (1962). Geographical aspects of apartheid in South Africa. *Tijdschrift voor economische en sociale geografie 53*, 197–209.

Netting, R. M. (1965). Household organization and intensive agriculture: the Kofyar case. *Africa 35*, 422–429.

Nicholas, G. (1960). Un village Haoussa de la République du Niger: Tussao Haoussa. *Cahiers d'Outre-Mer 13*, 421–450.

O'Connor, A. M. (1965). *Railways and development in Uganda*. Nairobi.

O'Connor, A. M. (1966). *An economic geography of East Africa*. Bell, London.

Ojo, G. J. A. (1967). *Yoruba culture*. University of London Press, London.

Oliver, R. A., and J. D. Fage (1962). *A short*

history of Africa. Penguin Books, Harmondsworth.

Oliver, R. W., *et al*. (1964). Comments on "The division of . . ." by W. Roder (1964), 53–58.

Oluwasanmi, H. (1966). *Agriculture and Nigerian economic development*. Oxford University Press, London.

Ominde, S. H. (1968). *Land and population movements in Kenya*. Heinemann, London.

Papy, L. (1953). Un pays d'Afrique orientale: le Ruanda-Urundi. *Cahiers d'Outre-Mer 24*, 399–407.

Pehaut, Y. (1961). L'arachide au Sénégal. *Cahiers d'Outre-Mer 14*, 5–25.

Pelissier, P. (1953). Les paysans Sérères. *Cahiers d'Outre-Mer 6*, 105–127.

Pelissier, P. (1953). *Les paysans du Sénégal: les civilisations agraires du Cayor à la Casamance*. St. Yrie.

Pollock, N. C. (1968). Irrigation in the Rhodesian Lowveld. *Geographical Journal 134*, 70–77.

Porter, P. W. (1965). Environmental potentials and economic opportunities—a background for cultural adaptation. *American Anthropologist 67*, 409–420.

Prothero, R. M. (1957a). Land use at Soba, Zaria Province, Northern Nigeria. *Economic Geography 33*, 72–86.

Prothero, R. M. (1957b). Land use, land holding and land tenure at Soba, Zaria Province, Northern Nigeria. *Bulletin Institut Français d'Afrique Noire*, Série B, *19*, 558–563.

Prothero, R. M. (1957c). Migratory labour from north-western Nigeria. *Africa 27*, 251–261.

Prothero, R. M. (1959). *Migrant labour from Sokoto Province, Northern Nigeria*. Government Printer, Kaduna, Nigeria.

Prothero, R. M. (1962). Some observations on desiccation in north-western Nigeria. *Erdkunde 16*, 111–119.

Prothero, R. M. (1964). Continuity and change in African population mobility, in Steel and Prothero (1964), *op. cit.*

Prothero, R. M. (1965). *Migrants and malaria*. Longmans, London; and (1968) *Migrants and malaria in Africa*. Contemporary Community Health Series, University of Pittsburgh Press, Pittsburgh.

Prothero, R. M. (1968). Migration in tropical Africa, in Caldwell and Okonjo (1968).

Prothero, R. M., ed. (1969). *A geography of Africa: regional essays on fundamental characteristics, issues and problems*. Routledge, London.

Richard-Molard, J. (1958). Essai sur la vie paysanne au Fouta-Dialon, in *Problèmes humaines en Afrique occidentale*, Présence Africain, Paris.

Richards, A. I. (1958). A changing pattern of agriculture in East Africa: the Bemba of Northern Rhodesia. *Geographical Journal 124*, 302–334.

Robinson, E. A. G., ed. (1964). *Economic development for Africa south of the Sahara*. International Economic Association, Macmillan, London.

Roder, W. (1964). The division of land resources in Southern Rhodesia. *Annals Association of American Geographers 54*, 41–52.

Rouch, J. (1957). Migrations au Ghana. *Journal de Société des Africanistes 24*, 33–196.

Sabbagh, M. E. (1968). Some geographical characteristics of a plural society: apartheid in South Africa. *Geographical Review 58*, 1–28.

Schilippe, P. de (1956). *Shifting cultivation in Africa: the Zande system of agriculture*. Routledge and Kegan Paul, London.

Stamp, L. D. (1940). The southern margin of the Sahara: comments on some recent studies on the question of desiccation in West Africa. *Geographical Review 30*, 297–300.

Steel, R. W. (1961). The towns of tropical Africa, in Barbour and Prothero (1961).

Steel, R. W. (1965). Population increase and food production in tropical Africa. *African Affairs*. Special Issue, 55–68.

Steel, R. W. (1968). The Volta dam: its prospects and problems, in Warren and Rubin (1968).

Steel, R. W. (1970). Problems of population pressure in tropical Africa. *Transactions Institute British Geographers 49*, 1–14.

Steel, R. W., and R. M. Prothero, eds. (1964). *Geographers and the tropics: Liverpool essays*. Longmans, London.

Stenning, D. J. (1959). *Savannah nomads*. International African Institute, Oxford University Press, London.

Stevenson, R. F. (1968). *Population and political systems in tropical Africa*. Columbia University Press, New York.

Taafe, E., *et al*. (1963). Transport expansion in underdeveloped countries (Ghana and Nigeria): a comparative analysis. *Geographical Review 53*, 503–529.

Thomas, M. F., and G. W. Whittington (1968). *Environment and land use in Africa*. Methuen, London.

Trewartha, G. T., and W. Zelinsky (1954).

Population patterns in tropical Africa. *Annals Association of American Geographers 44*, 135–193.

Tricart, J. (1956). Les échanges entre la zone forestière de Côte d'Ivoire et les savannes Soudaniennes. *Cahiers d'Outre-Mer 17*, 209–238.

Turner, B. J., and Baker, P. R. (1968). Tsetse control and livestock development: a case study from Uganda. *Geography 53*, 249–259.

Udo, R. K. (1963). Patterns of population distribution and settlement in Eastern Nigeria. *Nigerian Geographical Journal 6*, 73–88.

Udo, R. K. (1964). The migrant-tenant farmers of eastern Nigeria. *Africa 34*, 326–338.

Udo, R. K. (1965a). Disintegration of nucleated settlement in Eastern Nigeria. *Geographical Review 55*, 53–67.

Udo, R. K. (1965b). Sixty years of plantation agriculture in Southern Nigeria 1902–62. *Economic Geography 41*, 356–368.

Udo, R. K. (1966). Transformation of rural settlement in British tropical Africa. *Nigerian Geographical Journal 9*, 129–144.

U. N. (1966). *African agricultural development: reflections on the major lines of advance and the barriers to progress.* Economic Commission for Africa, New York.

van Velsen, J. (1960). Labour migration as a positive factor in the continuity of Tonga tribal society, in A. Southall ed., *Social change in modern Africa*, International African Institute, Oxford University Press, London.

Veyret, P. (1952). L'élevage dans la zone tropicale. *Cahiers d'Outre Mer 5*, 70–83.

Warren, W., and N. Rubin, eds. (1968). *Dams in Africa: an interdisciplinary study of man-made lakes in Africa.* London.

Watson, W. (1958). *Tribal cohesion in a money economy.* Manchester University Press, Manchester.

White, H. P. (1956). Internal exchange of staple foods in the Gold Coast. *Economic Geography 32*, 115–125.

White, H. P. (1958). Mechanised cultivation of peasant holdings in West Africa. *Geography 43*, 269–270.

White, H. P. (1963). The movement of export crops in Nigeria. *Tijdschrift voor economische en sociale geografie 11*, 248–253.

Wilde, J. C. de (1967). *Experiences with agricultural development in tropical Africa:* Vol. 1 *Synthesis;* Vol. II *Case studies.* International Bank for Reconstruction and Development, Johns Hopkins Press, Baltimore.

Wills, J. B. (1962). *Agriculture and land use in Ghana.* Oxford University Press, London.

Wood, A. (1950). *The groundnut affair.* Bodley Head, London.

Yudelman, M. (1964). *Africans on the land: economic problems of African agricultural development in southern, central and east Africa, with special reference to Southern Rhodesia.* Cambridge, Mass.

INDEX